PROGRAMMING THE WINDOWS® 95 USER INTERFACE

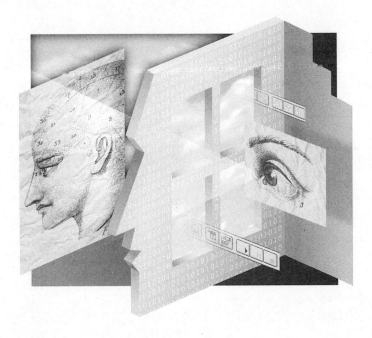

NANCY WINNICK CLUTS

Microsoft Press

PUBLISHED BY
Microsoft Press
A Division of Microsoft Corporation
One Microsoft Way
Redmond, Washington 98052-6399

Library of Congress Cataloging-in-Publication Data
Cluts, Nancy Winnick, 1962-
    Programming the Windows 95 user interface / Nancy Winnick Cluts.
        p.   cm.
    Includes index.
    ISBN 1-55615-884-X
    1. Microsoft Windows 95.   2. Operating systems (Computers)
    3. User interfaces (Computer systems)   I. Title.
    QA76.76.O63C57   1995
    005.265--dc20   95-30591
                                                         CIP

Printed and bound in the United States of America.

1 2 3 4 5 6 7 8 9   MLML   0 9 8 7 6 5

Distributed to the book trade in Canada by Macmillan of Canada, a division of Canada Publishing
Corporation.

A CIP catalogue record for this book is available from the British Library.

Microsoft Press books are available through booksellers and distributors worldwide. For further
information about international editions, contact your local Microsoft Corporation office. Or contact
Microsoft Press International directly at fax (206) 936-7329.

Acquisitions Editor: Eric Stroo
Project Editor: Mary Renaud
Technical Editor: Linda Rose Ebenstein

To my husband, Jonathan, and my son, Nicholas

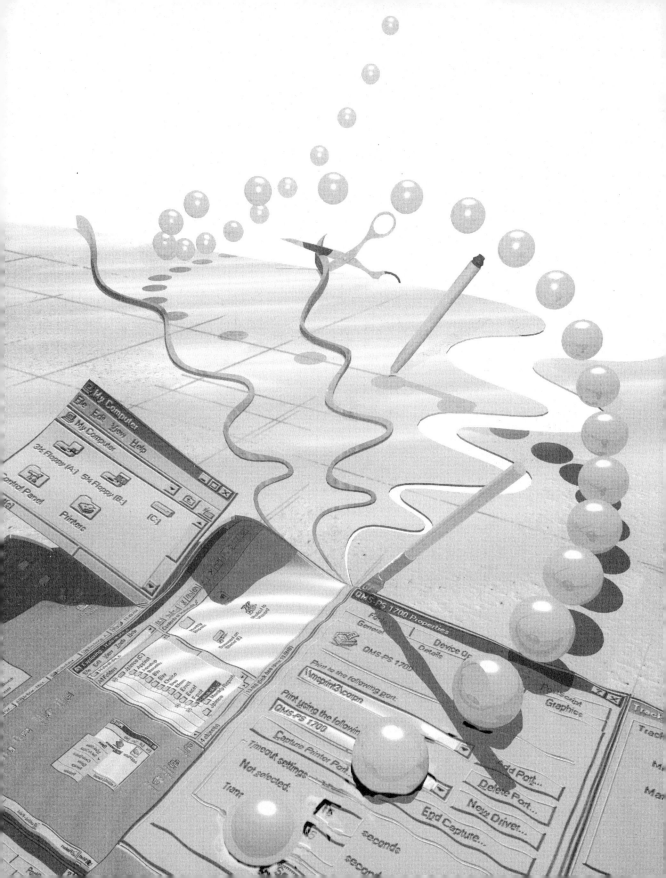

CONTENTS

CHAPTER THREE

Image Lists, List View Controls, Column Headers, and Tree View Controls: List Management Common Controls   **67**

CHAPTER FOUR

Tabs, Property Sheets, and Wizards: Whiz-Bang Common Controls   **109**

CHAPTER FIVE

Rich Edit Controls   **133**

CHAPTER SIX

The New Common Dialog Boxes   **159**

ACKNOWLEDGMENTS

Many, many people contributed greatly to this book and gave generously of their time and patience. They answered my questions, explained the unexplainable, read the drafts of my chapters (and left quite a bit of red ink, too), and generally allowed me to make a complete pest of myself.

I've tried to list here everyone who has been instrumental in the creation of this book. (If I have omitted anyone, I offer my apologies.) My sincere thanks to the following people:

My friends and colleagues (present and past) at the Microsoft Developer Network, especially Nigel Thompson and Dale Rogerson. They reviewed my chapters, commented on my sample code, offered assistance on thorny programming problems, didn't knock on my office door when my "Do Not Disturb" sign was up, and gave me ample opportunity to blow off steam when writer's block hit with a vengeance.

Chris Guzak, Kurt Eckhardt, George Pitt, Teri Schiele, George Moore, Joe Belfiore, and Mike Sheldon, for helping me to understand the underpinnings of the Windows 95 user interface.

My editors at MSDN: Judy Nessen, for editing all the chapters of the book and never complaining about the last-minute changes I had to make; Handan Selamoglu and Diane Stielstra, for all their work on my original articles; and Andy Himes, for his steadfast support of the book.

Dean McCrory, for answering my many, many MFC questions.

Greg Keyser and Jeffrey Saathoff, for offering their own sample code for my use.

The people at MS Press, including Eric Stroo, Mary Renaud, Linda Rose Ebenstein, Mary DeJong, Dail Magee, Jr., Jim Fuchs, Bill Teel, Barb Runyan, Jody Ivy, Jean Trenary, Barbara Remmele, John Sugg, Nancy Jacobs, Michael Victor, Kim Eggleston, Sally Anderson, Shawn Peck, Judith Bloch, Stephanie Marr, Lisa Theobald, Heidi Saastamoinen, and Koren Buckner.

TeamX, who, when all else fails, always comes to the rescue!

Finally, my son, Nicholas, who thinks it's "cool" that Mommy works with "'puters," and to my husband, Jonathan, who encourages me, inspires me, and never once complained about all the hours I spent working on the book.

INTRODUCTION

In December 1993, I got my hands on a beta copy of the Microsoft Windows 95 operating system (then called "Chicago"). The first thing that popped out at me was the new look and feel of the system. I'm always curious about how to program user interfaces and how to write applications that exploit their features, so I jumped right in. I began by exploring the new common controls. I soon decided to do some writing about what I was discovering, and before I knew it, what I had envisioned as an article or two turned into a long series of articles on the Microsoft Developer Network Development Library CD.

But it didn't stop there. My list of interesting topics to research kept growing—and all of the *most* interesting topics involved the user interface. Then one day, as I was reading one of the programming newsgroups out on that oft-touted "information superhighway" (there, now I've said it), someone asked the group to recommend a book that covered programming for the Windows 95 user interface. The unanimous response was that no such book existed yet but that when one surfaced, it would be snapped right up.

My fate was sealed. I decided that I wanted to fill that void, to provide a source of information for all those developers who want to know how to program the new Windows 95 UI. The place to start, of course, is with a brief introduction to the interface itself.

An Overview of the Windows 95 User Interface

Microsoft Windows 95 sports an exciting new user interface, redesigned to make it easier and faster for both beginners and power users to get their work done. But there's even better news for developers: you can incorporate the new functionality that has been implemented for this interface in your own applications.

No longer will a developer have to reverse-engineer a control used in the interface—the software development kit now contains the controls. No longer will a developer need to find a third party to add support for long filenames—the operating system itself now permits long filenames. No longer will a developer have to figure out some way to hack into the interface code—extensibility is now built in.

This book examines the Windows 95 user interface and the programming techniques you'll need to get the most out of its new elements. Specifically, I'll focus on these elements:

- New common controls
- New common dialog boxes
- Support for long filenames
- Shortcuts
- File viewers
- User interface extensions

The chapters that follow describe these features in detail, in addition to discussing important related topics: using the Windows 95 Registry, working with the user interface dynamic-link library (SHELL32.DLL), and browsing the shell name space. For now, however, I'd like to offer you a glimpse at what's ahead by briefly introducing the features listed above.

New Common Controls

The new common controls in Windows 95 include the following:

- Status bars and toolbars
- Trackbars, progress bars, animation controls, and up-down controls
- Image lists, list view controls, column headers, and tree view controls
- Property sheets, tabs, and wizards
- Rich edit controls

The best place to preview many of these new elements is Windows Explorer, the integrated replacement for File Manager and Program Manager. Figure I-1 points out a few of the new common controls. Microsoft designed and implemented these controls for Windows Explorer, but they have been exported for use by all Windows-based applications.

Tree view control

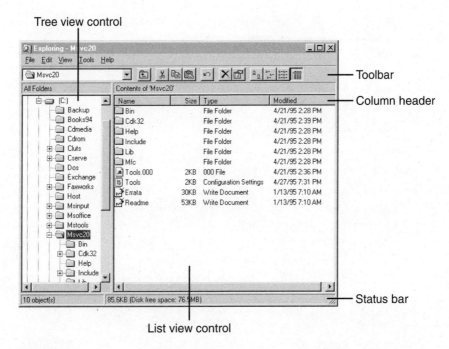

Toolbar

Column header

Status bar

List view control

Figure I-1.
Common controls in Windows Explorer.

Status Bars and Toolbars

Status bars and toolbars are organizational common controls—that is, they are used to organize or group other controls. Status bars and toolbars have appeared in applications for several years now; until Windows 95, however, the operating system did not support them.

A *status bar* usually resides at the bottom of the application's main window. It displays textual or graphical status information such as the name of the current document, the size of the document, the date, and the time. Status bars are a convenient way to give the user information about an object in your application.

A *toolbar* holds other controls such as buttons and combo boxes (usually grouped in a logical or convenient order), which help the user to quickly carry out common tasks—copying a file, printing a document, applying formatting, and so on. In many applications, for example, clicking a toolbar button lets the user immediately execute a save command, without having to choose the command from a menu or remember a key combination. You'll see toolbars most often at the top of an application's main window, although some programs allow the user to customize and move toolbars. You can see both a toolbar and a status bar in Figure I-1 on the preceding page.

Trackbars, Progress Bars, Animation Controls, and Up-Down Controls

Several new common controls are designed for general uses such as setting intensity levels, changing values, and simply helping the user understand what's going on in the system. With a *trackbar,* for instance, the user can move a slider through a range of tick marks that indicate degrees of brightness, volume, color mix, or other measures of intensity. You might use the vertical trackbar shown in Figure I-2 to control the volume of a pair of speakers.

Figure I-2.
A trackbar.

When your application needs to carry out a time-consuming operation, a *progress bar* can tell the user how far along things are. A highlight color gradually fills the progress bar from left to right as the operation moves toward completion. You'll find progress bars most frequently in setup programs or when you copy a large amount of data from one location to another. For example, when you copy a large file in Windows 95, you'll see the dialog box shown in Figure I-3. In addition to the progress bar, this dialog box contains an *animation control,* which allows you to play an audio-video interleaved (AVI) clip for the user.

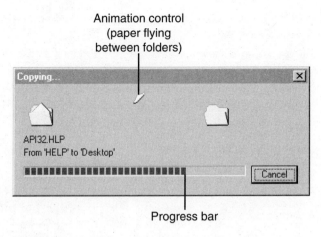

Figure I-3.
A progress bar and an animation control at work.

Another general-purpose control is the *up-down control,* which allows the user to scroll through and change items in an associated control. You'll usually want to pair an up-down control with an edit box to produce a spin box, in which the user can spin through numbers, days of the week, month names, and so on. Figure I-4 shows an example.

Figure I-4.
An up-down control paired with an edit box to create a spin box.

Image Lists, List View Controls, Column Headers, and Tree View Controls

Creating a user interface for managing lists can be a complicated task. But the new list management common controls in Windows 95 make life a lot simpler. An *image list,* which is designed to be used with list view controls and tree view controls, helps you manage lists of icons and bitmaps. With a *list view control,* you can display lists of data in varying arrangements and in varying degrees of detail. A *column header* in a list view control can specify what each column of information is about (and can also give the user a way to sort the information, by clicking a header item). A *tree view control* provides a list of data that is structured in a "tree" hierarchy. These controls, three of which are seen in Figure I-1 on page xvii, are the basis of the Windows Explorer user interface.

Property Sheets, Tabs, and Wizards

A *property sheet* displays the properties of an item, usually on several different *property sheet pages.* For example, a user can check out or change the properties of the current Windows 95 display with the Display Properties property sheet, shown in Figure I-5. Clicking one of the labeled *tab controls* switches to the corresponding property sheet page—that is, if the user clicks the Screen Saver tab, the Screen Saver page appears, where the user can find the name of the current screen saver or select a new one.

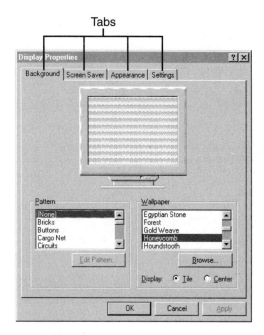

Figure I-5.
A property sheet with tabs.

A *wizard* is a type of property sheet that takes the user step by step through a series of dialog boxes to complete a process. Wizards are especially useful in a setup or installation application. For instance, when you install a new hardware device under Windows 95, the Add New Hardware wizard, shown in Figure I-6, walks you through that setup.

First page of the
Add New Hardware
wizard

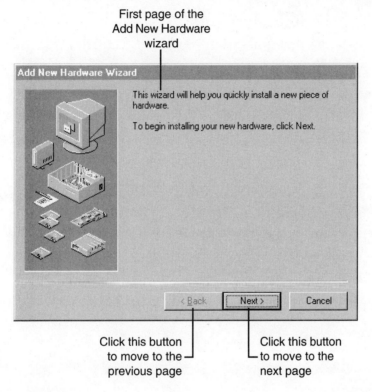

Click this button
to move to the
previous page

Click this button
to move to the
next page

Figure I-6.
The Add New Hardware wizard.

Rich Edit Controls

A *rich edit control* is essentially a text editing box—but there's much more. It provides functionality comparable to that of a multiline edit control, while also allowing the user to apply both character and paragraph formatting to the text, to perform drag-and-drop operations, and even to embed OLE objects in the text. To experiment with a rich edit control, try out the text editing area in the Windows 95 WordPad application, which you can see in Figure I-7 on the next page.

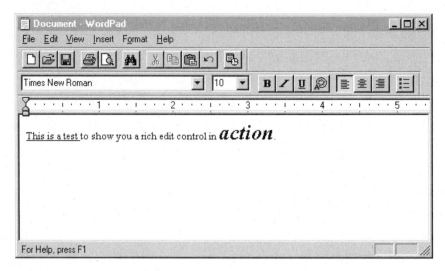

Figure I-7.
WordPad, which contains a rich edit control.

New Common Dialog Boxes

Microsoft has updated common dialog boxes in Windows 95. The biggest change is in the look of the dialog boxes, but you'll also find some new functionality. The new Open common dialog box in Figure I-8 shows the updated style. We'll discuss common dialog boxes for opening and saving files, setting fonts, changing or creating colors, finding and replacing text, and printing.

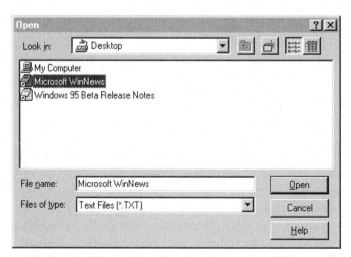

Figure I-8.
The new Open common dialog box.

Support for Long Filenames

As you can see in the Open common dialog box in Figure I-8, the days of those awkward, indecipherable, eight-character filenames are over. You can now assign sensible and easy-to-remember names to your files—*Summer Inventory Checklist and Order Sheet* rather than SINVCKOS.DOC, for instance. Long filenames come to you courtesy of the Windows 95 file system, called VFAT (*protected-mode,* or *virtual,* FAT). The VFAT system is compatible with the older file allocation table (FAT) system, using extended FAT structures to store long filenames and file information.

I'll offer some guidelines that will help you support long filenames in your applications and your interface design, and we'll examine some outdated assumptions that might still be lurking in your code.

Shortcuts

You can customize the desktop by adding shortcuts for your favorite programs, documents, and printers, changing the look to fit your work style and personality. *Shortcuts* provide an easy way to access the items you use often. After you've set up a shortcut for a document, for example, you can simply double-click the shortcut to open the document—you don't need to remember the document's full name or its precise location on your system. If you have a shortcut to your printer on your desktop, you can print a file simply by dragging the file's icon onto the printer icon. Users can easily create their own shortcuts in Windows 95, and you can also include them in your applications.

Figure I-9 shows a shortcut that I keep on my desktop. It gives me quick access to the Registry Editor, one of the applications I run most often.

Figure I-9.
A shortcut to the Registry Editor.

File Viewers

With a *file viewer,* a user can look at the contents of a file without opening the application in which the file was created. The file viewer itself supplies the interface, which can include elements such as menus, a toolbar, a status bar, and standard window controls.

To produce a file viewer, the user selects a file and then chooses Quick View from Windows Explorer's File menu. Another method is to select the file and then right-click it to display the file's context menu, from which the user can choose the Quick View option.

You can create and include your own file viewers in your applications. We'll discuss this process and look at how file viewers are registered in the Windows 95 Registry.

User Interface Extensions

Interface extensions enhance the basic functionality of the user interface by offering you additional ways to manipulate file objects or by supplying additional information. Extending the interface also allows an application to simplify the task of browsing through the Windows 95 file system and networks. Seven extensions to the user interface are built into Windows 95:

- Context menu handlers
- Drag-and-drop handlers
- Icon handlers
- Property sheet handlers
- Copy hook handlers
- Drop target handlers
- Data object handlers

An Overview of This Book

This book contains three parts. Chapters 1 through 7 cover the new common controls and common dialog boxes. Chapters 8 through 12 discuss additional functionality such as support for long filenames, shortcuts, and file viewers. The final part, Chapters 13 and 14, examines the advanced topics of implementing user interface extensions and browsing the shell name space. In each chapter, we'll discuss the programming issues you need to consider to take advantage of the visual richness of the Windows 95 environment, and you'll see some practical examples and coding techniques that you can adapt for your own applications.

Who Should Read This Book

This book is written for Windows programmers who already know C or who use C++ with the Microsoft Foundation Class Library (MFC). I'm a C programmer at heart, but I know that many more adventurous programmers out there have embraced C++ and MFC. Accordingly, where possible, I provide samples both in C and in C++ using the classes built into MFC. Toward the end of the book, you'll find some topics that require a minimal understanding of OLE: shortcuts, file viewers, and user interface extensions. In those chapters, I recommend some additional reading that will help get you up to speed on OLE issues.

The Companion CD-ROM

The sample code demonstrated in this book and included on the CD-ROM packaged as a companion disc with the book runs on Microsoft's 32-bit Windows operating systems: Windows 95, Windows NT 3.51 (using the new shell), and Win32s 1.3 running on Windows 3.1. To run the samples, you must be running one of these systems. To build the samples, you need the Microsoft Win32 Software Development Kit. If you plan to build the MFC samples, you need to run Microsoft Visual C++ version 2.1 or later with MFC version 3.1 or later.

The companion disc contains the source code for all the sample programs shown in the book. Each sample has a make file that you can use to build the project under Visual C++ version 2.1. The samples have been built and tested using Visual C++ 2.1 and MFC 3.1 on Windows 95.

I wrote most of the samples either specifically for this book or for the series of Microsoft Developer Network technical articles that preceded the book. In a few cases, samples I had written earlier eventually became incorporated into the Win32 Software Development Kit; they are included here with permission, as are two samples written by Greg Keyser.

PART I

NEW COMMON CONTROLS AND COMMON DIALOG BOXES

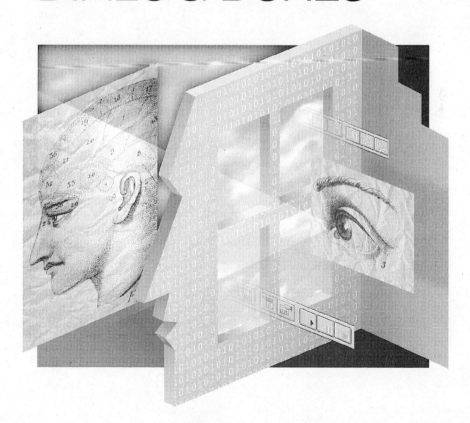

Status Bars and Toolbars: Organizational Common Controls

Our look at the new elements of the Microsoft Windows 95 user interface and the programming techniques you'll need to work with them begins with the new common controls. To get you started, this chapter does double duty. First it provides some basic information about the common controls as a group, including common control window classes, window styles, and notifications. Then the chapter moves on to introduce you to the two most popular common controls: status bars and toolbars.

Common Control Basics

The new common controls were designed specifically to enhance the look and feel of new interface elements such as those seen in Windows Explorer. If you as a developer want to do everything you can to make your applications look and feel as if they are part of the new interface, you need to understand how these controls work and how to integrate them into your applications.

When I started running Microsoft Windows 95, I was delighted to learn about the new controls that were available to me through the common control library. Some of these, such as property sheets, wizards, and tree view controls, provided just the type of functionality I was looking for in order to add some polish to my applications without too much effort. Now I could finally add wizards to my programs without having to write my own code to manage the windows! I discovered other controls, too: progress bars, trackbars, up-down controls, and animation controls, to name just a few.

In Part I of this book, we'll examine each new common control in turn, and I'll provide sample code in C and in C++ using the Microsoft Foundation Class Library (MFC) to help you understand how to create and manipulate the controls. I have also included lists of messages and member functions to show you the breadth of functionality each control supports. (These lists are based in large part on the documentation for the Win32 Software Development Kit [SDK] and the documentation for MFC version 3.1, but the lists are not comprehensive. If you would like even more detailed information about the common controls, you can also refer to the Win32 SDK itself, consult the MFC documentation, or check out the Microsoft Developer Network [MSDN] Development Library.) But first let's take a look at what all the "common" controls have in common.

Most of the new 32-bit common controls designed for the Windows 95 operating system are supported by the COMCTL32.DLL dynamic-link library (DLL), which is supported by the 32-bit Microsoft Windows operating systems: Windows 95, Win32s version 1.3 or later (running on Windows version 3.1), and Windows NT version 3.51 or later. It is important to remember that these new controls are 32-bit only—they are not supported in 16-bit Windows environments. If I've confused you with that last statement, let me clarify: these controls will work in Windows 3.1, but only if the system is running Win32s, which provides a mechanism called a *thunking layer* (don't you love that name?) to translate between 32-bit system calls and 16-bit system calls.

Essentially, a *common control* is a child window that sends a notification to its parent window when an event (such as a mouse click or a focus change) occurs in the control. Because these controls are windows, you can use the standard window management functions to manipulate them—that is, you can send messages or post messages to them. Some common controls send notifications as WM_COMMAND messages; others use a new message, WM_NOTIFY, to notify the control's parent of an action or a change. Each common control supports a set of messages that an application can use to manipulate the control.

Instead of using the SendMessage or PostMessage function to send messages to some of the common controls, an application can use a set of macros included in the COMMCTRL.H header file. I'm more comfortable using these macros than using the standard functions or the standard messages because the preface of the macro name specifies the type of control you are manipulating. For example, the ListView_DeleteColumn macro deletes a column in a list view control. When I ported my samples from C to MFC, I was able to easily strip off the preface of the macro and use the remainder in my calls to the member functions. In the example I just mentioned, an MFC application that has a list view control (CListCtrl class) defined as *m_List* would contain a member function called m_List.DeleteColumn.

The COMCTL32.DLL file contains the window procedures, resources, and functions that support common controls. Applications using the new common controls must link with the COMCTL32.LIB file. Before you make any calls into this library, you should call the Windows InitCommonControls function to ensure that this DLL has been loaded. InitCommonControls is a stub function that does nothing; it takes no parameters and returns no values. Calling this function simply confirms that the common control library has been loaded.

Each common control belongs to a window class defined by the common control library. An application creates a common control of a particular type by specifying the appropriate window class name in the CreateWindow or CreateWindowEx function, by using the Create member function for the MFC class designed to support the window class, or by using a dialog template. Table 1-1 lists the window classes provided by the common control library. You can find these definitions in the COMMCTRL.H file for C projects; for MFC projects, the AFXCMN.H file should be included in STDAFX.H.

Class Name	Description
ANIMATE_CLASS	Provides a method for displaying animated controls within a window.
HOTKEY_CLASS	Allows the developer to define hot keys, which are key combinations that the user can press to perform an action quickly. For example, a user can press the hot key Ctrl-Z to activate a given window and bring it to the top of the z-order. The hot-key control displays the user's choices and ensures that the user selects a valid key combination.

Table 1-1. *(continued)*
Common control window classes.

Table 1-1. *continued*

Class Name	Description
PROGRESS_CLASS	Provides a method for indicating the progress of a lengthy operation by gradually filling a rectangle from left to right with the system highlight color as the operation progresses.
STATUSCLASSNAME	Provides a method for displaying status information.
TOOLBARCLASSNAME	Provides buttons that carry out menu commands.
TOOLTIPS_CLASS	Creates a ToolTip control, which displays a small pop-up window containing text that explains the purpose of a tool in an application. ToolTips are generally used with toolbars.
TRACKBAR_CLASS	Allows the user to select from a range of values by moving a slider.
UPDOWN_CLASS	Provides a pair of arrows to increment or decrement the value in an adjacent (buddy) control.
WC_HEADER	Provides a method for displaying a header above a column of information and allows the user to sort the information by clicking the header.
WC_LISTVIEW	Provides a method for displaying and arranging a collection of items. Each item consists of an icon and a label.
WC_TABCONTROL	Provides a method for defining multiple pages for the same area of a window or a dialog box. Each page contains specific information or a group of controls that the application displays when the user clicks the corresponding tab.
WC_TREEVIEW	Provides a method for displaying a hierarchical list of items. Each item consists of a label and, optionally, a bitmap.

Common Control Window Styles

The Win32 application programming interface (API) offers several window styles that you can use when creating common controls. Table 1-2 lists and describes these styles. In general, you can combine styles when you create a new control, although Table 1-2 notes certain cases in which you cannot use a combination.

Style	Description
CCS_ADJUSTABLE	Allows a toolbar to be configured by the user.
CCS_BOTTOM	Positions the control at the bottom of its parent window's client area and sets the control width to the parent window width. Status bars have this style by default.
CCS_NODIVIDER	Prevents a 2-pixel highlight from being drawn at the top of the control.
CCS_NOHILITE	Prevents a 1-pixel highlight from being drawn at the top of the control.
CCS_NOMOVEY	Resizes the control and moves it horizontally, but not vertically, in response to a WM_SIZE message. This style is ignored if the CCS_NORESIZE style is set.
CCS_NOPARENTALIGN	Prevents the control from automatically moving to the top or bottom of the parent window. A control with this style maintains its position within the parent window even if the size of the parent window changes. If you specify the CCS_TOP or CCS_BOTTOM style with CCS_NOPARENTALIGN, the height of the control adjusts to the default, and the position and width of the control remain unchanged.
CCS_NORESIZE	Prevents the control from using the default width and height when setting its initial size or a new size. A control with this style uses the width and height specified in the creation or sizing request.
CCS_TOP	Positions the control at the top of the parent window's client area and sets the control width to the parent window width. Toolbars have this style by default.

Table 1-2.
Common control styles.

Common Control Notifications

A common control notifies its parent window of an input event by sending a notification. Some common controls send notifications in the form of WM_NOTIFY messages. The *lParam* parameter of a WM_NOTIFY message is either the address of an NMHDR structure or the address of a larger structure that includes the NMHDR structure (for tab controls, list view controls, and tree view controls). Each common control has its own specific set of notification values.

The common control library also provides notification values that can be sent by more than one type of common control. All of the common controls can send the following notifications:

NM_CLICK	The user clicked the left mouse button within the control.
NM_DBLCLK	The user double-clicked the left mouse button within the control.
NM_KILLFOCUS	The control lost the input focus.
NM_RCLICK	The user clicked the right mouse button within the control.
NM_RDBLCLK	The user double-clicked the right mouse button within the control.
NM_RETURN	The control has the input focus, and the user pressed the Enter key.
NM_SETFOCUS	The control gained the input focus.

Now that you have some background, the remainder of this chapter will explore two of the new common controls: status bars and toolbars. They are referred to as organizational controls because you can use them to organize other controls. Before Windows 95, you could find support for these controls from within Microsoft Visual C++ through the Microsoft Foundation Class Library; all you needed to do was click a check box. But these were MFC classes. C programmers were still out of luck if they wanted easy access to these controls. Now that the Win32 API supports the organizational controls, everyone can use the same status bars and toolbars that appear in the Windows 95 user interface.

Status Bars

A status bar is a horizontal window positioned, by default, at the bottom of a parent window. It displays status information that is defined by the application. This control can appear in one of two modes: as a *simple-mode status bar* (containing only one section) or as a *multiple-part status bar* (divided into various sections and able to display more than one type of status information). A multiple-part status bar can contain as many as 255 sections.

You can create a status bar in any of these three ways:

■ Use the CreateWindow or CreateWindowEx function, specifying the STATUSCLASSNAME window class.

■ Use the MFC CStatusBar class and its member functions.

■ Use the MFC CStatusBarCtrl class and its member functions.

Notice that I've listed two MFC classes: CStatusBar and CStatusBarCtrl. MFC has supported the CStatusBar class in both 16-bit and 32-bit Windows. I will refer to this as the "old-style" control. MFC now uses the CStatusBarCtrl class to support the new Win32-only status bar control. These two classes are entirely different. If you want the same functionality that the Win32 control offers, you should use CStatusBarCtrl, even though you will need to create the status bar yourself. AppWizard provides a check box for status bars when you create your project, but using this check box produces an old-style status bar, not the Win32 control. (Also note that CStatusBarCtrl does not have built-in support for the old-style Caps Lock and Num Lock indicators.) I chose to write a sample in C and port it to MFC using the CStatusBarCtrl class.

With all this in mind, let's see what you can do with status bars. I wrote the STATUS sample in C to demonstrate what the text styles look like, how to write text in a status bar, how to use the status bar modes, and how to draw a bitmap in a status bar. Figure 1-1 shows the multiple-part status bar produced by the STATUS sample.

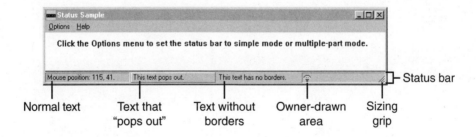

Figure 1-1.
The status bar created by the STATUS sample.

In the lower right corner of the status bar, you will notice a *sizing grip,* which is similar to a sizing border. The user can drag this triangular area to resize the parent window. You can get this functionality by including the

SBS_SIZEGRIP window style when you create your status bar. If you decide to include a sizing grip, you should avoid combining the CCS_TOP common control style and the SBS_SIZEGRIP style because this combination renders the sizing grip nonfunctional. The system will not even draw the sizing grip.

Creating a Multiple-Part Status Bar

I first wrote the STATUS sample in C using the messages provided by the Win32 API. I decided to create a multiple-part status bar to show these elements:

- Normal text
- Text that "pops out"
- Text without a border
- An owner-drawn section with a bitmap displayed

The following code, found in the STATUS.C file on the companion disc, creates the status bar and breaks it into parts. The array of integers passed in the SB_SETPARTS message (or the MFC SetParts member function) is an array of endpoints for each part of the status bar. Because I take care of sizing my status bar when I handle the WM_SIZE message, I fill in the actual endpoints at that time. As is the case for most of the common controls, you need to include the COMMCTRL.H header file in order to use status bars in your application, and you must include the COMCTL32.LIB file in your list of libraries.

```
static HWND hWndStatus;
static int aWidths [4];

switch (message)
{
   case WM_CREATE:
      hWndStatus = CreateWindowEx (
         0L,                             // extended style
         STATUSCLASSNAME,                // create status bar
         "",                             // window title
         WS_CHILD | WS_BORDER |
            WS_VISIBLE | SBS_SIZEGRIP,   // window styles
         0, 0, 0, 0,                     // x, y, width, height
         hWnd,                           // parent window
         (HMENU)ID_STATUSBAR,            // ID
         hInst,                          // instance
         NULL);                          // window data
```

```
if (hWndStatus == NULL)
    MessageBox (NULL, "Status Bar not created!", NULL, MB_OK);
// Break the status bar into four parts.
SendMessage (hWndStatus, SB_SETPARTS, 4, (LPARAM)aWidths);
```

Now that you've created the status bar, you should give it some text to display. What good is a status bar that doesn't say anything? Setting text is as easy as sending a message (or calling an MFC member function). The trick to displaying the different kinds of text shown in Figure 1-1 on page 9 is to set the drawing style when setting the text. The *wParam* parameter for the SB-_SETTEXT message is a combination of the (zero-based) part of the status bar that receives the text and the text drawing style.

```
// Set the text in the first part to normal.
SendMessage (hWndStatus, SB_SETTEXT, 0,
    (LPARAM)"Mouse position:");

// Set the text in the second part to pop out.
SendMessage (hWndStatus, SB_SETTEXT, 1 | SBT_POPOUT,
    (LPARAM)"This text pops out.");

// Set the text in the third part to have no borders.
SendMessage (hWndStatus, SB_SETTEXT, 2 | SBT_NOBORDERS,
    (LPARAM)"This text has no borders.");

// Load the bitmap for the owner-drawn part of the status bar.
hBmp = LoadBitmap (hInst, MAKEINTRESOURCE (ID_BITMAP));

// Set the fourth part to be owner-drawn and pass the bitmap.
SendMessage (hWndStatus, SB_SETTEXT, 3 | SBT_OWNERDRAW,
    (LPARAM)hBmp);
```

The MFC version of the code (the MFCSTATUS sample) creates the status bar in the view class of the OnCreate handler in the MFCSTVW.CPP file. The status bar is created and the text and parts initially set using the member functions provided by the CStatusBarCtrl class. As you can see, the code is very similar. One difference is in the SetText member function. Whereas the SB_SETTEXT message packed both the part and the drawing style into *wParam*, the SetText member function receives these two values separately: first the part and then the drawing style. Another difference between the C version and the MFC version is that you must include the AFXCMN.H file, which defines the new common control classes, in your STDAFX.H file.

```
// The view class is defined as follows in MFCSTVW.H.

class CMfcstatusView : public CView
{
    protected:    // create from serialization only
        CMfcstatusView ();
        DECLARE_DYNCREATE (CMfcstatusView);
        CStatus m_Status;

    // Attributes
    public:
        CMfcstatusDoc *GetDocument ();

    // Operations
    public:

    // Overrides
        // ClassWizard generated virtual function overrides.
        // {{AFX_VIRTUAL (CMfcstatusView)
        public:
            virtual void OnDraw (CDC *pDC);    // overridden to draw
                                               // this view
        protected:
        // }}AFX_VIRTUAL

    // Implementation
    public:
        virtual ~CMfcstatusView ();
#ifdef _DEBUG
        virtual void AssertValid () const;
        virtual void Dump (CDumpContext& dc) const;
#endif

    protected:

    // Generated message map functions
    protected:
        // {{AFX_MSG (CMfcstatusView)
        afx_msg int OnCreate (LPCREATESTRUCT lpCreateStruct);
        afx_msg void OnSimple ();
        afx_msg void OnMultiple ();
        afx_msg void OnSize (UINT nType, int cx, int cy);
        afx_msg void OnMouseMove (UINT nFlags, CPoint point);
        // }}AFX_MSG
        DECLARE_MESSAGE_MAP ()
};
```

```
// The status bar is created in MFCSTVW.CPP.

int CMfcstatusView::OnCreate (LPCREATESTRUCT lpCreateStruct)
{
if (CView::OnCreate (lpCreateStruct) == -1)
   return -1;

// Create the status bar.
m_Status.Create (WS_CHILD | WS_BORDER | WS_VISIBLE | SBARS_SIZEGRIP,
   Crect (0, 0, 0, 0),
   this,
   ID_STATUSBAR);

int aWidths [4] = {0, 0, 0, 0};
// Set the status bar to have four parts.
m_Status.SetParts (4, aWidths);
// Set the text in the first part to normal.
m_Status.SetText ((LPCTSTR)"Mouse position:", 0, 0);
// Set the text in the second part to pop out.
m_Status.SetText ((LPCTSTR)"This text pops out.", 1, SBT_POPOUT);
// Set the text in the third part to have no borders.
m_Status.SetText ((LPCTSTR)"This text has no borders.", 2,
   SBT_NOBORDERS);
// Set the fourth part to be owner-drawn.
m_Status.SetText ((LPCTSTR)"", 3, SBT_OWNERDRAW);
return 0;
}
```

Sizing the status bar window and its parts isn't difficult. It's simply a matter of handling the WM_SIZE message, moving the status bar window, and setting the endpoints for the parts in the status bar. Following is the C code I used; I leave the MFC code as an exercise for you.

```
case WM_SIZE:
   // Resize the status bar to fit along the bottom of the client area.
   MoveWindow (hWndStatus, 0, HIWORD(lParam) - 10, LOWORD(lParam),
      HIWORD(lParam), TRUE);
   // Set the rectangles for the multiple parts of the status bar.
   // Make each part 1/4 of the width of the client area.
   aWidths [0] = LOWORD(lParam) / 4;
   aWidths [1] = LOWORD(lParam) / 2;
   aWidths [2] = LOWORD(lParam) - aWidths [0];
   aWidths [3] = -1;
   SendMessage (hWndStatus, SB_SETPARTS, 4, (LPARAM)aWidths);
   break;
```

Using Owner Drawing in a Status Bar

Status bars are great for displaying text, but what if you want to put a bitmap in your status bar, as Microsoft Mail does? Using the Win32 API, you can add a bitmap by taking advantage of the control's support for owner drawing. Owner drawing lets you display a bitmap instead of text (or use a different font) in a section of a status bar. In the code you just saw, you send the SB_SETTEXT message with the SBT_OWNERDRAW drawing style specified to tell the system that a part of your status bar should be owner-drawn. The *lParam* parameter is a 32-bit, application-defined value that the application can use when drawing that part of the status bar (that is, you can pass a bitmap handle in this parameter if you like). At this point, you treat the control like any other owner-drawn control: you handle the WM_DRAWITEM message and then use the information in the DRAWITEMSTRUCT structure that is passed along. The following code demonstrates how I did this in the STATUS sample:

```
case WM_DRAWITEM:
    if ((int)wParam == ID_STATUSBAR)
    {
        LPDRAWITEMSTRUCT lpDis;
        HDC hdcMem;
        HBITMAP hbmOld;
        BITMAP bm;

        // Save the drawing information. This information is specific
        // to the part of the status bar to be drawn.
        lpDis = (LPDRAWITEMSTRUCT)lParam;
        // Create a compatible device context (DC) for the bit block
        // transfer (bitblt).
        hdcMem = CreateCompatibleDC (lpDis->hDC);
        // Select the bitmap into the DC.
        hbmOld = SelectObject (hdcMem, hBmp);
        // Get the information about the bitmap's size.
        GetObject (hBmp, sizeof (bm), &bm);
        // Use BitBlt to transfer the bitmap to the part.
        BitBlt (lpDis->hDC, lpDis->rcItem.left, lpDis->rcItem.top,
            bm.bmWidth, bm.bmHeight, hdcMem, 0, 0, SRCCOPY);
        // Reselect the original object into the DC.
        SelectObject (hdcMem, hbmOld);
        // Delete the compatible DC.
        DeleteDC (hdcMem);
    }
    break;
```

Some clever readers will notice that I call the BitBlt function to transfer a bitmap but that this bitmap is not drawn transparently. I cheated a bit by drawing the background as the standard gray used in most status bars. If someone were to change the color of the status bar, this little cheat would show.

The code in my MFC version of this sample looks strikingly familiar; however, I ran into a big "gotcha" when I ported this portion of the code. In short, the MFC class that is provided demands that you override the DrawItem method of the CStatusBarCtrl class in order to use the owner-drawn capabilities of the status bar. Initially, I just handled the WM_DRAWITEM message in the view, and the bitmap and the status bar drew correctly. But I kept getting these pesky ASSERT messages. When I tracked down the problem, I was annoyed, to say the least. To remedy the situation, I used ClassWizard to create a class based on CStatusBarCtrl and handled the DrawItem method myself. The MFC sample uses the following code to draw its bitmap on the status bar:

```
// CStatus message handlers

void CStatus::DrawItem (LPDRAWITEMSTRUCT lpDrawItemStruct)
{
static HBITMAP m_Bmp;

if (m_Bmp == NULL)
   // Load the bitmap for the owner-drawn part of the status bar.
   m_Bmp = ::LoadBitmap (AfxGetResourceHandle (),
      MAKEINTRESOURCE (ID_BITMAP));
// Create a compatible DC for the bit block transfer.
HDC hdcMem = ::CreateCompatibleDC (lpDrawItemStruct->hDC);
// Select the bitmap into the DC.
HBITMAP hbmOld = (HBITMAP) ::SelectObject (hdcMem, (HBITMAP)m_Bmp);

BITMAP bm;
// Get the information about the bitmap's size.
::GetObject ((HBITMAP)m_Bmp, sizeof (bm), &bm);
// Use BitBlt to transfer the bitmap.
::BitBlt (lpDrawItemStruct->hDC,
   lpDrawItemStruct->rcItem.left,
   lpDrawItemStruct->rcItem.top,
   bm.bmWidth,
   bm.bmHeight,
   hdcMem, 0, 0,
   SRCCOPY);
// Reselect the original bitmap.
::SelectObject (hdcMem, hbmOld);
// Delete the compatible DC.
::DeleteDC (hdcMem);
}
```

Creating a Simple-Mode Status Bar

A simple-mode status bar, such as the one shown in Figure 1-2, is useful for displaying a one-line description of a menu item as the user highlights the item or for displaying diagnostic information. To create a simple-mode status bar from a multiple-part status bar, you must send an SB_SIMPLE message to the status bar (or use the MFC SetSimple member function). But bear in mind that simple-mode status bars do not support owner drawing—so no cute bitmaps in this case.

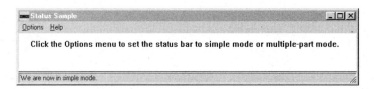

Figure 1-2.
A status bar in simple mode.

The string that a status bar displays in simple mode is maintained separately from the strings it displays when it is in multiple-part mode. Thus, as you can see in the STATUS sample, you can put the window in simple mode, set its text, and switch back to multiple-part mode without having to reset the text. The following code demonstrates how to set the status bar mode in response to a command sent through the Options menu. When you set the text in the status bar, you should set *wParam* to 255, which signals that this is a simple-mode status bar and that the string should be maintained separately from the strings originally used in the multiple-part status bar.

```
case WM_COMMAND:
   switch (LOWORD(wParam))
   {
     case IDM_SIMPLE:
        // Set the status bar to simple mode.
        SendMessage (hWndStatus, SB_SIMPLE, (WPARAM)TRUE, 0L);
        // Set the text of the status bar.
        SendMessage (hWndStatus, SB_SETTEXT, 255,
           (LPARAM)"We are now in simple mode.");
        // Check the Simple menu option.
        CheckMenuItem (GetMenu (hWnd), IDM_SIMPLE,
           MF_CHECKED | MF_BYCOMMAND);
        // Uncheck the Multiple menu option.
        CheckMenuItem (GetMenu (hWnd), IDM_MULTIPLE,
           MF_UNCHECKED | MF_BYCOMMAND);
        break;
```

```
case IDM_MULTIPLE:
    // Reset the status bar to multiple-part mode.
    SendMessage (hWndStatus, SB_SIMPLE, (WPARAM)FALSE, 0L);
    // Uncheck the Simple menu option.
    CheckMenuItem (GetMenu (hWnd), IDM_SIMPLE,
        MF_UNCHECKED | MF_BYCOMMAND);
    // Check the Multiple menu option.
    CheckMenuItem (GetMenu (hWnd), IDM_MULTIPLE,
        MF_CHECKED | MF_BYCOMMAND);
    break;
```

These operations are very similar in the MFC version of the sample. In that version, however, the SetSimple member function assumes TRUE by default, so I did not pass any parameters when I set my status bar to simple mode. When I reset the status bar to be multiple-part, I simply passed FALSE as the parameter.

Status Bar Messages and Member Functions

Table 1-3 lists the messages that can be sent to status bars and the member functions supported by the MFC-supplied class CStatusBarCtrl. Because the table's purpose is to describe what you can do with a status bar, it does not include return values or parameter information. You can find details about parameters and return values in the Win32 SDK documentation and in the MFC 3.1 documentation.

Message	Member Function	Description
SB_GETBORDERS*	GetBorders*	Retrieves the current widths of the horizontal and vertical borders of a status bar. These measurements determine the spacing between the outer edge of the window and the rectangles in the window that contain text as well as the spacing between rectangles.
SB_GETPARTS	GetParts	Retrieves the number of parts in a status bar and, for each part, the coordinate of the right edge.
SB_GETRECT	GetRect	Retrieves the bounding rectangle of the given part of a status bar.

Table 1-3.   *(continued)*

Status bar messages and member functions.

Table 1-3. *continued*

Message	Member Function	Description
SB_GETTEXT*	GetText*	Retrieves the text from the given part of a status bar. SB_GETTEXT returns a 32-bit value consisting of two 16-bit values. The low-order word specifies the length, in characters, of the text. The high-order word specifies the type of operation used to draw the text. If the text has a type of SBT_OWNERDRAW, the message returns the 32-bit value associated with the text instead of the length and type.
SB_GETTEXTLENGTH*	GetTextLength*	Retrieves the length, in characters, of the text from the given part of a status bar. SB_GETTEXTLENGTH returns a 32-bit value consisting of two 16-bit values. The low-order word specifies the length, in characters, of the text. The high-order word specifies the type of operation used to draw the text.
SB_SETBORDERS*	SetBorders*	Sets the widths of the horizontal and vertical borders of a status bar. These borders determine the spacing between the outer edge of the window and the rectangles within the window that contain text as well as the spacing between rectangles.
SB_SETMINHEIGHT*	SetMinHeight*	Sets the minimum height for a status bar. The sum of this minimum height (*wParam*) and the height of the vertical border of the window equals the minimum height of the entire window.
SB_SETPARTS	SetParts	Sets the number of parts in a status bar (no more than 255) and sets the coordinate of the right edge of each part. *lParam* is the address of an integer array that has the same number of elements as the number of parts specified by *wParam*. Each element in the array specifies the position, in client coordinates, of the right edge of the corresponding part. If an element is –1, the position of the right edge for that part extends to the right edge of the window.

(continued)

Table 1-3. *continued*

Message	Member Function	Description
SB_SETTEXT*	SetText*	Sets the text in the given part of a status bar. This message invalidates the portion of the window that has changed, causing the window to display the new text. *wParam* is the zero-based index of the part to set and the type of drawing operation. If this value is 255, the status bar is assumed to be in simple mode. *lParam* is the address of a null-terminated string that specifies the text to set. If *wParam* is SBT_OWNERDRAW, *lParam* represents 32 bits of data. The parent window must interpret and draw the data when it receives the WM-_DRAWITEM message.
SB_SIMPLE	SetSimple	Specifies whether a status bar displays simple text or displays all window parts set by a previous SB_SETPARTS message.

* This message or member function can also be used with header controls (column headers), discussed in Chapter 3.

Toolbars

Toolbars are probably the second most pervasive of the new common controls. Like status bars, the toolbars found in so many applications on the market today were created without the luxury of system support—that is, developers had to go about reinventing the wheel whenever they wanted to include toolbars in an application. With the additions to the Win32 API for Windows 95, developers can now implement toolbars as easily as any other type of system-supported control.

For those who have lived in a cave for the past few years, a toolbar is a window containing buttons or other controls, usually located at the top of the parent window. Toolbar buttons provide fast access to commonly used commands such as Open, Save, and Print. Figure 1-3 on the next page shows the toolbar created by the TOOLBAR sample (for C lovers) and MFCTOOL (the version for MFC maniacs). You can see the various parts of the toolbar, including buttons, a combo-box control, a separator (used to logically separate groups of buttons or controls), and a ToolTip (that neat little box that pops up when your mouse pointer lingers over a toolbar button—in this example, the Save button).

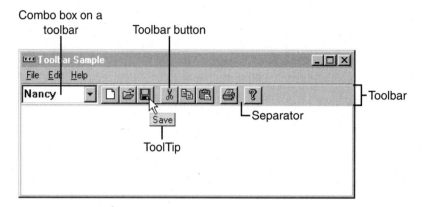

Figure 1-3.
The toolbar created by the TOOLBAR sample.

The design goals of the TOOLBAR sample, which I first wrote in C and then ported to MFC, included the following:

- To demonstrate what a fairly standard toolbar looks like.

- To support ToolTips.

- To include a nonbutton control on the toolbar. (I decided to use a drop-down combo box because it is the control I see most often on other toolbars in shipping applications.)

- To use the new Windows 95 version of the toolbar rather than the old-style control.

Toolbars, like status bars, have ancestors that were supported in MFC before the release of Windows 95. If you build your project with MFC and choose to include a toolbar, you will get the window class that MFC supported, CToolBar. If you check AppWizard's Dockable Toolbar check box, MFC provides a "standard" toolbar bitmap filled with tools such as New, Open, Save, and so on. MFC also creates the toolbar and manages the ToolTips for you. Another nice option of the original toolbar class is the ability to make your toolbar dockable. This feature lets users pick up the toolbar with the mouse, drag the toolbar around the window, and drop it wherever they want. If the user drops the toolbar at a window perimeter, the toolbar will "dock" itself on that side of the window.

Creating a Toolbar

Creating a toolbar is simple: you fill out a button structure, create a large bitmap containing the buttons, and then call the CreateToolbarEx function. This function takes care of adding the bitmaps and buttons to the toolbar. Then, unless you want to do something special, you can just let the system handle the toolbar processing. The window procedure for the toolbar automatically positions and sets the size of the toolbar window. By default, the toolbar appears at the top of its parent window's client area; however, you can place the toolbar at the bottom of the client area by specifying CCS-_BOTTOM. The TBSTYLE_TOOLTIPS window style allows the toolbar to display ToolTips. Windows sends a WM_NOTIFY message to the toolbar whenever Windows needs to display text in a pop-up.

The following code snippet from the TOOLBAR sample creates a toolbar with 24 "buttons," 8 of which are actual buttons. The bitmap provided for each button is 16-by-16 pixels. The total number of buttons (24) includes all separators. Because you will add a combo box, you must place separators as placeholders where the combo box will reside. Once you create the toolbar, you can create the combo box in the standard way and parent it to the toolbar window, which adds this nonbutton control to your toolbar.

```
TBBUTTON tbButtons [] =
{
    {0, 0, TBSTATE_ENABLED, TBSTYLE_SEP, 0L, 0},
    {0, 0, TBSTATE_ENABLED, TBSTYLE_SEP, 0L, 0},
    {0, 0, TBSTATE_ENABLED, TBSTYLE_SEP, 0L, 0},
    {0, 0, TBSTATE_ENABLED, TBSTYLE_SEP, 0L, 0},
    {0, 0, TBSTATE_ENABLED, TBSTYLE_SEP, 0L, 0},
    {0, 0, TBSTATE_ENABLED, TBSTYLE_SEP, 0L, 0},
    {0, 0, TBSTATE_ENABLED, TBSTYLE_SEP, 0L, 0},
    {0, 0, TBSTATE_ENABLED, TBSTYLE_SEP, 0L, 0},
    {0, 0, TBSTATE_ENABLED, TBSTYLE_SEP, 0L, 0},
    {0, 0, TBSTATE_ENABLED, TBSTYLE_SEP, 0L, 0},
    {0, 0, TBSTATE_ENABLED, TBSTYLE_SEP, 0L, 0},
    {0, 0, TBSTATE_ENABLED, TBSTYLE_SEP, 0L, 0},
    {0, 0, TBSTATE_ENABLED, TBSTYLE_SEP, 0L, 0},
    {0, IDM_NEW, TBSTATE_ENABLED, TBSTYLE_BUTTON, 0L, 0},
    {1, IDM_OPEN, TBSTATE_ENABLED, TBSTYLE_BUTTON, 0L, 0},
    {2, IDM_SAVE, TBSTATE_ENABLED, TBSTYLE_BUTTON, 0L, 0},
    {0, 0, TBSTATE_ENABLED, TBSTYLE_SEP, 0L, 0},
```

(continued)

```
        {3, IDM_CUT, TBSTATE_ENABLED, TBSTYLE_BUTTON, 0L, 0},
        {4, IDM_COPY, TBSTATE_ENABLED, TBSTYLE_BUTTON, 0L, 0},
        {5, IDM_PASTE, TBSTATE_ENABLED, TBSTYLE_BUTTON, 0L, 0},
        {0, 0, TBSTATE_ENABLED, TBSTYLE_SEP, 0L, 0},
        {6, IDM_PRINT, TBSTATE_ENABLED, TBSTYLE_BUTTON, 0L, 0},
        {0, 0, TBSTATE_ENABLED, TBSTYLE_SEP, 0L, 0},
        {7, IDM_ABOUT, TBSTATE_ENABLED, TBSTYLE_BUTTON, 0L, 0}
    };

    TOOLINFO tbToolInfo;

    char *szStrings[] = {"Nancy", "Dale", "Dennis", "Herman", "Ken", "Kyle",
        "Nigel", "Renan", "Ruediger"};

    static HWND hWndToolbar;

    // Create the toolbar control.
    hWndToolbar = CreateToolbarEx (
        hWnd,                        // parent
        WS_CHILD | WS_BORDER | WS_VISIBLE | TBSTYLE_TOOLTIPS |
            CCS_ADJUSTABLE,          // window style
        ID_TOOLBAR,                  // toolbar ID
        8,                           // number of bitmaps
        hInst,                       // mod instance
        IDB_TOOLBAR,                 // resource ID for bitmap
        (LPCTBBUTTON)&tbButtons,     // address of buttons
        24,                          // number of buttons
        16, 16,                      // width & height of buttons
        16, 16,                      // width & height of bitmaps
        sizeof (TBBUTTON));          // structure size

    if (hWndToolbar == NULL)
    {
        MessageBox (NULL, "Toolbar not created!", NULL, MB_OK);
        break;
    }

    // Create the combo box and add it to the toolbar.
    hWndCombo = CreateWindowEx (0L,          // no extended styles
        "COMBOBOX",                           // class name
        "",                                   // default text
        WS_CHILD | WS_BORDER | WS_VISIBLE |
            CBS_HASSTRINGS | CBS_DROPDOWN,    // styles and defaults
        0, 0, 100, 250,                       // size and position
        hWndToolbar,                          // parent window
        (HMENU)IDM_COMBO,                     // ID
        hInst,                                // current instance
        NULL);                                // no class data
```

```
if (hWndCombo)
{
   // Add strings to the combo box.
   for (idx = 0; idx < 9; idx++)
      SendMessage (hWndCombo, CB_INSERTSTRING, (WPARAM)(-1),
         (LPARAM)szStrings[idx]);
}
```

Using the MFC-supplied class CToolBarCtrl, I had to do a bit more work. The Create member function provided by MFC merely creates the toolbar; it doesn't load the bitmap or add the buttons. This is no big deal, however, because you simply need to call the AddBitmap and AddButtons member functions to add these items to your toolbar.

```
int CMfctoolView::OnCreate (LPCREATESTRUCT lpCreateStruct)
{
if (CView::OnCreate (lpCreateStruct) == -1)
   return -1;

// Create the toolbar.
m_ToolBar.Create (
   WS_CHILD | WS_BORDER | WS_VISIBLE | TBSTYLE_TOOLTIPS |
      CCS_ADJUSTABLE,   // style
   Crect (0, 0, 0, 0),
   this,
   ID_TOOLBAR);

// Add the bitmaps.
m_ToolBar.AddBitmap (8, IDB_BITMAP1);

// Add the buttons.
m_ToolBar.AddButtons (24, (LPTBBUTTON)&tbButtons);

// Create the combo box.
m_Combo.Create (
   WS_CHILD | WS_BORDER | WS_VISIBLE | CBS_HASSTRINGS | CBS_DROPDOWN,
   Crect (0, 0, 100, 250),
   (CWnd *)&m_ToolBar,
   ID_COMBO);

int idx;
for (idx = 0; idx < 8; idx++)
   m_Combo.InsertString (-1, (LPCTSTR)szStrings[idx]);

return 0;
}
```

The preceding code does not specify a size for the toolbar. Instead, you can size the toolbar when the parent window (the *client window* for you C people, or the *View window* for MFC fans) handles the WM_SIZE message. In response to this message, you can use the TB_AUTOSIZE message (or the MFC AutoSize member function) to tell the toolbar to size itself.

Creating a Toolbar Bitmap

If you have never produced a toolbar before, one of the "mysteries" you need to solve is how to create the bitmaps for the buttons. If you are like me, you might expect to create a bitmap for each button, include the bitmaps in your application, and pass the identifiers to these bitmaps to set each button. Well, that's not the way it's done. You do create a bitmap for each button, but you then build a larger bitmap by stringing together all of the small ones.

But what if you want to get your grubby little hands on the bitmaps that Windows Explorer uses for its Open, Save, and other buttons? One way to do this is to run AppWizard and write a stub program that includes a toolbar. By default, AppWizard gives you the standard bitmaps in a file ever-so-creatively called TOOLBAR.BMP (located in the RES subfolder of your project folder). You can edit this file with the resource editor built into Visual C++ or with Microsoft Paint. (Be sure to create a 16-color bitmap rather than a 256-color bitmap.) Figure 1-4 (zoomed up to a readable size) shows the standard set of bitmaps that AppWizard supplies. The last bitmap provides an easy way for the user to get help on an item shown in the application's window. When you click this bitmap, the cursor changes from an arrow pointer to a combination of an arrow and a question mark. Pointing with the new cursor and clicking a control or a window displays a Help topic for that item. (The TOOLBAR sample doesn't support this feature.)

Figure 1-4.
An example of a toolbar bitmap.

Even if you don't use AppWizard, you aren't out of luck: the standard toolbar bitmaps are now built into COMCTL32.DLL. You can add these images to your toolbar by using the TB_ADDBITMAP message. The following code sample shows you how to include three of the standard file bitmaps (new, open, and save) and four of the view bitmaps (large icon view, small icon view, list view, and details view). The code fills out the TBBUTTON structure with the predefined indexes to the bitmaps you want:

```
// Toolbar buttons
TBBUTTON tbButtons [] =
{
   {STD_FILENEW, IDM_NEW, TBSTATE_ENABLED, TBSTYLE_BUTTON, 0L, 0},
   {STD_FILEOPEN, IDM_OPEN, TBSTATE_ENABLED, TBSTYLE_BUTTON, 0L, 0},
   {STD_FILESAVE, IDM_SAVE, TBSTATE_ENABLED, TBSTYLE_BUTTON, 0L, 0},
   {0, 0, TBSTATE_ENABLED, TBSTYLE_SEP, 0L, 0},
   {VIEW_LARGEICONS, IDM_LARGEICON, TBSTATE_ENABLED, TBSTYLE_BUTTON,
      0L, 0},
   {VIEW_SMALLICONS, IDM_SMALLICON, TBSTATE_ENABLED, TBSTYLE_BUTTON,
      0L, 0},
   {VIEW_LIST, IDM_LISTVIEW, TBSTATE_ENABLED, TBSTYLE_BUTTON,
      0L, 0},
   {VIEW_DETAILS, IDM_REPORTVIEW, TBSTATE_ENABLED, TBSTYLE_BUTTON,
      0L, 0},
};
```

Next, in the code that will create the toolbar, the application calls the CreateToolbarEx function, specifying HINST_COMMCTRL as the HINSTANCE, IDB_STD_SMALL_COLOR as the bitmap identifier, and a pointer to the TBBUTTON structure. Notice that 11 bitmaps are specified because the IDB_STD_SMALL_COLOR bitmap contains 11 bitmaps. Notice also that four buttons are specified; this refers to the last four view buttons, which come from a different bitmap. When the toolbar is created, the view bitmaps are added through the TB_ADDBITMAP message. This message returns an index that is used to provide the correct index to the view bitmaps.

```
HWND CreateTheToolbar (HWND hWndParent)
{
HWND hWndToolbar;
TBADDBITMAP tb;
int index, stdidx;

hWndToolbar = CreateToolbarEx (hWndParent,
   WS_CHILD | WS_BORDER | WS_VISIBLE | WS_CHILD | TBSTYLE_TOOLTIPS,
   ID_TOOLBAR, 11, (HINSTANCE)HINST_COMMCTRL, IDB_STD_SMALL_COLOR,
   (LPCTBBUTTON)&tbButtons, 4, 0, 0, 100, 30, sizeof (TBBUTTON));

// Add the system-defined view bitmaps.
// The hInst == HINST_COMMCTRL
// The nID == IDB_VIEW_SMALL_COLOR
tb.hInst = HINST_COMMCTRL;
tb.nID = IDB_VIEW_SMALL_COLOR;
stdidx = SendMessage (hWndToolbar, TB_ADDBITMAP, 12, (LPARAM)&tb);

// Update the indexes to the bitmaps.
for (index = 4; index < NUM_BUTTONS; index++)
   tbButtons[index].iBitmap += stdidx;
```

(continued)

25

```
// Add the view buttons.
SendMessage (hWndToolbar, TB_ADDBUTTONS, 4, (LONG) &tbButtons[4]);

return hWndToolbar;
}
```

> TIP: When you create toolbar bitmaps, you'll often have trouble
> knowing exactly where you are in the image and getting the images
> to line up properly. With Windows 95, the images are actually taken
> out of the bitmap in such a manner that the originating bitmap
> doesn't have to exactly match the height and width based on the
> calls that load the bitmap—that is, you tell the CreateToolbarEx
> function how wide and how tall you want the individual bitmaps to
> be. This allows you to create a bitmap that will look something like
> the one shown here. In this bitmap, you can easily see the exact lo-
> cations of the button boundaries as well as the identifiers for the
> different images:

Supporting ToolTips

You can add ToolTips support to your toolbar by specifying the TBSTYLE-
_TOOLTIPS style and creating a string table in your RC file that contains the
text to display. You then process the WM_NOTIFY message that is sent to the
parent window procedure of the toolbar, as shown in the following code:

```
case WM_NOTIFY:
   switch (((LPNMHDR)lParam)->code)
   {
      case TTN_NEEDTEXT:
         // Display the ToolTip text.
         lpToolTipText = (LPTOOLTIPTEXT)lParam;
         LoadString (hInst,
            lpToolTipText->hdr.idFrom,   // string ID == cmd ID
            szBuf,
            sizeof (szBuf));
         lpToolTipText->lpszText = szBuf;
         break;
      ⋮
```

This step is a bit different for those developing in MFC. The standard lists currently provided with MFC do not include the WM_NOTIFY message. As a result, you need to put a function directly into the view class:

```
LRESULT CMfctoolView::WindowProc (UINT message, WPARAM wParam,
    LPARAM lParam)
{
static CHAR szBuf [128];
LPTOOLTIPTEXT lpToolTipText;

if (message == WM_NOTIFY)
{
    switch (((LPNMHDR)lParam)->code)
    {
      case TTN_NEEDTEXT:
          // Display the ToolTip text.
          lpToolTipText = (LPTOOLTIPTEXT)lParam;
          ::LoadString (AfxGetResourceHandle (),
              lpToolTipText->hdr.idFrom,   // string ID == cmd ID
              szBuf,
              sizeof (szBuf));
          lpToolTipText->lpszText = szBuf;
          break;
    ⋮
```

Adding a ToolTip to a Nonbutton Control

If your toolbar contains a nonbutton control, you have to do a bit more work to support ToolTips. In my sample, I created a combo box and then parented it to the toolbar. To add a ToolTip to this control, the application must send the TTM_ADDTOOL message to the ToolTip control (or use the MFC AddTool member function). It also needs to trap the WM_MOUSE-MOVE, WM_LBUTTONDOWN, and WM_LBUTTONUP messages in the window procedure for the combo box and pass these on to the ToolTip control so that it will know to pop up the ToolTip for the combo box. The following C code demonstrates these steps:

```
// This code is in the main window procedure after the combo box
// has been created.
// Set the window procedure for the combo box.
lpfnDefCombo = (WNDPROC) GetWindowLong (hWndCombo, GWL_WNDPROC);
SetWindowLong (hWndCombo, GWL_WNDPROC, (LONG)ComboWndProc);

// Get the handle to the ToolTip window.
hWndTT = (HWND) SendMessage (hWndToolbar, TB_GETTOOLTIPS, 0, 0);
```

(continued)

```
if (hWndTT)
{
    // Fill out the TOOLINFO structure.
    lpToolInfo.cbSize = sizeof (lpToolInfo);
    // The uID is the handle of the tool (the combo box).
    lpToolInfo.uFlags = TTF_IDISHWND | TTF_CENTERTIP;
    // The string ID in the resource
    lpToolInfo.lpszText = (LPSTR)IDM_COMBO;
    // The window that gets the ToolTip messages
    lpToolInfo.hwnd = hWnd;
    // The tool
    lpToolInfo.uId = (UINT)hWndCombo;
    // The instance that owns the string resource
    lpToolInfo.hinst = hInst;

    // Set up the ToolTip for the combo box.
    SendMessage (hWndTT, TTM_ADDTOOL, 0,
        (LPARAM)(LPTOOLINFO)&lpToolInfo);
}
    :

// This function relays the mouse messages from the combo box
// to get the ToolTip to work.
LRESULT CALLBACK ComboWndProc (HWND hWnd, UINT uMessage, WPARAM wParam,
    LPARAM lParam)
{
switch (uMessage)
{
    case WM_MOUSEMOVE:
    case WM_LBUTTONDOWN:
    case WM_LBUTTONUP:
    {
        MSG msg;
        HWND hWndTT;
        msg.lParam = lParam;
        msg.wParam = wParam;
        msg.message = uMessage;
        msg.hwnd = hWnd;
        hWndTT = (HWND) SendMessage (hWndToolbar, TB_GETTOOLTIPS, 0, 0);
        SendMessage (hWndTT, TTM_RELAYEVENT, 0, (LPARAM)(LPMSG)&msg);
        break;
    }
}
return CallWindowProc (lpfnDefCombo, hWnd, uMessage, wParam, lParam);
}
```

The corresponding MFC procedure is similar. One change I made was to create a class for my combo-box control derived from CComboBox and use ClassWizard to create a message map to WindowProc. Within this function, I did the same type of processing—except that it was less tedious to fill out the message structure. Instead, I was able to call CWnd::GetCurrentMessage.

Customizing a Toolbar

You can support toolbar customization if you create your toolbar with the CCS_ADJUSTABLE style. The customization features allow the user to drag a button to a new position or to remove a button by dragging it off the toolbar. In addition, the user can double-click the toolbar to display the Customize Toolbar dialog box, which makes it easy to add, delete, and re-arrange toolbar buttons. An application can display the dialog box by using the TB_CUSTOMIZE message (or MFC's Customize member function) in response to a double-click on the toolbar.

Handling toolbar customization in your application involves handling various notifications that are sent through the WM_NOTIFY message. In my sample application, I decided to support the following:

- Allowing the user to delete buttons. This is easily done by simply responding TRUE to the TBN_QUERYDELETE notification.

- Allowing the user to add buttons. Here again, I respond TRUE to the TBN_QUERYINSERT notification.

- Displaying customized Help. In response to the TBN_CUSTHELP notification, a message box appears, saying that the user is now seeing custom Help. You, of course, would add displays of more substance to your application.

- Resizing the toolbar by autosizing it in response to the TBN_TOOLBARCHANGE notification.

The following code from the MFCTOOL sample demonstrates how you can support minimal customization:

```
LRESULT CMfctoolView::WindowProc (UINT message, WPARAM wParam,
    LPARAM lParam)
{
static CHAR szBuf [128];
LPTOOLTIPTEXT lpToolTipText;
```

(continued)

```
if (message == WM_NOTIFY)
{
    switch (((LPNMHDR)lParam)->code)
    {
        case TTN_NEEDTEXT:
            // Display the ToolTip text.
            lpToolTipText = (LPTOOLTIPTEXT)lParam;
            ::LoadString (AfxGetResourceHandle (),
                lpToolTipText->hdr.idFrom,    // string ID == cmd ID
                szBuf,
                sizeof (szBuf));
            lpToolTipText->lpszText = szBuf;
            break;

        case TBN_QUERYDELETE:
            // Toolbar customization--can we delete this button?
            return TRUE;
            break;

        case TBN_GETBUTTONINFO:
            // The toolbar needs information about a button.
            return FALSE;
            break;

        case TBN_QUERYINSERT:
            // Can this button be inserted? Just say yo.
            return TRUE;
            break;

        case TBN_CUSTHELP:
            // Need to display custom Help.
            AfxMessageBox ("This Help is custom.");
            break;

        case TBN_TOOLBARCHANGE:
            // The user finished dragging a bitmap to the toolbar.
            m_ToolBar.AutoSize ();
            break;

        default:
            return TRUE;
            break;
    }
}
return CView::WindowProc (message, wParam, lParam);
}
```

If you want to have more control over customization, your application can handle many other notifications that I did not include in my sample. For instance, if you want to do your own button dragging, you can trap the TBN_BEGINDRAG and TBN_ENDDRAG notifications. You might also want to save the state of the toolbar and allow the user to reset its configuration. You can do this by using the TB_SAVERESTORE message to save the current state of the toolbar and waiting for a TBN_RESET notification to signal that the toolbar needs to be reset to its previous state.

Toolbar Messages and Member Functions

Table 1-4 lists the messages sent to toolbars and the member functions MFC provides for the CToolBarCtrl class. For details about each message, its parameters, and possible return values, refer to the Win32 SDK documentation.

Message	Member Function	Description
TB_ADDBITMAP	AddBitmap	Adds a new bitmap to the list of bitmaps available for a toolbar.
TB_ADDBUTTONS	AddButtons	Adds one or more buttons to a toolbar.
TB_ADDSTRING	AddString	Adds a new string to the list of strings available for a toolbar.
TB_AUTOSIZE	AutoSize	Forces a toolbar to be resized. An application sends this message when it changes a toolbar's size (for example, by setting the button size or adding strings).
TB_BUTTONCOUNT	ButtonCount	Retrieves a count of the buttons currently on a toolbar.
TB_BUTTONSTRUCTSIZE	SetButtonStructSize	Specifies the TBBUTTON structure's size, which Windows uses to determine which version of COMMCTRL.DLL is in use. If an application uses CreateWindow to create the toolbar, it must send this message before adding any buttons. The CreateToolbarEx function automatically sends this message, and the size of the TBBUTTON structure is a parameter to CreateToolbarEx.

Table 1-4. *(continued)*
Toolbar messages and member functions.

Table 1-4. *continued*

Message	Member Function	Description
TB_CHANGEBITMAP		Changes the bitmap for a button.
TB_CHECKBUTTON	CheckButton	Checks or unchecks a given button. (When a button is checked, it appears "pressed.")
TB_COMMANDTOINDEX	CommandToIndex	Retrieves the zero-based index for the button associated with the specified command identifier.
TB_CUSTOMIZE	Customize	Displays the Customize Toolbar dialog box.
TB_DELETEBUTTON	DeleteButton	Deletes a button from a toolbar.
TB_ENABLEBUTTON	EnableButton	Enables or disables the specified button. When a button has been enabled, it can be checked ("pressed").
TB_GETBITMAP		Retrieves the index of the bitmap associated with a toolbar button.
	GetBitmapFlags	Returns TBBF_LARGE if the display can support large toolbar bitmaps.
TB_GETBUTTON	GetButton	Retrieves information about the given button.
TB_GETBUTTONTEXT		Retrieves the text of a button.
TB_GETITEMRECT	GetItemRect	Retrieves the bounding rectangle of a button on a toolbar (unless the button's state is set to TBSTATE_HIDDEN).
TB_GETROWS	GetRows	Retrieves the number of rows of toolbar buttons.
TB_GETSTATE	GetState	Retrieves information about the state of a button, such as whether it is enabled or checked.
TB_GETTOOLTIPS	GetToolTips	Retrieves the handle to a ToolTip control associated with a toolbar.
TB_HIDEBUTTON	HideButton	Hides or shows a specified button.
TB_INDETERMINATE	Indeterminate	Sets or clears the indeterminate state of the specified button.
TB_INSERTBUTTON	InsertButton	Inserts a button in the specified location on a toolbar.

(continued)

Table 1-4. *continued*

Message	Member Function	Description
TB_ISBUTTONCHECKED	IsButtonChecked	Determines whether the given button is checked.
TB_ISBUTTONENABLED	IsButtonEnabled	Determines whether the given button is enabled.
TB_ISBUTTONHIDDEN	IsButtonHidden	Determines whether the given button is hidden.
TB_ISBUTTON-INDETERMINATE	IsButton-Indeterminate	Determines whether the given button is indeterminate.
TB_ISBUTTONPRESSED	IsButtonPressed	Determines whether the given button is "pressed."
TB_PRESSBUTTON	PressButton	"Presses" or "releases" the given button.
TB_SAVERESTORE	SaveState or RestoreState	Saves or restores the state of a toolbar.
TB_SETBITMAPSIZE	SetBitmapSize	Sets the size of the bitmapped images to be added to a toolbar. The size can be set only before you add any bitmaps to the toolbar. If an application does not explicitly set the bitmap size, the size defaults to 16-by-16 pixels.
TB_SETBUTTONSIZE	SetButtonSize	Sets the size of the buttons to be added to a toolbar. You can set the button size only before you add any buttons to the toolbar. If an application does not explicitly set the button size, the size defaults to 24-by-22 pixels.
TB_SETCMDID	SetCmdID	Sets the command ID of a button.
	SetOwner	Sets the owner window of a toolbar.
TB_SETPARENT		Sets the parent window of a toolbar.
TB_SETROWS	SetRows	Sets the number of rows of buttons in a toolbar.
TB_SETSTATE	SetState	Sets the state for the given button.
TB_SETTOOLTIPS	SetToolTips	Sets the handle to a ToolTip control associated with a toolbar.

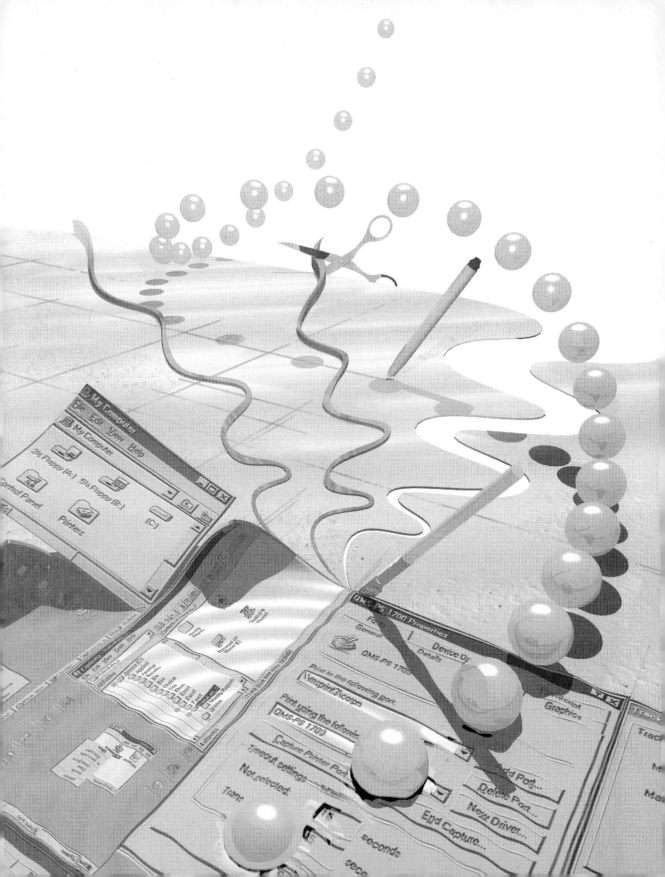

CHAPTER TWO

Trackbars, Progress Bars, Up-Down Controls, and Animation Controls: General-Purpose Common Controls

This chapter examines a group of new common controls that you can use for a broad range of purposes, from measuring intensity levels to scrolling through a list to changing a value. Let's say that you want to control the intensity of the light emitted by a computer-controlled light bulb. (You can stop by my house if you think this is far-fetched.) You could use a trackbar to set or vary the intensity of the light. Or let's say that your application needs to process a number of database files, and you want to let the user know how far it's gotten. You could use a progress bar to show this. In addition to trackbars and progress bars, Microsoft Windows 95 also supports two other general-purpose common controls: up-down and animation controls.

Trackbars

A trackbar is a window containing a slider and tick marks. You use a trackbar as a scrolling control: when you drag the slider (sometimes referred to as the *thumb*), the control sends a message to indicate the change in the slider's position. A horizontal trackbar (the default style) sends a WM_HSCROLL message, and a vertical trackbar uses a WM_VSCROLL message. The tick marks indicate how many points you can move left and right or up and down.

In Figure 2-1, you can see a simple horizontal trackbar with a range of 1 through 10.

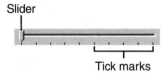

Figure 2-1.
The anatomy of a trackbar.

Trackbars are based on scroll bar controls, and many of the styles and notifications for trackbars are similar to those for scroll bars. By default, the tick marks appear on the right side of a vertical trackbar and on the bottom of a horizontal trackbar. When a user drags the slider or clicks on either side of it, the slider moves in the appropriate direction, tick by tick. In other words, scrolling is not continuous; instead, you scroll in increments indicated by the tick marks. For example, a trackbar with 10 ticks and a range of 1 through 100 allows you to scroll only in increments of 10. You can change the frequency of ticks programmatically.

You can set a portion of a trackbar as a selection range. A blue line in the channel of the trackbar indicates this selection range, and two arrows (replacing the tick marks) indicate its beginning and end. The selection range is a visual representation only; it does not prevent the user from moving the slider outside the selected area. This would be useful, for example, in a scheduling application; the user could see the range of ticks corresponding to the hours for which meetings have been scheduled. In Figure 2-2, the line in the trackbar's channel shows the selection range. To change this range, the application sends a message, TBM_SETSEL, or uses MFC's SetSelection member function.

Figure 2-2.
A trackbar with a selection range.

Table 2-1 lists the styles you can choose when creating a trackbar. You can combine styles for different looks, depending on the effect you want.

Style	Description
TBS_AUTOTICKS	Adds tick marks when you set the range on the trackbar by using the TBM_SETRANGE message (or the MFC SetRange member function).
TBS_BOTH	Places ticks on both sides of the trackbar.
TBS_BOTTOM	Places ticks on the bottom of a horizontal trackbar.
TBS_ENABLESEL-RANGE	Allows you to set a selection range on the trackbar.
TBS_FIXEDLENGTH	Specifies that the length of the slider remains the same even if the selection range changes.
TBS_HORZ	Specifies a horizontal trackbar. This is the default.
TBS_LEFT	Places ticks on the left side of a vertical trackbar.
TBS_NOTHUMB	Specifies that the trackbar has no slider.
TBS_NOTICKS	Specifies that no ticks are placed on the trackbar.
TBS_RIGHT	Places ticks on the right side of a vertical trackbar.
TBS_TOP	Places ticks on the top of a horizontal trackbar.
TBS_VERT	Specifies a vertical trackbar.

Table 2-1.
Trackbar styles.

I wrote a small sample called SLIDER (trackbars themselves are sometimes referred to as *sliders*) to demonstrate the trackbar styles and how they work. The design goals for SLIDER included the following:

- To create a trackbar with default styles.

- To create a horizontal trackbar with tick marks on the top and a selection range set.

- To create a vertical trackbar with tick marks on the left side.

- To set a range for a trackbar.

- To set the line size for a trackbar. (*Line size* specifies how many ticks the slider moves when the user presses the Up or Down arrow key.)

▧ To set the page size for a trackbar. (*Page size* specifies how many ticks the slider moves when the user presses the PgUp or PgDn key.)

▧ To demonstrate the notifications that are sent when you manipulate a trackbar. (In the SLIDER sample, the status bar at the bottom of the screen indicates the notification being sent to the trackbar that has the keyboard focus.)

I also wrote an MFC-equivalent sample called MFCTRACK that demonstrates how to create and manipulate trackbars using the MFC CSliderCtrl class. You can see the MFCTRACK sample in Figure 2-3.

Trackbar with default styles

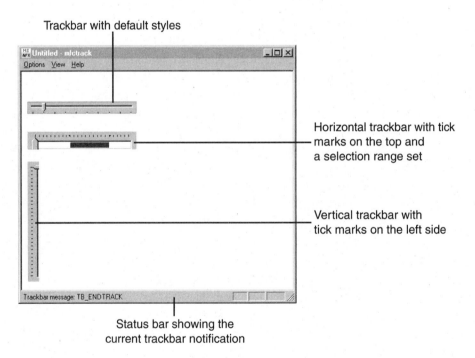

Horizontal trackbar with tick marks on the top and a selection range set

Vertical trackbar with tick marks on the left side

Status bar showing the current trackbar notification

Figure 2-3.
The MFCTRACK sample.

Creating a Trackbar

You can create a trackbar by using the CreateWindow or CreateWindowEx function and specifying the TRACKBAR_CLASS class name or by using the MFC Create member function on your CSliderCtrl object. You can then use trackbar messages or member functions to set the minimum and maximum positions for the slider, draw tick marks, and set a selection range. To use trackbars in your application, you must include the COMMCTRL.H header file, and you also need to have the COMCTL32.LIB file in your list of libraries. This C code creates the status bar and three trackbars in the SLIDER sample:

```
case WM_CREATE:

    hWndStatus = CreateWindow (
        STATUSCLASSNAME,
        "",
        WS_CHILD | WS_BORDER | WS_VISIBLE,
        -100, -100, 10, 10,
        hWnd,
        (HMENU)100,
        hInst,
        NULL);

    hWndSlider1 = CreateWindow (
        TRACKBAR_CLASS,
        "",
        WS_CHILD | WS_VISIBLE | TBS_AUTOTICKS,
        10, 50, 200, 20,
        hWnd,
        (HMENU)10,
        hInst,
        NULL);

    if (hWndSlider1 -- NULL)
        MessageBox (NULL, "Slider1 not created!", NULL, MB_OK);

    hWndSlider2 = CreateWindow (
        TRACKBAR_CLASS,
        "",
        WS_CHILD | WS_VISIBLE | TBS_AUTOTICKS | TBS_TOP |
            TBS_ENABLESELRANGE,
        10, 100, 200, 20,
        hWnd,
        (HMENU)11,
        hInst,
        NULL);

    if (hWndSlider2 == NULL)
        MessageBox (NULL, "Slider2 not created!", NULL, MB_OK);

    hWndSlider3 = CreateWindow (
        TRACKBAR_CLASS,
        "",
        WS_CHILD | WS_VISIBLE | TBS_VERT | TBS_LEFT | TBS_AUTOTICKS,
        10, 150, 20, 100,
```

(continued)

39

```
                    hWnd,
                    (HMENU)12,
                    hInst,
                    NULL);

            if (hWndSlider3 == NULL)
                MessageBox (NULL, "Slider3 not created!", NULL, MB_OK);

            // Set the default range.
            SendMessage (hWndSlider1, TBM_SETRANGE, TRUE, MAKELONG (1,10));
            SendMessage (hWndSlider2, TBM_SETRANGE, TRUE, MAKELONG (1,10));
            SendMessage (hWndSlider3, TBM_SETRANGE, TRUE, MAKELONG (1,10));

            // Set the selection range.
            SendMessage (hWndSlider2, TBM_SETSEL, TRUE, MAKELONG (3,5));
            break;
```

In the MFC version, MFCTRACK, I created the trackbar in the view class. I also needed to include the AFXCMN.H file in my STDAFX.H file.

```
// The view class is defined as follows in MFCTRVW.H.
class CMfctrackView : public CView
{
    protected:   // create from serialization only
        CMfctrackView ();
        DECLARE_DYNCREATE (CMfctrackView);
        CSliderCtrl m_Slider1;
        CSliderCtrl m_Slider2;
        CSliderCtrl m_Slider3;

    // Attributes
    public:
        CMfctrackDoc *GetDocument ();

    // Operations
    public:
        CSliderCtrl *GetSlider (int iSlider);

    // Overrides
        // ClassWizard generated virtual function overrides.
        // {{AFX_VIRTUAL (CMfctrackView)
        public:
            virtual void OnDraw (CDC *pDC);   // overridden to
        // }}AFX_VIRTUAL                      // draw this view
```

```
// Implementation
public:
    virtual ~CMfctrackView ();
#ifdef _DEBUG
    virtual void AssertValid () const;
    virtual void Dump (CDumpContext& dc) const;
#endif

protected:
    VOID TrackScrolling (UINT nSBCode);

// Generated message map functions
protected:
    // {{AFX_MSG (CMfctrackView)
    afx_msg int OnCreate (LPCREATESTRUCT lpCreateStruct);
    afx_msg void OnDestroy ();
    afx_msg void OnHScroll (UINT nSBCode, UINT nPos,
        CScrollBar *pScrollBar);
    afx_msg void OnRange ();
    afx_msg void OnFrequency ();
    afx_msg void OnLinesize ();
    afx_msg void OnPagesize ();
    afx_msg void OnVScroll (UINT nSBCode, UINT nPos,
        CScrollBar *pScrollBar);
    // }}AFX_MSG
    DECLARE_MESSAGE_MAP ()
};

// The trackbars are created in MFCTRVW.CPP.
int CMfctrackView::OnCreate (LPCREATESTRUCT lpCreateStruct)
{
if (CView::OnCreate (lpCreateStruct) == -1)
    return -1;

// Create the trackbars.
m_Slider1.Create (WS_CHILD | WS_VISIBLE | TBS_AUTOTICKS,
    CRect (10, 50, 200, 70),
    this,
    ID_SLIDER1);

m_Slider2.Create (WS_CHILD | WS_VISIBLE | TBS_AUTOTICKS | TBS_TOP |
    TBS_ENABLESELRANGE,
    CRect (10, 100, 200, 130),
    this,
    ID_SLIDER2);
```

(continued)

```
m_Slider3.Create (WS_CHILD | WS_VISIBLE | TBS_VERT | TBS_LEFT |
    TBS_AUTOTICKS,
    CRect (10, 150, 30, 350),
    this,
    ID_SLIDER3);

// Set the default range.
m_Slider1.SetRange (1, 10, TRUE);
m_Slider2.SetRange (1, 25, TRUE);
m_Slider3.SetRange (1, 30, TRUE);

// Set the selection range.
m_Slider2.SetSelection (10, 20);

return 0;
}
```

Working with a Trackbar

My trackbar sample programs allow a user to change or view a trackbar's range, tick frequency, page size, and line size through dialog boxes activated from the Options menu. You create these dialog boxes in the view class. For each dialog box, I wrote a class derived from CDialog and created a member variable for each value I needed from the controls.

For example, the Set Trackbar Range dialog box uses edit controls to let the user enter minimum and maximum values for the range and specify the trackbar to be set, as shown in Figure 2-4. For the trackbar, ClassWizard let me set up a member variable that is an integer between 0 and 2. (How nice that MFC provides this range checking!)

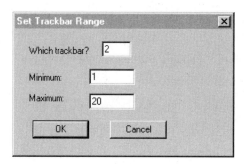

Figure 2-4.
The Set Trackbar Range dialog box.

I did not place restrictions on the actual minimum and maximum range values because you can in fact set the range's minimum value to be greater than the maximum (for instance, a minimum of 10 and a maximum of −1). If you do this, however, your trackbar will track backward (that is, the slider in a vertical trackbar will start at the bottom and move upward). When I run the Set Trackbar Range dialog box, the program simply sets the range on the specified trackbar by using the SetRange member function, as shown here:

```
CRange::CRange (CWnd *pParent /*=NULL*/)
    : CDialog (CRange::IDD, pParent)
{
// {{AFX_DATA_INIT (CRange)
m_Min = 0;
m_Max = 0;
m_Slider = 1;
// }}AFX_DATA_INIT
}

void CRange::DoDataExchange (CDataExchange *pDX)
{
CDialog::DoDataExchange (pDX);
// {{AFX_DATA_MAP (CRange)
DDX_Text (pDX, IDE_MIN, m_Min);
DDX_Text (pDX, IDE_MAX, m_Max);
DDX_Text (pDX, IDE_SLIDER, m_Slider);
DDV_MinMaxInt (pDX, m_Slider, 1, 2);
// }}AFX_DATA_MAP
}

BEGIN_MESSAGE_MAP (CRange, CDialog)
    // {{AFX_MSG_MAP (CRange)
    // }}AFX_MSG_MAP
END_MESSAGE_MAP ()

void CMfctrackView::OnRange ()
{
CRange rangeDlg;

if (rangeDlg.DoModal () == IDOK)
{
    switch (rangeDlg.m_Slider)
    {
        case 1:
            m_Slider1.SetRange (rangeDlg.m_Min, rangeDlg.m_Max, TRUE);
            break;
```

(continued)

```
        case 2:
            m_Slider2.SetRange (rangeDlg.m_Min, rangeDlg.m_Max, TRUE);
            break;

        case 3:
            m_Slider3.SetRange (rangeDlg.m_Min, rangeDlg.m_Max, TRUE);
            break;

        default:
            break;
    }
}
}
```

Finally, you can update the status bar to show which trackbar notification is being sent to each trackbar. In C, all of this code is in SLIDER.C, and the handles to the trackbars and the status bar are all within the scope of the window procedure. When using MFC, you need to find a different method because the pointer to the status bar object is not in scope when you need to set its text. You can create a message map entry for the WM_HSCROLL and WM_VSCROLL messages and copy the notification to a character buffer. Then you get a pointer to the status bar and set the text accordingly:

```
void CMfctrackView::OnHScroll (UINT nSBCode, UINT nPos,
    CScrollBar *pScrollBar)
{
TrackScrolling (nSBCode);

CView::OnHScroll (nSBCode, nPos, pScrollBar);
}

void CMfctrackView::OnVScroll (UINT nSBCode, UINT nPos,
    CScrollBar *pScrollBar)
{
TrackScrolling (nSBCode);

CView::OnVScroll (nSBCode, nPos, pScrollBar);
}

VOID CMfctrackView::TrackScrolling (UINT nSBCode)
{
BOOL bMsg = TRUE;
char *pMsg = NULL;

switch (nSBCode)
{
    case TB_BOTTOM:
        pMsg = "TB_BOTTOM";
        break;
```

```
    case TB_ENDTRACK:
        pMsg = "TB_ENDTRACK";
        break;

    case TB_LINEDOWN:
        pMsg = "TB_LINEDOWN";
        break;

    case TB_LINEUP:
        pMsg = "TB_LINEUP";
        break;

    case TB_PAGEDOWN:
        pMsg = "TB_PAGEDOWN";
        break;

    case TB_PAGEUP:
        pMsg = "TB_PAGEUP";
        break;

    case TB_THUMBPOSITION:
        pMsg = "TB_THUMBPOSITION";
        break;

    case TB_THUMBTRACK:
        pMsg = "TB_THUMBTRACK";
        break;

    default:
        bMsg = FALSE;
        break;
}

if (bMsg == TRUE)
{
    CStatusBar* pStatus = (CStatusBar*) GetParentFrame()->
        GetDescendantWindow (ID_VIEW_STATUS_BAR);
    char szBuf [256];
    sprintf (szBuf, "Trackbar message: %s", pMsg);
    pStatus->SetPaneText (0, szBuf);
    pStatus->UpdateWindow ();
}
}
```

Trackbar Messages and Member Functions

Table 2-2 lists the messages that can be sent to trackbars and the corresponding member functions supported by the MFC-supplied class CSliderCtrl. You can find detailed information about the parameters and return values in the Win32 SDK and the MFC 3.1 documentation.

Message	Member Function	Description
TBM_CLEARSEL	ClearSel	Clears the current selection range in a trackbar.
TBM_CLEARTICS	ClearTics	Removes the tick marks from a trackbar.
TBM_GETCHANNELRECT	GetChannelRect	Retrieves the rectangle bounding the channel in which the slider slides.
TBM_GETLINESIZE	GetLineSize	Retrieves the amount the slider will move when the user presses the Up or Down arrow key (or the Left or Right arrow key for a horizontal trackbar). The default increment is one tick.
TBM_GETNUMTICS	GetNumTics	Retrieves the number of tick marks in a trackbar.
TBM_GETPAGESIZE	GetPageSize	Retrieves the amount the slider will move when the user presses the PgUp or PgDn key. The default is calculated as the difference between the maximum and the minimum of the range divided by 5.
TBM_GETPOS	GetPos	Retrieves the current position of the slider.
TBM_GETPTICS	GetTicArray	Retrieves the address of the array containing the positions of the tick marks in a trackbar.
TBM_GETRANGEMIN and TBM_GETRANGEMAX	GetRange	Retrieves the current range (the minimum and maximum positions) for the slider.

Table 2-2.   *(continued)*

Trackbar messages and member functions.

Table 2-2. *continued*

Message	Member Function	Description
TBM_GETRANGEMAX	GetRangeMax	Retrieves the maximum position for the slider.
TBM_GETRANGEMIN	GetRangeMin	Retrieves the minimum position for the slider.
TBM_GETSELSTART and TBM_GETSELEND	GetSelection	Retrieves the current selection range in a trackbar.
TBM_GETSELEND	GetSelEnd	Retrieves the ending position of the current selection range in a trackbar.
TBM_GETSELSTART	GetSelStart	Retrieves the starting position of the current selection range in a trackbar.
TBM_GETTHUMBLENGTH		Retrieves the length of the slider.
TBM_GETTHUMBRECT	GetThumbRect	Retrieves the rectangle bounding the slider.
TBM_GETTIC	GetTic	Retrieves the position of a tick mark.
TBM_GETTICPOS	GetTicPos	Retrieves the position, in client coordinates, of a tick mark.
TBM_SETLINESIZE	SetLineSize	Sets the amount the slider will move when the user presses the Up or Down arrow key (or the Left or Right arrow key for a horizontal trackbar). The default increment is one tick.
TBM_SETPAGESIZE	SetPageSize	Sets the amount the slider will move when the user presses the PgUp or PgDn key. The default is calculated as the difference between the maximum and the minimum of the range divided by 5.
TBM_SETPOS	SetPos	Sets the current position of the slider.
TBM_SETRANGE	SetRange	Sets the minimum and maximum positions for the slider.

(continued)

Table 2-2. *continued*

Message	Member Function	Description
TBM_SETRANGEMAX	SetRangeMax	Sets the maximum position for the slider.
TBM_SETRANGEMIN	SetRangeMin	Sets the minimum position for the slider.
TBM_SETSEL	SetSelection	Sets the starting and ending positions of the selection range in a trackbar.
TBM_SETSELEND		Sets the position of the end of the selection range in a trackbar.
TBM_SETSELSTART		Sets the starting position of the current selection range in a trackbar.
TBM_SETTHUMBLENGTH		Sets the length of the slider.
TBM_SETTIC	SetTic	Sets the position of a tick mark.
TBM_SETTICFREQ	SetTicFreq	Sets the tick frequency.
	VerifyPos	Verifies that the current position of the slider is within the trackbar range.

N O T E: Table 2-2 describes many messages that support trackbar ranges and positions. Although trackbars are based on scroll bars, it is important to note that a trackbar updates its position automatically. In the case of a scroll bar, it is up to the application to update the scroll bar position when the WM_HSCROLL message or the WM_VSCROLL message is received.

Progress Bars

A progress bar is a window that an application can use to visually track the progress of a lengthy operation such as an installation or a file copying task. A progress bar has a range, which represents the entire duration of the operation, and a current position, which represents the progress the application has made toward completing the operation. The application sets both the range and the current position (as it does for a scroll bar) and has the ability to advance the current position.

The window procedure uses the range and the current position to determine how much of the bar should be filled with the highlight color. By default, the minimum range of a progress bar is 0, and the maximum range is 100. The increment value is set to 10.

The PROGRESS sample, which I wrote to demonstrate how to create and manipulate progress bars, simply creates one of these controls, sets its range, and allows the user to start and stop the process of filling the bar with the highlight color. I used a timer to simulate a lengthy operation. Figure 2-5 shows the PROGRESS sample.

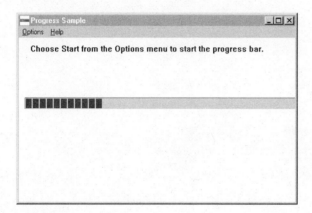

Figure 2-5.
The PROGRESS sample.

Creating a Progress Bar

To create a progress bar, you can use the CreateWindow or CreateWindowEx function and specify the PROGRESS_CLASS window class, or you can create a CProgressCtrl object and use the MFC Create member function. Be sure that you include the COMMCTRL.H header file in your application and the COMCTL32.LIB file in your list of libraries. The following C code (which differs from the PROGRESS sample on the companion disc) produces a simple progress bar in the parent window's procedure. A timer sends messages to advance the bar's current position.

```
// Function that creates a progress bar
// Parameters:
//    HWND hWndParent - Parent window of the progress bar
//    RECT rclPos - Size and position of the progress bar
//    WORD wID - ID of the progress bar
```

(continued)

49

```
//    HINSTANCE hInst - Current instance
//    LONG lRange - Sets the range
//    LONG lStep - Sets the stepping
HWND MyCreateProgressBar (HWND hWndParent, RECT rclPos, WORD wID,
    HINSTANCE hInst, LONG lRange, LONG lStep)
{
HWND hWndProgress;

hWndProgress = CreateWindowEx (
    0L,
    PROGRESS_CLASS,
    "",
    WS_CHILD | WS_VISIBLE,
    rclPos.x, rclPos.y, rclPos.cx, rclPos.cy,
    hWndParent,
    (HMENU)wID,
    hInst,
    NULL);

// Set the range for the progress bar.
SendMessage (hWndProgress, PBM_SETRANGE, 0L, lRange);

// Set the step.
SendMessage (hWndProgress, PBM_SETSTEP, lStep, 0L);

return (hWndProgress);
}

    ⋮

RECT rcl;    // holds the size of the progress bar

switch (message)
{
    case WM_CREATE:
        rcl.x = 10; rcl.y = 100; rcl.cx = 500; rcl.cy = 20;
        hWndProgress = MyCreateProgressBar (hWnd, rcl, ID_PROGRESS,
            hInst, MAKELONG (0, 20), 1);
        break;

    case WM_TIMER:
        if (uCurrent < uMax)
        {
```

```
            // Increment (step) the progress bar.
            SendMessage (hWndProgress, PBM_STEPIT, 0L, 0L);
            uCurrent++;
        }
        else
        {
            // We are at the end of the range - kill the timer.
            KillTimer (hWnd, ID_TIMER);
            uCurrent = 0;
        }
        break;

    case WM_COMMAND:
        switch (LOWORD (wParam))
        {
            case IDM_STOP:
                // Stop the progress bar.
                SendMessage (hWndProgress, PBM_SETPOS, 0L, 0L);
                KillTimer (hWnd, ID_TIMER);
                break;

            case IDM_START:
                uCurrent = uMin;
                SetTimer (hWnd, ID_TIMER, 500, NULL);
                break;
        ⋮
}
```

Pretty simple stuff, you say? Think how simple it must have been to port to MFC! Well, take a look at the same work done in the MFCPROG sample. Don't forget to include AFXCMN.H in your STDAFX.H file before you try this. I created a member variable, *m_Current*, to keep track of the current position of the progress bar and added this variable to my view class. As you can see, it's pretty easy here, too:

```
// CMfcprogView message handlers

void CMfcprogView::OnTimer (UINT nIDEvent)
{
if (m_Current < m_Max)
{
    m_Progress.StepIt ();
    m_Current++;
}
```

(continued)

```
else
{
   KillTimer (1000);
   m_Current = 0;
}

CView::OnTimer (nIDEvent);
}

void CMfcprogView::OnStart ()
{
m_Current = m_Min;
SetTimer (ID_TIMER, 500, NULL);
}

void CMfcprogView::OnStop ()
{
m_Progress.SetPos (0);
KillTimer (ID_TIMER);
}

int CMfcprogView::OnCreate (LPCREATESTRUCT lpCreateStruct)
{
if (CView::OnCreate (lpCreateStruct) == -1)
   return -1;

m_Progress.Create (WS_CHILD | WS_VISIBLE,
   CRect (10, 100, 500, 120),
   this,
   ID_PROGRESS);
m_Min = 0;
m_Max = 20;
m_Progress.SetRange (m_Min, m_Max);
m_Progress.SetStep (1);

return 0;
}
```

Progress Bar Messages and Member Functions

Table 2-3 lists the messages and member functions supported by the progress bar control. Refer to the Win32 SDK and the MFC 3.1 documentation for details about parameters and return values.

Message	Member Function	Description
PBM_DELTAPOS	OffsetPos	Advances the position of a progress bar by the specified increment and redraws the control.
PBM_SETPOS	SetPos	Sets the position of a progress bar and redraws the control to reflect the new position.
PBM_SETRANGE	SetRange	Sets the range (minimum and maximum values) for a progress bar and redraws the control.
PBM_SETSTEP	SetStep	Specifies the step increment for a progress bar, the amount by which the bar increases its position whenever it receives a PBM_STEPIT message (or when the MFC StepIt member function is called). The default is 10.
PBM_STEPIT	StepIt	Advances the position of a progress bar by the step increment and redraws the control. An application sets the step increment by sending the PBM_SETSTEP message (or by calling the MFC StepIt member function). When the position exceeds the maximum value of the range, this message resets the position so that the progress bar starts over from the beginning.

Table 2-3.
Progress bar messages and member functions.

Up-Down Controls

An up-down control is a small window containing up and down arrows that the user can click to increment or decrement a value. An up-down control is similar to a scroll bar, but it consists only of arrows. (It also has a sillier name.) You can use an up-down control alone as a simplified scroll bar or with another control (called a *buddy control*—yet another silly name). In Figure 2-6 on the next page, the up-down control is paired with an edit control to create a spin box; when the user clicks an arrow or presses an arrow key, the up-down control increments or decrements the value in the edit control. You can use any type of control as the designated buddy control, however.

Buddy control

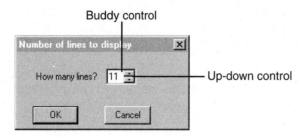

Up-down control

Figure 2-6.
A dialog box that uses an up-down control and a buddy control.

The range of an up-down control specifies the upper and lower bounds for the position (the integer the user adjusts with the up and down arrows). Unlike a scroll bar's position, the position of an up-down control is updated automatically. When the positional value is updated, the buddy control is also automatically updated if the up-down control has the UDS_AUTOBUDDY style. If the upper bound is less than the lower bound, clicking the up arrow decrements the position, and clicking the down arrow increments it.

You can specify various window styles to determine the characteristics of an up-down control or its buddy control. For example, you can change the way the up-down control positions itself relative to its buddy control (the UDS_ALIGNLEFT style), determine whether it sets the text of its buddy control (the UDS_SETBUDDYINT style), or determine whether it processes the Up and Down arrow keys on the keyboard (the UDS_ARROWKEYS style).

By default, the position of an up-down control does not change if the user attempts to increment or decrement it beyond the upper or lower bound. You can change this behavior by using the UDS_WRAP style, which wraps the position to the opposite extreme. (For example, if your range is 1 through 10, incrementing the position past 10 wraps it back to 1.)

The range of an up-down control cannot exceed 32,767 positions. You can invert the range—that is, the lower bound of the range can be greater than the upper bound. Note, however, that the up arrow always moves the current position toward the upper bound, and the down arrow always moves the current position toward the lower bound. If the range is 0 (the lower bound is equal to the upper bound) or the control is disabled, the control draws dimmed arrows.

The buddy control must have the same parent as the up-down control. If you use the UDS_ALIGNLEFT or UDS_ALIGNRIGHT style and the buddy control resizes, you must send the UDM_SETBUDDY message (or call the MFC SetBuddy member function) to re-anchor the up-down control on the appropriate border of the buddy control. The UDS_AUTOBUDDY style calls the GetWindow function with GW_HWNDPREV to choose the buddy control. In the case of a dialog resource, the UDS_AUTOBUDDY style chooses the previous control listed in the resource script. If the z-order of the windows changes, sending a UDM_SETBUDDY message with a NULL handle causes a new buddy to be selected; otherwise, the original autobuddy choice is maintained.

The UPDOWN sample, which I wrote to demonstrate up-down controls, allows the user to change the number of times the word *Welcome!* is written to the client area of the screen. Figure 2-7 shows the UPDOWN sample.

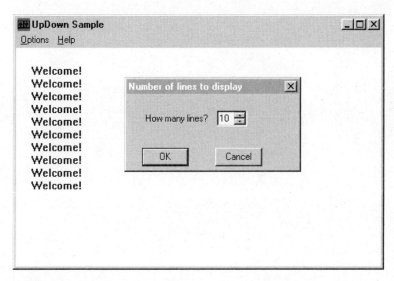

Figure 2-7.
The UPDOWN sample.

Creating an Up-Down Control

The code on the next page demonstrates how easy it is to create a spin box on the fly as part of a dialog box. You might want to do this if you are using one dialog box for several applications—one instance could show the current value as static information, while another might allow the user to change this data. When the user chooses OK in the dialog box, the program retrieves and saves the selection in the spin box and closes the dialog box. (To use an up-down control in your application, remember to include the COMMCTRL.H header file and to include the COMCTL32.LIB file in your list of libraries.)

```
BOOL APIENTRY Spin (
    HWND hDlg,
    UINT message,
    UINT wParam,
    LONG lParam)
{
static HWND hWndUpDown, hWndBuddy;
BOOL bErr;

switch (message)
{
    case WM_INITDIALOG:
        // Get a handle to the edit (buddy) control.
        hWndBuddy = GetDlgItem (hDlg, IDE_BUDDY);

        // Create the up-down control.
        hWndUpDown = CreateWindowEx (
            0L,
            UPDOWN_CLASS,
            "",
            WS_CHILD | WS_BORDER | WS_VISIBLE | UDS_WRAP | UDS_ARROWKEYS |
                UDS_ALIGNRIGHT | UDS_SETBUDDYINT,
            0, 0, 8, 8,
            hDlg,
            (HMENU)ID_UPDOWN,
            hInst,
            NULL);

        // Set the buddy window.
        SendMessage (hWndUpDown, UDM_SETBUDDY, (LONG)hWndBuddy, 0L);

        // Set the range.
        SendMessage (hWndUpDown, UDM_SETRANGE, 0L,
            MAKELONG (MAX_SPIN, MIN_SPIN));

        // Set the default value in the edit control.
        SetDlgItemInt (hDlg, IDE_BUDDY, 1, FALSE);

        return TRUE;

    case WM_COMMAND:
        switch (LOWORD (wParam))
        {
            case IDOK:
                iNumLines = (int) GetDlgItemInt (hDlg, IDE_BUDDY,
                    &bErr, FALSE);
                InvalidateRect (hWndMain, NULL, TRUE);

            case IDCANCEL:
                EndDialog (hDlg, TRUE);
```

```
            break;
        }
        break;

    }

    return FALSE;
}
```

If you don't need to create your spin box dynamically, and if you are using Microsoft Visual C++ version 2.1 or later, you can take advantage of the resource editor. The resource editor supports up-down controls, and you can place one of these controls in your dialog box as you would any other control. When I ported the UPDOWN sample to MFC (MFCSPIN), I used the resource editor. I created the CSpin class, derived from CDialog, and set up the *m_Lines* member variable to hold the number of lines. Here is the terribly complex code required to use the spin box:

```
// CSpin message handlers

BOOL CSpin::OnInitDialog ()
{
CDialog::OnInitDialog ();

// Set the buddy control.
m_Spin.SetBuddy (GetDlgItem (IDC_LINES));

// Set the range.
m_Spin.SetRange (1, 20);

return TRUE;    // return TRUE unless you set the focus to a control
                // EXCEPTION: OCX property pages should return FALSE
}

void CFcspinView::OnSpin ()
{
CSpin spinDlg;

if (spinDlg.DoModal() == IDOK)
{
   m_NumLines = spinDlg.m_Lines;
   GetDocument()->UpdateAllViews (NULL);
}
}
```

Of course, this wasn't difficult at all. As you can see, it's easy to use the new controls—and even easier to have the resource editor help you out.

Up-Down Control Messages and Member Functions

There aren't a lot of messages and member functions for up-down controls. Table 2-4 lists the messages that can be sent to up-down controls and the member functions that are supported by the MFC-supplied class CSpinButtonCtrl. The Win32 SDK and the MFC 3.1 documentation contain detailed information about parameters and return values.

Message	Member Function	Description
UDM_GETACCEL	GetAccel	Retrieves information about the accelerators for an up-down control. (You can set accelerator keys for this control.)
UDM_GETBASE	GetBase	Retrieves the current base value for an up-down control (10 for decimal or 16 for hexadecimal).
UDM_GETBUDDY	GetBuddy	Retrieves the window handle of the current buddy control.
UDM_GETPOS	GetPos	Retrieves the current position of an up-down control.
UDM_GETRANGE	GetRange	Retrieves the upper and lower bounds for an up-down control.
UDM_SETACCEL	SetAccel	Sets the accelerators for an up-down control.
UDM_SETBASE	SetBase	Sets the base value for an up-down control (10 for decimal or 16 for hexadecimal). The base value determines whether the buddy control displays numbers in decimal digits or in hexadecimal digits. Hexadecimal numbers are unsigned; decimal numbers are signed. If the buddy control is a list box, the up-down control sets its current selection instead of its text.
UDM_SETBUDDY	SetBuddy	Sets the buddy control for an up-down control.

Table 2-4. *(continued)*

Up-down control messages and member functions.

Table 2-4. *continued*

Message	Member Function	Description
UDM_SETPOS	SetPos	Sets the current position for an up-down control.
UDM_SETRANGE	SetRange	Sets the upper and lower bounds for an up-down control.

Animation Controls

When some of you saw the words *animation control,* you probably got all excited and wondered what this control could be. An animation control is simply a window that displays an audio-video interleaved (AVI) clip. AVI is the standard Windows audio-video format. An AVI clip is a series of bitmap frames, something like a movie. Although AVI clips can have sound, animation controls ignore sound information when they play these clips.

Because the thread continues to execute while an AVI clip is being displayed, you'll often see animation controls used to indicate system activity during a lengthy operation. For example, the Find dialog box (see Figure 2-8) shows a magnifying glass moving over a piece of paper.

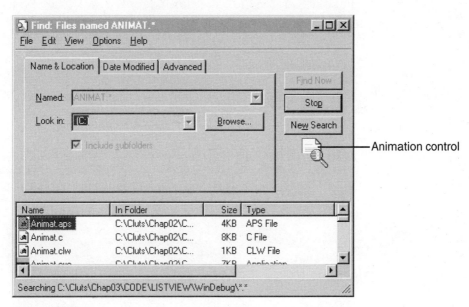

Animation control

Figure 2-8.
A dialog box containing an animation control.

The AVI clip can originate either from an uncompressed AVI file or from an AVI file that was compressed using run-length encoding (RLE). You can add the clip to your application as an AVI resource, or the clip can accompany your application as a separate AVI file. You can create the AVI file using one of the many tools on the market, such as those available with the Microsoft Video for Windows SDK or with Adobe Premier.

Because you are limited by the type of compression (RLE or none), you won't be able to play some of the really neat animations—Bugs Bunny, for instance—in the control. If you need a control to provide multimedia playback and recording capabilities for your application, you should use the MCIWnd control instead of an animation control.

Creating an Animation Control

An animation control belongs to the ANIMATE_CLASS window class. You create this control by using the CreateWindow or CreateWindowEx function, by using the Animate_Create macro, or, in MFC, by using the Create member function on your CAnimateCtrl object. The Animate_Create macro positions the animation control in the upper left corner of the parent window and, if you don't specify the ACS_CENTER style, sets the width and height of the control based on the dimensions of a frame in the AVI clip.

More likely, though, you will be creating your animation control to run in a dialog box. You can use the dialog box editor to place an animation control right in your dialog box and then set the styles of the control through the control properties. If you create an animation control within a dialog box or from a dialog box resource, the control is automatically destroyed when the user closes the dialog box. If you create an animation control within a window, you must explicitly destroy the control. Otherwise, you'll be guilty of being a resource hog.

You can use these window styles with animation controls:

- ACS_AUTOPLAY starts playing the animation when the animation clip is opened.

- ACS_CENTER centers the animation in the animation control's window.

- ACS_TRANSPARENT draws the animation using a transparent background rather than the background color specified in the animation clip.

I wrote my sample to demonstrate the animation control first in MFC (MFCANIM), and then I ported it back to C (ANIMAT). My design goals included the following:

- To create an animation control in a dialog box

- To allow the user to start and stop the animation by using buttons

- To allow the user to single-step through the animation frames

You can see this sample in Figure 2-9.

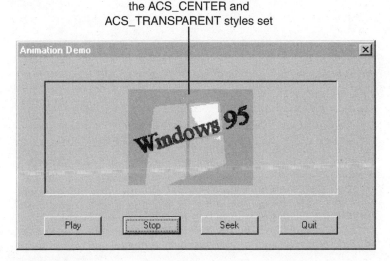

Figure 2-9.
The ANIMAT sample.

Writing this sample was very easy. In fact, the most difficult part was finding an animation that would work. Beginning on the following page is the code I used in the MFC sample to play the animation, stop the playback, and single-step through the frames. I chose to allow the user to single-step from the beginning through the last frame. Notice that because I put my animation control in a dialog box, I did not have to call the Create member function. (Don't forget to include AFXCMN.H in your STDAFX.H file to define the class.)

```
// CMfcanimView message handlers

void CMfcanimView::OnDemo ()
{
CDemo demoDlg;

// Run the Animation Demo dialog box.
demoDlg.DoModal ();
}

// CDemo dialog
CDemo::CDemo (CWnd *pParent /*=NULL*/)
    : CDialog (CDemo::IDD, pParent)
{
// {{AFX_DATA_INIT (CDemo)
// NOTE: ClassWizard will add member initialization here.
// }}AFX_DATA_INIT
m_bStart = FALSE;   // BOOL--whether or not animation has started
m_iSeek = 1;        // used for single-stepping through the frames
}

void CDemo::OnSeek ()
{
// If the animation is running...
if (m_bStart)
{
   // Seek to the specified frame.
   m_AnimateCtrl.Seek (m_iSeek);
   if (m_iSeek < NUM_FRAMES)
      m_iSeek++;
}
}

void CDemo::OnStart ()
{
// If the animation hasn't started yet...
if (! m_bStart)
{
   m_bStart = TRUE;
   // Open the animation file.
   m_AnimateCtrl.Open (IDR_AVICLIP);
   // Play it from beginning to end with infinite replay.
   m_AnimateCtrl.Play (0, (UINT)(-1), (UINT)(-1));
}
}

void CDemo::OnStop ()
{
```

```
// If the animation has started...
if (m_bStart)
{
   m_bStart = FALSE;
   // Stop it.
   m_AnimateCtrl.Stop ();
}
}
```

In the preceding code, I passed an identifier to the AVI resource rather than passing in the name of the AVI file. This means that the clip will be built into the sample. When I first wrote the code, I passed in the name of the clip. But this wasn't the best option because I had to pass in the full path. (If you don't pass in the full path, the call to open the AVI file will fail and the clip will not run.) To add the clip to my resource, I inserted the following line in my MFCANIM.RC2 file:

```
// Add manually edited resources here...
IDR_AVICLIP AVI res\win95.avi
```

I then added the symbol for the AVI file to the resource by choosing Symbols from the Resource menu. When you click the New button in the Symbol Browser, a second dialog box prompts you to add the new symbol, as shown in Figure 2-10.

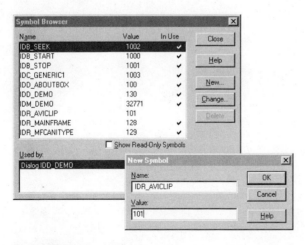

Figure 2-10.
Adding a symbol to your resource.

Rebuild after you've added the new symbol. Don't forget to scan all of your dependencies before doing this. I forgot at first; the project did not build all that it should have, and the sample didn't run.

The code in the C sample, ANIMAT, is quite similar. The dialog procedure handles all the manipulation of the animation control. You must include the COMMCTRL.H header file, and the COMCTL32.LIB file must be in your list of libraries.

```c
BOOL APIENTRY Demo (
    HWND hDlg,
    UINT message,
    UINT wParam,
    LONG lParam)
{
static BOOL bStart;
static int iSeek;

switch (message)
{
    case WM_INITDIALOG:
        bStart = FALSE;
        iSeek = 1;
        return TRUE;

    case WM_COMMAND:
        if (LOWORD(wParam) == IDOK)
        {
            EndDialog (hDlg, TRUE);
            return TRUE;
        }

        else if (HIWORD(wParam) == BN_CLICKED)
        {
            switch (LOWORD(wParam))
            {
                case IDC_PLAY:
                    if (! bStart)
                    {
                        bStart = TRUE;
                        Animate_Open (GetDlgItem (hDlg, IDC_ANIMATE),
                            "WIN95.AVI");
```

```
                    Animate_Play (GetDlgItem (hDlg, IDC_ANIMATE),
                        0, -1, -1);
                }
                break;

            case IDC_STOP:
                if (bStart)
                {
                    bStart = FALSE;
                    Animate_Stop(GetDlgItem(hDlg, IDC_ANIMATE));
                }
                break;

            case IDC_SEEK:
                if (bStart)
                {
                    Animate_Seek(GetDlgItem(hDlg, IDC_ANIMATE), iSeek);
                    if (iSeek < NUM_FRAMES)
                        iSeek++;
                }
                break;
            }
        }
        break;

    default:
        return FALSE;
    }
}
```

That's about all there is to it. If you build and run the sample, you will see a really cool animation (thanks to Jonathan Cluts).

Animation Control Macros and Member Functions

As you can see by looking at Table 2-5 on the following page, the functionality of the animation control is simple. Rather than listing messages, this table shows you the macros that the system supplies to manipulate animation controls. Some of the messages correspond to more than one member function, depending on the parameters you send to them. For me, it is far easier to understand the code if I use the macros, because they tell me exactly what I am trying to do.

Macro	Member Function	Description
Animate_Close	Close	Closes an AVI clip that was previously opened.
Animate_Create	Create	Creates an animation control.
Animate_Open	Open	Opens an AVI clip from a file or a resource and displays the first frame.
Animate_Play	Play	Plays an AVI clip without sound.
Animate_Seek	Seek	Displays a selected single frame of an AVI clip.
Animate_Stop	Stop	Stops playing an AVI clip.

Table 2-5.

Animation control macros and member functions.

CHAPTER THREE

Image Lists, List View Controls, Column Headers, and Tree View Controls: List Management Common Controls

Several of the new common controls in Microsoft Windows 95 are designed to provide a user interface for list management. These controls range from straightforward lists that can display various amounts of data (list view controls) to hierarchically structured lists of items (tree view controls) to lists of visual representations such as bitmaps and icons (image lists). In addition, you can use a column header (also called a header control), like those used with list view controls, to better organize and display your lists.

This chapter shows you how to use these new list management common controls in your applications. Because both list view and tree view controls use image lists, we'll look at image lists first.

Image Lists

An image list helps you manage a collection of images that are the same size, such as bitmaps or icons. Image lists, which are designed for use with list view and tree view controls, manage images but do not display them directly.

You can create the images in an image list in a single, wide bitmap or as individual bitmaps. If you have produced bitmaps for a toolbar, you're familiar with the type of bitmap I am referring to. One difference between creating a toolbar and creating an image list, however, is that you can set up an empty image list and add the bitmaps (or icons) to it later, one by one, rather than providing one long bitmap initially.

In the samples I wrote to demonstrate list view and tree view controls, I created an empty image list and then added each bitmap or icon one at a time. Figure 3-1 shows one of the icons I used. (That odd-looking structure poking up in the air is my approximation of Seattle's Space Needle.)

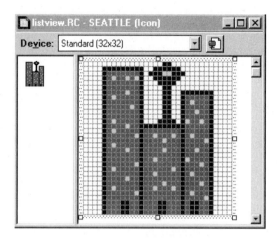

Figure 3-1.
An icon for an image list.

To reference a specific image in the bitmap, you use the index of the image within the image list. You can also include monochrome bitmaps in an image list to act as masks, which allow you to draw icons transparently. Or you might want to blend the icon with the background or with the system highlight color.

You might also want to add overlay masks to your image list. An overlay mask (which is different from a simple mask) is an image that is drawn transparently over another image. For instance, Windows 95 uses an overlay mask when it displays the image for a shared directory (the image of a hand holding a folder, shown in Figure 3-2.)

Figure 3-2.
An image with an overlay mask.

You can create either a nonmasked or a masked image list:

▪ A nonmasked image list includes a color bitmap that contains one or more images. This is a wide bitmap containing small bitmaps, similar to the one you saw in the TOOLBAR sample in Chapter 1. When a nonmasked image is drawn, it is simply copied into the target device context (DC); no special processing occurs.

▪ A masked image list includes two wide bitmaps of equal size. The first is a color bitmap that contains the images; the second is a monochrome bitmap that contains a series of masks (one for each image in the first bitmap). When a masked image is drawn, the mask specified for that image is combined with the image itself. This combination produces transparent areas in the bitmap in which the background color of the target DC shows through.

Table 3-1 describes the drawing styles you can use to produce different effects with your image lists. For instance, if you want the images in your list to be drawn transparently, you can specify the ILD_TRANSPARENT drawing style in your call to ImageList_Draw or to the MFC Draw member function of the CImageList class.

Style	Description
ILD_BLEND25	Draws the image, blending 25 percent with the system highlight color. This value has no effect unless the image list contains a mask.
ILD_BLEND50	Draws the image, blending 50 percent with the system highlight color. This value has no effect unless the image list contains a mask.
ILD_FOCUS	Draws the image striped with the highlight color to indicate that the image has the focus. This flag has no effect unless ILD_SELECTED is also specified or unless the image list contains a mask.
ILD_IMAGE	Draws the image.
ILD_MASK	Draws the mask.

Table 3-1. *(continued)*
Image list drawing styles.

Table 3-1. *continued*

Style	Description
ILD_NORMAL	Draws the image using the image list's background color. If the background color is CLR_NONE, the image is drawn transparently using the mask.
ILD_OVERLAYMASK	Draws the image transparently as an overlay mask.
ILD_SELECTED	Draws the image dithered with the highlight color to indicate that the image is selected. This flag has no effect unless the image list contains a mask.
ILD_TRANSPARENT	Draws the image transparently using the mask, regardless of the background color. This flag has no effect unless the image list contains a mask. To draw the masked image, the function first performs a logical AND operation between the bits of the image and the bits of the mask. Next it performs a logical XOR operation between the results of the first operation and the background bits of the destination DC. This creates transparent areas in the resulting image (that is, each white bit in the mask causes the corresponding bit in the resulting image to be transparent).

Creating an Image List

Creating an image list is easy: just call the ImageList_Create function or, if you are developing your application with MFC, use the Create member function on the CImageList object. For a nonmasked image list, ImageList_Create produces a single bitmap large enough to hold the specified number of images with the given dimensions. It then creates a screen-compatible DC and selects the bitmap into it. For a masked image list, ImageList_Create creates two bitmaps and two screen-compatible DCs. It selects the image bitmap into one DC and selects the mask bitmap into the other. The initial size of the image list is determined by the size values that you specify in your call to Image-List_Create. If you subsequently add more images, the size of the image list automatically increases to accommodate them, based on the number of images you specified as a growth limit.

The following code from the TREEVIEW sample demonstrates how to create an image list, add images to it, and then ensure that all the images have been added:

```
// First create the image list you will need.
hIml = ImageList_Create (BITMAP_WIDTH,    // width
                         BITMAP_HEIGHT,   // height
                         0,               // creation flags
                         NUM_BITMAPS,     // number of images
                         0);              // amount this list can grow

// Load the bitmaps and add them to the image list.
hBmp = LoadBitmap (hInst, MAKEINTRESOURCE (FORSALE));
idxForSale = ImageList_Add (hIml,         // handle to image list
                            hBmp,         // handle of bitmap to add
                            NULL);        // handle of bitmap mask

hBmp = LoadBitmap (hInst, MAKEINTRESOURCE (REDMOND));
idxRedmond = ImageList_Add (hIml, hBmp, NULL);

hBmp = LoadBitmap (hInst, MAKEINTRESOURCE (BELLEVUE));
idxBellevue = ImageList_Add (hIml, hBmp, NULL);

hBmp = LoadBitmap (hInst, MAKEINTRESOURCE (SEATTLE));
idxSeattle = ImageList_Add (hIml, hBmp, NULL);

// Be sure that all the bitmaps were added.
if (ImageList_GetImageCount (hIml) < NUM_BITMAPS)
   return FALSE;
```

Image List Functions and Member Functions

Because image lists are part of the dynamic-link library for common controls (COMCTL32.DLL), you must include the common control header file in your source code files and also link with the common control export library to use the image list functions, structures, and macros. If you are developing in MFC, you need to include the AFXCMN.H file in your STDAFX.H file to get the definition of the CImageList class. This class provides the functionality of the image list common control and includes a data member, *m_hImageList,* that is a handle containing the image list attached to the object. The GetSafeHwnd member function will retrieve *m_hImageList* if you need to get a handle to it in your application.

Table 3-2 on the following page describes all the functions and member functions supported by image list controls. If you would like more details about the functions or their parameters and return values, refer to the Win32 SDK or the MFC 3.1 documentation.

Function	Member Function	Description
ImageList_Add	Add	Adds one or more images to an image list. You can add bitmapped images, icons, or cursors.
ImageList_AddIcon	Add	Adds an icon to an image list. Because the system does not save the *hIcon* that is passed in, you can destroy *hIcon* after the function returns.
ImageList_AddMasked	Add	Adds one or more images to an image list, generating a mask from the given bitmap.
ImageList_BeginDrag	BeginDrag	Begins dragging an image and creates a temporary image list used for dragging. The drag image combines the specified image and its mask with the current cursor. The drag image can be moved using the ImageList_DragMove function.
ImageList_Create	Create	Creates a new image list.
ImageList_Destroy	DeleteObject	Destroys an image list.
ImageList_DragEnter	DragEnter	Locks the specified area of the screen, preventing it from receiving other updates. This function is called during a drag operation.
ImageList_DragLeave	DragLeave	Removes any locks on the locked area of the screen through a call to ImageList_DragEnter.
ImageList_DragMove	DragMove	Moves the image. This function is typically called in response to a WM_MOUSEMOVE message during a drag operation.
ImageList_DragShow-NoLock	DragShow-NoLock	Shows or hides the image being dragged.
ImageList_Draw	Draw	Draws an image list item in the specified DC. The drawing styles listed in Table 3-1 (page 69) have no effect on the appearance of a nonmasked image, which is copied to the destination DC using the SRCCOPY raster operation. The colors in the image appear the same regardless of the background color of the DC.

Table 3-2.   *(continued)*
Image list functions and member functions.

Table 3-2. *continued*

Function	Member Function	Description
ImageList_DrawEx	Draw	Draws an image based on the flags and colors passed into the function.
ImageList_EndDrag	EndDrag	Ends a drag operation. Although this function returns the handle of the temporary image list that is used for dragging, the temporary image list is destroyed, so the handle returned by this function is invalid.
ImageList_ExtractIcon	ExtractIcon	Creates an icon based on an image and a mask in an image list.
ImageList_GetBkColor	GetBkColor	Retrieves the current background color for an image list.
ImageList_GetDragImage	GetDragImage	Retrieves the temporary image list used for the drag image and the current drag position as well as the offset of the drag image relative to the drag position.
ImageList_GetIcon		Retrieves the specified icon in the image list.
ImageList_GetIconSize		Retrieves the dimensions of each image in an image list.
ImageList_GetImage-Count	GetImage-Count	Retrieves the number of images in an image list.
ImageList_GetImage-Info	GetImage-Info	Retrieves information about an image and fills out an IMAGEINFO structure with information about a single image. You can use this information to directly manipulate the bitmaps for the image.
	GetSafeHandle	Retrieves the handle to the image list.
ImageList_LoadBitmap	Create	Creates an image list from the given bitmap resource.
ImageList_LoadImage	LoadImage	Creates an image list from the specified bitmap, cursor, or icon.
ImageList_Merge	Attach	Merges two existing images, creating a new image list to store the image. The second image is drawn transparently over the first, and the mask for the new image is the result of performing a logical OR operation between the masks for the two images. You can also detach two image lists by using the Detach member function.

(continued)

Table 3-2. *continued*

Function	Member Function	Description
ImageList_Read	Read	Reads an image list from a stream.
ImageList_Remove	Remove	Removes an image from an image list.
ImageList_Replace	Replace	Replaces an image in an image list.
ImageList_ReplaceIcon	Replace	Replaces an image in an image list, using an icon.
ImageList_SetBkColor	SetBkColor	Sets the background color for an image list.
ImageList_SetDrag-CursorImage	SetDrag-CursorImage	Sets the image of the dragged item.
ImageList_SetIconSize	SetIconSize	Sets the dimensions of the images in an image list and removes all images from the list.
ImageList_SetOverlay-Image	SetOverlay-Image	Adds to the image list the index of an image that will be used as an overlay mask.
ImageList_Write	Write	Writes an image list to a stream.

List View Controls and Column Headers

A list view control displays a collection of items, such as files or folders, that can be manipulated in a variety of ways. For example, a user can drag an item to a new location or sort the collection by clicking a column header. If you've run Windows Explorer, you've seen a list view control—the large window on the right, pointed out in Figure 3-3.

A list view control can display its items in one of four ways (called *views*): in large icon view (also known as standard icon view), using the items' large icons; in small icon view, using a smaller icon size; in list view; or in details view (also known as report view). In large icon view, shown in Figure 3-4, each item is represented by a full-size icon and a text label below the icon. The user can drag items to any location in the list view window. This illustration comes from the LISTVIEW sample (its MFC counterpart is called MFCLIST), which demonstrates a list view control that contains real estate listings, with each item representing a house for sale. (The addresses are fictional, of course.)

In small icon view, shown in Figure 3-5 on page 76, each item appears with a small icon and a text label to the right of the icon, thus saving screen real estate. As in large icon view, the user can drag the items to any location in the window.

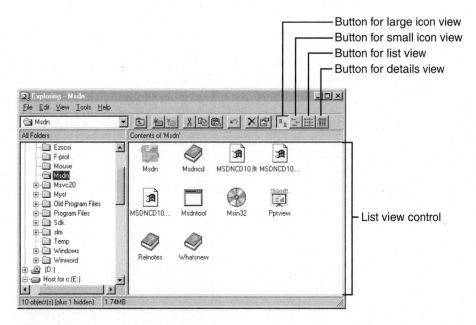

Figure 3-3.
A list view control in Windows Explorer.

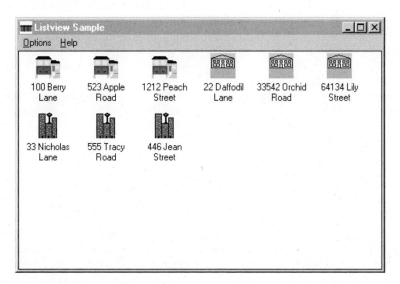

Figure 3-4.
Large icon view.

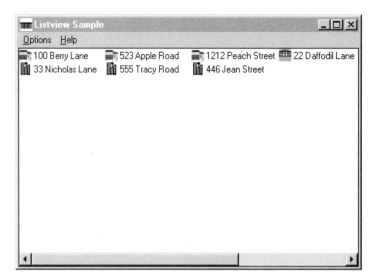

Figure 3-5.
Small icon view.

List view, like small icon view, displays each item with a small icon and a text label to the right. In list view, however, the items are arranged in a column, as shown in Figure 3-6, and the user cannot drag the items.

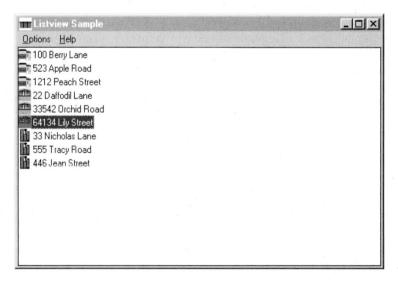

Figure 3-6.
List view.

In details view, items are displayed with their small icons and text labels, with each item on its own line and additional information about the item displayed in subsequent columns across the screen. The leftmost column contains the icon and the text label. A column header shows the title of each column, as you can see in Figure 3-7.

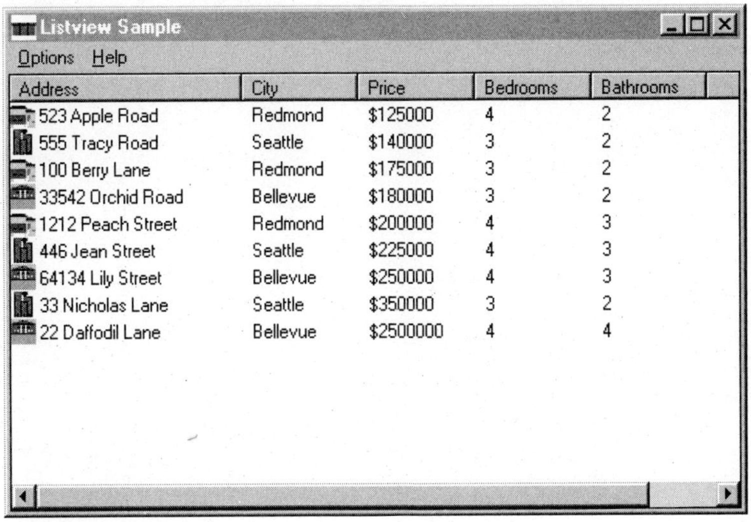

Figure 3-7.
Details view.

A column header is a horizontal window usually positioned above columns of text or numbers and containing a title for each column. A column header can be a stand-alone control (although I cannot for the life of me think of a good reason to use one this way), or it can be part of a list view control. When you use a column header in a list view control, it is "free"—that is, you don't have to create the header control yourself.

A header control can be divided into parts, called *header items,* whose width can be set by the user. A header item can behave like a command button, performing some action (such as sorting data according to a specified criterion) when the user clicks it. For example, clicking the Price header item shown in Figure 3-7 sorts the list by the price of the house. Header items appear as text on a gray background.

NOTE: Column headers do not support a keyboard interface and, as a result, do not accept the input focus.

A header item can have a string, a bitmapped image, and an application-defined 32-bit value associated with it. The string and the image appear within the boundaries of the item. If an item displays both a string and an image, the image is located above the string. If the string and the image overlap, the string overwrites part of the image.

For information about some of the messages and MFC member functions that header controls support, refer to Table 1-3 in Chapter 1 (page 17). You can find details about the remaining messages, such as HDM_LAYOUT, and MFC member functions, such as Layout, in the Win32 SDK documentation or the MFC 3.1 documentation.

Creating a List View Control

At first glance, creating a list view control might appear to be a daunting task. Getting all the necessary information placed in the correct structures involves several steps:

1. Create the window by using the CreateWindow or CreateWindowEx function, specifying WC_LISTVIEW as the class name. Alternatively, if you are writing in MFC, use the MFC CListCtrl class and its Create member function.

2. Create image lists for the large icon and small icon views by calling ImageList_Create. Load the bitmaps for the images by calling Load-Bitmap or LoadIcon, and add them to the image lists by calling ImageList_Add or ImageList_AddIcon. Alternatively, use the MFC CImageList class.

3. Initialize the column header you will use by loading the strings and calling ListView_InsertColumn. MFC developers should use the CListCtrl class.

4. Insert each item into the list view control, and initialize any associated text.

The following code demonstrates these steps. In the LISTVIEW and MFCLIST samples, I defined a structure containing information about the houses listed, including address, city, price, number of bedrooms, and number of bathrooms. I also created an icon for each city represented (a total of three icons).

```
// House structure used for listing
typedef struct tagHOUSEINFO
{
   char szAddress [MAX_ADDRESS];
   char szCity [MAX_CITY];
   int iPrice;
   int iBeds;
   int iBaths;
} HOUSEINFO;

HWND CreateListView (HWND hWndParent)
{
HWND hWndList;                      // handle to list view window
RECT rcl;                          // rectangle for setting size of window
HICON hIcon;                       // handle to an icon
int index;                         // index used in for loops
HIMAGELIST hSmall, hLarge;         // handles to image lists for small and
                                   // large icons
LV_COLUMN lvC;                     // list view column structure
char szText [MAX_PATH];            // place to store some text
LV_ITEM lvI;                       // list view item structure
int iSubItem;                      // index into column header string table

// Ensure that the common control DLL is loaded.
InitCommonControls ();

// Get the size and position of the parent window.
GetClientRect (hWndParent, &rcl);

// Create the list view window that starts out in details view
// and supports label editing.
hWndList = CreateWindowEx (
   0L,
   WC_LISTVIEW,                          // list view class
   "",                                   // no default text
   WS_VISIBLE | WS_CHILD | WS_BORDER | LVS_REPORT |
      LVS_EDITLABELS | WS_EX_CLIENTEDGE,    // styles
   0, 0,
   rcl.right - rcl.left, rcl.bottom - rcl.top,
   hWndParent,
   (HMENU)ID_LISTVIEW,
   hInst,
   NULL);

if (hWndList == NULL)
   return NULL;
```

(continued)

```
// Initialize the list view window.
// First initialize the image lists you will need:
// create image lists for the small and the large icons.

hSmall = ImageList_Create (BITMAP_WIDTH, BITMAP_HEIGHT,
   FALSE, 3, 0);

hLarge = ImageList_Create (LG_BITMAP_WIDTH, LG_BITMAP_HEIGHT,
   FALSE, 3, 0);

// Load the icons and add them to the image lists.
for (index = REDMOND; index <= SEATTLE; index++)
{
   hIcon = LoadIcon (hInst, MAKEINTRESOURCE (index));
   // You have 3 of each type of icon here, so add 3 at a time.
   for (iSubItem = 0; iSubItem < 3; iSubItem++)
   {
      if ((ImageList_AddIcon (hSmall, hIcon) == -1) ||
         (ImageList_AddIcon (hLarge, hIcon) == -1))
         return NULL;
   }
}

// Be sure that all the small icons were added.
if (ImageList_GetImageCount (hSmall) < 3)
   return FALSE;

// Be sure that all the large icons were added.
if (ImageList_GetImageCount (hLarge) < 3)
   return FALSE;

// Associate the image lists with the list view control.
ListView_SetImageList (hWndList, hSmall, LVSIL_SMALL);

ListView_SetImageList (hWndList, hLarge, LVSIL_NORMAL);
   ⋮
```

Next, after creating the list view control and then creating and initializing the image lists, it is time to add the column information. In order to do this, you must fill out an LV_COLUMN structure for each one of the columns and insert the columns by using the ListView_InsertColumn macro, as shown in the following code:

```
// Now initialize the columns you will need.
// Initialize the LV_COLUMN structure.
// The mask specifies that the fmt, width, pszText, and subitem members
// of the structure are valid.
lvC.mask = LVCF_FMT | LVCF_WIDTH | LVCF_TEXT | LVCF_SUBITEM;
lvC.fmt = LVCFMT_LEFT;    // left-align column
lvC.cx = 75;              // width of column in pixels
lvC.pszText = szText;

// Add the columns.
for (index = 0; index <= NUM_COLUMNS; index++)
{
   lvC.iSubItem = index;
   LoadString (hInst, IDS_ADDRESS + index, szText, sizeof (szText));
   if (ListView_InsertColumn (hWndList, index, &lvC) == -1)
     return NULL;
}
   :
```

After setting up the columns, add the items one by one. For each item, you must fill out an LV_ITEM structure. My samples include a callback function to provide the text for the items. Whenever the list view control needs the text for an item, my callback function is called.

```
// Finally, add the actual items to the control.
// Fill out the LV_ITEM structure for each item to add to the list.
// The mask specifies that the pszText, iImage, lParam, and state
// members of the LV_ITEM structure are valid.
lvI.mask = LVIF_TEXT | LVIF_IMAGE | LVIF_PARAM | LVIF_STATE;
lvI.state = 0;
lvI.stateMask = 0;

for (index = 0; index < NUM_ITEMS; index++)
{
   lvI.iItem = index;
   lvI.iSubItem = 0;
   // The parent window is responsible for storing the text.
   // The list view control will send an LVN_GETDISPINFO
   // when it needs the text to display.
   lvI.pszText = LPSTR_TEXTCALLBACK;
   lvI.cchTextMax = MAX_ITEMLEN;
   lvI.iImage = index;
   lvI.lParam = (LPARAM) &rgHouseInfo[index];
```

(continued)

```
   if (ListView_InsertItem (hWndList, &lvI) == -1)
      return NULL;

   for (iSubItem = 1; iSubItem < NUM_COLUMNS; iSubItem++)
   {
      ListView_SetItemText (hWndList, index, iSubItem,
         LPSTR_TEXTCALLBACK);
   }
}

return (hWndList);
}
```

Now that you've seen the code in C, you might wonder whether you need to do anything different or special in order to create and use a list view control in an MFC application. Under MFC, the list view control is supported through the CListCtrl class. In my MFCLIST sample, I created the control in the view class. In the definition of this class, I included a member variable for my CListCtrl object and my two CImageList objects:

```
class CMfclistView : public CView
{
   protected:   // create from serialization only
      CMfclistView ();
      DECLARE_DYNCREATE (CMfclistView);
      CListCtrl m_ListCtl;
      CImageList m_ImageLarge;
      CImageList m_ImageSmall;
      :
```

Then I created a message map entry for the WM_CREATE message and used the Create member function to create the list view control. This code looks nearly identical to the C code, as you can see here:

```
int CMfclistView::OnCreate(LPCREATESTRUCT lpCreateStruct)
{
int index;
int iSubItem;
HICON hIcon;
LV_COLUMN lvC;            // list view column structure
static char szText [256];  // place to store some text
LV_ITEM lvI;              // list view item structure

if (CView::OnCreate (lpCreateStruct) == -1)
   return -1;
```

```
// Create the CListCtrl window.
m_ListCtl.Create (
   WS_VISIBLE | WS_CHILD | WS_BORDER | LVS_REPORT | LVS_EDITLABELS,
   CRect (0, 0, 0, 0),   // bounding rectangle
   this,                 // parent
   ID_LISTVIEW);         // ID

// Create the large icon image list.
m_ImageLarge.Create (
   LARGE_BITMAP_WIDTH,
   LARGE_BITMAP_HEIGHT,
   FALSE,             // list does not include masks
   NUM_BITMAPS,
   0);                // list won't grow

// Create the small icon image list.
m_ImageSmall.Create (
   SMALL_BITMAP_WIDTH,
   SMALL_BITMAP_HEIGHT,
   FALSE,             // list does not include masks
   NUM_BITMAPS,
   0);                // list won't grow

// Load the icons and add them to the image lists.
for (index = IDI_BELLEVUE; index <= IDI_SEATTLE ; index++)
{
   hIcon = ::LoadIcon (AfxGetResourceHandle (),
      MAKEINTRESOURCE (index));
   // You have 3 of each type of icon here, so add 3 at a time.
   for (iSubItem = 0; iSubItem < 3; iSubItem++)
   {
      if ((m_ImageSmall.Add (hIcon) == -1) ||
         (m_ImageLarge.Add (hIcon) == -1))
         return NULL;
   }
}

// Be sure that all the small icons were added.
if (m_ImageSmall.GetImageCount () < 3)
   return NULL;

// Be sure that all the large icons were added.
if (m_ImageLarge.GetImageCount () < 3)
   return NULL;
```

(continued)

83

```
// Associate the image lists with the list view control.
m_ListCtl.SetImageList (&m_ImageSmall, LVSIL_SMALL);
m_ListCtl.SetImageList (&m_ImageLarge, LVSIL_NORMAL);

// Now initialize the columns you will need.
// Initialize the LV_COLUMN structure.
// The mask specifies that the fmt, width, pszText, and subitem members
// of the structure are valid.
lvC.mask = LVCF_FMT | LVCF_WIDTH | LVCF_TEXT | LVCF_SUBITEM;
lvC.fmt = LVCFMT_LEFT;     // left-align column
lvC.cx = 75;               // width of column in pixels

// Add the columns.
for (index = 0; index <= NUM_COLUMNS; index++)
{
    lvC.iSubItem = index;
    lvC.pszText = szColumns [index];

    if (m_ListCtl.InsertColumn (index, &lvC) == -1)
        return NULL;
}

// Finally, add the actual items to the control.
// Fill out the LV_ITEM structure for each item to add to the list.
// The mask specifies that the pszText, iImage, lParam, and state
// members of the LV_ITEM structure are valid.
lvI.mask = LVIF_TEXT | LVIF_IMAGE | LVIF_PARAM | LVIF_STATE;
lvI.state = 0;
lvI.stateMask = 0;

for (index = 0; index < NUM_ITEMS; index++)
{
    lvI.iItem = index;
    lvI.iSubItem = 0;
    // The parent window is responsible for storing the text.
    // The list view control will send an LVN_GETDISPINFO
    // when it needs the text to display.
    lvI.pszText = LPSTR_TEXTCALLBACK;
    lvI.cchTextMax = MAX_ITEMLEN;
    lvI.iImage = index;
    lvI.lParam = (LPARAM) &rgHouseInfo[index];

    if (m_ListCtl.InsertItem (&lvI) == -1)
        return NULL;
```

```
    for (iSubItem = 1; iSubItem < NUM_COLUMNS; iSubItem++)
    {
       m_ListCtl.SetItemText (index,
          iSubItem,
          LPSTR_TEXTCALLBACK);
    }
}


return 0;
}
```

Changing Views

The preceding code produces a list view control that initially appears in details view. As yet, you have no way of changing views. In the LISTVIEW sample, you can do this by choosing a view from the Options menu, shown in Figure 3-8.

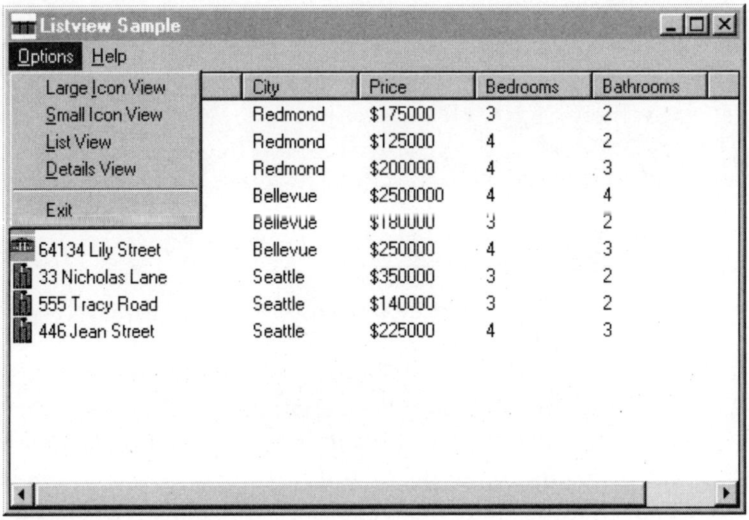

Figure 3-8.
The Options menu in the LISTVIEW sample.

Clicking an item on this menu generates a WM_COMMAND message. In an MFC application, you can handle this by adding a message map entry for the command (IDM_LARGEICON for large icon view), and you can change the view by setting the window style. To check the current view of the control, use the LVS_TYPEMASK constant. The current view can be LVS_ICON, LVS_SMALLICON, LVS_LIST, or LVS_REPORT.

```
void CMfclistView::OnLargeicon ()
{
DWORD dwStyle;

dwStyle = GetWindowLong (m_ListCtl.m_hWnd, GWL_STYLE);

if ((dwStyle & LVS_TYPEMASK) != LVS_ICON)
    SetWindowLong (m_ListCtl.m_hWnd, GWL_STYLE,
      .(dwStyle & ~LVS_TYPEMASK) | LVS_ICON);
}
```

Handling Notifications

OK. You have your list view control, you have your image lists, you're able to switch between views—but you still aren't ready to compile, link, and run. Before you do that, you must set up a way to handle the WM_NOTIFY messages that will be sent to the parent window. List view controls receive notifications when text is needed for display, when items are being dragged and dropped, when labels are being edited, and when columns are being sorted (to name just a few cases). The C code you'll see next is an implementation of a handler that I set up for the WM_NOTIFY message. When the parent window receives the WM_NOTIFY message, it calls this function to determine the following:

■ Whether it needs text for a list view item (LVN_GETDISPINFO)

■ Whether the items must be sorted (LVN_COLUMNCLICK)

■ Whether it needs to handle label editing (LVN_BEGINLABELEDIT and LVN_ENDLABELEDIT)

When the WM_NOTIFY message is sent, the *lParam* parameter serves as a pointer to an NM_LISTVIEW or LV_DISPINFO structure. Which structure *lParam* points to is determined by the notification sent. Each item in my list view control has an associated item containing information about the house it describes. I saved the pointer to this information in the *lParam* member of the LV_ITEM structure when I added the item to the control. The following code shows what the sample does in response to a request for text and in response to a column click. (We'll discuss label editing later in this chapter.)

```
LRESULT NotifyHandler (HWND hWnd, UINT uMsg, WPARAM wParam,
    LPARAM lParam)
{
LV_DISPINFO *pLvdi = (LV_DISPINFO *)lParam;
NM_LISTVIEW *pNm = (NM_LISTVIEW *)lParam;
```

```
HOUSEINFO *pHouse = (HOUSEINFO *)(pLvdi->item.lParam);
static char szText [10];

if (wParam != ID_LISTVIEW)
    return 0L;

switch (pLvdi->hdr.code)
{
    case LVN_GETDISPINFO:

        switch (pLvdi->item.iSubItem)
        {
            case 0:    // address
                pLvdi->item.pszText = pHouse->szAddress;
                break;

            case 1:    // city
                pLvdi->item.pszText = pHouse->szCity;
                break;

            case 2:    // price
                sprintf (szText, "$%u", pHouse->iPrice);
                pLvdi->item.pszText = szText;
                break;

            case 3:    // number of bedrooms
                sprintf (szText, "%u", pHouse->iBeds);
                pLvdi->item.pszText = szText;
                break;

            case 4:    // number of bathrooms
                sprintf (szText, "%u", pHouse->iBaths);
                pLvdi->item.pszText = szText;
                break;

            default:
                break;
        }
        break;
    :
    case LVN_COLUMNCLICK:
        // The user clicked a column header; sort by this criterion.
        ListView_SortItems (pNm->hdr.hwndFrom,
            ListViewCompareProc,
            (LPARAM)(pNm->iSubItem));
        break;
```

(continued)

```
   default:
      break;
}

return 0L;
}
```

When I ported this sample to MFC, I had to find a way to get to the WM-_NOTIFY message because ClassWizard does not offer WM_NOTIFY as an option for a message map. I decided to overload the WindowProc function in the Cwnd class and call my notification handler from there:

```
LRESULT CMfclistView::WindowProc (UINT message, WPARAM wParam,
    LPARAM lParam)
{
if (message == WM_NOTIFY)
    NotifyHandler (message, wParam, lParam);
return CView::WindowProc (message, wParam, lParam);
}
```

Sorting Items in Response to a Column Header Click

In the preceding C code, I handled a click on a column header by calling the ListView_SortItems macro and providing a pointer to a callback function. It is up to the application to provide the code to sort list view items when the user clicks a column header; the list view control does not sort the items for you. (Drat!) This makes some sense (albeit in a twisted kind of way)—how would the system know which criterion to use for the sort (for example, color or size)? Nevertheless, I wish that Windows 95 provided some built-in sorting callbacks for "standard" sorting needs such as string comparisons and numeric sorts. Because the list view control lacks this capability, you must provide a callback function to do the sorting. The saving grace is that this isn't hard to do.

The following code demonstrates one method of sorting. It uses the lstrcmpi function to compare strings and uses simple arithmetic to sort numbers. The callback function is given pointers to the two items to compare; it returns a negative value if the first item should precede the second, a positive value if the first item should follow the second, or 0 if the two items are equivalent. The *lParamSort* parameter is an application-defined value (which I did not use in my function). It would be useful in the sort to include any special information about the sort criterion. For instance, if you want to let the user specify whether to sort forward or backward, you can pass an indication of this in the *lParamSort* parameter.

```
int CALLBACK ListViewCompareProc (LPARAM lParam1, LPARAM lParam2,
    LPARAM lParamSort)
{
HOUSEINFO *pHouse1 = (HOUSEINFO *)lParam1;
HOUSEINFO *pHouse2 = (HOUSEINFO *)lParam2;
LPSTR lpStr1, lpStr2;
int iResult;

if (pHouse1 && pHouse2)
{
    switch (lParamSort)
      {
      case 0:   // sort by address
         lpStr1 = pHouse1->szAddress;
         lpStr2 = pHouse2->szAddress;
         iResult = lstrcmpi (lpStr1, lpStr2);
         break;

      case 1:   // sort by city
         lpStr1 = pHouse1->szCity;
         lpStr2 = pHouse2->szCity;
         iResult = lstrcmpi (lpStr1, lpStr2);
         break;

      case 2:   // sort by price
         iResult = pHouse1->iPrice - pHouse2->iPrice;
         break;

      case 3:   // sort by number of bedrooms
         iResult = pHouse1->iBeds - pHouse2->iBeds;
         break;

      case 4:   // sort by number of bathrooms
         iResult = pHouse1->iBaths - pHouse2->iBaths;
         break;

      default:
         iResult = 0;
         break;
    }
}

return (iResult);
}
```

Editing Labels

When you create a list view control, you can enable label editing by specifying the LVS_EDITLABELS style, which lets a user edit an item's text label in place. The user begins by clicking the label of an item that has the focus. The list view control notifies the parent window with an LVN_BEGINLABELEDIT notification. If you do not want to allow label editing on certain items, you can return a nonzero value to disallow it. To limit the amount of text the user can enter, the application gets the handle to the edit window through the LVM_GETEDITCONTROL message (or the MFC GetEditControl member function) and sends the EM_SETLIMITTEXT message to the edit control (or uses the MFC LimitText member function of the CEdit class), specifying the maximum number of characters that can be entered.

Once editing is completed, the list view control sends its parent window an LVN_ENDLABELEDIT notification. The *lParam* parameter is the address of an LV_DISPINFO structure identifying the item and specifying the edited text. The parent window is responsible for updating the item's label. If editing is canceled, the *iItem* member is −1. Be alert to the possibility of getting a valid index to an item but getting a NULL pointer back for the text. This happens if the user chooses an item and immediately presses the Enter key.

The following code from the MFCLIST sample shows how to support label editing in a list view control:

```
case LVN_BEGINLABELEDIT:
{
    CEdit *pEdit;
    // Get the handle to the edit control.
    pEdit = m_ListCtl.GetEditControl ();
    // Limit the amount of text that the user can enter.
    pEdit->LimitText (20);
}
    break;

case LVN_ENDLABELEDIT:
    // If label editing wasn't canceled and the
    // text buffer is non-NULL...
    if ((pLvdi->item.iItem != -1) && (pLvdi->item.pszText != NULL))
    // Save the new label information.
    lstrcpy (pHouse->szAddress, pLvdi->item.pszText);
    break;
```

That's all there is to it. The LISTVIEW and MFCLIST samples should be enough to get you started if you plan to include list view controls in your application.

List View Control Messages and Member Functions

Table 3-3 describes the messages and member functions supported by list view controls. The MFC class that supports these controls is the CListCtrl class. To use a list view control in your application, you must link with the COMCTL32.LIB library. If you write your application in C, you must include the COMMCTRL.H header file; if you write the application in MFC, you need to include the AFXCMN.H file in your STDAFX.H file (if you are using STDAFX.H).

Message	Member Function	Description
LVM_ARRANGE	Arrange	Arranges the items in large icon view based on the flags set.
LVM_CREATE-DRAGIMAGE	Create-DragImage	Creates a drag image for the specified item.
LVM_DELETEALLITEMS	DeleteAllItems	Removes all items from a list view window.
LVM_DELETECOLUMN	DeleteColumn	Removes a column from a list view window.
LVM_DELETEITEM	DeleteItem	Removes a single item from a list view window.
LVM_EDITLABEL	EditLabel	Begins in-place editing of an item's text label. This message selects and sets the focus to the item. When the user completes or cancels the editing, the edit window is destroyed and the handle becomes invalid. You can safely subclass the edit window, but do not destroy it. To cancel editing, send a WM_CANCELMODE message to the list view control.
LVM_ENSUREVISIBLE	EnsureVisible	Ensures that an item is entirely or partially visible by scrolling the list view window if necessary.
LVM_FINDITEM	FindItem	Searches for an item in a list view control.
LVM_GETBKCOLOR	GetBkColor	Retrieves the background color of the list view window.

Table 3-3. *(continued)*

List view control messages and member functions.

Table 3-3. *continued*

Message	Member Function	Description
LVM_GETCALLBACKMASK	GetCallbackMask	Retrieves the callback mask for a list view window.
LVM_GETCOLUMN	GetColumn	Retrieves the attributes of a column in a list view control. The *mask* member of the LV_COLUMN structure passed in specifies which attributes to get. If the LVCF_TEXT flag is specified, the *pszText* member must contain the address of the buffer that receives the item's text, and the *cchTextMax* member must specify the size of the buffer.
LVM_GETCOLUMNWIDTH	GetColumnWidth	Retrieves the width of a column in list view or details view.
LVM_GETCOUNTPERPAGE	GetCountPerPage	Calculates the number of items that can fit vertically in the visible area in list view or details view.
LVM_GETEDITCONTROL	GetEditControl	Retrieves the handle of the edit window used to edit an item's text label in place. The item being edited currently has the focus. When the user completes or cancels the editing, the edit window is destroyed and the handle becomes invalid. You can safely subclass the edit window, but do not destroy it. To cancel editing, send a WM_CANCELMODE message to the list view control.
LVM_GETIMAGELIST	GetImageList	Retrieves the handle of an image list used for drawing items.
LVM_GETITEM	GetItem	Retrieves the attributes of an item.
LVM_GETITEMCOUNT	GetItemCount	Retrieves the number of items in a list view control.
LVM_GETITEMPOSITION	GetItemPosition	Retrieves the position of an item in large icon view or small icon view.
LVM_GETITEMRECT	GetItemRect	Retrieves the bounding rectangle for an item in the current view.

(continued)

Table 3-3. *continued*

Message	Member Function	Description
LVM_GETITEMSTATE	GetItemState	Retrieves the state of an item.
LVM_GETITEMTEXT	GetItemText	Retrieves the text of an item or a subitem.
LVM_GETNEXTITEM	GetNextItem	Searches for the next item, starting from a specified item.
LVM_GETORIGIN	GetOrigin	Retrieves the list view origin point, which is needed for setting the item position.
LVM_GETSTRINGWIDTH	GetStringWidth	Retrieves the minimum column width necessary to display the given string. The returned width takes the current font and column margins of the list view control (but not the width of a small icon) into account.
LVM_GETTEXTBKCOLOR	GetTextBkColor	Retrieves the background text color in a list view window.
LVM_GETTEXTCOLOR	GetTextColor	Retrieves the color of the text in a list view window.
LVM_GETTOPINDEX	GetTopIndex	Retrieves the index of the first visible item in a list view window.
LVM_GETVIEWRECT	GetViewRect	Retrieves the bounding rectangle of all items in large icon view.
LVM_HITTEST	HitTest	Determines which item is at a specified position in a list view window.
LVM_INSERTCOLUMN	InsertColumn	Inserts a new column in a list view window.
LVM_INSERTITEM	InsertItem	Inserts a new item in a list view window.
LVM_REDRAWITEMS	RedrawItems	Forces a redraw of a range of items in a list view control. The specified items are not repainted until the control receives a WM_PAINT message. To repaint immediately, call the UpdateWindow function after using this message.
LVM_SCROLL	Scroll	Scrolls the contents of a list view window. In details view, the *dx* parameter must be 0, and the *dy* parameter is the number of lines to scroll.

(continued)

Table 3-3. *continued*

Message	Member Function	Description
LVM_SETBKCOLOR	SetBkColor	Sets the background color of a list view window.
LVM_SETCALLBACKMASK	SetCallbackMask	Sets the callback mask for a list view window.
LVM_SETCOLUMN	SetColumn	Sets the attributes of a column in a list view control.
LVM_SETCOLUMNWIDTH	SetColumnWidth	Sets the width of a column in details view or list view.
LVM_SETIMAGELIST	SetImageList	Sets the image list used for drawing items in a list view control.
LVM_SETITEM	SetItem	Sets an item's attributes.
LVM_SETITEMCOUNT	SetItemCount	Sets the item count of a list view control.
LVM_SETITEMPOSITION	SetItemPosition	Sets the position of an item in large icon view or small icon view relative to the list view rectangle.
LVM_SETITEMSTATE	SetItemState	Sets the state of an item.
LVM_SETITEMTEXT	SetItemText	Sets the text of an item or a subitem.
LVM_SETTEXTBKCOLOR	SetTextBkColor	Sets the background text color in a list view window.
LVM_SETTEXTCOLOR	SetTextColor	Sets the text color in a list view window.
LVM_SORTITEMS	SortItems	Sorts items in a list view control, using an application-defined comparison function.
LVM_UPDATE	Update	Updates an item. If the list view control has the LVS_AUTOARRANGE style, the list view items will be automatically arranged in the window.

Tree View Controls

A tree view control displays a hierarchical list of labeled items. Optionally, each item can have a bitmap (or a pair of bitmaps) associated with it. You've seen this type of hierarchy in File Manager (displaying directory information) and in Microsoft Mail (displaying mail folders). The top item in the hierarchy, which has no parent, is referred to as the *root item*. An item below the root item in the hierarchy is called a *child item* of the root. An item that has child items is called a *parent item*. Child items, when displayed, are indented below their parent item. (In fact, the entire hierarchy of items is expandable and collapsible.) If you specify the TVS_HASLINES style, you can connect the items with lines. Figure 3-9 shows a tree view window that lists houses for sale in various cities in the beautiful Pacific Northwest.

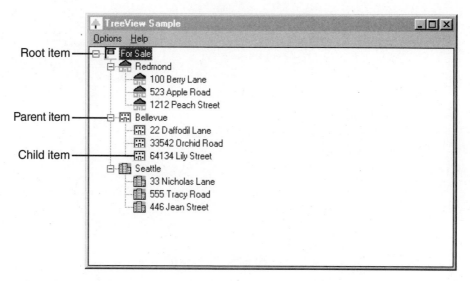

Figure 3-9.
Anatomy of a tree view control.

The first time I saw a tree hierarchy like this, I wanted to implement one in my application. Like most of you, I figured out how to do it on my own, but it was complex, and it was a pain. I really wished that a tree hierarchy had been built into the system. With Windows 95, it's finally happened.

In a tree view control, you can add a pair of bitmaps to the left of an item's label, displaying one bitmap when the item is selected and the other when the item is not selected. For example, when you select a folder in Windows Explorer, the image changes from a closed folder to an open one, as shown in Figure 3-10 on the following page.

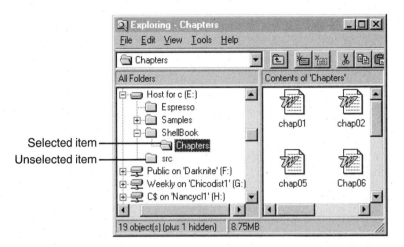

Selected item ——
Unselected item ——

Figure 3-10.
Selected and unselected items in a tree view control.

Creating a Tree View Control

To create a tree view control in C, use the CreateWindow or CreateWindowEx function and specify the WC_TREEVIEW style for the window class. If you are using MFC, create a CTreeCtrl object by using the Create member function. The following code produces a tree view control and uses the image list functions to create an image list associated with it:

```
HWND CreateTreeView (HWND hWndParent)
{
HWND hwndTree;      // handle to tree view window
RECT rcl;           // rectangle for setting size of window
HBITMAP hBmp;       // handle to a bitmap
HIMAGELIST hIml;    // handle to image list

// Ensure that the common control DLL is loaded.
InitCommonControls ();

// Get the size and position of the parent window.
GetClientRect (hWndParent, &rcl);

// Create the tree view window.
hwndTree = CreateWindowEx (
    0L,
    WC_TREEVIEW,    // tree view class
    "",             // no default text
```

```
              WS_VISIBLE | WS_CHILD | WS_BORDER | TVS_HASLINES | TVS_HASBUTTONS |
                 TVS_LINESATROOT,
              0, 0,
              rcl.right - rcl.left, rcl.bottom - rcl.top - 15,
              hWndParent,
              (HMENU)ID_TREEVIEW,
              hInst,
              NULL);

     if (hwndTree == NULL)
        return NULL;

     // Initialize the tree view window.
     // First create the image list you will need.
     hIml = ImageList_Create (
        BITMAP_WIDTH,    // width
        BITMAP_HEIGHT,   // height
        0,               // creation flags
        NUM_BITMAPS,     // number of images
        0);              // amount this list can grow

     // Load the bitmaps and add them to the image list.
     hBmp = LoadBitmap (hInst, MAKEINTRESOURCE (FORSALE));
     idxForSale = ImageList_Add (
        hIml,     // handle to image list
        hBmp)     // handle of bitmap to add
        NULL);    // handle of bitmap mask

     hBmp = LoadBitmap (hInst, MAKEINTRESOURCE (REDMOND));
     idxRedmond = ImageList_Add (hIml, hBmp, NULL);

     hBmp = LoadBitmap (hInst, MAKEINTRESOURCE (BELLEVUE));
     idxBellevue = ImageList_Add (hIml, hBmp, NULL);

     hBmp = LoadBitmap (hInst, MAKEINTRESOURCE (SEATTLE));
     idxSeattle = ImageList_Add (hIml, hBmp, NULL);

     // Be sure that all the bitmaps were added.
     if (ImageList_GetImageCount (hIml) < NUM_BITMAPS)
        return FALSE;

     // Associate the image list with the tree view control.
     TreeView_SetImageList (hwndTree, hIml, idxForSale);

     return hwndTree;
     }
```

Adding Items to a Tree View Control

You can add items to a tree view control by sending the TVM_INSERTITEM message or by calling the associated TreeView_InsertItem macro. In MFC, use the InsertItem member function. For each item, you must fill out the TV_ITEM and TV_INSERTSTRUCT structures. When adding an item, you must specify the handle of the new item's parent item. If you specify NULL or TVI_ROOT instead of an item handle, the item is added as a root item.

The following example demonstrates how to add items to a tree view control. This sample handles the real estate listing you saw earlier, with three houses listed for each of three cities. A global structure keeps track of the handle to the parent item and its image.

```
typedef struct tagHOUSEINFO
{
    char szAddress [MAX_ADDRESS];
    int iImage;
    HTREEITEM hParent;
} HOUSEINFO;

BOOL AddTreeViewItems (HWND hwndTree)
{
static HTREEITEM hPrev;
char szText [MAX_LEN];
int index;

// First add the root item "Houses for Sale."
LoadString (hInst, IDS_FORSALE, szText, MAX_LEN);
hTRoot = AddOneItem ((HTREEITEM)NULL, szText, (HTREEITEM)TVI_ROOT,
    idxForSale, hwndTree);

// Now add the cities.
LoadString (hInst, IDS_REDMOND, szText, MAX_LEN);
hTRed = AddOneItem (hTRoot, szText, (HTREEITEM)TVI_FIRST, idxRedmond,
    hwndTree);

LoadString (hInst, IDS_BELLEVUE, szText, MAX_LEN);
hTBel = AddOneItem (hTRoot, szText, hTRed, idxBellevue, hwndTree);

LoadString (hInst, IDS_SEATTLE, szText, MAX_LEN);
hTSea = AddOneItem (hTRoot, szText, hTBel, idxSeattle, hwndTree);

// Fill out the structure for each house.
FillInStruct (hTRed, idxRedmond, 0, 3);
FillInStruct (hTBel, idxBellevue, 3, 6);
FillInStruct (hTSea, idxSeattle, 6, 9);

// Add the houses for each city.
hPrev = hTSea;
```

```
    for (index = 0; index < NUM_HOUSES; index++)
    {
        hPrev = AddOneItem (rgHouseInfo[index].hParent,
                            rgHouseInfo[index].szAddress,
                            hPrev,
                            rgHouseInfo[index].iImage,
                            hwndTree);
        rgHouseInfo[index].hItem = hPrev;
    }
    return TRUE;
}


// This function saves the current image and the handle to the
// parent of the tree view item.
VOID FillInStruct (HTREEITEM hParent, int iImage, int index, int iMax)
{
for (; index < iMax; index++)
    {
        rgHouseInfo[index].iImage = iImage;
        rgHouseInfo[index].hParent = hParent;
    }
}


// This function fills out the TV_ITEM and TV_INSERTSTRUCT structures
// and adds the item to the tree view control.
HTREEITEM AddOneItem (HTREEITEM hParent, LPSTR szText,
    HTREEITEM hInsAfter, int iImage, HWND hwndTree)
{
HTREEITEM hItem;
TV_ITEM tvI;
TV_INSERTSTRUCT tvIns;

// The pszText, iImage, and iSelectedImage members are filled out.
tvI.mask = TVIF_TEXT | TVIF_IMAGE | TVIF_SELECTEDIMAGE | TVIF_PARAM;
tvI.pszText = szText;
tvI.cchTextMax = lstrlen (szText);
tvI.iImage = iImage;
tvI.iSelectedImage = iImage;

tvIns.item = tvI;
tvIns.hInsertAfter = hInsAfter;
tvIns.hParent = hParent;

// Insert the item into the tree.
hItem = (HTREEITEM) SendMessage (hwndTree, TVM_INSERTITEM, 0,
    (LPARAM)(LPTV_INSERTSTRUCT)&tvIns);

return (hItem);
}
```

In MFCTREE, the MFC version of the TREEVIEW sample, the control is created in the view class. The preceding C code is nearly identical to the MFC code. You should note where I keep track of some of the data in MFCTREE, however. In the header file for the view class, MFCTRVW.H, the view class is defined. Within this class, I save the CTreeCtrl object, the image list, the indexes to the images associated with the tree view items, and information about the item being dragged.

```
class CMfctreeView : public CView
{
    protected:    // create from serialization only
        CMfctreeView();
        DECLARE_DYNCREATE(CMfctreeView);
        CTreeCtrl m_TreeCtl;       // tree view control
        CImageList m_ImageList;    // image list associated with tree
        BOOL m_fDragging;          // whether you are dragging an item
        HTREEITEM m_hDragItem;     // current item being dragged
        int m_idxForSale;          // index to For Sale icon
        int m_idxRedmond;          // index to Redmond icon
        int m_idxBellevue;         // index to Bellevue icon
        int m_idxSeattle;          // index to Seattle icon

    // Attributes
    public:
        CMfctreeDoc *GetDocument ();

    // Operations
    public:
        BOOL AddTreeViewItems ();
        HTREEITEM AddOneItem (HTREEITEM, LPSTR, HTREEITEM, int);
        VOID FillInStruct (HTREEITEM, int, int, int);
        VOID BeginDrag (NM_TREEVIEW *);
        VOID DropItem (HTREEITEM);

    // Overrides
        // ClassWizard generated virtual function overrides.
        // {{AFX_VIRTUAL (CMfctreeView)
        public:
            virtual void OnDraw (CDC *pDC);   // overridden to draw this
                                              // view
        protected:
            virtual LRESULT WindowProc (UINT message, WPARAM wParam,
                LPARAM lParam);
        // }}AFX_VIRTUAL
```

```
// Implementation
public:
    virtual ~CMfctreeView ();

protected:

// Generated message map functions
protected:
    // {{AFX_MSG (CMfctreeView)
    afx_msg int OnCreate (LPCREATESTRUCT lpCreateStruct);
    afx_msg void OnSize (UINT nType, int cx, int cy);
    afx_msg void OnDestroy ();
    afx_msg void OnMouseMove (UINT nFlags, CPoint point);
    afx_msg void OnLButtonUp (UINT nFlags, CPoint point);
    // }}AFX_MSG
    DECLARE_MESSAGE_MAP ()
};
```

Implementing Drag and Drop for a Tree View Item

Now that you have a tree view control that can be expanded and collapsed, it would be neat if the user could pick up one of the items and drag it to a new location. The tree view control has some built-in functions that facilitate this operation. When processing a drag operation for a tree view item, an application typically does the following:

1. Processes the start of the drag

2. Processes the dragging

3. Processes the drop

An application processes the start of the drag (picking up the item) in the window procedure of the parent window by using the TVN_BEGINDRAG notification (if the user is dragging with the left mouse button) or the TVN_BEGINRDRAG notification (if the user is dragging with the right mouse button). These notifications are sent through a WM_NOTIFY message. The following sample code creates a drag image, captures the mouse, and sets a Boolean flag to signal that dragging is occurring:

```
case WM_NOTIFY:
    switch(((LPNMHDR)lParam)->code)
    {
        case TVN_BEGINDRAG:
```

(continued)

101

```
            // The user wants to drag an item. Call the drag handler.
            BeginDrag (hWndTreeView, (NM_TREEVIEW *)lParam);
            // Save the dragged item information.
            tvI = ((NM_TREEVIEW *)lParam)->itemNew;
            // Get a handle to the drag object.
            hDragItem = tvI.hItem;
            break;

        default:
            break;
    }
    break;
:
VOID BeginDrag (HWND hwndTree, NM_TREEVIEW *lItem)
{
HIMAGELIST hIml;
RECT rcl;

// Create an image to use for dragging.
hIml = TreeView_CreateDragImage (hwndTree, lItem->itemNew.hItem);

// Get the bounding rectangle of the item being dragged.
TreeView_GetItemRect (hwndTree, lItem->itemNew.hItem, &rcl, TRUE);

// Start dragging the image.
ImageList_BeginDrag (hIml, 0, lItem->ptDrag.x, lItem->ptDrag.y);

// Hide the cursor.
ShowCursor (FALSE);

// Capture the mouse.
SetCapture (GetParent (hwndTree));

// Set a global flag that tells whether dragging is occurring.
g_fDragging = TRUE;
}
```

The **MFCTREE** sample handles the drag-and-drop operation through a virtual function mapped to the WindowProc function:

```
// Handle the WM_NOTIFY::TVN_BEGINDRAG notification.
LRESULT CMfctreeView::WindowProc (UINT message, WPARAM wParam,
    LPARAM lParam)
{
TV_ITEM tvI;
if (message == WM_NOTIFY)
{
    if (((LPNMHDR)lParam)->code == TVN_BEGINDRAG)
    {
        BeginDrag ((NM_TREEVIEW *)lParam);
        tvI = ((NM_TREEVIEW *)lParam)->itemNew;
```

```
      // Get a handle to the drag object.
      m_hDragItem = tvI.hItem;
   }
}
return CView::WindowProc (message, wParam, lParam);
}


VOID CMfctreeView::BeginDrag (NM_TREEVIEW *lItem)
{
CImageList *CImage;

// Create an image to use for dragging.
CImage = m_TreeCtl.CreateDragImage (lItem->itemNew.hItem);

// Start dragging the image.
CImage->BeginDrag (0, lItem->ptDrag);

// Hide the cursor.
ShowCursor (FALSE);

SetCapture ();
m_fDragging = TRUE;
}
```

The application processes the dragging operation by capturing the mouse and monitoring the WM_MOUSEMOVE messages. In a typical drag-and-drop scenario, the image appears to be dragged because the cursor is changed to the image of the item being dragged.

```
VOID CMfctreeView::OnMouseMove (UINT nFlags, CPoint point)
{
HTREEITEM hTarget;
UINT flags;

if (m_fDragging)
{
   // Drag the item to the current mouse position.
   m_ImageList.DragMove (point);

   flags = TVHT_ONITEM;
   // If the cursor is on an item, highlight it as the drop target.
   if ((hTarget = m_TreeCtl.HitTest (point, &flags)) != NULL)
   m_TreeCtl.SelectDropTarget (hTarget);
}

CView::OnMouseMove (nFlags, point);
}
```

When the user finishes dragging the item, the application can look for the WM_LBUTTONUP message. At this point, the currently selected item is recorded, the mouse is released, and the cursor is restored to the previous state. This is also the point at which you want to reset the parentage of the item and reset any internal structures that are keeping track of your tree items. Also, remember to reset the drop highlight item. During the drag operation, the drop highlight item changes dynamically as the user moves the mouse. When the item is dropped, you need to set the drop highlight back to NULL, or you will end up with two items that both appear selected, because selected items and drop highlight items are painted the same way. This is remedied by another call to TreeView_SelectItem, passing NULL for the *hItem* parameter.

```
case WM_LBUTTONUP:
    // If dragging, stop it.
    if (g_fDragging)
    {
        // Process the item drop.
        DropItem (hDragItem, hWndTreeView);

        // Inform the image list that dragging has stopped.
        ImageList_EndDrag ();

        // Release the mouse capture.
        ReleaseCapture ();

        // Show the cursor.
        ShowCursor (TRUE);

        // Reset the global Boolean flag to a nondragging state.
        g_fDragging = FALSE;
    }
    break;

// Function that processes the item drop
VOID DropItem (HTREEITEM hDragItem, HWND hwnd)
{
HTREEITEM hParent, hNewItem, hTarget;
TV_ITEM tvTarget;
int index;

// Get the handle to the drop target.
hTarget = TreeView_GetDropHilight (hwnd);
```

```
    // Get the parent of the drop target.
    hParent = TreeView_GetParent (hwnd, hTarget);

    // Get the image information.
    tvTarget.hItem = hTarget;
    tvTarget.mask = TVIF_IMAGE;
    TreeView_GetItem (hwnd, &tvTarget);

    // Get the index into the structure containing the text for the items.
    for (index = 0; index < NUM_HOUSES; index++)
    {
        if (rgHouseInfo[index].hItem == hDragItem)
          break;
    }

    if (index == NUM_HOUSES)
        index--;

    // Reinsert the new item.
    hNewItem = AddOneItem (hParent, rgHouseInfo[index].szAddress,
        hTarget, tvTarget.iImage, hwnd);

    // Delete the dragged item.
    TreeView_DeleteItem(hwnd, hDragItem);

    // Reset the drop target to NULL.
    TreeView_SelectDropTarget (hwnd, (HTREEITEM)NULL);
}
```

As you can see, processing a drag-and-drop operation for a tree view control is not at all difficult, so you really won't have any excuse for not supporting it.

Tree View Control Macros and Member Functions

Table 3-4 on the following page describes the macros and member functions supported by tree view controls. CTreeCtrl is the MFC class that supports these controls. To use tree view controls in your application, you must link with the COMCTL32.LIB library. If you are working in C, you must include the COMMCTRL.H header file; if you write your application in MFC, you must include the AFXCMN.H file in your STDAFX.H file (if you are using STDAFX.H).

For each message supported by tree view controls, the system provides a macro that an application can call. I used the macros rather than the messages in my samples because I find the macros more readable and because they make it easier to move between C and MFC. As you can see in Table 3-4, the name of the member function is nearly always the same as the end of the macro name (that is, the DeleteItem member function corresponds to the TreeView_DeleteItem macro).

Macro	Member Function	Description
TreeView_Create	Create	Creates a tree view control.
TreeView_CreateDragImage	CreateDragImage	Creates a drag image for the specified item.
TreeView_DeleteAllItems	DeleteAllItems	Deletes all items in a tree view window.
TreeView_DeleteItem	DeleteItem	Deletes a specified item from a tree view window. This message has two macros, TreeView_DeleteItem and Tree-View_DeleteAllItems, which you can use to delete one item or all items from the control. If the item label is being edited when this message is sent, the edit operation is canceled, and the parent window receives a TVN_ENDLABEL-EDIT notification. Then a TVN_DELETEITEM notification is sent to the parent window. If *hItem* is TVI-_ROOT, all items are deleted from the control.
TreeView_EditLabel	EditLabel	Begins in-place editing of an item's text label. The text is replaced by a single-line edit window containing the original text in a selected and focused state. A TVN_BEGINLABELEDIT notification is sent to the parent window of the tree view control. You can safely subclass the edit control, but do not destroy it. When the user completes or cancels the editing, the handle to the edit window becomes invalid.

Table 3-4. *(continued)*
Tree view control macros and member functions.

Table 3-4. *continued*

Macro	Member Function	Description
TreeView_EnsureVisible	EnsureVisible	Ensures that an item is visible, and expands the parent item or scrolls the tree view window if necessary. If the message expands the parent item, TVN_ITEMEXPANDING and TVN_ITEMEXPANDED notifications are sent to the parent window.
TreeView_Expand	Expand	Expands or collapses the list of child items associated with a parent item. This message sends TVN_ITEMEXPANDING and TVN_ITEMEXPANDED notifications to the parent window.
TreeView_GetChild	GetChildItem	Retrieves the child of a specified tree view item.
TreeView_GetCount	GetCount	Returns the number of items in a tree view window.
TreeView_GetDrop-Hilight	GetDrop-HilightItem	Retrieves the target of a drag-and-drop operation.
TreeView_GetEditControl	GetEditControl	Retrieves the handle of the edit control being used for in-place editing of an item's text label.
TreeView_GetFirstVisible	GetFirstVisibleItem	Retrieves the first visible item of a tree view control.
TreeView_GetImageList	GetImageList	Retrieves the handle of the image list associated with a tree view window.
TreeView_GetIndent	GetIndent	Retrieves the amount, in pixels, that child items are indented relative to their parent item.
TreeView_GetItem	GetItem	Retrieves information about an item depending on the *mask* member in the TV_ITEM structure passed in.
TreeView_GetItemRect	GetItemRect	Retrieves the bounding rectangle and visibility state of an item.

(continued)

Table 3-4. *continued*

Macro	Member Function	Description
TreeView_GetNextItem	GetNextItem	Retrieves the next item that matches a specified relationship.
TreeView_GetNextSibling	GetNext-SiblingItem	Retrieves the next sibling of an item.
TreeView_GetNextVisible	GetNext-VisibleItem	Retrieves the next visible item following the specified tree view item.
TreeView_GetParent	GetParentItem	Retrieves the parent of an item.
TreeView_GetPrevSibling	GetPrev-SiblingItem	Retrieves the previous sibling of an item.
TreeView_GetPrevVisible	GetPrev-VisibleItem	Retrieves the first visible item preceding the specified tree view item.
TreeView_GetRoot	GetRootItem	Retrieves the root of an item.
TreeView_GetSelection	GetSelectedItem	Retrieves the currently selected item.
TreeView_GetVisibleCount	GetVisibleCount	Retrieves the count of items that will fit into the tree view window.
TreeView_HitTest	HitTest	Retrieves the tree view item that occupies the specified point. This message is generally used for drag-and-drop operations.
TreeView_InsertItem	InsertItem	Inserts a new item in a tree view window. If the item is being edited, the edit operation is canceled, and the parent window receives a TVN_ENDLABEL-EDIT notification.
TreeView_Select	Select	Selects, scrolls into view, or redraws an item.
TreeView_SelectDropTarget	SelectDropTarget	Selects an item as the drop target.
TreeView_SelectItem	SelectItem	Selects an item.
TreeView_SetImageList	SetImageList	Sets the image list for a tree view window and redraws it.
TreeView_SetIndent	SetIndent	Sets the amount of indention for a child item.
TreeView_SetItem	SetItem	Sets the attributes of an item.
TreeView_SortChildren	SortChildren	Sorts the child items of a given parent item.
TreeView_SortChildrenCB	SortChildrenCB	Sorts items using an application-defined comparison function.

CHAPTER FOUR

Tabs, Property Sheets, and Wizards: Whiz-Bang Common Controls

Tabs, property sheets, and wizards are what I refer to as the "whiz-bang" common controls. These controls are extremely popular right now; it seems as if every new application (or every new version of an existing application) is using property sheets and wizards liberally. This is a nice development for new users because a feature like a wizard can walk them gently through a new or complicated task.

For those of us who have been programming for longer than we care to mention, property sheets replace those awful, cascading, modal dialog boxes that we've come to know and despise. You've all had the experience of successfully navigating down through all those layers to actually set a value, such as a network address, only to discover that you've forgotten some key piece of information, forcing you to cancel out of each and every dialog box and then to navigate down again. This is when you pick up your foam baseball bat and whack your computer monitor. (A tip for the uninitiated: Don't use the wood or aluminum bat! Although the immediate rush is terrific, you'll have a devil of a time explaining it to your boss.) Now, however, by using a property sheet instead of the modal dialog boxes, you can move easily among all the different properties that need to be set rather than backtracking through layers of dialog boxes.

This chapter covers the whiz-bang common controls that Microsoft Windows 95 supports, and it offers some details about how you can create and use them in your C application. At the time this book was written, MFC did not support Windows 95–style property sheets and wizards.

Tabs

A tab control is similar to a set of notebook dividers: it separates topics or sections of information and helps you locate a particular topic or section easily. In Windows 95, a tab control on a property sheet lets a user move from page to page, viewing information and setting options. An application typically defines a group of dialog boxes as property sheet pages, each of which appears when the user clicks the corresponding tab.

The Windows 95 user interface employs tabs extensively in Control Panel. The Display Properties dialog box, which is shown in Figure 4-1, is a Control Panel property sheet whose tabs let you access pages on which you can view or change options for the background, the screen saver, the screen appearance, and various other display settings.

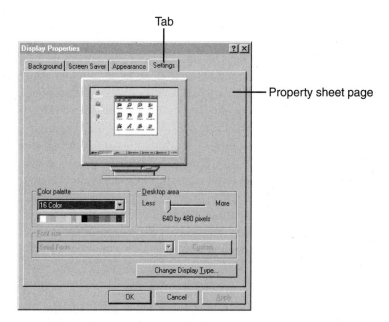

Figure 4-1.
The Display Properties dialog box.

You can also use a tab to carry out a specific command, much as you can choose a menu item to immediately perform an action. Figure 4-2 is a screen shot showing tabs in this button-style format.

Tab controls have styles. Actually, each control can have more than one style. If you create a tab control using the default style TCS_TABS, your tabs will look like notebook dividers, as shown in Figure 4-1, with all of the tabs displayed in a single row of left-justified text (TCS_SINGLELINE). For multiple rows of tabs, you can use the TCS_MULTILINE style. Using the TCS-_BUTTONS style creates the buttonlike tabs shown in Figure 4-2.

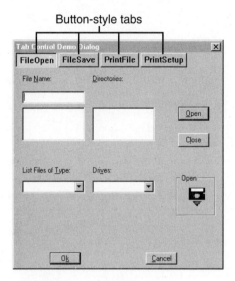

Figure 4-2.
A dialog box with button-style tabs.

Creating a Tab Control

You create a tab control by calling the CreateWindow or CreateWindowEx function and specifying the WC_TABCONTROL window class. This window class is registered when the dynamic-link library for Win32 common controls (COMCTL32.DLL) is loaded. You also need to link with the COMCTL32.LIB library.

To include tabs in a window, the application must also fill out the TC-_ITEM or TC_ITEMHEADER structure. These two structures specify the attributes of the tabs. TC_ITEM and TC_ITEMHEADER are nearly identical, except that TC_ITEMHEADER lets you specify extra application-specific data. To do this, the application should define its own structure, consisting of the TC_ITEMHEADER structure followed by application-defined data, and then set the total number of bytes per tab using the TCM_SETITEMEXTRA message. For example, if my application stored information about a baseball player for each tab, I would define a structure that looks something like the code on the following page.

```
typedef struct _PLAYER_TAB
{
    TC_ITEMHEADER tci;      // tab item information
    LPSTR lpstrName;        // player's name
    LPSTR lpstrTeam;        // player's team
    LONG lERA;              // player's ERA
    LONG lSalary;           // player's salary
    BOOL bCap;              // salary cap?
} PLAYER_TAB;
```

After adding the tabs to the tab control, the application sends the TCM-_SETITEMEXTRA message to set the amount of data to *sizeof (PLAYER_TAB)*. If the application needs to store a pointer to the structure without including TC_ITEMHEADER in the structure, it can instead use TC_ITEM and store the pointer to the structure in the *lParam* field.

Let's look at some simple code that fills out the TC_ITEM structure and creates a tab within a tab control by calling the TabCtrl_InsertItem macro. The following code snippet creates a tab control that contains text and has no image list associated with it:

```
TC_ITEM tie;

tie.mask = TCIF_TEXT | TCIF_IMAGE;
tie.iImage = -1;
tie.pszText = "Tab 1";

if (TabCtrl_InsertItem (hwndTab, i, &tie) == -1)
{
    // The insert failed; display an error box.
    MessageBox (NULL, "TabCtrl_InsertItem failed!", NULL, MB_OK);
    return NULL;
}
```

So far, you've created a tab control and inserted tab items, but the tab control still doesn't have much functionality. The application must now manage the window associated with the tabs. You can do this the easy way or the not-so-easy way. The easy way is to use a property sheet in conjunction with tabs, as described later in this chapter.

The not-so-easy way is to handle the TCN_SELCHANGE notification that is sent through a WM_COMMAND message. This notification is sent when the user clicks a tab and the application needs to switch pages. The application processes the notification and makes the appropriate changes to the focus window. With this method, you could, for example, allow the application to use one edit control for all the tabs. The application would assign the memory handle (send an EM_SETHANDLE message to the edit control) for the incoming page. Although this method certainly works, a better way to handle paging between tabs is to let the system do the grunt work for you and to use a property sheet instead.

Property Sheets

A property sheet is a window that lets the user switch among pages of information to view and edit the properties of an item or an object. Property sheets are also referred to as *tabbed dialog boxes* (because you use tabs to navigate among modeless dialog boxes); each page in a property sheet is analogous to a dialog box. In a spreadsheet application, for instance, one property sheet might allow the user to set both the font properties and the border properties of a cell, with font properties listed on one page and border properties on another. The Windows 95 user interface includes numerous property sheets, so developers who are aiming for a consistent look and feel should seriously consider using this common control.

The PROPS sample, which I wrote in C, displays a property sheet that lets the user view and change the properties of a trackbar. Each group of properties is marked by a tab and appears on a separate page. As you can see in Figure 4-3, this property sheet has two tabs: Trackbar Range and Trackbar Page And Line Size. When the user selects a tab, the associated page moves to the foreground of the property sheet. For example, to change the trackbar page size, the user clicks the Trackbar Page And Line Size tab to bring that page to the foreground and then changes the values as desired.

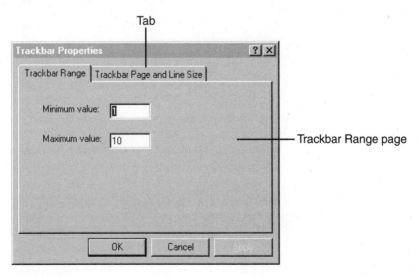

Figure 4-3.
An example of a property sheet.

Essentially, a property sheet is a system-defined modeless dialog box, and each page is an application-defined modeless dialog box. The property sheet is a container for the pages and is responsible for managing them. It includes a frame, a title bar, and four buttons: OK, Cancel, Apply, and (optionally) Help. A property sheet must have at least 1 page and can have as many as 24 pages.

Much like a typical dialog box, each page manages its own control windows (such as edit controls and list box controls). The application provides a dialog template and a dialog procedure for the page. Each page has a label (the text displayed on the tab) and can also have an icon. When the property sheet creates the tab for the page, it displays the label and the icon in the tab. If the property sheet has only one page, the tab for the page is not displayed.

Creating a Property Sheet

My PROPS sample demonstrates how to create and manipulate property sheets. It produces a simple property sheet that supports two pages. I had already written the TRACKBAR sample (discussed in Chapter 2), so I put a trackbar on the client area of the screen and used a property sheet to set values for this control.

Converting Dialog Boxes to Property Sheets

First I took an existing sample and used its dialog boxes for the pages in my property sheet. I made two major changes to the dialog templates:

- I removed the OK, Cancel, and Help buttons from the dialog templates because these buttons are already included in the property sheet control.

- I added the DS_3DLOOK dialog box style to the dialog templates. This style gives the pages the same three-dimensional look as the rest of the built-in dialog boxes.

In the Microsoft Visual C++ 2.1 resource editor, the DS_3DLOOK style is not supported with the other dialog box styles. To use this style, you need to edit your dialog boxes manually.

I also took this opportunity to review my dialog boxes and concluded that I could rearrange the contents of the original four dialog boxes into two pages. This added a little extra work to the conversion, but it improved the organization of the pages and gave my sample a more polished look. If you aren't converting dialog boxes to property sheet pages, you can simply use the resource editor to create a new dialog box, follow the two steps described in the bulleted list on page 114, and add your controls.

After I converted the dialog boxes, I produced the property sheet by defining an array of PROPSHEETPAGE structures for the pages, filling out a PROPSHEETHEADER structure, and then calling the PropertySheet function. This function creates handles for the pages before adding the pages to the property sheet. The order of the array determines the order of the pages in the property sheet, so be sure to decide the sequence of the tabs before you define the pages in the array.

Once a property sheet exists, an application can add and remove pages dynamically by sending the PSM_ADDPAGE and PSM_REMOVEPAGE messages or executing their corresponding macros. By default, when a property sheet is destroyed, its pages are destroyed in first-in-last-out (FILO) order— that is, the last page specified in the array of pages is the first page destroyed.

I wrote the CreatePropertySheet function to create the property sheet and its pages. This function fills out a PROPSHEETPAGE structure for the two pages, fills out the PROPSHEETHEADER structure, and then calls the PropertySheet function. I replaced the DialogBox function calls in my code with a call to the CreatePropertySheet function.

```
int CreatePropertySheet (HWND hwndOwner)
{
PROPSHEETPAGE psp [2];
PROPSHEETHEADER psh;

psp[0].dwSize = sizeof (PROPSHEETPAGE);
psp[0].dwFlags = PSP_USETITLE;
psp[0].hInstance = hInst;
psp[0].pszTemplate = MAKEINTRESOURCE (IDD_RANGE);
psp[0].pszIcon = NULL;
psp[0].pfnDlgProc = Range;
psp[0].pszTitle = "Trackbar Range";
psp[0].lParam = 0;

psp[1].dwSize = sizeof (PROPSHEETPAGE);
psp[1].dwFlags = PSP_USETITLE;
```

(continued)

```
psp[1].hInstance = hInst;
psp[1].pszTemplate = MAKEINTRESOURCE (IDD_PROPS);
psp[1].pszIcon = NULL;
psp[1].pfnDlgProc = PageSize;
psp[1].pszTitle = "Trackbar Page and Line Size";
psp[1].lParam = 0;

psh.dwSize = sizeof (PROPSHEETHEADER);
psh.dwFlags = PSH_PROPSHEETPAGE;
psh.hwndParent = hwndOwner;
psh.hInstance = hInst;
psh.pszIcon = NULL;
psh.pszCaption = (LPSTR)"Trackbar Properties";
psh.nPages = sizeof (psp) / sizeof (PROPSHEETPAGE);
psh.ppsp = (LPCPROPSHEETPAGE) &psp;

return PropertySheet (&psh);
}
```

Changing the Dialog Procedure

Next I had to convert my dialog procedure from managing a dialog box to managing a property sheet page. The major changes involved the handling of the OK and Cancel buttons. Typically, a WM_COMMAND message notifies a dialog procedure that the OK or Cancel button has been clicked. When the procedure gets this message, it generally verifies the information entered in the dialog box controls and calls the EndDialog function to destroy the dialog box. The following code demonstrates how a typical dialog procedure manages the OK button:

```
case WM_COMMAND:
    if (LOWORD (wParam) == IDOK)
    {
        uMin = GetDlgItemInt (hDlg, IDE_MIN, &bErr, TRUE);
        uMax = GetDlgItemInt (hDlg, IDE_MAX, &bErr, TRUE);
        SendMessage (hWndCurrent, TBM_SETRANGE, TRUE,
            MAKELONG (uMax, uMin));
        EndDialog (hDlg, TRUE);
        return TRUE;
    }
    break;
```

In a property sheet, the OK and Cancel notifications are no longer sent to the dialog procedure. Instead, the procedure must handle a group of page notifications. My application needed to handle the following notifications:

PSN_APPLY	Sent when the user clicks the OK button or the Apply button. This is also the time to validate any changes the user has made.
PSN_KILLACTIVE	Sent when the user clicks a tab on the property sheet and switches pages.
PSN_RESET	Sent when the user clicks the Cancel button.
PSN_SETACTIVE	Sent when a page is coming into focus. The application should take this opportunity to initialize the controls for that page.

Initially, I found it difficult to differentiate between the OK and Apply buttons. They both require the page to validate and apply the changes the user has made. The only difference is that clicking OK destroys the property sheet after the changes are applied, whereas clicking Apply does not. As a result, if the user applies a change and later cancels out of the property sheet, the application should reset the property to its initial value rather than saving the applied value. In other words, changes are permanent when the user chooses the OK button; the Apply button allows the user to "try out" an action.

Another change I had to make was removing the EndDialog call. I couldn't call the EndDialog function for a property sheet page because it destroys the entire property sheet instead of destroying only the page. The following dialog procedure handles the Trackbar Range page:

```
BOOL APIENTRY Range (
    HWND hDlg,
    UINT message,
    UINT wParam,
    LONG lParam)
{
static PROPSHEETPAGE *ps;
BOOL bErr;
static UINT uMin, uMax, uMinSave, uMaxSave;

switch (message)
{
    case WM_INITDIALOG:
      // Save the PROPSHEETPAGE information.
      ps = (PROPSHEETPAGE *)lParam;
      return TRUE;

    case WM_NOTIFY:
      switch (((NMHDR FAR *)lParam)->code)
```

(continued)

```
    {
        case PSN_SETACTIVE:
            // Initialize the controls.
            uMinSave = SendMessage (hWndSlider, TBM_GETRANGEMIN,
                0L, 0L);
            uMaxSave = SendMessage (hWndSlider, TBM_GETRANGEMAX,
                0L, 0L);
            SetDlgItemInt (hDlg, IDE_MIN, uMinSave, TRUE);
            SetDlgItemInt (hDlg, IDE_MAX, uMaxSave, TRUE);
            break;

        case PSN_APPLY:
            uMin = GetDlgItemInt (hDlg, IDE_MIN, &bErr, TRUE);
            uMax = GetDlgItemInt (hDlg, IDE_MAX, &bErr, TRUE);
            SendMessage (hWndSlider, TBM_SETRANGE, TRUE,
                MAKELONG (uMin, uMax));
            SetWindowLong (hDlg, DWL_MSGRESULT, TRUE);
            break;

        case PSN_KILLACTIVE:
            SetWindowLong (hDlg, DWL_MSGRESULT, FALSE);
            return 1;
            break;

        case PSN_RESET:
            // Reset to the original values.
            SendMessage (hWndSlider, TBM_SETRANGE, TRUE,
                MAKELONG (uMinSave, uMaxSave));
            SetWindowLong (hDlg, DWL_MSGRESULT, FALSE);
            break;
    }
}
return FALSE;
}
```

When a page is created, the dialog procedure for the page receives a WM_INITDIALOG message (as it does when a dialog box is created); however, the *lParam* parameter points to the PROPSHEETPAGE structure that is used to produce the page. The dialog procedure can save the pointer to this structure and use it later to modify the page.

A Word About Property Sheet Notifications

A property sheet sends a notification to the dialog procedure for a page when the page gains or loses the focus or when the user chooses the OK, Cancel, Apply, or Help button. The notifications are sent as WM_NOTIFY messages. The *lParam* member is a pointer to an NMHDR structure describing the notification. The *hwndFrom* member contains the window handle of the property sheet, and the *hwndTo* member contains the window handle of the page.

Some notifications require the dialog procedure to return either TRUE or FALSE in response to the WM_NOTIFY message. For example, if your procedure cannot handle the Apply button, the code that handles the PSN-_APPLY notification should respond with a value of TRUE. The return value from the dialog procedure must be set by using the SetWindowLong function rather than by returning TRUE or FALSE. This return value is set in the DWL_MSGRESULT window attribute as follows:

```
SetWindowLong (hDlg, DWL_MSGRESULT, value);
```

This is a very important point. I've talked to a great many people who have had problems with their property sheet code, only to find that they are not setting the return value correctly.

Can I Use One Piece of Code for Both a Property Sheet Page and a Dialog Box?

Let's say that you already have a dialog box and a dialog procedure and that you have some odd attachment to the procedure that prevents you from throwing away the code. In fact, you like this code so much that you're wondering whether you can use it for a property sheet page in some cases and for a dialog box in other cases. You can indeed write a single piece of code that works for both a property sheet page and a dialog box, but this is not as easy as having dedicated code for each purpose. If you are using shared code, follow these guidelines:

- Be sure that the dialog procedure does not call the End-Dialog function when it is handling a property sheet.

- Write handlers for the OK, Cancel, and Help notifications and use them for the PSN_APPLY, PSN_RESET, and PSN_HELP notifications.

- If you decide to use a single template for both a property sheet page and a dialog box, place the OK and Cancel buttons outside the dimensions of the dialog box and disable these buttons when handling a page. When the dialog procedure is handling a dialog box, resize the dialog box to include these buttons when the WM_INITDIALOG message is received.

Hey, My Screen Is Flashing!

You don't have to use a different template for each page of your property sheet. If you like, you can instead use a single template for all the pages and enable/disable or show/hide the controls that are specific to each page on the fly. If you do this, however, the user could encounter annoying screen flashes when switching pages. Your application can minimize or eliminate these flashes by responding to the WM_SHOWWINDOW message. This code snippet demonstrates one method of eliminating the screen flash:

```
case WM_SHOWWINDOW:
    // Check to see whether the window is shown via ShowWindow.
    if (wParam && ! LOWORD (lParam))
        // It is, so post a message to yourself.
        PostMessage (hDlg, WM_APP, 0, 0L);
    break;

case WM_APP:
    // Remove the rectangle for the page from the invalid list.
    ValidateRect (hDlg, NULL);
    // Invalidate any and all controls within the page.
    InvalidateRect (GetDlgItem (hDlg, ID_CONTROL1), NULL, FALSE);
    InvalidateRect (GetDlgItem (hDlg, ID_CONTROL2), NULL, FALSE);
    ⋮
    InvalidateRect (GetDlgItem (hDlg, ID_CONTROLn), NULL, FALSE);
    break;
```

An application that uses this method repaints only the controls that need repainting inside the page, instead of repainting the whole window when the WM_SHOWWINDOW message is sent. A page will also need to call InvalidateRect with the *bErase* parameter set to TRUE for controls that do not completely paint their client area during a WM_PAINT message (for example, for a list box that is not full).

Property Sheet Messages

Table 4-1 lists and describes the messages that support property sheets in Windows 95. If you need to find more detailed information about the parameters and return values for these messages, you can refer to the Win32 SDK documentation.

Message	Description
PSM_ADDPAGE	Adds a page to the end of an existing property sheet. An added page should be no larger than the maximum size already in use, because the property sheet will not resize dynamically added pages and because the size of the property sheet itself cannot change.
PSM_APPLY	Simulates clicking the Apply button. This message returns TRUE if and only if every page successfully saved its information.
PSM_CANCELTOCLOSE	Sent when a change is made that cannot be canceled in the property sheet. It disables the Cancel button and changes the OK button to Close.
PSM_CHANGED	Sent to a property sheet when information in a page has changed. The property sheet changes the page name to italic text in the list of pages, and the Apply button is enabled. (This button is initially disabled when a page becomes active and there are no property changes to apply yet.) When the page receives user input through one of its controls, indicating that the user has edited a property, the page sends the PSM_CHANGED message to the property sheet. If the user then clicks the Apply button or the Cancel button, the page reinitializes its controls and sends the PSM_UNCHANGED message to redisable the Apply button. Sometimes the Apply button causes a page to change a property sheet, and the change cannot be undone. In that case, the page sends the PSM_CANCEL-TOCLOSE message to the property sheet, which changes the Cancel button to Close, indicating to the user that the applied changes cannot be canceled.
PSM_GETTABCONTROL	Retrieves a handle to a tab control.
PSM_PRESSBUTTON	Causes the specified button to appear "pressed" (to be selected). *wParam,* the ID of the button, can be one of the following values:

PSBTN_BACK	Select the Back button
PSBTN_NEXT	Select the Next button
PSBTN_FINISH	Select the Finish button
PSBTN_OK	Select the OK button
PSBTN_APPLYNOW	Select the Apply button
PSBTN_CANCEL	Select the Cancel button
PSBTN_HELP	Select the Help button

Table 4-1.   *(continued)*
Property sheet messages.

Table 4-1. *continued*

Message	Description
PSM_QUERYSIBLINGS	Forwarded to each property sheet page until a page returns a nonzero value, which becomes the return value of this message. This message is convenient for passing information between pages that don't know about one another. For example, the printer property page extensions use this message to communicate with the property sheet pages provided by the system.
PSM_REBOOTSYSTEM	Sent when the user must reboot to have the changes specified in the property sheet take effect. The page sends this notification only in response to a PSN_APPLY or PSN_KILLACTIVE notification. The PSM_REBOOT-SYSTEM message supersedes all PSM_RESTARTWIN-DOWS notifications that precede or follow. It causes the property sheet return value to be ID_PSREBOOTSYS-TEM if the user chooses OK to close the property sheet.
PSM_REMOVEPAGE	Removes a page from an existing property sheet. If *hPage* is NULL or does not exist, the property sheet removes the page at the location specified by the *index* parameter. When a page is defined, an application can specify the address of a ReleasePropSheetPageProc callback function that the property sheet calls when it is removing the page. Using a ReleasePropSheetPageProc function gives an application the opportunity to perform cleanup operations for individual pages.
PSM_RESTARTWINDOWS	Sent when the user must restart Windows to have changes specified in the property sheet take effect. The page sends this notification only in response to a PSN-_APPLY or PSN_KILLACTIVE notification. This causes the property sheet to return ID_PSRESTARTWINDOWS if the user chooses OK to close the property sheet.
PSM_SETCURSEL	Sent to the property sheet to change focus to a different page. If *hPage* is NULL or does not exist, the property sheet sets the active page at the location specified by the *index* parameter.
PSM_SETCURSELID	Sets the active page by the ID of the tab or the *hPage* as specified in *lParam*.

(continued)

Table 4-1. *continued*

Message	Description
PSM_SETFINISHTEXT	Enables the Finish button, hides the Back button, and sets the text on the Finish button to the text specified in *lParam*.
PSM_SETTITLE	Changes the caption for the property sheet.
PSM_SETWIZBUTTONS	Specifies which buttons should be enabled in a wizard-style property sheet. *lParam* can be a combination of the following values:
	PSWIZB_BACK Enable the Back button
	PSWIZB_NEXT Enable the Next button
	PSWIZB_FINISHEnable the Finish button
PSM_UNCHANGED	Sent to a property sheet when the information in a page has reverted to its previously saved state. The property sheet cancels any changes caused by PSM_CHANGED. The Apply button is disabled if no pages with registered changes remain.

Wizards

What is a wizard? Although you might envision a person who wears a funny, pointed hat with stars on it and makes magic happen, in the context of an application the term *wizard* refers to a piece of code that can walk the user through a series of steps (in the form of dialog boxes) in order to accomplish a complex task. For instance, many applications take advantage of a wizard for their setup operation or for installing various devices. Figure 4-4 on the following page shows an example, the Add Printer wizard.

A wizard is basically a property sheet with extra buttons and no tabs. In a standard property sheet, the user can navigate among its pages by clicking tabs. There is no need to conform to a special navigation order, and the user doesn't even have to look at every page. In contrast, a wizard moves the user through a series of dialog boxes in a specific sequence. The user can go backward or forward, but the application determines the order in which the steps must be taken or the information supplied. If the application requires input for a particular page, it can disable the Next button to prevent the user from paging forward.

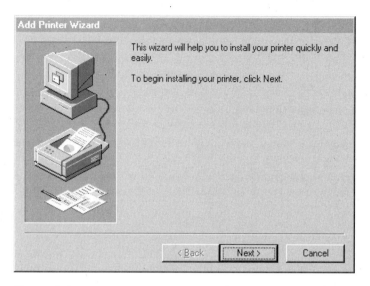

Figure 4-4.
The Add Printer wizard.

Property sheets and wizards also present different buttons to the user. A property sheet has OK, Cancel, and Apply buttons and an optional Help button, which are used for all the pages in the property sheet. The buttons that reside at the bottom of a page in a wizard—typically, the Back, Next, and Cancel buttons—apply only to the currently active page.

Creating a Wizard

I created the WIZARD sample in C to demonstrate how to manipulate wizard controls. (A version of this program also appears in the Win32 SDK.) The design goals for this sample were simple: first, to create a wizard in which you can step back and forth; and second, to make it fun. The second goal was the hardest. After a lot of thought, an inspiration finally came to me. So if you'll indulge me in a little "company" humor, let's get started.

Twice a year, each Microsoft employee participates in a performance review, evaluating our sterling accomplishments of the past six months, explaining how important we are to the success of the company, and listing all the reasons why we deserve a raise. Every time reviews roll around, we complain about having to do the paperwork, and every time I wonder why someone hasn't created a cool tool that would generate a performance review, given some basic data. So I decided to write a wizard to help with this sometimes painful exercise. In reality, of course, it ended up being used for nothing more than chuckles around here, but at least it made the sample a bit more fun.

The first step in creating any wizard is to create a dialog box for each page of information you want to collect. You can do this with the same resource editor you use for standard dialog boxes. For a wizard page, however, you should remove the OK and Cancel buttons that are included in the default dialog template.

After you've created the dialog boxes, you must write code that will first fill out a PROPSHEETPAGE structure for each page (dialog box) you plan to display and will then fill out a PROPSHEETHEADER structure for the overall property sheet. The *dwFlags* field of the PROPSHEETHEADER structure must include the PSH_WIZARD flag to specify that this particular property sheet is a wizard. Finally, the application must call the PropertySheet function. The following code demonstrates how to fill out these structures to create a wizard:

```
// FUNCTION: FillInPropertyPage (PROPSHEETPAGE *, int, LPSTR, LPFN)
//
// PURPOSE: Fills out the given PROPSHEETPAGE structure
//
// COMMENTS:
//    This function fills out a PROPSHEETPAGE structure with the
//    information the system needs to create the page.

void FillInPropertyPage (PROPSHEETPAGE *psp, int idDlg, LPSTR pszProc,
    DLGPROC pfnDlgProc)
{
// Set the size of this structure.
psp->dwSize = sizeof (PROPSHEETPAGE);
// No special flags
psp->dwFlags = 0;
// The instance associated with this application
psp->hInstance = rvInfo.hInst;
// The dialog template to use
psp->pszTemplate = MAKEINTRESOURCE (idDlg);
// Don't use a special icon in the caption.
psp->pszIcon = NULL;
// The dialog procedure that handles this page
psp->pfnDlgProc = pfnDlgProc;
// The title for this page
psp->pszTitle = pszProc;
// No special application-specific data
psp->lParam = 0;
}
```

(continued)

```
// FUNCTION: CreateWizard (HWND)
//
// PURPOSE: Creates the wizard control
//
// COMMENTS:
//    This function creates the wizard property sheet.

int CreateWizard (HWND hwndOwner, HINSTANCE hInst)
{
PROPSHEETPAGE psp [NUM_PAGES];
PROPSHEETHEADER psh;

// For each page, fill out a PROPSHEETPAGE structure.
FillInPropertyPage (&psp[0], IDD_INFO,
    "Your Information", YourInfo);
FillInPropertyPage (&psp[1], IDD_WORKHABITS,
    "Work Habits", WorkHabits);
FillInPropertyPage (&psp[2], IDD_TEAMWORK,
    "Team Work", TeamWork);
FillInPropertyPage (&psp[3], IDD_RELIABILITY,
    "Reliability", Reliability);
FillInPropertyPage (&psp[4], IDD_GOALS,
    "Attainment of Goals", Goals);
FillInPropertyPage (&psp[5], IDD_ADAPTATION,
    "Adaptability to Change", Adaptation);

// Fill in the size of the PROPSHEETHEADER structure.
psh.dwSize = sizeof (PROPSHEETHEADER);
// Specify a wizard property sheet with no Apply button.
psh.dwFlags = PSH_PROPSHEETPAGE | PSH_WIZARD | PSH_NOAPPLYNOW;
// Specify the parent window.
psh.hwndParent = hwndOwner;
// The caption for the wizard
psh.pszCaption = (LPSTR)"Review Wizard";
// The number of pages in this wizard
psh.nPages = sizeof (psp) / sizeof (PROPSHEETPAGE);
// Point to the array of property sheet pages.
psh.ppsp = (LPCPROPSHEETPAGE) &psp;
// Create and run the wizard.
return PropertySheet (&psh);
}
```

Although the wizard control simplifies the task of creating a wizard, it doesn't perform magic: you still have to do a lot yourself. The preceding code simply fills out the structures and calls the function to create and run the wizard. If you want those dialog boxes to gather the data and use the information the user enters, you need to do some work in your dialog procedures.

Each dialog function, as specified by the *pfnDlgProc* member of the PROPSHEETPAGE structure, must process the messages and notifications it receives. Property sheets rely heavily on notifications, packaged as WM_NOTIFY messages. The code used to trap the wizard notifications is similar to the code used for standard property sheets. Three special notifications are associated with wizards, however:

PSN_WIZBACK   Sent to the property sheet page when the user clicks the Back button

PSN_WIZNEXT   Sent to the property sheet page when the user clicks the Next button

PSN_WIZFINISH   Sent to the property sheet page when the user clicks the Finish button

When these notifications are sent, the default action is to advance to the next page or to move back to the previous page. The application's notification handler can disallow either action by setting the notification result to −1. But that's not all.

Let's say you want your wizard to branch to a specific page depending on certain user input. For example, your wizard installs a piece of software, and your application must prompt for extra information depending on whether the user prefers a standard setup or a custom setup. The default behavior is to display the next page in the array of property sheet pages. But you can override that behavior and branch to a specific page by setting the notification result to the ID of the page you need—think of it as a visual GOTO. Your application could by default display the pages for custom setup in order, but it could branch past those pages if the user wants a standard setup.

Processing Wizard Notifications

The information the WIZARD sample gathers to generate the review is kept in a global structure named REVIEWINFO, which resides in the WIZARD.H file. The MAX_PATH constant in the following code is defined to be 256 characters.

```
typedef struct tagREVIEWINFO
{
   HINSTANCE hInst;    // current instance
   int iWorkHabits;
   int iTeamWork;
   int iReliability;
   int iGoals;
   int iAdaptation;
```

(continued)

```
          char pszName [MAX_PATH];
          char pszTitle [MAX_PATH];
          char pszProject [MAX_PATH];
          char pszDepartment [MAX_PATH];
     } REVIEWINFO;
```

The following code from the WIZARD sample demonstrates how an application can trap the notifications that are sent to a wizard. In this code, the dialog procedure initializes the text buffers with NULL strings upon the first entrance into the wizard and whenever the dialog box receives a PSN_RESET notification. When this dialog box receives the PSN_WIZNEXT notification, it saves the information that the user entered in the text fields. If this dialog box is called again and receives a PSN_SETACTIVE notification, the text buffers are reinitialized with the information that was previously entered in the text fields. This dialog box also sets the Next button as the only enabled function when it receives the PSN_SETACTIVE notification. Since this is the first dialog box entered in the wizard, the Back button should not be enabled.

```
// FUNCTION: YourInfo (HWND, UINT, UINT, LONG)
//
// PURPOSE:  Processes messages for "Your Information" page
//
// MESSAGES:
//
//     WM_INITDIALOG initializes the page.
//     WM_NOTIFY processes the notifications sent to the page.

BOOL APIENTRY YourInfo (HWND hDlg, UINT message, UINT wParam,
    LONG lParam)
{
switch (message)
{
    case WM_INITDIALOG:
        // Initialize the text buffers with NULL.
        strcpy (rvInfo.pszName, "");
        strcpy (rvInfo.pszTitle, "");
        strcpy (rvInfo.pszProject, "");
        strcpy (rvInfo.pszDepartment, "");
        break;

    case WM_NOTIFY:
        switch (((NMHDR FAR *) lParam)->code)
        {
            case PSN_KILLACTIVE:
                SetWindowLong (hDlg, DWL_MSGRESULT, FALSE);
                return 1;
                break;
```

```
        case PSN_RESET:
            // Reset to the original values.
            strcpy (rvInfo.pszName, "");
            strcpy (rvInfo.pszTitle, "");
            strcpy (rvInfo.pszProject, "");
            strcpy (rvInfo.pszDepartment, "");
            SetWindowLong (hDlg, DWL_MSGRESULT, FALSE);
            break;

        case PSN_SETACTIVE:
            PropSheet_SetWizButtons (GetParent (hDlg), PSWIZB_NEXT);
            SendMessage (GetDlgItem (hDlg, IDE_NAME), WM_SETTEXT,
                0, (LPARAM)rvInfo.pszName);
            SendMessage (GetDlgItem (hDlg, IDE_TITLE), WM_SETTEXT,
                0, (LPARAM)rvInfo.pszTitle);
            SendMessage (GetDlgItem (hDlg, IDE_PROJECT), WM_SETTEXT,
                0, (LPARAM)rvInfo.pszProject);
            SendMessage (GetDlgItem (hDlg, IDE_DEPARTMENT), WM_SETTEXT,
                0, (LPARAM)rvInfo.pszDepartment);
            break;

        case PSN_WIZNEXT:
            // The Next button was clicked; get the text info entered.
            SendDlgItemMessage (hDlg, IDE_NAME, WM_GETTEXT,
                (WPARAM)MAX_PATH, (LPARAM)rvInfo.pszName);
            SendDlgItemMessage (hDlg, IDE_TITLE, WM_GETTEXT,
                (WPARAM)MAX_PATH, (LPARAM)rvInfo.pszTitle);
            SendDlgItemMessage (hDlg, IDE_PROJECT, WM_GETTEXT,
                (WPARAM)MAX_PATH, (LPARAM)rvInfo.pszProject);
            SendDlgItemMessage (hDlg, IDE_DEPARTMENT, WM_GETTEXT,
                (WPARAM)MAX_PATH, (LPARAM)rvInfo.pszDepartment);
            break;

        default:
            return FALSE;
    }
    break;

    default:
        return FALSE;
}

return TRUE;
}
```

When you build and run this sample, you'll see the first page of the wizard, shown in Figure 4-5.

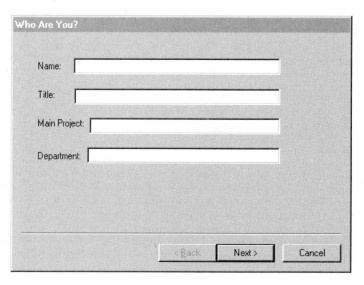

Figure 4-5.
The first page of the performance review wizard.

In the WIZARD sample, information is gathered to produce text for a performance review. While the wizard is running, the results the user enters are kept in the REVIEWINFO structure, as shown previously, and used to create the review. The review is generated through indexes into a string table, and the resulting buffer is displayed in a multiline edit box in the client area of the main window. The WIZARD sample uses the following code to generate the final text buffer:

```
// FUNCTION: GenerateReview (HWND)
//
// PURPOSE: Generates the review
//
// COMMENTS:
//    This function generates the review based on the answers
//    given to the wizard. The function translates lame reality into
//    impressive-sounding managerspeak via a string table.

void GenerateReview (HWND hDlg)
{
```

```
    char lpBuf1 [MAX_LINE];    // buffers for lines in review
    char lpBuf2 [MAX_LINE];
    char lpBuf3 [MAX_LINE];
    char lpBuf4 [MAX_LINE];
    char lpBuf5 [MAX_LINE];

    wsprintf (lpReview, "Name: %s%C%C%C%CTitle: %s%C%C%C%CDepartment: "
       "%s%C%C%C%CMain Project: %s%C%C%C%C",
       rvInfo.pszName, 0x0d, 0x0a, 0x0d, 0x0a,
       rvInfo.pszTitle, 0x0d, 0x0a, 0x0d, 0x0a,
       rvInfo.pszDepartment, 0x0d, 0x0a, 0x0d, 0x0a,
       rvInfo.pszProject, 0x0d, 0x0a, 0x0d, 0x0a);

// Add a line describing work habits.
if (LoadString (rvInfo.hInst, rvInfo.iWorkHabits, lpBuf1,
    sizeof (lpBuf1)) == 0)
    MessageBox (hDlg, "Error loading string!", NULL, MB_OK);
else
    strcat (lpReview, lpBuf1);

// Add a line describing teamwork.
if (LoadString (rvInfo.hInst, rvInfo.iTeamWork, lpBuf2,
    sizeof (lpBuf2)) == 0)
    MessageBox (hDlg, "Error loading string!", NULL, MB_OK);
else
    strcat (lpReview, lpBuf2);

// Add a line describing reliability.
if (LoadString (rvInfo.hInst, rvInfo.iReliability, lpBuf3,
    sizeof (lpBuf3)) == 0)
    MessageBox (hDlg, "Error loading string!", NULL, MB_OK);
else
    strcat (lpReview, lpBuf3);

// Add a line describing goals.
if (LoadString (rvInfo.hInst, rvInfo.iGoals, lpBuf4,
    sizeof (lpBuf4)) == 0)
    MessageBox (hDlg, "Error loading string!", NULL, MB_OK);
else
    strcat (lpReview, lpBuf4);

// Add a line describing adaptability.
if (LoadString (rvInfo.hInst, rvInfo.iAdaptation, lpBuf5,
    sizeof (lpBuf5)) == 0)
    MessageBox (hDlg, "Error loading string!", NULL, MB_OK);
else
    strcat (lpReview, lpBuf5);
}
```

If you build and run the sample now, you can fill in the appropriate information, check the boxes that most accurately reflect your skills and work habits, and have a review generated for you. Just for grins, I used the wizard and picked the last option in the list for each question asked. You can see the result in Figure 4-6.

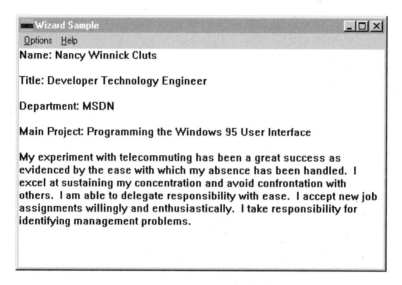

Figure 4-6.

The review generated by the performance review wizard.

C H A P T E R   F I V E

Rich Edit Controls

Single-line edit controls are nice. Multiline edit controls are nicer. But rich edit controls are the nicest of all.

At its simplest, a rich edit control is a window in which a user can both enter and edit text. But that's not all. Just as a multiline edit control provides a programming interface for entering and editing multiple lines of text, a rich edit control provides a programming interface for formatting text. With this new Microsoft Windows 95 common control, a user can assign both character and paragraph formatting (making words boldface or italic, adding underlining, or realigning paragraphs, for instance) and can include embedded OLE objects in the text.

To make these formatting operations available to the user, an application must implement the necessary user interface components. For example, if you want to let the user format selected characters as boldface in a rich edit control, your application must provide a mechanism to do this, such as a toolbar button or a menu item.

Rich edit controls are based on multiline edit controls, and they support almost all the messages and notifications used with multiline edit controls. (A list near the end of this chapter specifies messages that are not supported.) If your application already includes single-line or multiline edit controls, you can easily change it to use rich edit controls, and thus incorporate their unique functionality.

The RICHED Sample

You create a rich edit control by using the CreateWindow or CreateWindowEx function, specifying the RichEdit window class. Because the common control library registers this window class, you must call the InitCommonControls function to ensure that the library is loaded before creating the control. To use rich edit controls in your application, you must link with the

COMCTL32.LIB library. If you are writing your application in C, you must include the COMMCTRL.H header file. Applications must also include the RICHEDIT.H header file, in which rich edit controls are defined. Note that four of the window styles you can use with multiline edit controls cannot be used with rich edit controls: ES_LOWERCASE, ES_PASSWORD, ES_OEM-CONVERT, and ES_UPPERCASE.

To explore the rich edit control, I wrote a sample called RICHED. (Do I lose points for uncreative sample names?) The design goals for RICHED were a bit more challenging than those of my previous samples:

- To provide a rich edit control with a toolbar that mimics the Windows 95 WordPad accessory

- To allow the user to format characters as boldface, italic, or underlined (or as any combination of these three attributes)

- To allow the user to change the typeface and the point size of the font

- To allow the user to left-align, right-align, or center paragraphs or selected text

- To support word-break and line-break procedures

- To provide serialization

- To support drag-and-drop operations

- To support printing

The initialization code in the RICHED sample needed to perform the following tasks:

- Create the toolbar and the combo boxes on the toolbar

- Create the rich edit control

- Enumerate the available fonts, and fill the typeface and point size combo boxes with the font information

- Initialize drag and drop

Figure 5-1 offers a sneak peek at the main screen that appears when you start the RICHED sample.

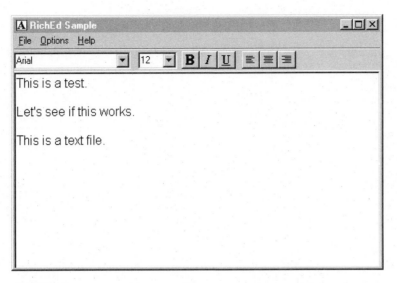

Figure 5-1.
The RICHED sample.

Creating the Sample's Toolbar and Combo Boxes

I created a toolbar for the RICHED sample by calling the CreateToolbarEx function (For a detailed discussion of toolbars, refer to Chapter 1.) I specified a TBBUTTON structure containing information about the toolbar's buttons. Buttons on a toolbar are "free"—that is, you don't need to do anything special to include them other than filling out the structure and giving the CreateToolbarEx function a pointer to that structure.

Other controls on a toolbar, such as the combo boxes I used, require a bit more work. To reserve space on the toolbar for the controls, the application must place separators in the TBBUTTON structure where these extra controls will reside. If you are creating a static structure to hold the buttons, you can determine heuristically how many separators to use (try it out to see what looks good). If you are creating your toolbar dynamically, you can send the TB_GETITEMRECT message to determine the width of a separator and then use the values returned (*rect.right, rect.left*) to calculate how many separators you need to add. The application then creates the control and parents it to the toolbar. To include ToolTips for the various controls and buttons, the application uses the TTM_ADDTOOL message to add ToolTip support.

```
HWND InitToolbar (HWND hWndParent)
{
TOOLINFO lpToolInfo;
HWND hWndToolbar, hWndTT;
HFONT hFont;

// Create the toolbar control.
hWndToolbar = CreateToolbarEx (
    hWndParent,                 // parent
    WS_CHILD | WS_BORDER | WS_VISIBLE | TBSTYLE_TOOLTIPS,   // style
    IDB_TOOLBAR,                // toolbar ID
    6,                          // number of bitmaps
    hInst,                      // mod instance
    IDB_TOOLBAR,                // resource ID for bitmap
    (LPCTBBUTTON)&tbButtons,    // address of buttons
    34,                         // number of buttons
    16, 16,                     // width & height of buttons
    16, 16,                     // width & height of bitmaps
    sizeof (TBBUTTON));         // structure size

if (hWndToolbar == NULL)
{
    MessageBox (NULL, "Toolbar not created!", NULL, MB_OK);
    return NULL;
}

// Create the combo box for the typeface.
hWndComboFont = CreateWindowEx (0L,   // no extended styles
    "COMBOBOX",                        // class name
    "",                                // default text
    WS_CHILD | WS_BORDER | WS_VISIBLE |
      CBS_HASSTRINGS | CBS_DROPDOWN,   // window styles
    0, 3, 150, 250,                    // size and position
    hWndToolbar,                       // parent window
    (HMENU)IDM_COMBOFONT,              // ID
    hInst,                             // current instance
    NULL);                             // no class data

// Set the window procedure for the combo box.
lpfnDefComboFont = (WNDPROC) GetWindowLong (hWndComboFont, GWL_WNDPROC);
SetWindowLong (hWndComboFont, GWL_WNDPROC, (LONG)ComboWndProcFont);

// Create the combo box for the point size.
hWndComboSize = CreateWindowEx (0L,   // no extended styles
    "COMBOBOX",                        // class name
    "",                                // default text
```

```
        WS_CHILD | WS_BORDER | WS_VISIBLE |
          CBS_HASSTRINGS | CBS_DROPDOWN,    // window styles
        160, 3, 50, 250,                    // size and position
        hWndToolbar,                        // parent window
        (HMENU)IDM_COMBOSIZE,               // ID
        hInst,                              // current instance
        NULL);                              // no class data

    // Set the window procedure for the combo box.
    lpfnDefComboSize = (WNDPROC) GetWindowLong (hWndComboSize, GWL_WNDPROC);
    SetWindowLong (hWndComboSize, GWL_WNDPROC, (LONG)ComboWndProcSize);

    // Get the handle to the ToolTip window.
    hWndTT = (HWND) SendMessage (hWndToolbar, TB_GETTOOLTIPS, 0, 0);

    if (hWndTT)
    {
        // Fill out the TOOLINFO structure.
        lpToolInfo.cbSize = sizeof (lpToolInfo);
        lpToolInfo.uFlags = TTF_IDISHWND | TTF_CENTERTIP;
        lpToolInfo.lpszText = (LPSTR)IDM_COMBOFONT;
        lpToolInfo.hwnd = hWndParent;
        lpToolInfo.uId = (UINT)hWndComboFont;
        lpToolInfo.hinst = hInst;
        // Set up ToolTips for the typeface combo box.
        SendMessage (hWndTT, TTM_ADDTOOL, 0,
            (LPARAM)(LPTOOLINFO)&lpToolInfo);

        lpToolInfo.lpszText = (LPSTR)IDM_COMBOSIZE;
        lpToolInfo.uId = (UINT)hWndComboSize;
        // Set up ToolTips for the point size combo box.
        SendMessage (hWndTT, TTM_ADDTOOL, 0,
            (LPARAM)(LPTOOLINFO)&lpToolInfo);
    }
    else
        MessageBox (NULL, "Could not get ToolTip window handle.", NULL,
            MB_OK);

    // Set the fonts for the combo boxes on the toolbar.
    hFont = (HFONT) SendMessage (hWndToolbar, WM_GETFONT, 0, 0);
    SendMessage (hWndComboFont, WM_SETFONT, (WPARAM)hFont, 0);
    SendMessage (hWndComboSize, WM_SETFONT, (WPARAM)hFont, 0);

    return hWndToolbar;
    }
```

Creating a Rich Edit Control

I created the rich edit control used in this sample in response to the WM-_CREATE message in the main window procedure. The ES_SAVESEL style specifies that the text selection is saved when the control loses the focus and redisplayed when it regains the focus. (By default, the entire contents of a rich edit control are selected when it is reactivated.)

```
// Create the rich edit control.
hWndRichEdit = CreateWindowEx (
    WS_EX_CLIENTEDGE,    // make rich edit control appear "sunken"
    "RICHEDIT",          // class name of rich edit control
    "",                  // text of rich edit control
    WS_CHILD | WS_VISIBLE | ES_MULTILINE | ES_SUNKEN | ES_SAVESEL |
        WS_HSCROLL | WS_VSCROLL,   // window styles
    0, 0,                // initially create 0 size,
    0, 0,                // main window's WM_SIZE handler will resize
    hWnd,                // use main parent
    (HMENU)ID_RICHED,    // ID
    hInst,               // this app instance owns this window
    NULL);
```

Building a Font List

The two combo boxes on the toolbar specify the fonts supported by the current device. One box lists typefaces (such as Arial and Times New Roman), and the other lists point sizes (units of measure that specify the size of the type—10-point, 12-point, 14-point, and so on). When you build the font list, the combo boxes are filled, and the buttons on the toolbar and the associated menu items are updated to reflect the current character formatting. For instance, if the current formatting is boldface, the Bold button appears "pressed," and the Bold menu item is checked.

```
// Enumerate the fonts for the rich edit control.
hDC = GetDC (hWndRichEdit);
parFontsGlobal = BuildFontList (hDC, &nFaces);

// Fill in the typeface and point size combo boxes.
FillCombos ();

// Set the current font.
ChangeFaceName (hWndRichEdit, parFontsGlobal[0].lf->lfFaceName);
ChangePointSize (hWndRichEdit, 12);

// Select the current typeface and point size.
iSelect = SelectFont (parFontsGlobal[0].lf->lfFaceName, 12);
```

```
// Show the effects of the current font.
bItalic = bUnderLine = FALSE;
bBold = ToggleButton (hWnd, IDM_BOLD, FALSE);

// Release the DC.
ReleaseDC (hWndRichEdit, hDC);
```

Initializing Drag and Drop

To support drag-and-drop operations, the application must call the Drag-AcceptFiles function and must notify the rich edit control that it should pass along any ENM_DROPFILES notifications. By default, the notification is not sent to the parent of the rich edit control.

```
// Register to allow drag and drop.
DragAcceptFiles (hWndRichEdit, TRUE);

// Tell the rich edit control that you want to allow drag and drop.
SendMessage (hWndRichEdit, EM_SETEVENTMASK, 0, (LPARAM)ENM_DROPFILES);
```

Character Formatting

You can apply character formatting to text in a rich edit control by using the EM_SETCHARFORMAT message. To determine the current formatting of selected characters, use the EM_GETCHARFORMAT message. With either message, the application uses a pointer to the CHARFORMAT structure to specify character attributes. The following attributes are supported for characters:

- Effects such as boldface, italics, and underlining
- Typeface (also known as *facename*)
- Point size
- Color

Setting the effects is simply a matter of filling out the CHARFORMAT structure with the size of the structure (for versioning), specifying which attribute to alter, and sending the EM_SETCHARFORMAT message. In the RICHED sample, these effects are toggled, so the handler checks the current effect and toggles it. The code on the following page is the handler for the Bold command. The only differences between this handler and the handlers for italics and underlining are the *dwMask* field (CFM_ITALIC for italics and CFM_UNDERLINE for underlining) and the *dwEffects* field (CFE_ITALIC for italics and CFE_UNDERLINE for underlining).

```
void BoldCmd (HWND hWndRichEdit)
{
CHARFORMAT cf;

// Fill out the CHARFORMAT structure to set character effects.
cf.cbSize = sizeof (cf);
cf.dwMask = CFM_BOLD;

// Get the bold status.
SendMessage (hWndRichEdit, EM_GETCHARFORMAT, TRUE, (LPARAM)&cf);

// Toggle the bold effect.
cf.dwEffects ^= CFE_BOLD;

// Set the new bold status.
SendMessage (hWndRichEdit, EM_SETCHARFORMAT, SCF_SELECTION,
    (LPARAM)&cf);
}
```

The default character formatting is applied to newly inserted text only if the current selection is empty. Otherwise, the new text assumes the character formatting of the text it replaces. If the selection changes, the default character formatting changes to match the first character in the new selection.

In the RICHED sample, the user can also pick a new typeface by using one of the drop-down combo boxes on the toolbar, shown in Figure 5-2.

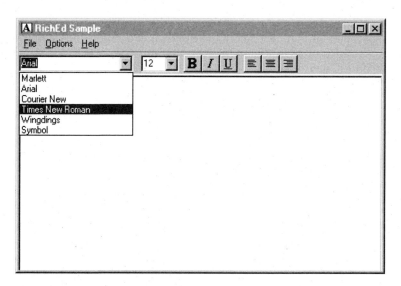

Figure 5-2.
The combo box displaying typeface choices.

When the user chooses a typeface from the list, the application's ChangeFaceName function sends an EM_SETCHARFORMAT message to change the typeface. This function preserves the previous character effects (boldface, italics, and underlining).

```
VOID ChangeFaceName (HWND hWndRichEdit, LPTSTR lpFaceName)
{
CHARFORMAT cf;

// Fill out the CHARFORMAT structure to get the character effects.
cf.cbSize = sizeof (cf);
cf.dwMask = CFM_ITALIC | CFM_BOLD | CFM_UNDERLINE;
SendMessage (hWndRichEdit, EM_GETCHARFORMAT, TRUE, (LPARAM)&cf);

// Include the mask to ask the rich edit control for the current
// typeface.
cf.dwMask |= CFM_FACE;

// Set the new typeface, preserving the previous effects.
strcpy (cf.szFaceName, lpFaceName);
SendMessage (hWndRichEdit, EM_SETCHARFORMAT, SCF_SELECTION,
    (LPARAM)&cf);
}
```

You might be wondering how I filled in the font choices. Well, like any smart developer, I looked for some sample code I could use. In the Win32 SDK, I found a sample called TTFONTS, which enumerates all the available fonts and allows the user to play around with the fields in the TEXTMETRIC and LOGFONT structures. I was able to use the font-enumerating code from TTFONTS and to use the structure that was defined to hold font information:

```
// Structure holding font information
typedef struct tagArFonts
{
    int         nFonts;
    int         cySpace;
    HDC         hdc;
    LOGFONT     *lf;
    TEXTMETRIC *tm;
    int         *Type;
} ARFONTS, *PARFONTS;
```

The code that begins on the following page uses the EnumFonts function to get the number of fonts, allocates space for the font information, and fills out a structure for each font found. The only change I made was to add a filter for TrueType fonts (because my sample supports only these fonts). Filtering for TrueType fonts allowed me to make some assumptions about the font that the user will choose.

```
PARFONTS BuildFontList (HDC hdcIn, LPINT retnFaces)
{
nFaces = 0;            // initialize global face count to 0
hdcGlobal = hdcIn;     // save HDC for callbacks

// Count the number of typefaces.
EnumFonts (hdcGlobal, NULL, (FONTENUMPROC)MyEnumCount,
    (LPARAM)&nFaces);

// Allocate the pointer to the array of ARFONTS structures.
parFontsGlobal = (PARFONTS) LocalAlloc (
    LPTR, sizeof(ARFONTS) * (nFaces+1));

// Step through all fonts again. For each one, fill out a LOGFONT
// structure and a TEXTMETRIC structure.
iFace = 0;
EnumFonts (hdcGlobal, NULL, (FONTENUMPROC)MyEnumFaces, (LPARAM)NULL);

*retnFaces = nFaces;
return parFontsGlobal;
}

int APIENTRY MyEnumFaces (
    LPLOGFONT lpLogFont,
    LPTEXTMETRIC lpTEXTMETRICs,
    DWORD fFontType,
    LPVOID lpData)
{
int nFonts;

UNREFERENCED_PARAMETER (lpTEXTMETRICs);
UNREFERENCED_PARAMETER (fFontType);
UNREFERENCED_PARAMETER (lpData);

if (fFontType & TRUETYPE_FONTTYPE)
{
    nFonts = 0;
    EnumFonts (hdcGlobal, lpLogFont->lfFaceName,
        (FONTENUMPROC)MyEnumCount, (LPARAM)&nFonts);

    parFontsGlobal[iFace].lf = (LPLOGFONT) LocalAlloc (LPTR,
        sizeof(LOGFONT) * nFonts);
    parFontsGlobal[iFace].tm = (LPTEXTMETRIC) LocalAlloc (LPTR,
        sizeof(TEXTMETRIC) * nFonts);
    parFontsGlobal[iFace].Type = (LPINT) LocalAlloc (LPTR,
        sizeof(int) * nFonts);

    if ((parFontsGlobal[iFace].lf == NULL) ||
        (parFontsGlobal[iFace].tm == NULL) ||
```

```
         (parFontsGlobal[iFace].Type == NULL))
     {
         MessageBox (NULL, "alloc failed", NULL, MB_OK);
         return FALSE;
     }

     parFontsGlobal[iFace].nFonts = nFonts;

     jFont = 0;
     EnumFonts (hdcGlobal, lpLogFont->lfFaceName,
         (FONTENUMPROC)MyEnumCopy, (LPARAM)NULL);
     iFace++;
}

return TRUE;
}

int APIENTRY MyEnumCount (
     LPLOGFONT lpLogFont,
     LPTEXTMETRIC lpTEXTMETRICs,
     DWORD fFontType,
     LPINT lpData)
{
UNREFERENCED_PARAMETER (lpLogFont);
UNREFERENCED_PARAMETER (lpTEXTMETRICs);
UNREFERENCED_PARAMETER (fFontType);

if (fFontType & TRUETYPE_FONTTYPE)
     (*lpData)++;
return TRUE;
}

int APIENTRY MyEnumCopy (
     LPLOGFONT lpLogFont,
     LPTEXTMETRIC lpTEXTMETRICs,
     DWORD fFontType,
     LPVOID lpData)
{
LOGFONT *lplf;
TEXTMETRIC *lptm;
int *pType;

UNREFERENCED_PARAMETER (lpData);

if (fFontType & TRUETYPE_FONTTYPE)
{
     lplf = parFontsGlobal[iFace].lf;
```

(continued)

```
    lptm = parFontsGlobal[iFace].tm;
    pType = parFontsGlobal[iFace].Type;

    lplf[jFont] = *lpLogFont;
    lptm[jFont] = *lpTEXTMETRICs;
    pType[jFont] = fFontType;

    jFont++;
}
return TRUE;
}
```

When the structures are filled out, the names of the typefaces are inserted in the typeface combo box. The point size combo box is filled with an array of standard point sizes, as shown in Figure 5-3. The same point sizes are listed for each typeface. That's why I picked only TrueType fonts. Other kinds of fonts, such as raster fonts, are device-dependent, and you cannot make assumptions about their availability or about the point sizes they support. For a "real" word processor, the point size combo box can be filled dynamically when the user picks a typeface.

To change the point size, you simply use the same EM_SETCHARFORMAT message and specify the CFM_SIZE mask. Bear in mind that the point size is represented internally as twips, so you need to multiply the number the user chooses by 20. If you don't do this, you'll end up getting really tiny letters.

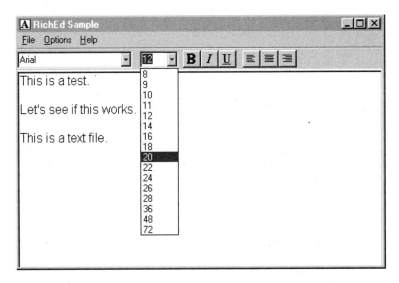

Figure 5-3.
The combo box displaying the point size options.

```
VOID ChangePointSize (HWND hWndRichEdit, int PointSize)
{
CHARFORMAT cf;

// Fill out the CHARFORMAT structure to set the point size.
cf.cbSize = sizeof (cf);
cf.dwMask = CFM_SIZE;

// Multiply by 20 to convert to twips.
cf.yHeight = PointSize * 20;

// Set the point size.
SendMessage (hWndRichEdit, EM_SETCHARFORMAT, SCF_SELECTION,
    (LPARAM)&cf);

// Reset the dirty bit.
SendMessage (hWndRichEdit, EM_SETMODIFY, (WPARAM)TRUE, OL);
}
```

Notice in the RICHED sample that the appropriate toolbar buttons appear "pressed" and the corresponding menu items are checked when the user has chosen specific character effects, as shown in Figure 5-4. The sample accomplishes this task with a function called ToggleButton, which simply takes the command identifier of the button and a Boolean to toggle the button on and off. (The identifiers for the menu item and the button are the same.)

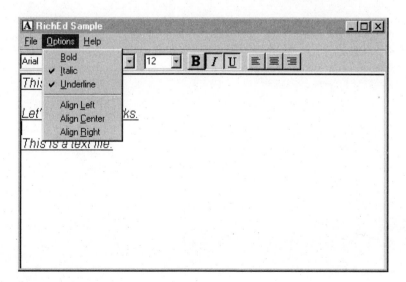

Figure 5-4.
Checked menu items and "pressed" toolbar buttons indicating character effects.

```
BOOL ToggleButton (HWND hWnd, int nID, BOOL bToggle)
{
if (bToggle)
{   // Uncheck the menu item and unpress the toolbar button.
    CheckMenuItem (GetMenu(hWnd), nID, MF_BYCOMMAND | MF_UNCHECKED);
    SendMessage (hWndToolbar, TB_CHECKBUTTON, nID, MAKELONG (FALSE, 0));
    return FALSE;
}
else
{   // Check the menu item and press the toolbar button.
    CheckMenuItem (GetMenu (hWnd), nID, MF_BYCOMMAND | MF_CHECKED);
    SendMessage (hWndToolbar, TB_CHECKBUTTON, nID, MAKELONG (TRUE, 0));
    return TRUE;
}
}
```

I did not implement the protected attribute or the color attribute in the RICHED sample. The protected character attribute allows the application to specify some text as read-only (without changing the appearance of the text by graying it out). If the user tries to modify protected text, the rich edit control sends its parent window an EN_PROTECTED notification, allowing the parent window to permit or prevent the change. This is useful for an application that lets the user change only specific items in a rich edit control, based on a password. To receive this notification, the application enables it by using the EM_SETEVENTMASK message, specifying ENM_PROTECTED.

The foreground color of a rich edit control is also a character attribute, but the background color is a property of the control. To set the background color, an application sends the EM_SETBKGNDCOLOR message. To set the foreground color, the application fills out the CHARFORMAT structure, specifying the CFM_COLOR attribute.

Paragraph Formatting

In a rich edit control, the user can also set the attributes of entire paragraphs, including alignment (left-justified, centered, or right-justified), tab stops, indention, and numbering.

You can apply paragraph formatting to text in a rich edit control by using the EM_SETPARAFORMAT message. As with all good Windows APIs, you use the EM_GETPARAFORMAT message to find out the current paragraph formatting. Both messages use the PARAFORMAT structure to specify paragraph attributes.

The RICHED sample supports all three paragraph alignment options, as the following code demonstrates. It's interesting to note that it takes more code to ensure that the buttons are "pressed" and the menu items are checked than it does to actually set the paragraph format.

```
VOID AlignCmd (HWND hWnd, HWND hWndRichEdit, int iAlign)
{
PARAFORMAT pf;

// Fill out the PARAFORMAT structure with the mask and size.
pf.cbSize = sizeof (pf);
pf.dwMask = PFM_ALIGNMENT;

switch (iAlign)
{
   case IDM_ALIGNLEFT:
      pf.wAlignment = PFA_LEFT;
      ⋮
}

// Set the new paragraph alignment.
SendMessage (hWndRichEdit, EM_SETPARAFORMAT, 0, (LPARAM)&pf);
// Reset the dirty bit.
SendMessage (hWndRichEdit, EM_SETMODIFY, (WPARAM)TRUE, 0L);
}
```

Figure 5-5 shows you the look that is produced by centering text in the RICHED sample.

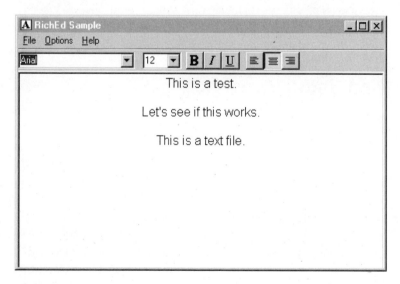

Figure 5-5.
Centered paragraphs in the RICHED sample.

Word and Line Breaks

An application can use a word-break procedure to determine how to break words and lines. This information is used in word-wrap operations or when the user moves to the previous word or the next word by pressing the Ctrl-Left arrow or the Ctrl-Right arrow key combination. An application can send a message to a rich edit control to replace the default word-break procedure (EM_SETWORDBREAKPROC), to retrieve word-break information (EM-_FINDWORDBREAK), or to determine on what line a given character falls (EM_EXLINEFROMCHAR).

A word-break procedure for a rich edit control groups characters into classes, identifying each class by a value in the range 0x00 through 0x0F. Word breaks can occur after delimiters or between characters of different classes. A character's class can be combined with zero or more word-break flags to form an 8-bit value. When performing word-wrap operations, a rich edit control uses word-break flags to determine where it can break lines. The following flags are supported:

WBF_BREAKAFTER	Lines can break after the character. This value allows wrapping after a character that does not mark the end of a word, such as a hyphen.
WBF_BREAKLINE	The character is a delimiter, which marks the end of a word. Lines can break after delimiters.
WBF_ISWHITE	The character is a white-space character. Trailing white-space characters are not included in the length of a line when wrapping.

Serialization Using Streams

Data is transferred into or out of a rich edit control through streams. A stream is defined by an EDITSTREAM structure, which specifies a buffer and an application-defined callback function. In the RICHED sample, the user can open either a text (TXT) file or a rich text format (RTF) file. The data is read into the rich edit control through the EM_STREAMIN message. After receiving this message, the control repeatedly calls the application-defined callback function, EditStreamCallback, which transfers a portion of the data into the buffer each time. The *dwCookie* member of the EDITSTREAM structure is an application-defined value. The RICHED sample uses this member for storing the handle to the file opened by the OpenFile function. The EM-

_STREAMIN message allows either textual or RTF data to be read in by specifying SF_TEXT or SF_RTF in the *wParam* parameter.

```
BOOL OpenTheFile (HWND hWndRichEdit, int iAttrib, char *lpszFileName)
{
HFILE hFile;
OFSTRUCT of;
EDITSTREAM eStream;

if (hFile = OpenFile (lpszFileName, &of, OF_READ))
{
   // dwCookie is an app-defined value that holds
   // the handle to the file.
   eStream.dwCookie = hFile;
   eStream.pfnCallback = EditStreamCallback;
   eStream.dwError = 0;
   SendMessage (hWndRichEdit, EM_STREAMIN, (WPARAM)iAttrib,
      (LPARAM)&eStream);

   // Reset the dirty bit.
   SendMessage (hWndRichEdit, EM_SETMODIFY, (WPARAM)TRUE, OL);

   CloseHandle ((HANDLE)hFile);
   return TRUE;
}
return FALSE;
}

DWORD CALLBACK EditStreamCallback (DWORD dwCookie,
   LPBYTE pbBuff, LONG cb, LONG FAR *pcb)
{
ReadFile ((HANDLE)dwCookie, pbBuff, cb, pcb, NULL);
if (*pcb < cb)
   return 0;   // file has been fully read in
else
   return (DWORD) *pcb;   // more to read
}
```

As you can see from the code on the following page, the RICHED sample offers two options for saving the contents of the rich edit control: save as a TXT file or save as an RTF file. The application sends the EM_STREAM-OUT message to save the contents of the control. The control repeatedly writes to the buffer and then calls the application's callback function. For each call, this function saves the contents of the buffer.

```
BOOL SaveTheFile (HWND hWndRichEdit, int nID)
{
HFILE hFile;
OFSTRUCT of;
EDITSTREAM eStream;
char *lpszFileName;
int iAttrib;

if (nID == IDM_SAVETXT)
{
   lpszFileName = "TEXTDOC.TXT";
   iAttrib = SF_TEXT;
}
else
{
   lpszFileName = "RTFDOC.RTF";
   iAttrib = SF_RTF;
}
if (hFile = OpenFile (lpszFileName, &of, OF_CREATE))
{
   eStream.dwCookie = hFile;
   eStream.dwError = 0;
   eStream.pfnCallback = SaveCallback;
   SendMessage (hWndRichEdit, EM_STREAMOUT, (WPARAM)iAttrib,
      (LPARAM)&eStream);

   CloseHandle ((HANDLE)hFile);
   return TRUE;
}
return FALSE;
}

DWORD CALLBACK SaveCallback (DWORD dwCookie,
   LPBYTE pbBuff, LONG cb, LONG FAR *pcb)
{
WriteFile ((HANDLE)dwCookie, pbBuff, cb, pcb, NULL);
return 0;
}
```

As Figure 5-6 shows, the options in the RICHED sample for reading in or saving data are limited to specifying the type of data (TXT or RTF). The sample furnishes the names of the sample files. To allow the user a choice of files to read in, you should use the common dialog boxes designed for opening and saving files. (You'll find detailed information about the common dialog boxes in Chapter 6.)

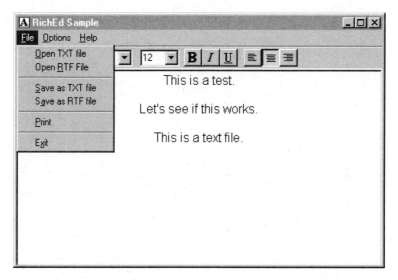

Figure 5-6.
The File menu in the RICHED sample.

Drag-and-Drop Operations

To support a drag-and-drop operation in a rich edit control, an application must first set an event mask by using the EM_SETEVENTMASK message to allow the EN_DROPFILES notification to be sent to the control's parent window. In the RICHED sample, when the parent window receives this notification, the DragQueryFile function is called to determine how many files have been dropped in the rich edit control. This sample allows the user to drop only one file at a time, so if more than one file has been dropped, the action is disallowed. If the user has dropped only one file, the application queries for the filename, opens the file, and reads it into the rich edit control. As you can see in the following code, the sample allows the user to drop only a TXT or an RTF file:

```
case WM_NOTIFY:
    ⋮
    // Is the notification a drop notification?
    else if ((((LPNMHDR)lParam)->code == EN_DROPFILES)
    {
        WORD cFiles;
        char lpszFile [80];
        HANDLE hDrop;
```

(continued)

```
      // Get the handle to the drop object.
      hDrop = ((ENDROPFILES *)lParam)->hDrop;
      // Determine how many objects have been dropped.
      cFiles = DragQueryFile (hDrop, 0xFFFF, (LPSTR)NULL, 0);
      // If more than one object has been dropped, don't bother.
      if (cFiles > 1)
          return 0;
      // Get the name of the file dropped.
      DragQueryFile (hDrop, 0, lpszFile, sizeof (lpszFile));

      // Open the file (TXT or RTF).
      if (strstr (lpszFile, "TXT"))
          OpenTheFile (hWndRichEdit, SF_TEXT, lpszFile);
      else if (strstr (lpszFile, "RTF"))
          OpenTheFile (hWndRichEdit, SF_RTF, lpszFile);
      DragFinish (hDrop);
      return 1;
  }
  return 0L;
  break;
```

This code demonstrates one way that an application can handle a drop operation. Rich edit controls also support OLE drag and drop through the IRichEditOle and IRichEditOleCallback interfaces, which allow objects to be embedded in the control. The subject of embedding objects is beyond the scope of this book, however, so I will not cover it here.

Printing

A rich edit control can format its data to be suitable for use with devices such as displays and printers. Applications use the EM_FORMATRANGE message to tell the control how to format its contents. The FORMATRANGE structure used with this message specifies the range of text to format as well as the device context for the target device.

The RICHED sample supports printing through its Print command on the File menu. The sample uses the PrintDlg function to get the DC for the printer. It then fills out the FORMATRANGE structure with the DC, the rectangle to print, and the amount of data within the rectangle to print. The usual DOCINFO structure is filled out, and the rest is standard printing code.

```
void PrintTheContents (HWND hWndRichEdit)
{
FORMATRANGE fr;
DOCINFO docInfo;
```

```
LONG lTextOut, lTextAmt;
PRINTDLG pd;

// Initialize the PRINTDLG structure.
pd.lStructSize = sizeof (PRINTDLG);
pd.hwndOwner = hWndRichEdit;
pd.hDevMode = (HANDLE)NULL;
pd.hDevNames = (HANDLE)NULL;
pd.nFromPage = 0;
pd.nToPage = 0;
pd.nMinPage = 0;
pd.nMaxPage = 0;
pd.nCopies = 0;
pd.hInstance = (HANDLE)hInst;
pd.Flags = PD_RETURNDC | PD_NOPAGENUMS | PD_NOSELECTION | PD_PRINTSETUP;
pd.lpfnSetupHook = (LPSETUPHOOKPROC)(FARPROC)NULL;
pd.lpSetupTemplateName = (LPTSTR)NULL;
pd.lpfnPrintHook = (LPPRINTHOOKPROC)(FARPROC)NULL;
pd.lpPrintTemplateName = (LPTSTR)NULL;

// Get the printer DC.
if (PrintDlg (&pd) == TRUE)
{
   // Fill out the FORMATRANGE structure for the RTF output.
   fr.hdc = fr.hdcTarget = pd.hDC;    // HDC
   fr.chrg.cpMin = 0;                  // print
   fr.chrg.cpMax = -1;                 // entire contents
   fr.rc.top = fr.rcPage.top = fr.rc.left = fr.rcPage.left = 0;
   fr.rc.right = fr.rcPage.right = GetDeviceCaps (pd.hDC, HORZRES);
   fr.rc.bottom = fr.rcPage.bottom = GetDeviceCaps (pd.hDC, VERTRES);

   // Fill out the DOCINFO structure.
   docInfo.cbSize = sizeof (DOCINFO);
   docInfo.lpszDocName = "(RTF Test)";
   docInfo.lpszOutput = NULL;

   // Be sure that the printer DC is in text mode.
   SetMapMode (pd.hDC, MM_TEXT);

   StartDoc (pd.hDC, &docInfo);
   StartPage (pd.hDC);

   lTextOut = 0;
   lTextAmt = SendMessage (hWndRichEdit, WM_GETTEXTLENGTH, 0, 0);
```

(continued)

```
   while (lTextOut < lTextAmt)
   {
      lTextOut = SendMessage (hWndRichEdit, EM_FORMATRANGE, TRUE,
         (LPARAM)&fr);

      if (lTextOut < lTextAmt)
      {
         EndPage (pd.hDC);
         StartPage (pd.hDC);
         fr.chrg.cpMin = lTextOut;
         fr.chrg.cpMax = -1;
      }
   }

   // Reset the formatting of the rich edit control.
   SendMessage (hWndRichEdit, EM_FORMATRANGE, TRUE, (LPARAM)NULL);

   // Finish the document.
   EndPage (pd.hDC);
   EndDoc (pd.hDC);

   // Delete the printer DC.
   DeleteDC (pd.hDC);
}
}
```

An application can implement *banding* (that is, dividing the output into smaller parts in order to overcome printer buffer-size limitations) by using the EM_DISPLAYBAND message in concert with the EM_FORMATRANGE message. With the EM_SETTARGETDEVICE message, the application can also specify the target device for which the control will format its text. You'll find this message useful for WYSIWYG (What You See Is What You Get) formatting, in which an application positions text using the default printer's font metrics instead of the screen's font metrics.

Monitoring Events

Certain events within a rich edit control, such as mouse and keyboard events and drag-and-drop operations, can be monitored by the control's parent window. An application uses an event-notification mask (by sending the EM_SETEVENTMASK message) to specify which events it wants to monitor. The control will then send the appropriate notification each time one of the specified events occurs. All the notifications that are listed in Table 5-1 are sent through the WM_NOTIFY message.

Event-Notification Mask	Description
ENM_CHANGE	Sends an EN_CHANGE notification when the user changes the text in a rich edit control.
ENM_DROPFILES	Sends EN_DROPFILES notifications. The application can allow the user to drop files in a rich edit control by processing the EN_DROPFILES notification. The specified ENDROPFILES structure contains information about the files being dropped.
ENM_KEYEVENTS	Sends EN_MSGFILTER notifications for keyboard events. The parent window can prevent the keyboard message from being processed or can change the message by modifying the specified MSGFILTER structure.
ENM_MOUSEEVENTS	Sends EN_MSGFILTER notifications for mouse events. The parent window can prevent the mouse message from being processed or can change the message by modifying the specified MSGFILTER structure.
ENM_PROTECTED	Sends EN_PROTECTED notifications, which are used to detect when the user attempts to modify protected text.
ENM_REQUESTRESIZE	Sends EN_REQUESTRESIZE notifications. This lets an application resize a rich edit control as needed so that the control is always the same size as its contents. A rich edit control supports this "bottomless" functionality by sending its parent window an EN_REQUESTRESIZE notification whenever the size of its contents changes. In response, the application uses the SetWindowPos function to resize the control to the dimensions in the specified REQRESIZE structure.
ENM_SCROLL	Sends an EN_HSCROLL notification when the user clicks the horizontal scroll bar of a rich edit control.
ENM_SELCHANGE	Sends EN_SELCHANGE notifications. This informs the parent window that the current selection has changed.
ENM_UPDATE	Sends an EN_UPDATE notification when a rich edit control is about to display altered text.
ENM_NONE	No notifications are sent to the parent window (the default).

Table 5-1.
Rich edit control event-notification masks.

Rich Edit Control Messages

Rich edit controls support most, but not all, of the functionality of multiline edit controls. Table 5-2 lists the messages that are supported by rich edit controls. But you should also take special note of the following messages, which are processed by multiline edit controls but *not* by rich edit controls:

EM_FMTLINES

EM_GETHANDLE (Rich edit controls do not store text as a simple array of characters.)

EM_GETMARGINS

EM_GETPASSWORDCHAR (Rich edit controls do not support the ES_PASSWORD style.)

EM_SETHANDLE (Rich edit controls do not store text as a simple array of characters.)

EM_SETMARGINS

EM_SETPASSWORDCHAR (Rich edit controls do not support the ES_PASSWORD style.)

EM_SETRECTNP

EM_SETTABSTOPS (Rich edit controls use the EM_SETPARA-FORMAT message instead.)

WM_CTLCOLOR (Rich edit controls use the EM_SETBKGND-COLOR message instead.)

WM_GETFONT (Rich edit controls use the EM_GETCHARFORMAT message instead.)

Message	Description
EM_CANPASTE	Determines whether a rich edit control can paste a given clipboard format.
EM_CHARFROMPOS	Retrieves the zero-based character index and the zero-based line index of the character nearest the specified point in a rich edit control.

Table 5-2.   *(continued)*

Rich edit control messages.

Table 5-2. *continued*

Message	Description
EM_DISPLAYBAND	Displays part of a rich edit control's contents as previously formatted for a device (by using the EM_FORMATRANGE message).
EM_EXGETSEL	Retrieves the positions of the starting and ending characters in a selection.
EM_EXLIMITTEXT	Sets an upper limit (in characters) on the amount of text that can be contained in a rich edit control.
EM_EXLINEFROMCHAR	Determines which line contains a specified character.
EM_EXSETSEL	Selects a range of characters.
EM_FINDTEXT	Finds text within a rich edit control.
EM_FINDTEXTEX	Finds text within a rich edit control by using the FINDTEXTEX structure.
EM_FINDWORDBREAK	Finds the next word break before or after the specified character position, or retrieves information about the character at that position.
EM_FORMATRANGE	Formats a range of text for a specific device.
EM_GETCHARFORMAT	Determines the current character formatting.
EM_GETEVENTMASK	Retrieves the event mask for a rich edit control. The event mask specifies which notifications the control sends to its parent window.
EM_GETLIMITTEXT	Retrieves the current upper limit (in characters) on the amount of text that can be contained in a rich edit control.
EM_GETOLEINTERFACE	Retrieves an IRichEditOle object that a client can use to access a rich edit control's OLE functionality.
EM_GETOPTIONS	Retrieves the current options (styles) of a rich edit control (read-only, vertical scroll bar, and so on).
EM_GETPARAFORMAT	Retrieves the paragraph formatting of the current selection.
EM_GETSELTEXT	Retrieves the currently selected text.
EM_GETTEXTRANGE	Retrieves a specified range of characters.
EM_HIDESELECTION	Hides or shows the current selection.
EM_PASTESPECIAL	Pastes a specific clipboard format in the control.

(continued)

Table 5-2. *continued*

Message	Description
EM_POSFROMCHAR	Retrieves the coordinates of the specified character in a rich edit control.
EM_REQUESTRESIZE	Forces the control to send an EN_REQUESTRESIZE notification to its parent window.
EM_SCROLLCARET	Scrolls the caret into view in a rich edit control.
EM_SELECTIONTYPE	Determines the selection type. (See the Win32 SDK documentation for the selection types that can be returned.)
EM_SETBKGNDCOLOR	Sets the background color.
EM_SETCHARFORMAT	Sets character formatting.
EM_SETEVENTMASK	Sets the event mask, which specifies the notifications the control sends to its parent window.
EM_SETOLECALLBACK	Gives a rich edit control an IRichEditOleCallback object that the control uses to get OLE-related resources and information from the client.
EM_SETOPTIONS	Sets the options (styles) for a rich edit control (read-only, vertical scroll bar, and so on).
EM_SETPARAFORMAT	Sets the paragraph formatting for the current selection.
EM_SETTARGETDEVICE	Sets the target device and line width used for WYSIWYG formatting.
EM_STREAMIN	Replaces the contents of the control with the specified data stream.
EM_STREAMOUT	Writes the contents of the control to the specified data stream.

CHAPTER SIX

The New Common Dialog Boxes

The Win32 API supports common dialog boxes, which Microsoft Windows 95 provides to help the user perform functions that are common to most applications: opening and saving files, changing fonts, changing colors, searching for and replacing text, and printing. Not only do you save time by having the operating system carry out these mundane tasks, but you also automatically conform to the look and feel of the system when you include the common dialog boxes in your application.

These dialog boxes are easy to use. In the simplest case, when you want the dialog box's default appearance and behavior, you need only fill out a structure and call a single function. A dynamic-link library, COMDLG32.DLL, supplies the default dialog procedure and the default template for each common dialog box. If you want to extend the functionality of a dialog box, the system provides hooks and allows you to include your own template containing any additional controls that you need.

This chapter describes the various common dialog boxes and includes code examples that can help you incorporate these dialog boxes in your Win32-based applications. The examples come from CMNDLG32, a sample I wrote in C, which demonstrates how a developer can manipulate the common dialog boxes using their standard form or using hooks and custom templates. Figure 6-1, which appears on the following page, offers an advance look at the CMNDLG32 sample.

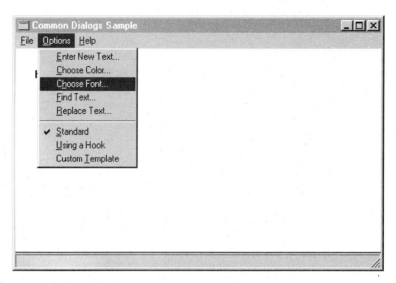

Figure 6-1.
The CMNDLG32 sample.

The new set of common dialog boxes found in Windows 95 has not only a fresh look but also some added functionality and a few other changes, as you'll see. But if you are an old hand at programming the common dialog boxes supported in Microsoft Windows version 3.1 and Microsoft Windows NT, you'll find that using the new dialog boxes requires little or no additional work. For example, the common dialog box sample I wrote for Windows NT many moons ago worked without a hitch under Windows 95, with no changes and no recompilation. If you are including templates and want to take advantage of the new look, a simple recompile is all you have to do. (If, however, you are including templates and don't want to change your dialog boxes, you don't have to do anything: just run the application, and your original dialog boxes will appear.)

Opening and Saving Files
with Common Dialog Boxes

The most frequently used common dialog boxes are those that open files and save files. As you can see in the example shown in Figure 6-2, these dialog boxes support long filenames and contain a list view control, which

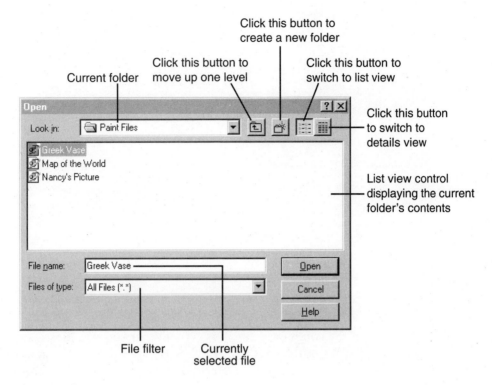

Figure 6-2.

An Open common dialog box in list view.

graphically represents the contents of the current folder. The Open common dialog box and the Save As common dialog box use the same dialog template, and you use the same structure, OPENFILENAME, to initialize them. The only real difference is how you display the dialog boxes: for opening a file, you use the GetOpenFileName function; for saving a file, you use the Get-SaveFileName function.

The list view control in the Open or Save As common dialog box presents the current folder's contents in either list view or details view. Clicking the rightmost toolbar button changes the display to details view, which provides details about each object (file). For example, in the Save As dialog box shown in Figure 6-3 on the following page, you can see not only the object's name but also its size, its type, and when it was last modified. Clicking the next-to-last toolbar button on the right switches the display back to list view.

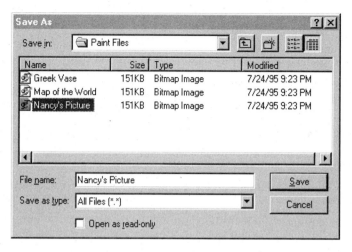

Figure 6-3.
A Save As common dialog box in details view.

Using the Open and Save As Common Dialog Boxes

To use one of the common dialog boxes that open and save files, an application must first fill out the OPENFILENAME structure, which includes the items needed to initialize the dialog box. The following example is the code I used for the Open common dialog box:

```
OpenFileName.lStructSize        = sizeof (OPENFILENAME);
OpenFileName.hwndOwner          = hWnd;
OpenFileName.hInstance          = (HANDLE)hInst;
OpenFileName.lpstrFilter        = szFilter;
OpenFileName.lpstrCustomFilter  = (LPTSTR)NULL;
OpenFileName.nMaxCustFilter     = 0L;
OpenFileName.nFilterIndex       = 1L;
OpenFileName.lpstrFile          = szFile;
OpenFileName.nMaxFile           = sizeof (szFile);
OpenFileName.lpstrFileTitle     = szFileTitle;
OpenFileName.nMaxFileTitle      = sizeof (szFileTitle);
OpenFileName.lpstrInitialDir    = NULL;
OpenFileName.lpstrTitle         = "Open";
OpenFileName.nFileOffset        = 0;
OpenFileName.nFileExtension     = 0;
OpenFileName.lpstrDefExt        = "*.txt";
OpenFileName.lCustData          = 0;
```

When the structure is filled out, a call to GetOpenFileName with a pointer to the structure will display the dialog box. If the function returns a value of TRUE, no errors occurred, and the file can be opened. The filename is copied into the *lpstrFile* member of the OPENFILENAME structure. If the GetOpenFileName function returns FALSE, an error handler is called with the extended error (returned from the CommDlgExtendedError function):

```
if (GetOpenFileName (&OpenFileName))
{
    // Open the file.
    if ((hFile = CreateFile ((LPCTSTR)OpenFileName.lpstrFile,
        GENERIC_READ,
        FILE_SHARE_READ,
        NULL,
        OPEN_EXISTING,
        FILE_ATTRIBUTE_NORMAL,
        (HANDLE)NULL)) == (HANDLE)(-1))
    {
        MessageBox (hWnd, "File open failed.", NULL, MB_OK);
        return FALSE;
    }

    // Read its contents into a buffer.
    ⋮
}
else
{
    // Send the error to your error handler.
    ProcessCDError (CommDlgExtendedError (), hWnd);
    return FALSE;
}
```

A wide variety of flags can be used in the *Flags* member of the OPEN-FILENAME structure. These flags allow a developer to provide functionality (such as multiple selection), to decide whether to use the Windows 3.1 or the Windows 95 look in the dialog box, and to specify that the file must exist in order to be opened. For an exhaustive list of all flags supported by the OPENFILENAME structure, refer to the Win32 SDK documentation.

Monitoring Input

Now let's look at what you need in order to monitor the input to the controls in a common dialog box. Notifications about these controls can be monitored through hooks. The dialog procedure provided in COMDLG32.DLL calls the application's hook function if the application specifies the appropriate flag (OFN_ENABLEHOOK) and a pointer to the hook function in the *lpfnHook* member of the OPENFILENAME structure.

```
OpenFileName.Flags = OFN_SHOWHELP | OFN_PATHMUSTEXIST | OFN_EXPLORER |
   OFN_FILEMUSTEXIST | OFN_HIDEREADONLY | OFN_ENABLEHOOK;
OpenFileName.lpfnHook = (LPOFNHOOKPROC)FileOpenHookProc;
```

The hook function used in the CMNDLG32 sample simply passes the WM_NOTIFY message to the notification handler:

```
BOOL APIENTRY FileOpenHookProc (HWND hDlg, UINT message, UINT wParam,
   LONG lParam)
{
if (message == WM_NOTIFY)
   return FileOpenNotify (hDlg, (LPOFNOTIFY)lParam);

return FALSE;
}
```

Under Windows 95, the WM_NOTIFY message is sent to the hook procedure for the Open and Save As common dialog boxes whenever an action such as selection occurs. The hook procedure receives the WM_NOTIFY message with the OFNOTIFY structure packaged in its *lParam* parameter. The OFNOTIFY structure contains information about the notification and the object, including pointers to an NMHDR structure, to the OPENFILENAME structure, and to the current filename.

When the hook procedure receives the WM_NOTIFY message, it can use the *code* member of the NMHDR structure to determine the current action. The following code traps the notification code and writes it to the status bar. When the user clicks the OK button, the application prompts the user to confirm that the operation should continue.

```
BOOL NEAR PASCAL FileOpenNotify (HWND hDlg, LPOFNOTIFY pofn)
{
static char lpszNotification [FILE_LEN];
HANDLE hFile;
char szTempText [MAX_PATH];
char szString [MAX_PATH];
DWORD dwBytesWritten;

switch (pofn->hdr.code)
{
   // The current selection has changed.
   case CDN_SELCHANGE:
   {
      char szFile [MAX_PATH];

      // Get the file specification from the common dialog box.
      CommDlg_OpenSave_GetSpec (GetParent (hDlg),
         szFile, sizeof (szFile));
```

```
        wsprintf (lpszNotification,
            "File Open Notification: %s. File: %s",
            "CDN_SELCHANGE", szFile);
    }
    break;

    // The current folder has changed.
    case CDN_FOLDERCHANGE:
    {
        char szFile [MAX_PATH];

        if (CommDlg_OpenSave_GetFolderPath (GetParent (hDlg),
            szFile, sizeof (szFile)) <= sizeof (szFile))
        {
            wsprintf (lpszNotification,
                "File Open Notification: %s. File: %s",
                "CDN_FOLDERCHANGE", szFile);
        }
    }
    break;

    // The Help button has been clicked.
    case CDN_HELP:
        wsprintf (lpszNotification, "File Open Notification: %s.",
            "CDN_HELP");
        break;

    // The OK button has been clicked.
    // To prevent the common dialog box from closing, the result should
    // be nonzero via a call to SetWindowLong (hDlg, DWL_MSGRESULT,
    // lResult).
    case CDN_FILEOK:
        SetWindowLong (hDlg, DWL_MSGRESULT, 1L);
        wsprintf (lpszNotification,
            "File Open Notification: %s. File: %s",
            "CDN_FILEOK", pofn->lpOFN->lpstrFile);
        GetDlgItemText (hDlg, edt1, szTempText, sizeof (szTempText) -1);
        wsprintf (szString, "Are you sure you want to open %s?",
            szTempText);
        if (MessageBox (hDlg, szString, "Information", MB_YESNO) == IDNO)
        {
            SetWindowLong (hDlg, DWL_MSGRESULT, -1);
            break;
        }
        // Check to see whether the Create File box is checked.
        if ((BOOL) (SendMessage (GetDlgItem (hDlg, chx2),
            BM_GETCHECK, 0, 0L)) == TRUE)
        {
```

(continued)

```
            // If so, create the file.
            if ((hFile = CreateFile (szTempText,
               GENERIC_READ | GENERIC_WRITE,
               FILE_SHARE_READ | FILE_SHARE_WRITE,
               NULL,
               CREATE_ALWAYS,
               FILE_ATTRIBUTE_NORMAL,
               (HANDLE)NULL)) == (HANDLE)(-1))
            {
               MessageBox (hDlg, "Directory could not be created.",
                  NULL, MB_OK);
               SetWindowLong (hDlg, DWL_MSGRESULT, -1);
               break;
            }

            if (WriteFile (hFile, (LPTSTR)FileBuf, dwFileSize,
               &dwBytesWritten, NULL) == FALSE)
               MessageBox (hDlg, "Error writing file.", NULL, MB_OK);

            if (hFile)
               CloseHandle (hFile);    // close the file
         }
         break;

      // Received a sharing violation
      case CDN_SHAREVIOLATION:
         wsprintf (lpszNotification, "File Open Notification: %s.",
            "CDN_SHAREVIOLATION");
         break;

      // Received when initialization has finished via the WM_INITDIALOG
      // message; all controls moved at this point
      case CDN_INITDONE:
         wsprintf (lpszNotification, "File Open Notification: %s.",
            "CDN_INITDONE");
         break;

      // Received when the file type changes in the Files Of Type box
      case CDN_TYPECHANGE:
         wsprintf (lpszNotification, "File Open Notification: %s.",
            "CDN_TYPECHANGE");
         break;
   }

   // Write the notification to the status window.
   SendMessage (hWndStatus, SB_SETTEXT, 0, (LPARAM)lpszNotification);

   return TRUE;
}
```

Using the OFN_EXPLORER Flag

In Windows 3.1 and Windows NT 3.1 and 3.5, if you want to change a common dialog box in some way, you need to have a copy of the DLG file and then use the #include statement to incorporate it in your resource file. In Windows 95, however, you no longer need to do this in order to include your own custom template that works with the new Open (and Save As) template. Now, you can simply include the OFN_EXPLORER flag and create a dialog template that contains only the items that you want to add to the dialog box. If the OFN_EXPLORER flag is set in the *Flags* field of the OPENFILENAME structure, the *hInstance, lpfnHook,* and *lpTemplateName* fields are interpreted as follows:

- If the OFN_ENABLETEMPLATE flag is set in the *Flags* field, the *lpTemplateName* field is the name of the dialog template, and the *hInstance* field is the module instance. The dialog template must have the WS_CHILD style set, or GetOpenFileName will fail. The common dialog handler creates a child dialog box (a subdialog box) and the standard dialog box. This child dialog box, which is placed in the upper left corner of the standard dialog box, is resized to contain not only its own, new controls but also all the controls in the standard dialog box. Thus the *hDlg* parameter passed to the application's hook function is the child of the dialog box containing the standard controls. If your application must communicate with a standard control from the hook procedure, it should call GetParent on the *hDlg* passed to the hook procedure. For example, to get the text from the Types combo box, you use the following code:

```
GetDlgItemText (GetParent (hDlg), cmb1, buf, MAX_PATH);
```

- If the OFN_ENABLETEMPLATEHANDLE flag is set in the *Flags* field, the *hInstance* field should contain the memory handle for the dialog template.

- If the OFN_ENABLEHOOK flag is set in the *Flags* field, the *lpfnHook* field is a DLGPROC (not an LPOFNHOOKPROC) that is associated with the child dialog box.

- If neither the OFN_ENABLETEMPLATE flag nor the OFN_ENABLETEMPLATEHANDLE flag is set in the *Flags* field, the common dialog handler creates an empty template.

For example, in the Win32 SDK COMDLG32 sample, the following dialog template adds some fields to the Open dialog box:

```
IDD_COMDLG32 DIALOG DISCARDABLE  0, 0, 300, 74
STYLE WS_CHILD | WS_VISIBLE | WS_CLIPSIBLINGS | DS_3DLOOK | DS_CONTROL
FONT 8, "MS Sans Serif"
BEGIN
    LTEXT           "Path:",-1,28,4,36,8
    LTEXT           "This is to the left",-1,4,16,20,40
    LTEXT           "Selected:",-1,32,49,40,8
    EDITTEXT        IDE_SELECTED,74,47,200,12,ES_AUTOHSCROLL
    LTEXT           "This is to the right.",-1,232,20,65,8
    LTEXT           "",stc32,28,16,204,31
    EDITTEXT        IDE_PATH,65,2,200,12,ES_AUTOHSCROLL
END
```

Once I created this template, I used the notification code to trap the notifications and to update the new fields that I added. Also, when I filled out the OPENFILENAME structure, I included the OFN_ENABLETEMPLATE flag to enable the template. Figure 6-4 shows the resulting customized Open dialog box.

In the preceding code, notice the next-to-last resource, which is a control with the ID *stc32*. In the common dialog handler, this ID has a special purpose: to let the handler know where to place all the standard controls. Without an *stc32* control, the common dialog handler places all the new controls added by the application-defined template below the standard controls. If you include the *stc32* control, the handler assesses the size of this control. If

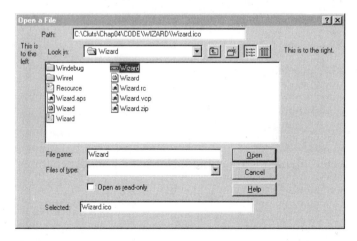

Figure 6-4.
A customized Open common dialog box created with a template.

it is too small to hold all the standard controls, the handler moves them to the right of the *stc32* control or below it to make room for the new controls. Figure 6-5 shows the child dialog box that is provided to customize the Open dialog box from the Win32 SDK COMDLG32 sample.

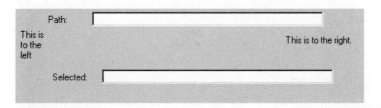

Figure 6-5.
A child dialog box used to customize an Open common dialog box.

If you want to maintain the old-style look of a common dialog box or if you need to insert new controls that are interspersed among the existing controls (as opposed to being positioned around them), your application should use a hook or a template and must not include the OFN_EXPLORER flag. The hook can be as simple as a function that returns NULL. If you don't use a hook or a template, your dialog box will display the Explorer look by default. To be compatible with previous versions of the common controls, your application must use a template to position controls among the standard controls.

You can also set the tab order of the controls in a customized common dialog box. Let's say you want the user to be able to tab from the OK button to an added button and then to the Cancel button. To do this, the child dialog box containing the added button must have the DS_CONTROL style. With this style set, you can use a call to SetWindowPos to change the z-order. The dialog box manager determines which control will receive the focus next by walking in z-order through windows that have the WS_TABSTOP style.

NOTE: To allow the user to select more than one file to open in the Open common dialog box, specify the OFN_ALLOWMULTI-SELECT flag. The *lpstrFile* member of the OPENFILENAME structure points to a buffer into which the path to the current folder and the selected filenames are copied. Normally, a space separates the first filename from the path, and each subsequent filename is separated from the preceding filename by a space. If you include the OFN_EXPLORER flag, a NULL (\0) character rather than a space will separate the filenames. The entire buffer is terminated by two NULL characters (\0\0).

Learning New IDs

In previous versions of Windows, identifiers for the various controls in common dialog boxes resided in a header file that you included directly in your application. In Windows 95, those identifiers are defined in COMCTL32.LIB. Figure 6-6 illustrates which identifiers belong to which controls. Notice that some identifiers are defined in lowercase letters.

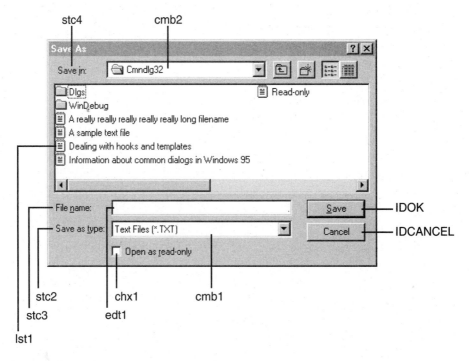

Figure 6-6.
Identifiers for controls in the Open and Save As common dialog boxes.

If you are the type who prefers code to pictures, here's the template used for the new Open and Save As common dialog boxes:

```
NEWFILEOPENORD DIALOG DISCARDABLE  0, 0, 280, 164
STYLE DS_MODALFRAME | 4L | WS_POPUP | WS_VISIBLE | WS_CAPTION |
WS_SYSMENU | DS_CONTEXTHELP | WS_CLIPCHILDREN
CAPTION "Open"
FONT 8, "MS Sans Serif"
```

```
BEGIN
    LTEXT           "Look &in:",stc4,7,6,41,8,SS_NOTIFY
    COMBOBOX        cmb2,50,3,138,100,CBS_DROPDOWNLIST |
                    CBS_OWNERDRAWFIXED | CBS_HASSTRINGS |
                    WS_VSCROLL | WS_TABSTOP
    LTEXT           "",stc1,188,2,82,17,NOT WS_GROUP | NOT WS_VISIBLE
    LISTBOX         lst1,4,20,272,85,LBS_SORT | LBS_NOINTEGRALHEIGHT |
                    LBS_MULTICOLUMN | WS_HSCROLL | NOT WS_VISIBLE
    LTEXT           "File &name:",stc3,5,112,36,8,SS_NOTIFY
    EDITTEXT        edt1,54,110,155,12,ES_AUTOHSCROLL
    LTEXT           "Files of &type:",stc2,5,128,46,8,SS_NOTIFY
    COMBOBOX        cmb1,54,126,155,53,CBS_DROPDOWNLIST |
                    WS_VSCROLL | WS_TABSTOP
    CONTROL         "Open as &read-only",chx1,"Button",BS_AUTOCHECKBOX |
                    WS_TABSTOP,54,145,74,10
    DEFPUSHBUTTON   "&Open",IDOK,222,110,50,14
    PUSHBUTTON      "Cancel",IDCANCEL,222,128,50,14
    PUSHBUTTON      "&Help",pshHelp,222,145,50,14
END
```

Customization Guidelines

You can customize any of the common dialog boxes. You might, for instance, want to hide some of the original controls, add a few new controls, or enlarge a dialog box. If your application subclasses controls in any of the common dialog boxes, the subclass must be done during the processing of the WM_INITDIALOG message in the application's hook function. This allows the application to receive the control-specific messages first.

In general, it's not a good idea to customize the common dialog boxes too severely. After all, one of their chief benefits is a look and feel consistent with the rest of the Windows 95 user interface. I'd suggest that you customize these dialog boxes only if necessary, leaving the original look intact as much as possible. Users won't be confused by small modifications, however, such as a change in the size of the dialog box or the addition of a new control or two.

The Font Common Dialog Box

The Font common dialog box displays lists of typefaces, styles, and point sizes that correspond to the available fonts. After the user selects the current font for an application, the dialog box displays sample text rendered with that font, as shown in Figure 6-7.

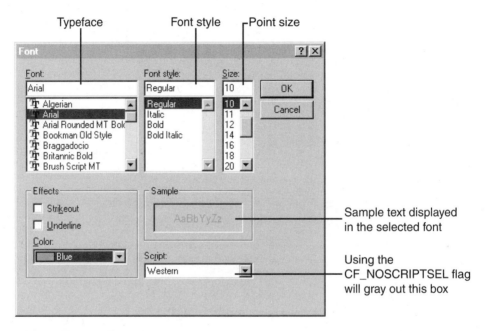

Figure 6-7.
The Font common dialog box.

To use the Font common dialog box, you fill out the CHOOSEFONT structure and call the ChooseFont function. The CHOOSEFONT structure contains information such as the attributes of the initial font, the point size, and the types of fonts (screen fonts or printer fonts), as well as hook and template information.

The following code demonstrates how the CMNDLG32 sample fills out the CHOOSEFONT structure. In the sample, how some of the fields are filled depends on whether a hook or a template should be included. The flags indicate that the strikeout, underline, and color effects should be enabled (CF_EFFECTS) and that the fonts listed should include only the screen fonts supported by the system (CF_SCREENFONTS). Note that, although it is not used in this sample, the CF_NOSCRIPTSEL flag is available if you want to gray out the script box.

```
CHOOSEFONT chf;
LOGFONT lf;
 ⋮

HDC hDC;

hDC = GetDC (hWnd);
chf.hDC = CreateCompatibleDC (hDC);
ReleaseDC (hWnd, hDC);
chf.lStructSize = sizeof (CHOOSEFONT);
chf.hwndOwner = hWnd;
chf.lpLogFont = &lf;
chf.Flags = CF_SCREENFONTS | CF_EFFECTS;
chf.rgbColors = RGB (0, 255, 255);
chf.lCustData = 0;
chf.hInstance = (HANDLE)hInst;
chf.lpszStyle = (LPTSTR)NULL;
chf.nFontType = SCREEN_FONTTYPE;
chf.nSizeMin = 0;
chf.nSizeMax = 0;

switch (wMode)
{
    case IDM_STANDARD:
        chf.lpfnHook = (LPCFHOOKPROC)(FARPROC)NULL;
        chf.lpTemplateName = (LPTSTR)NULL;
        break;

    case IDM_HOOK:
        chf.Flags |= CF_ENABLEHOOK;
        chf.lpfnHook = (LPCFHOOKPROC)ChooseFontHookProc;
        chf.lpTemplateName = (LPTSTR)NULL;
        break;

    case IDM_CUSTOM:
        chf.Flags |= CF_ENABLEHOOK | CF_ENABLETEMPLATE;
        chf.lpfnHook = (LPCFHOOKPROC)ChooseFontHookProc;
        chf.lpTemplateName = (LPTSTR) MAKEINTRESOURCE (FORMATDLGORD31);
        break;
}
```

After you fill out the structure, you simply call the ChooseFont function and delete the DC. The common dialog procedure sets the font for you. If you need to customize the dialog box, your application should provide a hook function and, if you want to add controls, a dialog template. Instead of specifying additional controls in a child dialog box, as you do for the Open and Save As common dialog boxes, you must include the full template for the Font common dialog box in order to customize it. For example, the CMNDLG32.RC file includes the following template for the Font dialog box:

```
1543 DIALOG DISCARDABLE  13, 54, 264, 147
STYLE DS_MODALFRAME | WS_POPUP | WS_CAPTION | WS_SYSMENU
CAPTION "Font"
FONT 8, "Helv"
BEGIN
    LTEXT           "&Font:",1088,6,3,40,9
    COMBOBOX        1136,6,13,94,54,CBS_SIMPLE | CBS_OWNERDRAWFIXED |
                    CBS_AUTOHSCROLL | CBS_SORT | CBS_HASSTRINGS |
                    CBS_DISABLENOSCROLL | WS_VSCROLL | WS_TABSTOP
    LTEXT           "Font St&yle:",1089,108,3,44,9
    COMBOBOX        1137,108,13,64,54,CBS_SIMPLE | CBS_DISABLENOSCROLL |
                    WS_VSCROLL | WS_TABSTOP
    LTEXT           "&Size:",1090,179,3,30,9
    COMBOBOX        1138,179,13,32,54,CBS_SIMPLE | CBS_OWNERDRAWFIXED |
                    CBS_SORT | CBS_HASSTRINGS | CBS_DISABLENOSCROLL |
                    WS_VSCROLL | WS_TABSTOP
    DEFPUSHBUTTON   "OK",IDOK,218,6,40,14,WS_GROUP
    PUSHBUTTON      "Cancel",IDCANCEL,218,23,40,14,WS_GROUP
    PUSHBUTTON      "&Apply",1026,218,40,40,14,WS_GROUP
    PUSHBUTTON      "&Help",1038,218,57,40,14,WS_GROUP
    GROUPBOX        "Effects",1072,6,72,84,34,WS_GROUP
    CONTROL         "Stri&keout",1040,"Button",
                    BS_AUTOCHECKBOX | WS_TABSTOP,10,82,49,10
    CONTROL         "&Underline",1041,"Button",
                    BS_AUTOCHECKBOX,10,94,51,10
    LTEXT           "&Color:",1091,6,110,30,9
    COMBOBOX        1139,6,120,84,100,
                    CBS_DROPDOWNLIST | CBS_OWNERDRAWFIXED |
                    CBS_AUTOHSCROLL | CBS_HASSTRINGS | WS_BORDER |
                    WS_VSCROLL | WS_TABSTOP
    GROUPBOX        "Sample",1073,98,72,160,49,WS_GROUP
    CTEXT           "",1093,98,124,160,20,SS_NOPREFIX | NOT WS_GROUP
    CTEXT           "AaBbYyZz",1092,104,81,149,37,SS_NOPREFIX | NOT
                    WS_VISIBLE
END
```

The Color Common Dialog Box

In the Color common dialog box, users can change the current color or create their own colors. The basic dialog box, shown in Figure 6-8, contains a control that displays as many as 48 colors. The user's display driver determines the actual number of colors; for example, a VGA driver displays 48 colors, whereas a monochrome driver displays only 16.

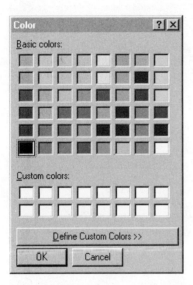

Figure 6-8.
The basic Color common dialog box.

When the user clicks the Define Custom Colors button, the width of the dialog box expands to display the custom colors control, as shown in Figure 6-9 on the following page. With this control, the user can create a new color by specifying red, green, and blue (RGB) values; by using the color spectrum to set hue, saturation, and luminosity (HSL); or by specifying HSL values in the edit controls. After the user has created a custom color, clicking the Add To Custom Colors button displays the new color in a Custom Colors section of the dialog box. The Color|Solid control displays both the dithered color (a mixture of solids) and the solid color that correspond to the user's selection.

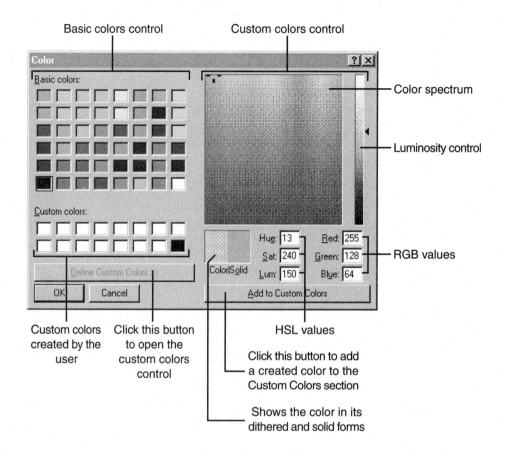

Basic colors control   Custom colors control

Color spectrum

Luminosity control

RGB values

HSL values

Custom colors created by the user

Click this button to open the custom colors control

Click this button to add a created color to the Custom Colors section

Shows the color in its dithered and solid forms

Figure 6-9.
The expanded Color common dialog box.

The Color common dialog box uses two color models: RGB and HSL. Screen displays and other devices that emit light use the RGB model. Valid values for red, green, and blue are in the range 0 through 255, with 0 the minimum intensity and 255 the maximum intensity. The application should specify COLORREF values using the RGB macro for RGB colors.

The HSL color model uses different ranges of values. As you can see in Figure 6-10, the saturation and luminosity values must be in the range 0 through 240, and the hue value must be in the range 0 through 239. The Color common dialog procedure that is provided in COMDLG32.DLL converts HSL values to the corresponding RGB values, so your application does not have to do this.

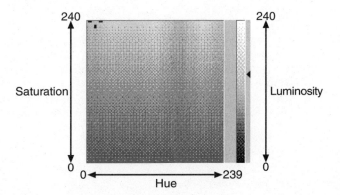

Figure 6-10.
The color spectrum and HSL value ranges.

Before displaying a Color common dialog box, an application must initialize a CHOOSECOLOR structure, which contains information such as the parent of the dialog box, the custom colors that should appear initially, and the use of hooks and templates to customize the dialog box. The following code demonstrates how the CMNDLG32 sample fills out the CHOOSECOLOR structure and makes the subsequent call to ChooseColor, the function that displays and handles the dialog box. Notice again that certain fields are filled differently if a hook or a template is included. The custom colors array is initially filled entirely with white, whose RGB value is (0, 0, 0); the color initially selected is black, with an RGB value of (255, 255, 255).

```
BOOL ChooseNewColor (HWND hWnd)
{
DWORD dwColor;
DWORD dwCustClrs [16];
BOOL fSetColor = FALSE;
int i;

for (i = 0; i < 15; i++)
   dwCustClrs [i] = RGB (255, 255, 255);

dwColor = RGB (0, 0, 0);

chsclr.lStructSize = sizeof (CHOOSECOLOR);
chsclr.hwndOwner = hWnd;
chsclr.hInstance = (HANDLE)hInst;
chsclr.rgbResult = dwColor;
chsclr.lpCustColors = (LPDWORD)dwCustClrs;
chsclr.lCustData = 0L;
```

(continued)

```
switch (wMode)
{
    case IDM_HOOK:
        chsclr.Flags = CC_ENABLEHOOK;
        chsclr.lpfnHook = (LPCCHOOKPROC)ChooseColorHookProc;
        chsclr.lpTemplateName = (LPTSTR)NULL;
        break;

    case IDM_CUSTOM:
        chsclr.Flags = CC_PREVENTFULLOPEN | CC_ENABLEHOOK |
            CC_ENABLETEMPLATE;
        chsclr.lpfnHook = (LPCCHOOKPROC)ChooseColorHookProc;
        chsclr.lpTemplateName = "CHOOSECOLOR";
        break;

    case IDM_STANDARD:
        chsclr.Flags = CC_PREVENTFULLOPEN;
        chsclr.lpfnHook = (LPCCHOOKPROC)(FARPROC)NULL;
        chsclr.lpTemplateName = (LPTSTR)NULL;
        break;
}
if (fSetColor = ChooseColor (&chsclr))
{
    crColor = chsclr.rgbResult;
    return TRUE;
}
else
{
    ProcessCDError (CommDlgExtendedError (), hWnd);
    return FALSE;
}
}
```

The Find and Replace Common Dialog Boxes

The Find common dialog box, shown in Figure 6-11, prompts the user to enter a string of text and then searches for that string. The Replace dialog box, which is quite similar, not only searches for a specified string but also replaces it with a specified replace string. Unlike the other common dialog boxes, these two dialog boxes are modeless, which means that the user can switch between the dialog box and the window that created it.

The Find and Replace common dialog boxes use the FINDREPLACE structure. When this structure is initialized, the application calls the FindText function to display the Find dialog box or the ReplaceText function to display the Replace dialog box. Within the FINDREPLACE structure, the application can specify items such as the owner of the dialog box, an initial string to

Figure 6-11.
The Find common dialog box.

search for, whether to match the case of the string, whether to match the entire string, and hook and template information.

For an application to process messages from a Find or a Replace dialog box, the application must use the RegisterWindowMessage function to register the dialog box's unique message, FINDMSGSTRING. The following code from CMNDLG32 handles the FindReplaceMsg message:

```
LONG APIENTRY MainWndProc (
    HWND hWnd,      // window handle
    UINT message,   // type of message
    UINT wParam,    // additional information
    LONG lParam)    // additional information
{
⋮
switch (message)
{
    case WM_CREATE:
    ⋮
    default:
        // Handle the special find-replace message (FindReplaceMsg) that
        // was registered at initialization time.
        if (message == FindReplaceMsg)
        {
            if (lpFR = (LPFINDREPLACE)lParam)
            {
                if (lpFR->Flags & FR_DIALOGTERM)   // terminating dialog
                    return 0;
                SearchFile (lpFR);
                InvalidateRect (hWnd, NULL, TRUE);
            }
        return (0);
        }
        ⋮
}
⋮
}
```

The following example initializes the FINDREPLACE structure and then calls FindText. The flags specified for the dialog box stipulate that the Match Case, Up and Down, and Match Whole Word Only options should be disabled. The hook and template are enabled if the user has specified them.

```
void CallFindText (HWND hWnd)
{
frText.lStructSize = sizeof (frText);
frText.hwndOwner = hWnd;
frText.hInstance = (HANDLE)hInst;
frText.lpstrFindWhat = szFindString;
frText.lpstrReplaceWith = (LPTSTR)NULL;
frText.wFindWhatLen = sizeof (szFindString);
frText.wReplaceWithLen = 0;
frText.lCustData = 0;
lpBufPtr = FileBuf;

switch (wMode)
{
    case IDM_STANDARD:
        frText.Flags = FR_NOMATCHCASE | FR_NOUPDOWN | FR_NOWHOLEWORD;
        frText.lpfnHook = (LPFRHOOKPROC)(FARPROC)NULL;
        frText.lpTemplateName = (LPTSTR)NULL;
        break;

    case IDM_HOOK:
        frText.Flags = FR_NOMATCHCASE | FR_NOUPDOWN | FR_NOWHOLEWORD |
            FR_ENABLEHOOK;
        frText.lpfnHook = (LPFRHOOKPROC)FindTextHookProc;
        frText.lpTemplateName = (LPTSTR)NULL;
        break;

    case IDM_CUSTOM:
        frText.Flags = FR_NOMATCHCASE | FR_NOUPDOWN | FR_NOWHOLEWORD |
            FR_ENABLEHOOK | FR_ENABLETEMPLATE;
        frText.lpfnHook = (LPFRHOOKPROC)FindTextHookProc;
        frText.lpTemplateName = (LPTSTR) MAKEINTRESOURCE (FINDDLGORD);
        break;
}
if ((hDlgFR = FindText (&frText)) == NULL)
    ProcessCDError (CommDlgExtendedError (), hWnd);
}
```

The Replace common dialog box, shown in Figure 6-12, resembles the Find dialog box. It lacks Direction options, however, and it contains three additional controls that let the user specify a replacement string and choose whether to replace one or all occurrences of the string.

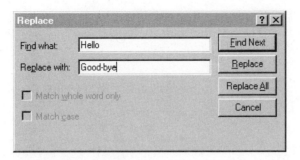

Figure 6-12.
The Replace common dialog box.

The code to initialize the FINDREPLACE structure for the Replace common dialog box is nearly identical to the code that initializes this structure for the Find common dialog box. The only difference is that you must include a pointer to a string in the *lpstrReplaceWith* member and specify the size of that string buffer in the *wReplaceWithLen* member. After you initialize the FINDREPLACE structure, the application calls the ReplaceText function to display the dialog box.

The Printing Common Dialog Boxes

The common dialog library provides three common dialog boxes that you can use for printing: Print, which lets the user configure the printer for a particular print job; Print Setup, in which the user can configure the printer for all jobs; and Page Setup, which allows the user to set properties such as margins, paper orientation, and paper source for the current document. The Print Setup common dialog box is supported for backward compatibility with previous versions of Windows; new applications should use the new print dialog boxes—Print and Page Setup. A user can access the printer configuration dialog box through the Page Setup dialog box.

The Print dialog box, shown in Figure 6-13 on the following page, differs from other common dialog boxes in that part of its dialog procedure resides in COMDLG32.DLL and part of it resides in the printer driver. When the user clicks the Properties button in the Print dialog box, the printer driver uses an exported function called ExtDeviceMode to display the Printer Properties property sheet.

Win32-based applications fill out the PRINTDLG structure and call a single function, PrintDlg, to show the Print dialog box or the Print Setup

181

dialog box. The Print dialog box appears by default; to display the Print Setup dialog box, which is shown in Figure 6-14, the application specifies the PD_PRINTSETUP flag.

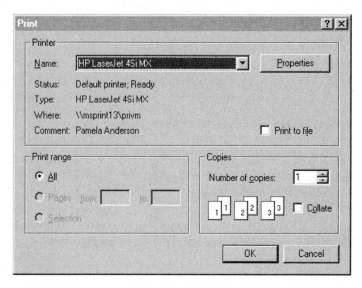

Figure 6-13.
The Print common dialog box.

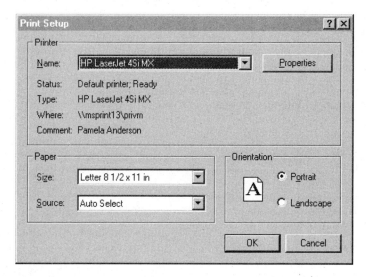

Figure 6-14.
The Print Setup common dialog box.

The PRINTDLG structure contains data such as the printer device context, initial values for the dialog box controls (such as number of copies and page range), and hook and template information. The following code shows how the CMNDLG32 sample fills out the structure and prints the contents of its edit buffer. Notice that I included the PD_USEDEVMODECOPIES and PD_COLLATE styles. If the application does not specify these styles, it takes responsibility for simulating the printing of multiple copies or collating.

```
void PrintFile (HWND hWnd)
{
DOCINFO di;
int nError;

// Initialize the PRINTDLG structure.
pd.lStructSize = sizeof (PRINTDLG);
pd.hwndOwner = hWnd;
pd.hDevMode = (HANDLE)NULL;
pd.hDevNames = (HANDLE)NULL;
pd.nFromPage = 0;
pd.nToPage = 0;
pd.nMinPage = 0;
pd.nMaxPage = 0;
pd.nCopies = 0;
pd.hInstance = (HANDLE)hInst;
pd.Flags = PD_RETURNDC | PD_USEDEVMODECOPIES | PD_COLLATE |
    PD_NOSELECTION | PD_PRINTSETUP;

switch (wMode)
{
    case IDM_STANDARD:
        pd.lpfnSetupHook = (LPSETUPHOOKPROC)(FARPROC)NULL;
        pd.lpSetupTemplateName = (LPTSTR)NULL;
        pd.lpfnPrintHook = (LPPRINTHOOKPROC)(FARPROC)NULL;
        pd.lpPrintTemplateName = (LPTSTR)NULL;
        break;

    case IDM_HOOK:
        pd.Flags |= PD_ENABLEPRINTHOOK | PD_ENABLESETUPHOOK;
        pd.lpfnSetupHook = (LPSETUPHOOKPROC)PrintSetupHookProc;
        pd.lpSetupTemplateName = (LPTSTR)NULL;
        pd.lpfnPrintHook = (LPPRINTHOOKPROC)PrintDlgHookProc;
        pd.lpPrintTemplateName = (LPTSTR)NULL;
        break;
```

(continued)

```
    case IDM_CUSTOM:
        pd.Flags |= PD_ENABLEPRINTHOOK | PD_ENABLEPRINTTEMPLATE |
            PD_ENABLESETUPHOOK | PD_ENABLESETUPTEMPLATE;
        pd.lpfnSetupHook = (LPSETUPHOOKPROC)PrintSetupHookProc;
        pd.lpfnPrintHook = (LPPRINTHOOKPROC)PrintDlgHookProc;
        pd.lpPrintTemplateName = (LPTSTR) MAKEINTRESOURCE (PRINTDLGORD);
        pd.lpSetupTemplateName =
            (LPTSTR) MAKEINTRESOURCE (PRNSETUPDLGORD);
        break;
}

// Print a test page if successful.
if (PrintDlg (&pd) == TRUE)
{
    // Fill out the DOCINFO structure.
    di.cbSize = sizeof (DOCINFO);
    di.lpszDocName = "Printing Test";
    di.lpszOutput = (LPTSTR)NULL;
    di.fwType = 0;

    // Start the document.
    StartDoc (pd.hDC, &di);

    nError = StartPage (pd.hDC);
    if (nError <= 0)
        MessageBox (hWnd, "Error in StartPage.", NULL, MB_OK);
    else
    {
        // Print the text.
        TextOut (pd.hDC, 5, 5, FileBuf, lstrlen (FileBuf));

        // Exit if the user has clicked the Cancel button in the
        // AbortPrintJob dialog box; if the button has been clicked,
        // call the AbortDoc function. Otherwise, inform the spooler
        // that the page is complete.
        nError = EndPage (pd.hDC);
        if (nError <= 0)
        {
            MessageBox (hWnd, "Error in EndPage.", NULL, MB_OK);
            AbortDoc (pd.hDC);
        }
        else
        {
            // The document has ended.
            nError = EndDoc (pd.hDC);
            if (nError <= 0)
                MessageBox (hWnd, "Error in EndDoc.", NULL, MB_OK);
        }
    }
```

```
        DeleteDC (pd.hDC);
        if (pd.hDevMode)
            GlobalFree (pd.hDevMode);
        if (pd.hDevNames)
            GlobalFree (pd.hDevNames);
    }
    else
        ProcessCDError (CommDlgExtendedError (), hWnd);
    }
```

Using the PD_RETURNDC flag, as I did in this code, causes PrintDlg to return a handle to a printer device context in the *hDC* member of the PRINTDLG structure. This handle is used in subsequent calls to do the actual printing. In this case, the *hDC* is sent to the Escape functions, which are used to send instructions to the print manager and spooler.

Using the Page Setup Common Dialog Box

Page Setup is a new common dialog box for Windows 95. (In earlier versions of Windows, the dialog template for the Print common dialog box included the code for page setup.) The Page Setup common dialog box, which is shown in Figure 6-15, allows the user to set the paper size, paper source, document orientation, and margins for printing. The sample representation of the page at the top of the dialog box gives the user an idea of what the printed output will look like.

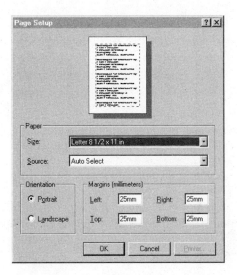

Figure 6-15.
The Page Setup common dialog box.

You can customize the Page Setup dialog box to use a hook function to paint the sample page. To use the hook function, the application must specify the PSD_ENABLEPAGEPAINTHOOK flag in the *Flags* member of the PAGE-SETUPDLG structure and the name of the hook function in the *lpfnPagePaintHook* member. This hook function will receive messages for all the steps in the drawing process. Table 6-1 lists the messages that are sent to the page setup hook in the order that the hook receives them.

Message	Description
WM_PSD_PAGESETUPDLG	Notifies the hook function to carry out initialization tasks.
WM_PSD_FULLPAGERECT	Specifies the bounding rectangle of the sample page.
WM_PSD_MINMARGINRECT	Specifies the minimum margin rectangle.
WM_PSD_MARGINRECT	Specifies the margin rectangle.
WM_PSD_GREEKTEXTRECT	Specifies the Greek-text rectangle.
WM_PSD_ENVSTAMPRECT	Specifies the envelope-stamp rectangle (for envelopes only).

Table 6-1.
Page setup messages.

From a programming standpoint, using the Page Setup common dialog box is very much like programming the other common dialog boxes: you fill out a structure and make a function call. The new structure provided for the Page Setup dialog box is PAGESETUPDLG. When you have filled out this structure, a call to PageSetupDlg with a pointer to the structure displays the dialog box. This code demonstrates how the CMNDLG32 sample fills out the structure and produces the Page Setup common dialog box:

```
void PageSetup (HWND hWnd)
{
// Initialize the PAGESETUPDLG structure.
psDlg.lStructSize = sizeof (PAGESETUPDLG);
psDlg.hwndOwner = hWnd;
psDlg.hDevMode = (HANDLE)NULL;
psDlg.hDevNames = (HANDLE)NULL;
psDlg.hInstance = (HANDLE)hInst;
psDlg.lCustData = (LPARAM)NULL;
psDlg.hPageSetupTemplate = (HGLOBAL)NULL;
psDlg.Flags = PSD_DEFAULTMINMARGINS | PSD_INHUNDREDTHSOFMILLIMETERS;
```

```
switch (wMode)
{
    case IDM_STANDARD:
        psDlg.lpfnPageSetupHook = (LPPAGESETUPHOOK)(FARPROC)NULL;
        psDlg.lpPageSetupTemplateName = (LPTSTR)NULL;
        psDlg.lpfnPagePaintHook = (LPPAGEPAINTHOOK)(FARPROC)NULL;
        break;

    case IDM_HOOK:
        psDlg.Flags |= PSD_ENABLEPAGESETUPHOOK;
        psDlg.lpfnPageSetupHook = (LPPAGESETUPHOOK)(FARPROC)PageSetupHook;
        psDlg.lpPageSetupTemplateName = (LPTSTR)NULL;
        psDlg.lpfnPagePaintHook = (LPPAGEPAINTHOOK)(FARPROC)NULL;
        break;

    case IDM_CUSTOM:
        psDlg.Flags |= PSD_ENABLEPAGESETUPHOOK |
            PSD_ENABLEPAGESETUPTEMPLATE;
        psDlg.lpfnPageSetupHook = (LPPAGESETUPHOOK)(FARPROC)PageSetupHook;
        psDlg.lpPageSetupTemplateName = (LPTSTR)PRNSETUPDLGORD95;
        psDlg.lpfnPagePaintHook = (LPPAGEPAINTHOOK)(FARPROC)NULL;
        break;
}

// Call the Page Setup common dialog procedure.
if (PageSetupDlg (&psDlg) == FALSE)
    ProcessCDError (CommDlgExtendedError (), hWnd);
}
```

Like the Open and Save As common dialog boxes, the three printing common dialog boxes have new templates. Here's what they look like:

```
// Print dialog box
PRINTDLGORD DIALOG DISCARDABLE  32, 32, 288, 186
STYLE DS_MODALFRAME | WS_POPUP | WS_VISIBLE | WS_CAPTION | WS_SYSMENU |
    DS_CONTEXTHELP | DS_3DLOOK
CAPTION "Print"
FONT 8, "MS Sans Serif"
BEGIN
    GROUPBOX        "Printer",grp4,8,4,272,84,WS_GROUP
    LTEXT           "&Name:",stc6,16,20,36,8
    COMBOBOX        cmb4,52,18,152,152,CBS_DROPDOWNLIST | CBS_SORT |
                    WS_VSCROLL | WS_GROUP | WS_TABSTOP
    PUSHBUTTON      "&Properties",psh2,212,17,60,14,WS_GROUP
    LTEXT           "Status:",stc8,16,36,36,10,SS_NOPREFIX
    LTEXT           "",stc12,52,36,224,10,SS_NOPREFIX |
                    SS_LEFTNOWORDWRAP
```

(continued)

```
        LTEXT           "Type:",stc7,16,48,36,10,SS_NOPREFIX
        LTEXT           "",stc11,52,48,224,10,SS_NOPREFIX |
                        SS_LEFTNOWORDWRAP
        LTEXT           "Where:",stc10,16,60,36,10,SS_NOPREFIX
        LTEXT           "",stc14,52,60,224,10,SS_NOPREFIX |
                        SS_LEFTNOWORDWRAP
        LTEXT           "Comment:",stc9,16,72,36,10,SS_NOPREFIX
        LTEXT           "",stc13,52,72,152,10,SS_NOPREFIX |
                        SS_LEFTNOWORDWRAP
        CONTROL         "Print to fi&le",chx1,"Button",BS_AUTOCHECKBOX |
                        WS_GROUP | WS_TABSTOP,212,70,64,12
        GROUPBOX        "Print range",grp1,8,92,144,64,WS_GROUP
        CONTROL         "&All",rad1,"Button",BS_AUTORADIOBUTTON | WS_GROUP |
                        WS_TABSTOP,16,106,64,12
        CONTROL         "Pa&ges",rad3,"Button",BS_AUTORADIOBUTTON,
                        16,122,36,12
        CONTROL         "&Selection",rad2,"Button",BS_AUTORADIOBUTTON,
                        16,138,64,12
        RTEXT           "&from:",stc2,52,124,20,8
        EDITTEXT        edt1,74,122,26,12,WS_GROUP | ES_NUMBER
        RTEXT           "&to:",stc3,100,124,16,8
        EDITTEXT        edt2,118,122,26,12,WS_GROUP | ES_NUMBER
        GROUPBOX        "Copies",grp2,160,92,120,64,WS_GROUP
        LTEXT           "Number of &copies:",stc5,168,108,68,8
        EDITTEXT        edt3,240,106,32,12,WS_GROUP | ES_NUMBER
        ICON            "",ico3,162,124,76,24,WS_GROUP | SS_CENTERIMAGE
        CONTROL         "C&ollate",chx2,"Button",BS_AUTOCHECKBOX |
                        WS_GROUP | WS_TABSTOP,240,130,36,12
        DEFPUSHBUTTON   "OK",IDOK,180,164,48,14,WS_GROUP
        PUSHBUTTON      "Cancel",IDCANCEL,232,164,48,14
END


// Print Setup dialog box
PRNSETUPDLGORD DIALOG DISCARDABLE  32, 32, 288, 178
STYLE DS_MODALFRAME | WS_POPUP | WS_VISIBLE | WS_CAPTION | WS_SYSMENU |
      DS_CONTEXTHELP | DS_3DLOOK
CAPTION "Print Setup"
FONT 8, "MS Sans Serif"
BEGIN
        GROUPBOX        "Printer",grp4,8,4,272,84,WS_GROUP
        LTEXT           "&Name:",stc6,16,20,36,8
        COMBOBOX        cmb1,52,18,152,152,CBS_DROPDOWNLIST | CBS_SORT |
                        WS_VSCROLL | WS_GROUP | WS_TABSTOP
        PUSHBUTTON      "&Properties",psh2,212,17,60,14,WS_GROUP
        LTEXT           "Status:",stc8,16,36,36,10,SS_NOPREFIX
        LTEXT           "",stc12,52,36,224,10,SS_NOPREFIX |
                        SS_LEFTNOWORDWRAP
```

```
    LTEXT            "Type:",stc7,16,48,36,10,SS_NOPREFIX
    LTEXT            "",stc11,52,48,224,10,SS_NOPREFIX |
                     SS_LEFTNOWORDWRAP
    LTEXT            "Where:",stc10,16,60,36,10,SS_NOPREFIX
    LTEXT            "",stc14,52,60,224,10,SS_NOPREFIX |
                     SS_LEFTNOWORDWRAP
    LTEXT            "Comment:",stc9,16,72,36,10,SS_NOPREFIX
    LTEXT            "",stc13,52,72,224,10,SS_NOPREFIX |
                     SS_LEFTNOWORDWRAP
    GROUPBOX         "Paper",grp2,8,92,164,56,WS_GROUP
    LTEXT            "Si&ze:",stc2,16,108,36,8
    COMBOBOX         cmb2,52,106,112,112,CBS_DROPDOWNLIST | CBS_SORT |
                     WS_VSCROLL | WS_GROUP | WS_TABSTOP
    LTEXT            "&Source:",stc3,16,128,36,8
    COMBOBOX         cmb3,52,126,112,112,CBS_DROPDOWNLIST | CBS_SORT |
                     WS_VSCROLL | WS_GROUP | WS_TABSTOP
    GROUPBOX         "Orientation",grp1,180,92,100,56,WS_GROUP
    ICON             "",ico1,195,112,18,20,WS_GROUP
    CONTROL          "P&ortrait",rad1,"Button",BS_AUTORADIOBUTTON |
                     WS_GROUP | WS_TABSTOP,224,106,52,12
    CONTROL          "L&andscape",rad2,"Button",BS_AUTORADIOBUTTON,
                     224,126,52,12
    DEFPUSHBUTTON    "OK",IDOK,180,156,48,14,WS_GROUP
    PUSHBUTTON       "Cancel",IDCANCEL,232,156,48,14
END

// Page Setup dialog box
PAGESETUPDLGORD DIALOG DISCARDABLE  32, 32, 240, 240
STYLE DS_MODALFRAME | WS_POPUP | WS_VISIBLE | WS_CAPTION |
    WS_SYSMENU | 0x4 | DS_CONTEXTHELP
CAPTION "Page Setup"
FONT 8, "MS Sans Serif"
BEGIN
    CONTROL          "",rct1,"Static",SS_WHITERECT | WS_GROUP,80,8,80,80
    CONTROL          "",rct2,"Static",SS_GRAYRECT | WS_GROUP,160,12,4,80
    CONTROL          "",rct3,"Static",SS_GRAYRECT | WS_GROUP,84,88,80,4
    GROUPBOX         "Paper",grp2,8,96,224,56,WS_GROUP
    LTEXT            "Si&ze:",stc2,16,112,36,8
    COMBOBOX         cmb2,64,110,160,160,CBS_DROPDOWNLIST | CBS_SORT |
                     WS_VSCROLL | WS_GROUP | WS_TABSTOP
    LTEXT            "&Source:",stc3,16,132,36,8
    COMBOBOX         cmb3,64,130,160,160,CBS_DROPDOWNLIST | CBS_SORT |
                     WS_VSCROLL | WS_GROUP | WS_TABSTOP
    GROUPBOX         "Orientation",grp1,8,156,64,56,WS_GROUP
    CONTROL          "P&ortrait",rad1,"Button",BS_AUTORADIOBUTTON |
                     WS_GROUP | WS_TABSTOP,16,170,52,12
    CONTROL          "L&andscape",rad2,"Button",BS_AUTORADIOBUTTON,
                     16,190,52,12
```

(continued)

```
        GROUPBOX        "Margins",grp4,80,156,152,56,WS_GROUP
        LTEXT           "&Left:",stc15,88,172,32,8
        EDITTEXT        edt4,120,170,28,12,WS_GROUP
        LTEXT           "&Right:",stc16,164,172,32,8
        EDITTEXT        edt6,196,170,28,12,WS_GROUP
        LTEXT           "&Top:",stc17,88,192,32,8
        EDITTEXT        edt5,120,190,28,12,WS_GROUP
        LTEXT           "&Bottom:",stc18,164,192,32,8
        EDITTEXT        edt7,196,190,28,12,WS_GROUP
        DEFPUSHBUTTON   "OK",IDOK,80,220,48,14,WS_GROUP
        PUSHBUTTON      "Cancel",IDCANCEL,132,220,48,14
        PUSHBUTTON      "&Printer...",psh3,184,220,48,14
END
```

Error Detection

Throughout the examples in this chapter, you might have noticed that whenever an error occurs, the ProcessCDError function is called. This isn't a system function; rather, it's a function I wrote that gets the extended error from the common dialog library and then displays a message box that describes the problem. When a common dialog function fails, an application can call the CommDlgExtendedError function, which returns an error value that identifies the cause of the most recent error. I created a string ID table containing descriptions of each error. In a switch statement, I use the error code to determine which string to load and then display in the message box.

```
void ProcessCDError(DWORD dwErrorCode, HWND hWnd)
{
WORD wStringID;
char buf [MAX_PATH];

switch (dwErrorCode)
{
    case CDERR_STRUCTSIZE:      wStringID = IDS_STRUCTSIZE;      break;
    case CDERR_INITIALIZATION:  wStringID = IDS_INITIALIZATION;  break;
    case CDERR_NOTEMPLATE:      wStringID = IDS_NOTEMPLATE;      break;
    case CDERR_NOHINSTANCE:     wStringID = IDS_NOHINSTANCE;     break;
    case CDERR_LOADSTRFAILURE:  wStringID = IDS_LOADSTRFAILURE;  break;
    case CDERR_FINDRESFAILURE:  wStringID = IDS_FINDRESFAILURE;  break;
    case CDERR_LOADRESFAILURE:  wStringID = IDS_LOADRESFAILURE;  break;
    case CDERR_LOCKRESFAILURE:  wStringID = IDS_LOCKRESFAILURE;  break;
    case CDERR_MEMALLOCFAILURE: wStringID = IDS_MEMALLOCFAILURE; break;
    case CDERR_MEMLOCKFAILURE:  wStringID = IDS_MEMLOCKFAILURE;  break;
```

```
case CDERR_NOHOOK:           wStringID = IDS_NOHOOK;           break;
case PDERR_PARSEFAILURE:     wStringID = IDS_PARSEFAILURE;     break;
case PDERR_RETDEFFAILURE:    wStringID = IDS_RETDEFFAILURE;    break;
case PDERR_LOADDRVFAILURE:   wStringID = IDS_LOADDRVFAILURE;   break;
case PDERR_GETDEVMODEFAIL:   wStringID = IDS_GETDEVMODEFAIL;   break;
case PDERR_INITFAILURE:      wStringID = IDS_INITFAILURE;      break;
case PDERR_NODEVICES:        wStringID = IDS_NODEVICES;        break;
case PDERR_NODEFAULTPRN:     wStringID = IDS_NODEFAULTPRN;     break;
case PDERR_DNDMMISMATCH:     wStringID = IDS_DNDMMISMATCH;     break;
case PDERR_CREATEICFAILURE:  wStringID = IDS_CREATEICFAILURE;  break;
case PDERR_PRINTERNOTFOUND:  wStringID = IDS_PRINTERNOTFOUND;  break;
case CFERR_NOFONTS:          wStringID = IDS_NOFONTS;          break;
case FNERR_SUBCLASSFAILURE:  wStringID = IDS_SUBCLASSFAILURE;  break;
case FNERR_INVALIDFILENAME:  wStringID = IDS_INVALIDFILENAME;  break;
case FNERR_BUFFERTOOSMALL:   wStringID = IDS_BUFFERTOOSMALL;   break;
case 0:      // user might have clicked Cancel,
    return;  // or this is a *very* random error
default:
    wStringID = IDS_UNKNOWNERROR;
}

LoadString (NULL, wStringID, buf, sizeof (buf));
MessageBox (hWnd, buf, NULL, MB_OK);
return;
}
```

Supporting Help

An application can display a Help button in any common dialog box by specifying the appropriate flag in the *Flags* member of the structure for that common dialog box. When the Help button is displayed, the application must process the request for help from the user. This can be done in one of the application's window procedures or in a hook function.

To have a window procedure process the request for help, the application must register the HELPMSGSTRING message identifier by calling the RegisterWindowMessage function. (This is the same as the action that the Find common dialog box needs to take to process the FINDMSGSTRING message.) The application uses the *hwndOwner* member of the common dialog structure in order to specify the owner for the Help window in its call to WinHelp.

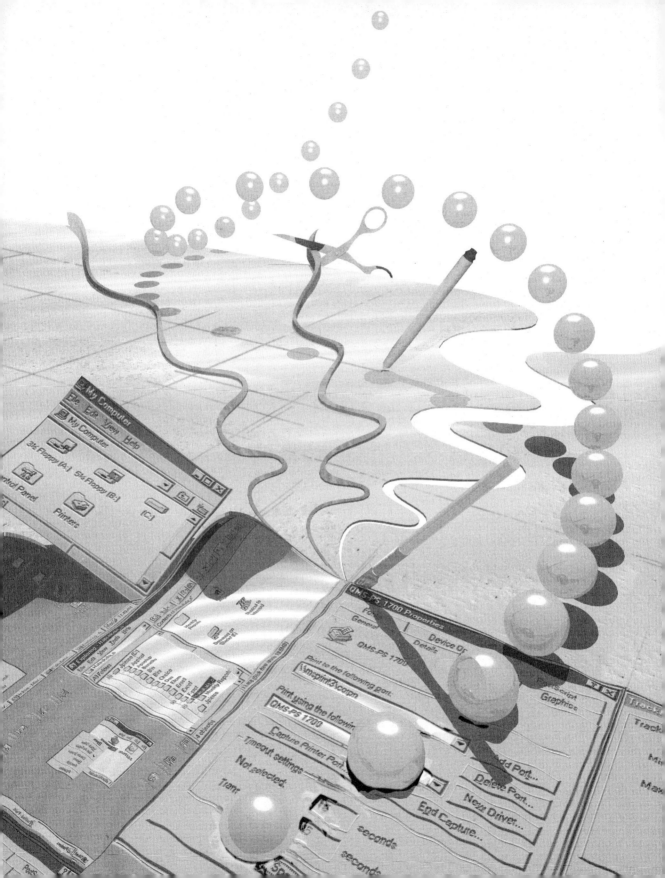

CHAPTER SEVEN

Putting It All Together

As you've seen in preceding chapters, the Win32 API for Microsoft Windows 95 supplies a lot of new common controls. In Windows 95, the showcase for many of these new controls and for several of the new common dialog boxes is Windows Explorer. Because Windows Explorer closely follows the Windows 95 user interface design guidelines and because it includes a variety of new common controls, many developers are likely to use it as a model for creating applications based on the new operating system.

This chapter builds on the previous chapters by pulling together the new common controls into an Explorer-like application that displays real estate listings for houses. We'll look at two samples: CHICOAPP, the original C version of the application; and MFCEXP, the MFC-based version. (Please note that CHICOAPP and MFCEXP are not user interface extensions. Chapter 13 will cover Windows 95 user interface extensions.)

Designing CHICOAPP

I began my work by using samples I had written for previous chapters demonstrating toolbars, status bars, tree view controls, and list view controls. I didn't know how much time it would take to simply integrate my samples, so, to get a head start, I brought my computer home one weekend and started to work on the application in earnest. I was amazed at how much I was able to accomplish in two days. By the end of the weekend, I could display and resize the major user interface components, all of which were working in an orderly fashion. It did, however, take more time to add all the features you see in the final version of CHICOAPP.

My goals for this real estate application were to include the following functional elements:

▨ A toolbar (with ToolTips) for easy access to commands

▨ A status bar displaying the currently selected city and the number of houses listed for that city

▨ A tree view control displaying the cities that have houses for sale

▨ A list view control displaying the houses for sale

▨ Context menus

▨ A property sheet for viewing and changing properties of the various houses

▨ Support for long filenames in opening and saving files

Figure 7-1 shows you the main screen of CHICOAPP, with a selected listing for the city of Bellevue, Washington. (Remember that the listings you see in these text files and screen shots are purely fictional. If you are shopping for a house, don't rely on this information!)

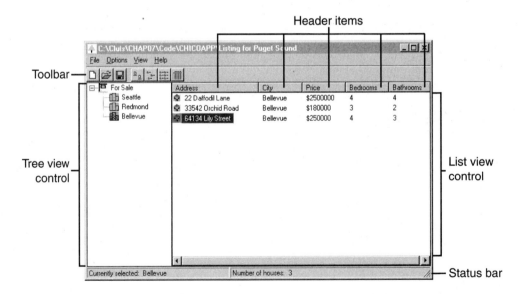

Figure 7-1.
The main screen of CHICOAPP.

Creating the Windows

To set up the basic windows for my application, I wrote a function to call the worker functions that actually create the windows. Because these windows are part of the new Windows 95 common control library, I first had to call Init-CommonControls to ensure that COMCTL32.DLL was loaded.

My first control was a multiple-part status bar. The left section of the status bar displays the currently selected city, and the right section displays the number of houses listed for that city. The following code demonstrates how the status bar is implemented:

```
g_Listing.hWndStatus = CreateStatusWindow (
   WS_CHILD | WS_BORDER | WS_VISIBLE,    // window styles
   "",                                   // default window text
   hwndParent,                           // parent window
   ID_STATUS);                           // ID

if (g_Listing.hWndStatus == NULL)
   MessageBox (NULL, "Status Bar not created!", NULL, MB_OK);

// Set the status bar to have two parts.
lpSBParts [0] = (rcl.right - rcl.left) / 2;
lpSBParts [1] = -1;
SendMessage (g_Listing.hWndStatus, SB_SETPARTS, (WPARAM)2,
   (LPARAM)&lpSBParts),
```

Next I created the toolbar, using the TB_ADDBITMAP message to add built-in bitmaps for the standard file and view operations. This code fills out the TBBUTTON structure with the predefined bitmap indexes:

```
// Toolbar buttons
TBBUTTON tbButtons [] =
{
   {STD_FILENEW, IDM_NEW, TBSTATE_ENABLED, TBSTYLE_BUTTON, 0L, 0},
   {STD_FILEOPEN, IDM_OPEN, TBSTATE_ENABLED, TBSTYLE_BUTTON, 0L, 0},
   {STD_FILESAVE, IDM_SAVE, TBSTATE_ENABLED, TBSTYLE_BUTTON, 0L, 0},
   {0, 0, TBSTATE_ENABLED, TBSTYLE_SEP, 0L, 0},
   {VIEW_LARGEICONS, IDM_LARGEICON, TBSTATE_ENABLED, TBSTYLE_BUTTON,
      0L, 0},
   {VIEW_SMALLICONS, IDM_SMALLICON, TBSTATE_ENABLED, TBSTYLE_BUTTON,
      0L, 0},
   {VIEW_LIST, IDM_LISTVIEW, TBSTATE_ENABLED, TBSTYLE_BUTTON, 0L, 0},
   {VIEW_DETAILS, IDM_REPORTVIEW, TBSTATE_ENABLED, TBSTYLE_BUTTON,
      0L, 0},
};
```

This piece of code creates the toolbar, as you saw earlier, in Chapter 1:

```
HWND CreateTheToolbar (HWND hWndParent)
{
HWND hWndToolbar;
TBADDBITMAP tb;
int index, stdidx;

hWndToolbar = CreateToolbarEx (hWndParent,
    WS_CHILD | WS_BORDER | WS_VISIBLE | WS_CHILD | TBSTYLE_TOOLTIPS,
    ID_TOOLBAR, 11, (HINSTANCE)HINST_COMMCTRL, IDB_STD_SMALL_COLOR,
    (LPCTBBUTTON)&tbButtons, 4, 0, 0, 100, 30, sizeof (TBBUTTON));

// Add the system-defined view bitmaps.
// The hInst == HINST_COMMCTRL
// The nID == IDB_VIEW_SMALL_COLOR
tb.hInst = HINST_COMMCTRL;
tb.nID = IDB_VIEW_SMALL_COLOR;
stdidx = SendMessage (hWndToolbar, TB_ADDBITMAP, 12, (LPARAM)&tb);

// Update the indexes to the bitmaps.
for (index = 4; index < NUM_BUTTONS; index++)
    tbButtons[index].iBitmap += stdidx;

// Add the view buttons.
SendMessage (hWndToolbar, TB_ADDBUTTONS, 4, (LONG) &tbButtons[4]);

return hWndToolbar;
}
```

As my third step, I created the list view and tree view windows, using helper functions. I made the tree view control one-fourth the width of the window's client area and accounted vertically for both the toolbar and the status bar, as you can see in the following code. (Note that for this sample I hard-coded the values that determine the size of the controls. If I were writing an application for general consumption, I would instead obtain these values by calling GetSystemMetrics.)

```
HWND TV_CreateTreeView (HWND hWndParent, HINSTANCE hInst, int NumCities,
    CITYINFO *pCity)
{
HWND hwndTree;      // handle to tree view window
RECT rcl;           // rectangle for setting size of window
HBITMAP hBmp;       // handle to a bitmap
HIMAGELIST hIml;    // handle to image list
```

```
// Get the size and position of the parent window.
GetClientRect (hWndParent, &rcl);

// Create the tree view window, make it 1/4 the width of the parent
// window, and account for the status bar and the toolbar.
hwndTree = CreateWindowEx (0L,
    WC_TREEVIEW,                    // window class
    "",                            // no default text
    WS_VISIBLE | WS_CHILD | WS_BORDER | TVS_HASLINES |
        TVS_HASBUTTONS | TVS_LINESATROOT, | WS_EX_CLIENTEDGE,
    0, 27,                         // x, y
    (rcl.right - rcl.left) / 4,    // cx
    rcl.bottom - rcl.top - 45,     // cy
    hWndParent,                    // parent
    (HMENU)ID_TREEVIEW,            // ID
    hInst,                         // instance
    NULL);

if (hwndTree == NULL)
{
    MessageBox (NULL, "CreateWindow of TreeView failed!", NULL, MB_OK);
    return NULL;
}

// First create the image list you will need.
hIml = ImageList_Create (BITMAP_WIDTH, BITMAP_HEIGHT, FALSE, 2, 10);

if (hIml == NULL)
    MessageBox (NULL, "ImageList_Create failed!", NULL, MB_OK);

// Load the bitmaps and add them to the image list.
hBmp = LoadBitmap (hInst, MAKEINTRESOURCE (FORSALE_BMP));
idxForSale = ImageList_Add (hIml, hBmp, NULL);
hBmp = LoadBitmap (hInst, MAKEINTRESOURCE (CITY_BMP));
idxCity = ImageList_Add (hIml, hBmp, NULL);
hBmp = LoadBitmap (hInst, MAKEINTRESOURCE (SELCITY_BMP));
idxSelect = ImageList_Add (hIml, hBmp, NULL);

// Be sure that all the bitmaps were added.
if (ImageList_GetImageCount (hIml) != 3)
{
    MessageBox (NULL, "TreeView image list not loaded!", NULL, MB_OK);
    return FALSE;
}

// Associate the image list with the tree view control.
TreeView_SetImageList (hwndTree, hIml, idxForSale);
```

(continued)

197

```
// Initialize the tree view control by adding "Houses For Sale."
TV_InitTreeView (hInst, hwndTree);

return hwndTree;
}
```

I created the list view window, made it three-fourths the width of the parent window's client area, placed it on the right side of the area, and accounted vertically for the toolbar and the status bar, using this code:

```
HWND LV_CreateListView (HWND hWndParent, HINSTANCE hInst, int NumHouses,
    HOUSEINFO *pHouse)
{
HWND hWndList;                  // handle to list view window
RECT rcl;                       // rectangle for setting size of window
HICON hIcon;                    // handle to an icon
int index;                      // index used in for loops
HIMAGELIST hSmall, hLarge;      // handles to image lists
LV_COLUMN lvC;                  // list view column structure
char szText [MAX_ITEMLEN];      // place to store some text
int iWidth;                     // column width

// Get the size and position of the parent window.
GetClientRect (hWndParent, &rcl);

iWidth = (rcl.right - rcl.left) - ((rcl.right - rcl.left) / 4);

// Create the list view window, make it 3/4 the width of the
// parent window, and account for the status bar and the toolbar.
hWndList = CreateWindowEx (0L,
    WC_LISTVIEW,                        // list view class
    "",                                 // no default text
    WS_VISIBLE | WS_CHILD | WS_BORDER | LVS_REPORT | WS_EX_CLIENTEDGE,
    (rcl.right - rcl.left) / 4, 27,     // x, y
    iWidth, rcl.bottom - rcl.top - 42,  // cx, cy
    hWndParent,                         // parent
    (HMENU)ID_LISTVIEW,                 // ID
    hInst,                              // instance
    NULL);

if (hWndList == NULL )
    return NULL;

// First initialize the image lists you will need.
// Create image lists for the small and the large icons.
// TRUE specifies small icons; FALSE specifies large.
```

```
hSmall = ImageList_Create (BITMAP_WIDTH, BITMAP_HEIGHT, TRUE, 1, 0);
hLarge = ImageList_Create (LG_BITMAP_WIDTH, LG_BITMAP_HEIGHT, FALSE,
    1, 0);

// Load the icons and add them to the image lists.
hIcon = LoadIcon (hInst, MAKEINTRESOURCE (HOUSE_ICON));
if ((ImageList_AddIcon (hSmall, hIcon) == -1) ||
    (ImageList_AddIcon (hLarge, hIcon) == -1))
{
    MessageBox (NULL, "ImageList_AddIcon failed!", NULL, MB_OK);
    return NULL;
}

// Associate the image lists with the list view control.
ListView_SetImageList (hWndList, hSmall, LVSIL_SMALL);
ListView_SetImageList (hWndList, hLarge, LVSIL_NORMAL);

// Initialize the LV_COLUMN structure.
// The mask specifies that the fmt, cx, pszText, and iSubitem
// members of the structure are valid.
lvC.mask = LVCF_FMT | LVCF_WIDTH | LVCF_TEXT | LVCF_SUBITEM;
lvC.fmt = LVCFMT_LEFT;                  // left-align column
lvC.cx = iWidth / NUM_COLUMNS + 1;    // width of column in pixels
lvC.pszText = szText;

// Add the columns.
for (index = 0; index < NUM_COLUMNS; index++)
{
    lvC.iSubItem = index;
    LoadString (hInst,
        IDS_ADDRESS + index,
        szText,
        sizeof (szText));
    if (ListView_InsertColumn (hWndList, index, &lvC) == -1)
        return NULL;
}
return hWndList;
}
```

Using MFC to Create the Same Controls

After writing the C version of the sample application, I decided (with just a bit of prodding—my electronic mailbox was filling up with requests for an MFC version) to port CHICOAPP to MFC. The MFC version contains a few small changes: I added separate icons for the cities, and I used the same image list

199

both for the tree view control and for the list view control in small icon view.
I created all the application windows in one function, CreateAppWindows,
and left sizing the windows to the WM_SIZE handler.

```
BOOL CMfcexpView::CreateAppWindows ()
{
static char szBuf [MAX_PATH];
HICON hIcon;                    // handle to an icon
int index;                      // index used in for loops
LV_COLUMN lvC;                  // list view column structure
char szText [MAX_ITEMLEN];      // place to store some text

// Ensure that the common control DLL is loaded.
InitCommonControls ();

// Create the status bar.
m_StatusBar.Create (WS_CHILD | WS_BORDER | WS_VISIBLE | SBS_SIZEGRIP,
    CRect (0, 0, 0, 0),
    this,
    ID_STATUSBAR);

// Set the status bar to have two parts.
int aWidths [2] = {0, 0};
m_StatusBar.SetParts (2, aWidths);
// Set the text for the status bar.
ChangeSBText (-1);

// Create the toolbar.
m_Toolbar.Create (
    WS_CHILD | WS_BORDER | WS_VISIBLE | TBSTYLE_TOOLTIPS,    // styles
    CRect (0, 0, 0, 0),
    this,
    ID_TOOLBAR);

// Add the bitmaps.
m_Toolbar.AddBitmap (NUM_BITMAPS, IDB_TOOLBAR);

// Add the buttons.
m_Toolbar.AddButtons (NUM_BUTTONS, (LPTBBUTTON)&tbButtons);

// Create the CListCtrl window.
m_ListCtl.Create (
    WS_VISIBLE | WS_CHILD | WS_BORDER | LVS_REPORT | LVS_EDITLABELS,
    CRect (0, 0, 0, 0),    // bounding rectangle
    this,                  // parent
    ID_LISTVIEW);          // ID
```

```
// Create the large icon image list.
m_ImageLarge.Create (LARGE_BITMAP_WIDTH,
    LARGE_BITMAP_HEIGHT,
    FALSE,    // list does not include masks
    NUM_BITMAPS,
    10);      // list won't grow

// Create the small icon image list.
m_ImageSmall.Create (SMALL_BITMAP_WIDTH,
    SMALL_BITMAP_HEIGHT,
    FALSE,    // list does not include masks
    NUM_BITMAPS,
    10);      // list won't grow

// Load the house icon.
hIcon = ::LoadIcon (AfxGetResourceHandle (),
    MAKEINTRESOURCE (IDI_SEATTLE));
m_idxSeattle = m_ImageSmall.Add (hIcon);
m_ImageLarge.Add (hIcon);
hIcon = ::LoadIcon (AfxGetResourceHandle (),
    MAKEINTRESOURCE (IDI_BELLEVUE));
m_idxBellevue = m_ImageSmall.Add (hIcon);
m_ImageLarge.Add (hIcon);
hIcon = ::LoadIcon (AfxGetResourceHandle (),
    MAKEINTRESOURCE (IDI_REDMOND))·
m_idxRedmond = m_ImageSmall.Add (hIcon);
m_ImageLarge.Add (hIcon);

// Associate the image lists with the list view control.
m_ListCtl.SetImageList (&m_ImageSmall, LVSIL_SMALL);
m_ListCtl.SetImageList (&m_ImageLarge, LVSIL_NORMAL);

// Now initialize the columns you will need.
// Initialize the LV_COLUMN structure.
// The mask specifies that the fmt, cx, pszText, and iSubitem
// members of the structure are valid.
lvC.mask = LVCF_FMT | LVCF_WIDTH | LVCF_TEXT | LVCF_SUBITEM;
lvC.fmt = LVCFMT_LEFT;    // left-align column
lvC.cx = 75;              // width of column in pixels
lvC.pszText = szText;
```

(continued)

```
// Add the columns.
for (index = 0; index < NUM_COLUMNS; index++)
{
    lvC.iSubItem = index;
    ::LoadString (AfxGetResourceHandle (),
        IDS_ADDRESS + index,
        szText,
        sizeof (szText));
    if (m_ListCtl.InsertColumn (index, &lvC) == -1)
        return NULL;
}

// Create the tree view control.
m_TreeCtl.Create (
WS_VISIBLE | WS_CHILD | WS_BORDER | TVS_HASLINES | TVS_HASBUTTONS |
    TVS_LINESATROOT,     // styles
CRect (0, 0, 0, 0),      // bounding rectangle
this,                    // parent
ID_TREEVIEW);            // ID

// Load the bitmaps and add them to the image list.
hIcon = ::LoadIcon (AfxGetResourceHandle (),
    MAKEINTRESOURCE (IDI_FORSALE));
m_idxForSale = m_ImageSmall.Add (hIcon);
hIcon = ::LoadIcon (AfxGetResourceHandle (),
    MAKEINTRESOURCE (IDI_SELECTED));
m_idxSeaSel = m_ImageSmall.Add (hIcon);
hIcon = ::LoadIcon (AfxGetResourceHandle (),
    MAKEINTRESOURCE (IDI_SELBELL));
m_idxBellSel = m_ImageSmall.Add (hIcon);
hIcon = ::LoadIcon (AfxGetResourceHandle (),
    MAKEINTRESOURCE (IDI_REDSEL));
m_idxRedSel = m_ImageSmall.Add (hIcon);

// Associate the image list with the tree view control.
m_TreeCtl.SetImageList (TVSIL_NORMAL, &m_ImageSmall);

TV_InitTreeView ();
return TRUE;
}
```

As you can see in Figure 7-2, the main screen of MFCEXP is quite similar to that of CHICOAPP. One exception is the toolbar. Instead of using the built-in toolbar bitmaps, I created my own and included buttons for adding a house, removing a house, and adding a city to the listing.

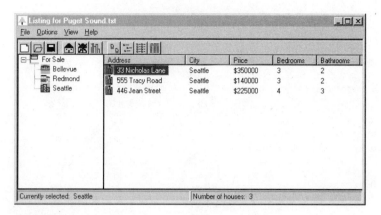

Figure 7-2.
The main screen of MFCEXP.

Resizing the Windows

When I finished creating the windows, I had to find an easy way to resize the application's main window. In the C version, I used the handy DeferWindow-Pos function to resize all the windows at the same time. For those who are new to Win32, DeferWindowPos updates a structure that contains multiple window positions. You use this function as you would use the window enumeration functions—that is, you begin, defer, and end. This code illustrates how I resized all the windows:

```
BOOL ResizeWindows (HWND hwnd)
{
RECT rcl;
HDWP hdwp;

// Get the client area of the parent window.
GetClientRect (hwnd, &rcl);

// You will defer all the application's windows.
hdwp = BeginDeferWindowPos (NUM_WINDOWS);

// First, reset the size of the status bar.
DeferWindowPos (hdwp, g_Listing.hWndStatus, NULL, 0, 0,
    rcl.right - rcl.left, 20, SWP_NOZORDER | SWP_NOMOVE);

// Next, reset the size of the toolbar.
DeferWindowPos (hdwp, g_Listing.hWndToolbar, NULL, 0, 0,
    rcl.right - rcl.left, 20, SWP_NOZORDER | SWP_NOMOVE);
```

(continued)

203

```
// Next, reset the size of the tree view control.
DeferWindowPos (hdwp, g_Listing.hWndTreeView, NULL, 0, 0,
   (rcl.right - rcl.left ) / 4, rcl.bottom - rcl.top - 46,
   SWP_NOZORDER | SWP_NOMOVE);

// Last, reset the size of the list view control.
DeferWindowPos (hdwp, g_Listing.hWndListView, NULL,
   (rcl.right - rcl.left ) / 4, 27,
   (rcl.right - rcl.left) - ((rcl.right - rcl.left) / 4),
   rcl.bottom - rcl.top - 46,
   SWP_NOZORDER);

return EndDeferWindowPos (hdwp);
}
```

In MFCEXP, I added a handler for the WM_SIZE message, OnSize, to set the window positions for all the windows. The CToolBarCtrl class includes AutoSize, a special member function that resizes the toolbar to fit within the parent window.

```
void CMfcexpView::OnSize (UINT nType, int cx, int cy)
{
CView::OnSize (nType, cx, cy);

// Resize the toolbar.
m_Toolbar.AutoSize ();

// Resize the status bar.
// Make it fit along the bottom of the client area.
m_StatusBar.MoveWindow (0, cx - 10, cy, cy - 10);

// Set the rectangle for each part of the status bar.
// Make each 1/2 the width of the client area.
int aWidths [2];

aWidths [0] = cx / 2;
aWidths [1] = -1;
m_StatusBar.SetParts (2, aWidths);

m_TreeCtl.MoveWindow (0, 25, cx / 4, cy - 45);

m_ListCtl.MoveWindow (cx / 4, 25, cx, cy - 45);
}
```

Parsing and Storing the Data

After creating and resizing my windows, I needed a method for reading in and storing the data for the various house listings. In my original samples, I used static arrays filled with dummy information. This technique is great if you never intend to change the information you are displaying. But in a working application, it makes sense to provide for dynamic data changes.

The easiest way to store the data is to save it in a file. I decided to use an ASCII file because it is easy to test and easy to alter. The file contains the following information:

- Number of cities
- Name of city (one name per line)
- Number of houses
- Information about each house (one house per line, with each item of information separated by a comma)

Here's what the ASCII file looks like:

```
3
Bellevue
Redmond
Seattle
9
100 Berry Lane,Redmond,175000,3,2,Joan Smith,555-1212
523 Apple Road,Redmond,125000,4,2,Ed Jones,555-1111
1212 Peach Street,Redmond,200000,4,3,Mary Wilson,555-2222
22 Daffodil Lane,Bellevue,2500000,4,4,Joan Smith,555-1212
33542 Orchid Road,Bellevue,180000,3,2,Ed Jones,555-1111
64134 Lily Street,Bellevue,250000,4,3,Mary Wilson,555-2222
33 Nicholas Lane,Seattle,350000,3,2,Joan Smith,555-1212
555 Tracy Road,Seattle,140000,3,2,Ed Jones,555-1111
446 Jean Street,Seattle,225000,4,3,Mary Wilson,555-2222
```

Parsing the file was simply a matter of using sscanf, converting some of the strings to integers, copying the data to my data structure, and updating my file pointer. The data structures I used contained information about the houses, the cities, and the current state of the application. I filled out a CITYINFO structure for each city listed and a HOUSEINFO structure for each house listed. When saving the information to a file, I reversed the procedure. The code on the next page shows what the structures look like.

```
typedef struct tagCITYINFO
{
    char szCity [MAX_CITY];    // city name
    int NumHouses;             // number of houses listed in this city
    HTREEITEM hItem;           // handle to tree view item
} CITYINFO;

typedef struct tagHOUSEINFO
{
    char szAddress [MAX_ADDRESS];   // address
    char szCity [MAX_CITY];         // city
    int iPrice;                     // price
    int iBeds;                      // number of bedrooms
    int iBaths;                     // number of bathrooms
    int iImage;                     // bitmap index for this house
    char szAgent [MAX_CITY];        // listing agent
    char szNumber [MAX_CITY];       // listing agent's phone number
} HOUSEINFO;
```

When I ported CHICOAPP to MFC, I stored data in the view class in member variables rather than using the LISTINFO structure:

```
typedef struct tagCITYINFO
{
    CString szCity;        // city name
    int NumHouses;         // number of houses listed in this city
    HTREEITEM hItem;       // handle to tree view item
} CITYINFO;

typedef struct tagHOUSEINFO
{
    CString szAddress;
    CString szCity;
    int iPrice;
    int iBeds;
    int iBaths;
    int iImage;
    CString szAgent;
    CString szNumber;
} HOUSEINFO;

class CMfcexpView : public CView
{
    protected:   // create from serialization only
        CMfcexpView ();
        DECLARE_DYNCREATE (CMfcexpView);
```

```
        // Common controls
        CToolBarCtrl m_Toolbar;        // toolbar
        CStatusBarCtrl m_StatusBar;    // status bar
        CListCtrl m_ListCtl;           // list view control
        CImageList m_ImageLarge;       // large (32-by-32) image list
        CImageList m_ImageSmall;       // small (16-by-16) image list
        CTreeCtrl m_TreeCtl;           // tree view control

        // Indexes to icons in the tree view image list
        int m_idxForSale;
        int m_idxSeattle;
        int m_idxSeaSel;
        int m_idxRedmond;
        int m_idxRedSel;
        int m_idxBellevue;
        int m_idxBellSel;

        // Handles to the root, parent, and previous tree view items
        HTREEITEM m_hTPrev;
        HTREEITEM m_hParent;
        HTREEITEM m_hTRoot;

        // House listing information
        int m_NumCities;    // number of cities
        int m_NumHouses;    // number of houses
        int m_iSelected;    // index to selected city
        int m_iSelHouse;    // index to selected house
        HOUSEINFO m_rgHouses [MAX_HOUSES];
        CITYINFO m_rgCities [MAX_CITIES];

        // Pointer to buffer for listing data
        char *m_lpBufPtr;

        // Current file opened
        LPTSTR m_lpstrFile;
        ⋮
}
```

In the MFC version of the sample, I replaced the character arrays that hold textual information with CString instances. This made it very easy to compare strings and get information to and from the dialog boxes. (You'll see this code later in the chapter.) It wasn't so easy, however, to use the C run-time sscanf to get information from the data file. With character arrays (for example, *char szAddress [MAX_ADDRESS]*), sscanf works perfectly; but when you use CStrings, this function does not work. To get around this, I used a character buffer and copied the string from the character buffer into CStrings.

```
// Read the house information for each line.
for (count = 0; count < g_Listing.NumHouses; count++)
{
    result = sscanf (lpBufPtr,
        "%[^,'],%[^,'],%[^,'],%[^,'],%[^,'],%[^,'],%s",
        rgHouses[count].szAddress,
        rgHouses[count].szCity,
        szTemp, szBeds, szBaths,
        rgHouses[count].szAgent,
        rgHouses[count].szNumber);

    rgHouses[count].iPrice = atoi (szTemp);
    rgHouses[count].iBeds = atoi (szBeds);
    rgHouses[count].iBaths = atoi (szBaths);
    ⋮
}
```

Using the Common Dialog Boxes

To support long filenames (and to save some time), I used two of the Windows 95 common dialog boxes to open and save the house-listing information. I was actually able to use some code I had written for the Windows 3.1 common dialog boxes; when I recompiled, the application displayed the new dialog boxes. I had to strip off the filename extension (TXT, in this case) before I set the caption text for the main window. As you can see in Figure 7-3 on the next page, the Open common dialog box has no problem with long filenames, such as *Listing for Puget Sound* or *Another Saved Listing*.

You'll see some differences between the code used to handle common dialog boxes in CHICOAPP and that used in MFCEXP. MFC has built-in support for the File Open and File New functions. The AppWizard tool adds entries to the message map for the application in the main module's CPP file—in this case, MFCEXP.CPP:

```
BEGIN_MESSAGE_MAP (CMfcexpApp, CWinApp)
    // {{AFX_MSG_MAP (CMfcexpApp)
    ON_COMMAND (ID_APP_ABOUT, OnAppAbout)
    // NOTE: ClassWizard will add and remove mapping macros here.
    // DO NOT EDIT what you see in these blocks of generated code!
    // }}AFX_MSG_MAP
    // Standard file-based document commands
    // ON_COMMAND (IDM_NEW, CWinApp::OnFileNew)
    // ON_COMMAND (IDM_OPEN, CWinApp::OnFileOpen)
END_MESSAGE_MAP ()
```

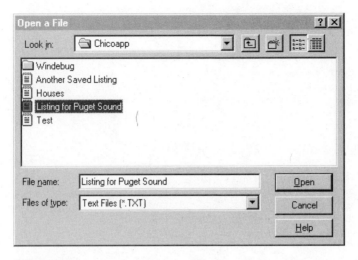

Figure 7-3.
The Open common dialog box used in CHICOAPP.

In my MFCEXP sample, the file input/output commands are handled in the view class. In response to a command to open or save a file, the application calls the common dialog box directly through the CFileDialog class. When creating the class, the application passes initialization information that is used to fill out the OPENFILENAME structure. This structure can be accessed directly through the *m_ofn* member variable:

```
void CMfcexpView::OnOpen ()
{
CFileDialog Dlg (TRUE, "*.txt", m_lpstrFile,
   OFN_HIDEREADONLY | OFN_OVERWRITEPROMPT,
   szFilter);

if (Dlg.DoModal () == IDOK)
{
   HANDLE hFile;
   DWORD dwBytesRead;
   DWORD dwFileSize;

   if ((hFile = CreateFile ((LPCTSTR) Dlg.m_ofn.lpstrFile,
      GENERIC_READ,
      FILE_SHARE_READ,
      NULL,
      OPEN_EXISTING,
      FILE_ATTRIBUTE_NORMAL,
      (HANDLE)NULL)) == (HANDLE)(-1))
```

(continued)

209

```
    {
        AfxMessageBox ("File open failed.");
        return;
    }

    // Get the size of the file.
    dwFileSize = GetFileSize (hFile, NULL);
    if (dwFileSize == 0xFFFFFFFF)
    {
        AfxMessageBox ("GetFileSize failed!");
        return;
    }

    // Allocate a buffer to read the file into.
    m_lpBufPtr = (char *) malloc (dwFileSize);
    if (m_lpBufPtr == NULL)
    {
        AfxMessageBox ("malloc failed!");
        CloseHandle (hFile);
        return;
    }

    // Read the file contents into the buffer.
    ReadFile (hFile, (LPVOID)m_lpBufPtr, dwFileSize, &dwBytesRead, NULL);

    if (dwBytesRead == 0)
    {
        AfxMessageBox ("Zero bytes read.");
        return;
    }

    // Close the file.
    CloseHandle (hFile);

    // Parse the file buffer.
    if (ParseFile ());
    {
        lstrcpy (m_lpstrFile, Dlg.m_ofn.lpstrFileTitle);
        // Reset the title in the title bar.
        GetParentFrame() -> SetWindowText(m_lpstrFile);
        // Redraw the title bar.
        GetParentFrame() -> Invalidate(TRUE);
    }


}
}
```

Handling Notifications

The application uses notifications extensively to manipulate the behavior and the appearance of the controls. Because toolbars, status bars, tree view controls, and list view controls all expect notifications, I had to ensure that each control could get the notifications it needed. In the main window procedure for my C application, I simply trapped the WM_NOTIFY message and either handled the toolbar notifications directly or passed the notifications to the handlers I wrote.

For the toolbar, I was interested only in the TTN_NEEDTEXT notification, which is sent whenever the system needs to display a ToolTip associated with a toolbar button. In response to this notification, the application must load the appropriate text string into the *lpszText* member of the LPTOOLTIP-TEXT structure:

```
case WM_NOTIFY:
    lpToolTipText = (LPTOOLTIPTEXT)lParam;
    if (lpToolTipText->hdr.code == TTN_NEEDTEXT)
    {
      LoadString (g_Listing.hInst,
        lpToolTipText->hdr.idFrom,    // string ID == cmd ID
        szBuf,
        sizeof (szBuf));
      lpToolTipText->lpszText = szBuf;
    }
    :
```

My tree view control has a very simple notification handler that handles only the TVN_SELCHANGED notification (which is sent to the tree view control whenever the selection changes). In response to this notification, I needed to update the list view control and the status bar to reflect the house listings for the newly selected city, as shown here:

```
VOID UpdateListView (HWND hwndLV, int iSelected)
{
int count, index;

// Remove the previous items.
LV_RemoveAllItems (hwndLV);

// Loop through the house listings.
for (index = 0, count = 0; count < g_Listing.NumHouses; count++)
{
    // If the house is listed for the new city...
    if (strcmp (rgHouses[count].szCity, rgCities[iSelected].szCity) == 0)
```

(continued)

211

```
    {
        // Add the house to the list view control.
        if (! LV_AddItem (hwndLV, index, &rgHouses[count]))
            MessageBox (NULL, "LV_AddItem failed!", NULL, MB_OK);
        index++;
    }
  }
}
```

Handling notifications for the list view control is a bit more complicated. I implemented this control using a callback that receives the text for each item, so the notification handler needs to trap the LVN_GETDISPINFO notification and fill in the *pszText* member of the LV_ITEM structure with the appropriate text, depending on the column. This notification handler must also process the LVN_COLUMNCLICK notification, which is sent when the user clicks a column header. In response, the application must sort the items in the list view control based on the criterion specified by the header. For example, if the user clicks the Bedrooms column header, the application sorts the list in ascending order by the number of bedrooms in each house.

I provided a simple callback procedure that is called through the List-View_SortItems function. This procedure then sorts the data using simple math (returning the greater of two values) for columns with integer values and using the strcmp function for columns with string values.

```
LRESULT LV_NotifyHandler (HWND hWnd, UINT uMsg, WPARAM wParam,
    LPARAM lParam, HINSTANCE hInst)
{
LV_DISPINFO *pLvdi = (LV_DISPINFO *)lParam;
NM_LISTVIEW *pNm = (NM_LISTVIEW *)lParam;
HOUSEINFO *pHouse = (HOUSEINFO *) (pLvdi->item.lParam);
static char szText [TEMP_LEN];

if (wParam != ID_LISTVIEW)
    return 0L;

switch(pLvdi->hdr.code)
{
    case LVN_GETDISPINFO:
        switch (pLvdi->item.iSubItem)
        {
            case 0:   // address
                pLvdi->item.pszText = pHouse->szAddress;
                break;
```

```
              case 1:    // city
                 pLvdi->item.pszText = pHouse->szCity;
                 break;

              case 2:    // price
                 sprintf (szText, "$%u", pHouse->iPrice);
                 pLvdi->item.pszText = szText;
                 break;

              case 3:    // number of bedrooms
                 sprintf (szText, "%u", pHouse->iBeds);
                 pLvdi->item.pszText = szText;
                 break;

              case 4:    // number of bathrooms
                 sprintf (szText, "%u", pHouse->iBaths);
                 pLvdi->item.pszText = szText;
                 break;

              default:
                 break;
           }
           break;

     case LVN_COLUMNCLICK:
        // The user clicked a column header; sort by this criterion.
        ListView_SortItems (pNm->hdr.hwndFrom,
           ListViewCompareProc,
           (LPARAM) (pNm->iSubItem));
        break;

     default:
        break;
  }
  return 0L;
}
```

Adding Context Menus

Next I wanted to add a context menu. This requires handling the WM_CON-TEXTMENU message, which is sent when the user clicks the right mouse button in the client window. For instance, when the user right-clicks a list view item (the *wParam* parameter is filled in with the handle of the window that received the right click), a context menu for that item appears.

This task is straightforward. Basically, you load the menu and call Track-PopupMenu, as you would in a 16-bit Windows-based application. When the user chooses an item from the context menu, the appropriate command is generated and sent to the window procedure as a WM_COMMAND message. The following code, from the main window procedure, demonstrates how to handle the WM_CONTEXTMENU message:

```
case WM_CONTEXTMENU:
    // The right mouse button has been clicked.
    if ((HWND)wParam == g_Listing.hWndListView)
    {
        // Get the context menu from the resource file.
        hMenu = LoadMenu (g_Listing.hInst, "HousePopupMenu");
        if (! hMenu)
            break;;

        // Get the first item in the menu for TrackPopupMenu().
        hMenuTrackPopup = GetSubMenu (hMenu, 0);

        // Draw and track the "floating" menu.
        TrackPopupMenu (hMenuTrackPopup,
            TPM_LEFTALIGN | TPM_RIGHTBUTTON,
            LOWORD(lParam), HIWORD(lParam),
            0, g_Listing.hWndListView, NULL);

        // Destroy the menu.
        DestroyMenu (hMenu);
    }
    break;
```

Incorporating a Property Sheet

In this application, I implemented a property sheet with two property sheet pages. One allows the user to view and change the properties for a particular house listing (for example, the address and the city); the other displays information about the listing agent (for example, the agent's name and phone number), which the user can also change. Figure 7-4 shows the House Listing property sheet page.

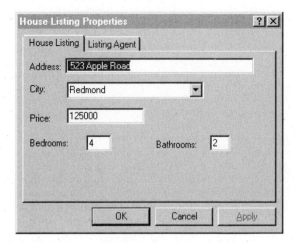

Figure 7-4.
The House Listing property sheet page.

Processing a property sheet page is similar to processing a dialog box, with one major difference: when you process a property sheet page, you handle notifications instead of the commands generated for the OK and Cancel buttons. I could process my property sheet pages as follows:

- Save the original values for the house or agent in response to the WM_INITDIALOG message.

- Reset the values for the house or agent in response to the PSN_APPLY and PSN_KILLACTIVE notifications.

- Reset the values for the house or agent in response to a PSN_RESET notification.

- In response to the PSN_SETACTIVE notification, set the edit fields in the page for the item.

To initialize the property sheet pages, I had to determine which house was currently selected and save that information for future reference. The House Listing page is displayed first. Responding to the WM_INITDIALOG message offers the first chance to determine the currently selected house. I used the code on the following page to determine the index of the selected house within my global array of houses.

```
char szTemp [MAX_ADDRESS];
static char szAddSave [MAX_ADDRESS];
static char szCitySave [MAX_CITY];
static int iPrice, iBeds, iBaths;
BOOL bErr;
int index, count;
LV_ITEM lvItem;
    ⋮
    case WM_INITDIALOG:
        // Fill in the list box with the cities.
        for (index = 0; index < g_Listing.NumCities; index++)
            SendDlgItemMessage (hDlg, IDE_CITY, CB_INSERTSTRING,
                (WPARAM)(-1), (LPARAM)(rgCities[index].szCity));

        // Get the index to the selected list view item.
        index = ListView_GetNextItem (g_Listing.hWndListView,
            -1, MAKELPARAM (LVNI_SELECTED, 0));

        // Get the house address.
        lvItem.iItem = index;
        lvItem.iSubItem = 0;
        lvItem.mask = LVIF_TEXT;
        lvItem.cchTextMax = sizeof (szAddSave);
        lvItem.pszText = szAddSave;
        ListView_GetItem (g_Listing.hWndListView,&lvItem);

        // Find the house in the list.
        for (count = 0; count < g_Listing.NumHouses; count++)
        {
            if (strcmp (lvItem.pszText, rgHouses[count].szAddress) == 0)
                break;
        }
        g_Listing.iSelHouse = count;
        ⋮
```

My other property sheet page, Listing Agent, allows the user to view and change the name and phone number of the listing agent associated with the selected house. I used similar code to handle this page, except that I modified the *szAgent* and *szNumber* members of the HOUSEINFO structure instead of altering the other house-specific fields. Figure 7-5 shows the Listing Agent property sheet page.

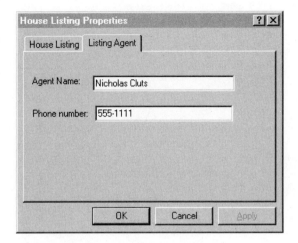

Figure 7-5.
The Listing Agent property sheet page.

Creating a Property Sheet in MFC

For the MFC-based sample, I decided to use the built-in classes CProperty-Sheet and CPropertyPage, which require considerably less code than I had to implement in the C version of the sample. The property sheet is displayed in response to the House Properties command.

```
void CMfcexpView::OnProperties ()
{
if (m_iSelected == -1)
    return;

// Create a property sheet object.
CPropertySheet dlgPropertySheet ("House Properties", this);
CHouse dlgHouse;
CAgent dlgAgent;
int index, count;
LV_ITEM lvItem;
char szAddSave [MAX_ADDRESS];

dlgPropertySheet.AddPage (&dlgHouse);
dlgPropertySheet.AddPage (&dlgAgent);
```

(continued)

217

```
// Fill in the list box with the cities.
for (index = 0; index < m_NumCities; index++)
   SendDlgItemMessage (IDC_CITY, CB_ADDSTRING, 0,
      (LPARAM) (LPCTSTR) m_rgCities[index].szCity);

// Get the index to the selected list view item.
index = m_ListCtl.GetNextItem (-1, LVNI_SELECTED);

// Get the house address.
lvItem.iItem = index;
lvItem.iSubItem = 0;
lvItem.mask = LVIF_TEXT;
lvItem.cchTextMax = sizeof (szAddSave);
lvItem.pszText = szAddSave;
m_ListCtl.GetItem (&lvItem);

// Find the house in the list.
for (count = 0; count < m_NumHouses; count++)
{
   if (strcmp (lvItem.pszText, m_rgHouses[count].szAddress) == 0)
      break;
}
m_iSelHouse = count;

dlgHouse.m_Address = m_rgHouses[m_iSelHouse].szAddress;
dlgHouse.m_City = m_rgHouses[m_iSelHouse].szCity;
dlgHouse.m_Price = m_rgHouses[m_iSelHouse].iPrice;
dlgHouse.m_Bedrooms = m_rgHouses[m_iSelHouse].iBeds ;
dlgHouse.m_Bathrooms = m_rgHouses[m_iSelHouse].iBaths;

dlgAgent.m_AgentName = m_rgHouses[m_iSelHouse].szAgent;
dlgAgent.m_PhoneNumber = m_rgHouses[m_iSelHouse].szNumber;

if (dlgPropertySheet.DoModal () == IDOK)
{
   m_rgHouses[m_iSelHouse].szAddress = dlgHouse.m_Address;
   m_rgHouses[m_iSelHouse].szCity = dlgHouse.m_City;
   m_rgHouses[m_iSelHouse].iPrice = dlgHouse.m_Price;
   m_rgHouses[m_iSelHouse].iBeds = dlgHouse.m_Bedrooms;
   m_rgHouses[m_iSelHouse].iBaths = dlgHouse.m_Bathrooms;

   m_rgHouses[m_iSelHouse].szAgent = dlgAgent.m_AgentName;
   m_rgHouses[m_iSelHouse].szNumber = dlgAgent.m_PhoneNumber;

   GetDocument() -> SetModifiedFlag();
   GetDocument() -> UpdateAllViews(NULL);
}
}
```

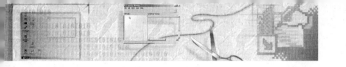

PART II

USING THE NEW USER INTERFACE FEATURES

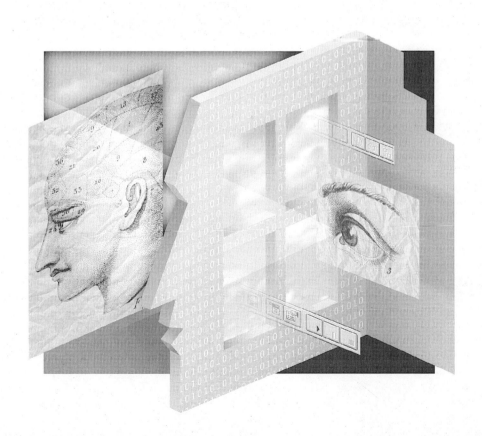

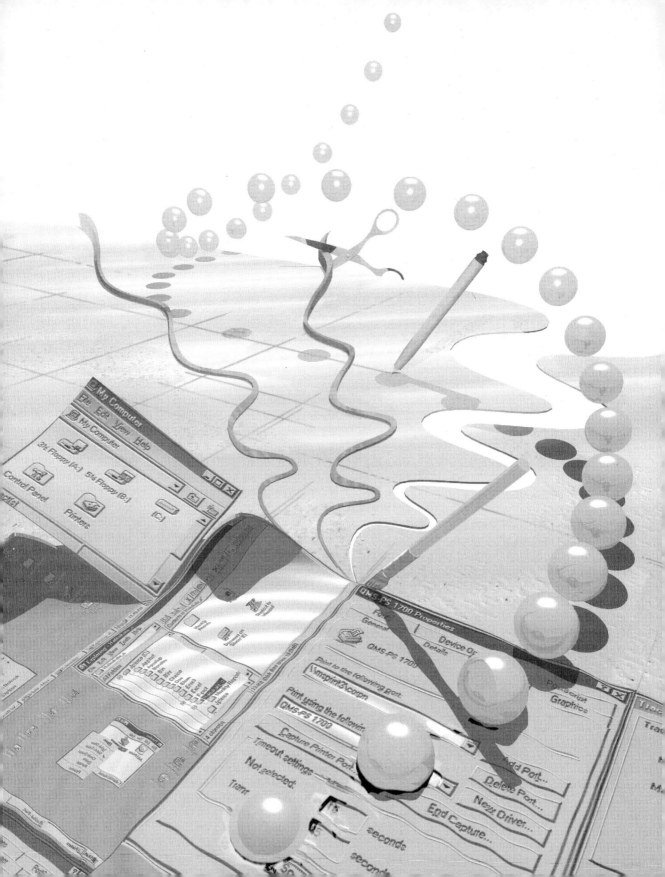

Support for Long Filenames

Until recently, if you wanted to create and name a file in a Windows-based application, you were limited to a filename of only eight characters, plus a three-character extension. As a result, your directories were filled with cryptically named files such as STKREPT.XLS and STAT794.DOC. Microsoft Windows NT version 3.1 was the first system to remove this limitation; now Microsoft Windows 95 brings the power of long filenames to the masses. This chapter covers the file systems that Win32 supports and explains how you, as a developer, can support long filenames in your applications.

STK4Q94.XLS?

The limitations on the length and content of filenames in previous versions of Windows have understandably been a source of much grumbling among application developers and end users alike. How many times have you had to save a file with a name such as STK4Q94.XLS or STJUL94.DOC when you wanted to use a more informative description such as *Stock Report Analysis 4Q 1994* or *Monthly Status Report for July 1994*? The good news is that the most recent Microsoft operating systems (Windows NT and Windows 95) will let you use those descriptive filenames. If you are using the Win32 API to develop applications for these systems, you will be able to support long filenames for your end users.

Is Your System FAT?

Applications rely on file systems to store and retrieve information from mass storage devices. File systems organize data on hard disks and (sometimes) on floppy disks. Your file system gives you the ability to create and access files and directories on the individual volumes (disks) associated with the devices in an application. Depending on the configuration of a computer, a Win32-based application might have access to volumes managed by any of the following file systems:

- File allocation table (FAT) file system
- Protected-mode FAT file system (VFAT, short for virtual FAT)
- High-performance file system (HPFS)
- Windows NT file system (NTFS)

The FAT File System

The FAT file system organizes data on both hard disks and floppy disks. If you have a FAT file system running on your computer, you have no doubt slammed up against its filename convention, lovingly referred to as *8.3* (pronounced "eight-dot-three"). This convention requires that a filename consist of no more than eight characters, followed by a separating period (.) and a filename extension of no more than three characters.

The main advantage of FAT volumes is that they can be accessed by MS-DOS, Microsoft Windows, and OS/2 systems. The FAT file system is currently supported on floppy disks and other removable media. The major disadvantages of FAT volumes are the limitations on the length and content of filenames and the lack of Unicode support. (Unicode is a character-encoding standard used worldwide, which helps to simplify the localization process.)

Valid FAT filenames have the following form:

[*drive:*] [*directory*] *filename*[*.extension*]

drive, which must be followed by a colon (:), specifies the name of an existing drive. It can be any letter from A through Z.

directory specifies which directory contains the file. It is separated from the filename by a backslash (\), and it must be either the full path, including the root directory, or the relative path from the current directory. A directory name contains no more than eight characters (and can have an optional three-character extension, preceded by a period) using any combination of letters, digits, and the following special characters:

$ % ' - _ @ {} ~ ` ! # ( )

filename consists of no more than eight letters, digits, and special characters. It can include embedded spaces if each space is preceded and followed by one or more legal characters. For example, the string *disk 1* is a legal filename. Bear in mind, however, that although a space is a valid character in the FAT file system, many applications do not support spaces in filenames, so it's not a good idea to include them. Furthermore, FAT volumes do not distinguish between uppercase and lowercase letters; the filenames ALPHABET.DOC and alphabet.doc refer to the same file.

extension consists of no more than a total of three letters, digits, and special characters. It is preceded by a period.

The Protected-Mode FAT File System (VFAT)

Like the FAT file system, the VFAT file system used in Windows 95 organizes data on both hard disks and floppy disks. Because it is compatible with the FAT file system, using file allocation tables and directory entries to store information about the contents of a disk, you do not need to reformat your disk structure when you install Windows 95. VFAT supports long filenames by storing the names and other information, such as the date and time each file was last accessed, in extended FAT structures.

In the VFAT system, a filename can contain as many as 255 characters, including a terminating null character. VFAT allows pathnames of as many as 260 characters, including the terminating null. Remember that the pathname contains the full filename; if your filename is 255 characters, only 4 characters are left for the path. (The last character is the terminating null.)

The VFAT file system supports dual name spaces—that is, it keeps track of both short (8.3) and long filenames—so that it can work with older applications that allow only short names as well as newer applications that permit long names. When you run an older application with a VFAT file system, you will see the 8.3 filename.

When an application creates a file, the API that is used (Win32 or Win16) determines whether long filenames are supported. Using the Win32 CreateFile function sets up a file with both a long filename and an associated 8.3 "alias." An 8.3 alias is generated for every long filename, and the file can be accessed by either name. Your application can use the GetShortName function to get the alias. The alias is based on the long filename and on the directory in which the file resides. If you change a long filename or copy the file to a different directory, the alias might change. The alias is created using the following basic algorithm:

1. Select the first eight characters (not including any embedded spaces) of the long filename.

2. If there is an extension, select its first three characters (not including any embedded spaces) and its preceding dot.

223

3. Convert letters to uppercase.

4. Convert to underscores (_) any characters that are illegal under the FAT file system.

5. If the resulting name already exists in the same directory, replace the last two characters with a tilde (~) and a unique integer— NEWREP~2, for instance. (Even if the resulting name is unique, replace the last two characters if the long filename has embedded spaces or illegal characters.)

An interesting side effect of filename aliasing occurs when you use the FindFirstFile and FindNextFile functions. Windows 95 checks for both the long filename and the alias, for compatibility reasons. If, for instance, you search for a file using the pattern *1, you might find a file named *Whatcha-macallit*, whose alias is WHATCH~1. To determine the name that actually caused the match, you can check both the *cFileName* and *cAlternateFileName* members of the WIN32_FIND_DATA structure.

The High-Performance File System (HPFS)

HPFS organizes data on hard disks but not on floppy disks (that is, you cannot format a floppy disk to use HPFS). In many cases, accessing files under HPFS is faster than accessing similar files under the FAT file system.

HPFS allows filenames containing as many as 254 characters, including a terminating null. The names can include characters that are not valid for the FAT file system, such as periods. You can use spaces anywhere in an HPFS filename or directory name, but the system ignores spaces and periods at the end of filenames—that is, the filenames *Test 1* and *Test 1.* are treated as if they were the same filename. You can use the following special characters in HPFS filenames:

, + = [] ; _

HPFS filenames do not require extensions, although many applications still create and use them. An HPFS filename can be all uppercase, all lowercase, or mixed-case. The case is preserved for directory listings but ignored in file searches and all other system operations. Therefore, a given directory cannot contain more than one file with the same name when the only difference is case.

The Windows NT File System (NTFS)

Like HPFS, NTFS organizes data on hard disks but not on floppy disks. NTFS supports object-oriented applications by treating files as objects with user-defined and system-defined attributes. It provides all the capabilities of the FAT and HPFS file systems without many of their limitations.

NTFS is also a fully recoverable file system, designed to restore consistency to a disk after a CPU failure, a system crash, or an I/O error. If you crash your NTFS volume, chances are that you will be able to recover your data. NTFS allows the operating system to recover without requiring you to use the *autochk* or *chkdsk* command, which saves a lot of time when you must reboot after a system failure. Have you ever crashed an HPFS volume and then had to sit and wait while *chkdsk* ran on your 1-gigabyte drive? I hope you brought a book to pass the time. (NTFS does provide *chkdsk* and *autochk* in case the recovery fails or corruption occurs outside the control of the file system.)

NTFS includes features not available in FAT or HPFS, such as security, Unicode filenames, automatic creation of MS-DOS aliases, multiple data streams, and unique functionality specific to the POSIX subsystem (a collection of international standards for UNIX-style operating system interfaces). NTFS follows the HPFS filename conventions described in the preceding section, but it also supports Unicode filenames, implemented internally in Windows NT. NTFS cannot manipulate a file's extended attributes if the file was created in HPFS.

NTFS supports filenames with as many as 256 characters, including a terminating null. In most cases, it also generates an MS-DOS–compatible filename in 8.3 format that allows an application based on MS-DOS or 16-bit Windows to access the same file. (When the NTFS directory name or filename contains spaces and fewer than eight characters, NTFS does not create an 8.3 filename.) To translate a long filename into an 8.3 filename, NTFS uses the following guidelines:

■ Deletes any illegal characters and any spaces from the long filename. The following are illegal characters:

. " / \ [] : ; = ,

■ Removes additional periods from the filename if valid, nonspace characters follow the final period. For example,

This is a really long filename.123.456.789.TXT

becomes

THISIS~1.TXT

■ Ignores a final period and retains the second-to-last period. For example,

This is a really long filename.123.456.789.

becomes

THISIS~1.789

■ Truncates the filename, if necessary, to six characters and appends a tilde and a numeral. Each unique filename created ends with *~1*, while duplicate filenames end with *~2*, *~3*, and so on.

■ Truncates the filename extension to three or fewer characters.

■ Converts all letters in the filename and extension to uppercase.

NOTE: If you're working with an application based on MS-DOS or Windows 3.*x*, you might occasionally need to save a file from that application on an NTFS volume. If the application saves to a temporary file, deletes the original file, and renames the temporary file to the original filename, the long filename will be lost. You will also lose any unique permissions set on that file, although you can reset the permissions from the parent directory.

Long Filenames and Novell NetWare

Versions of Novell NetWare earlier than 3.12 can support long filenames, but the servers require that you enable Macintosh or OS/2 (HPFS) name spaces to do so. This is costly in terms of RAM on the server, and you must use NetWare-specific name space APIs to access the long filenames.

The good news is that if you write a Win32 application using the Win32 file system calls, you can check to see whether a given volume supports long filenames and can use the long names without worrying about the server system. The Microsoft-developed Windows 95 client for NetWare will use the OS/2 name space, when available, to store filenames containing as many as 254 characters (including the terminating null) and will make the Win32 API available. If you are running the real-mode Novell client, or if the server has not been enabled for long filenames, you can use only 8.3 filenames.

Determining Which File System Is in Use

To determine under which file system your application is currently running, the application calls the GetVolumeInformation function. This function returns information about the current volume, such as the maximum length of filenames. Once you call this function, you can use the value returned in the *lpMaximumComponentLength* parameter as the maximum file length in your application and dynamically allocate a buffer for your filenames and paths. This is preferable to using static buffers for filenames and paths. If you must use static buffers, however, reserve at least 256 characters for filenames and 260 characters for paths.

Here is the syntax for the GetVolumeInformation function:

```
BOOL GetVolumeInformation (
    LPCTSTR lpRootPathName,
    LPTSTR lpVolumeNameBuffer,
    DWORD nVolumeNameSize,
    LPDWORD lpVolumeSerialNumber,
    LPDWORD lpMaximumComponentLength,
    LPDWORD lpFileSystemFlags,
    LPTSTR lpFileSystemNameBuffer,
    DWORD nFileSystemNameSize)
```

lpRootPathName points to a string containing the root directory of the volume to be queried. If this parameter is NULL, the root of the current directory is used.

lpVolumeNameBuffer points to a buffer that is filled in with the name of the volume. This parameter can be NULL if the volume name is not needed.

nVolumeNameSize is the length, in characters, of the volume name buffer. This parameter is ignored if the volume name buffer is not supplied.

lpVolumeSerialNumber points to a variable that is filled in with the volume serial number. This parameter can be NULL if the volume serial number is not needed.

lpMaximumComponentLength points to a variable that is filled in with the maximum length, in characters, of a filename component (the part of the filename between the backslashes) supported by the specified file system.

lpFileSystemFlags points to a variable that is filled in with flags associated with the specified file system. This variable can contain any combination of flags, such as FS_CASE_SENSITIVE, which specifies that the file system supports case-sensitive filename lookup. For a description of all the flags, see the Win32 SDK documentation.

lpFileSystemNameBuffer points to a buffer that is filled in with the name of the file system (such as FAT, HPFS, or NTFS). This parameter can be NULL if the system name is not needed.

nFileSystemNameSize is the length, in characters, of the file system name buffer. This parameter is ignored if the name buffer is not supplied.

General Guidelines for Supporting Long Filenames

The following general guidelines for working with long filenames apply to all file systems supported by the various Windows systems. An application that follows these guidelines can create valid names for files and directories regardless of the file system in use.

- You can include any character from the current code page in a name, but do not use a path separator, a character in the ASCII range 0 through 31, or any character disallowed by the specific file system. A name can contain characters from the extended character set (ASCII 128 through 255).

- Use the backslash (\), the forward slash (/), or both to separate components in a path.

- Use a period (.) to represent the current directory in a path.

- Use two consecutive periods (..) to represent the parent of the current directory in a path.

- Separate components in a directory name or in a filename with a period (.).

- The following characters are reserved for Windows and should not be used in directory names or filenames:

     < > : " / \ |

- Do not use reserved words, such as *aux, con,* and *prn,* as filenames or directory names.

- The application should process a path as a null-terminated string. The maximum length for a path is given by MAX_PATH. The Unicode versions of the CreateDirectory, FindFirstFile, GetFile-Attributes, and SetFileAttributes functions allow paths to exceed the

MAX_PATH length if the path has the \\?\ or \\?\UNC\ prefix. These prefixes turn off path parsing. Use the \\?\ prefix with paths for local storage devices and the \\?\UNC\ prefix with paths having the Universal Naming Convention (UNC) format. An example of a UNC path is *machine**sharename.*

▓ Do not assume case sensitivity, because not all file systems distinguish case. For example, under NTFS, the filenames FILENAME and Filename are considered to be the names of two different files; under HPFS, however, these two filenames are considered to be the same, although the file system preserves the case as entered and allows the user to see mixed-case filenames.

Outdated Assumptions

Since Windows has resided on FAT-only volumes for so long, developers have grown used to making some understandable assumptions based on the 8.3 convention. But times have changed. If you are planning to support long filenames in your applications, you would be wise to examine your code for these common assumptions.

Assumption: The filename extension contains no more than 3 characters.

I make this assumption most often when I am trying to filter files based on the file extension (the file type) or when I am stripping off the file extension. The assumption is true in the FAT file system, but if you are running under VFAT, HPFS, or NTFS, you can best determine the maximum length by a call to Get-VolumeInformation.

Assumption: The filename contains no more than 12 characters.

If your operating system supports long filenames, 12-character buffers might not have enough space for all the characters in the filename. Consider the following code snippet, in which the buffer is assumed to be 12 characters long:

```
char szFile [12] = "\0";

// Fill out the OPENFILENAME structure to support a template and a hook.
OpenFileName.lStructSize     = sizeof (OPENFILENAME);
OpenFileName.hwndOwner       = hWnd;
OpenFileName.hInstance       = g_hInst;
```

(continued)

229

```
OpenFileName.lpstrFilter        = NULL;
OpenFileName.lpstrCustomFilter  = NULL;
OpenFileName.nMaxCustFilter     = 0;
OpenFileName.nFilterIndex       = 0;
OpenFileName.lpstrFile          = szFile;
OpenFileName.nMaxFile           = sizeof (szFile);
OpenFileName.lpstrFileTitle     = NULL;
OpenFileName.nMaxFileTitle      = 0;
OpenFileName.lpstrInitialDir    = NULL;
OpenFileName.lpstrTitle         = "Open a File";
OpenFileName.nFileOffset        = 0;
OpenFileName.nFileExtension     = 0;
OpenFileName.lpstrDefExt        = NULL;
OpenFileName.lCustData          = NULL;
OpenFileName.lpfnHook           = ComDlg32DlgProc;
OpenFileName.lpTemplateName     = MAKEINTRESOURCE (IDD_COMDLG32);
OpenFileName.Flags              = OFN_SHOWHELP | OFN_EXPLORER |
                                  OFN_ENABLEHOOK | OFN_ENABLETEMPLATE;

// Call the common dialog function.
if (GetOpenFileName (&OpenFileName))
{
   ⋮
}
else
{
    ProcessCDError (CommDlgExtendedError (), hWnd);
    return FALSE;
}
```

If the user enters a filename that contains more than 12 characters, the Open common dialog procedure returns an error of FNERR_BUFFERTOO-SMALL, saving you from a nasty trap. But the buffer size is not the only problem. If you are doing your own file parsing, and if you accept only the first 12 characters in a filename, you could open the wrong file. For instance, imagine that a user enters the filename *Marketing Report* and that the current directory contains files named *Marketing Report* and *Marketing Salaries*. If your application accepts only the first 8 characters of a filename and assumes an extension, which file will the application open?

Assumption: A filename contains only one period.

The FAT file system allows only one period in a filename, as a delimiter. In that case, you know that the three characters following the period are the file extension. Under file systems that support long filenames, however, this is not true. What happens if your application scans a filename looking for a period in order to find the file extension? Here's a bit of code from one of my samples that (unfortunately) relies on this assumption:

```
// Strip off the extension, if any.
if (pDot = strstr (szLink, "."))
   *pDot = (char)NULL;

// Add in the LNK extension.
lstrcat (szLink, ".LNK");
```

Had there been more than one period in the filename, my code would have failed to create a file of the correct type. A better way to get the name of the file, without the file extension, is to use a string function that returns the pointer to the extension by checking the string from the reverse:

```
if (pDot = strrchr (szLink, '.'))
   *pDot = (char)NULL;

lstrcat (szLink, ".LNK");
```

Assumption: Filenames do not contain spaces.

In the FAT file system, a filename can include spaces, as long as each space is preceded and followed by a nonspace character. This is not the case in the VFAT file system. You can now have a filename such as *This One Has Lots   Of Spaces* , which includes several spaces between characters and a trailing space character.

Assumption: The plus sign (+) character is invalid in a filename.

Under the systems that support long filenames, you can include a plus sign (+) in a filename. So if I wanted to be romantic, and if I had a file containing information about me and my husband, I could name it *Nancy + Jonathan.*

User Interface Considerations

You now have the basics for supporting long filenames internally in your applications. But what about the application's user interface? The following sections discuss some further considerations to bear in mind as you design the interface.

Hiding File Extensions

Windows 95 interface components such as Windows Explorer strip off the file extension by default when displaying the name of a file. (You can set an option to display the MS-DOS file extensions.) If you run Windows Explorer in details view, you will see a file "type," but this is not necessarily the file extension. For example, in the Type column for a Microsoft Word file, you'll see the more explanatory phrase *Microsoft Word Document* rather than the DOC extension.

An application can get the filename to display (that is, the filename with the extension stripped off) through various methods, such as the SHGetFile-Info function. This function provides an easy way to get the attributes of a file, given the full path. SHGetFileInfo uses a structure called SHFILEINFO that contains the handle to the icon, the index to the icon, the file attributes, the display name (or the path for a folder), and the file type. Table 8-1 lists the flags that you can specify when calling SHGetFileInfo.

Flag	Description
SHGFI_ICON	Retrieves the icon associated with the file.
SHGFI_DISPLAYNAME	Retrieves the file's display name.
SHGFI_TYPENAME	Retrieves the file's type name.
SHGFI_ATTRIBUTES	Retrieves the attributes of the file.
SHGFI_ICONLOCATION	Retrieves the icon location.
SHGFI_EXETYPE	Retrieves the executable type of the file.
SHGFI_SYSICONINDEX	Retrieves the system icon index.
SHGFI_LINKOVERLAY	Places a link overlay on the icon.
SHGFI_SELECTED	Displays the icon in selected state.
SHGFI_LARGEICON	Retrieves the large icon.
SHGFI_SMALLICON	Retrieves the small icon.
SHGFI_OPENICON	Retrieves the open icon.
SHGFI_SHELLICONSIZE	Retrieves the icon size used by the shell.
SHGFI_PIDL	The path specified in the *pszPath* parameter is a pointer to an ITEMID list.
SHGFI_USEFILEATTRIBUTES	The file attributes passed in the *dwFile-Attributes* parameter should be used.

Table 8-1.
File information flags.

Although generally you should not display file extensions, they are nevertheless useful to the application programmer. An application designer can use unique file extensions to differentiate his or her files from other files in the system. So feel free to employ them—but don't show them to the user unless you must.

Adjusting the Width of Edit Fields

You need to ensure that you allocate enough space to accommodate long filenames in your edit fields, list boxes, and static text strings. In the old-style Open and Save As common dialog boxes (in 16-bit Windows), for instance, the field for entering a filename isn't really all that large, as you can see in Figure 8-1. If a filename is fairly long, the user has to scroll horizontally to see the entire name—a task that is even more frustrating without a horizontal scroll bar. Not viewing the complete name can also cause the user to confuse similar filenames.

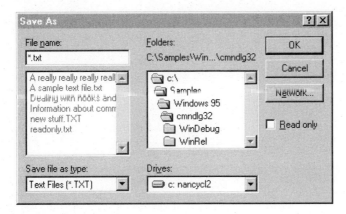

Figure 8-1.
The old-style (16-bit Windows) Save As common dialog box.

The design of the new common dialog boxes for opening and saving files (in 32-bit Windows) improves the situation. Notice in Figure 8-2 on the following page that the edit box in which current filename and path information is entered or displayed has been expanded to let the user see more of the filename without scrolling.

233

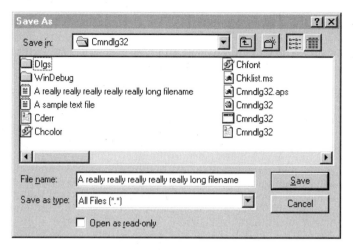

Figure 8-2.
The new (32-bit Windows) Save As common dialog box.

In short, take a look at the dialog boxes in your applications and be sure to update the width of edit boxes to allow for longer filenames. Of course, if you use only the common dialog boxes, you don't have to worry about this because the common dialog library takes care of it.

An alternative to providing new dialog boxes to support longer file-names is to use only nonbold fonts (which require less space) in your edit boxes. You'll find that allowing enough room for 30 to 40 characters in a non-bold font is adequate for most purposes.

CHAPTER NINE

Shortcuts

Shortcuts are one of the handiest features of the Microsoft Windows 95 user interface. Keeping shortcuts on your desktop makes it quick and easy to access the items that you use most often—a specific document, a favorite application, or a printer, for instance.

A shortcut is a convenient way to reference an object in the shell name space (the hierarchical structure of objects in the user interface) without having to keep track of the object's actual name and location. Figure 9-1, for example, shows the icon that appears on the desktop when you create a shortcut to the Paint program in Windows 95. (Notice the small arrow in the lower left corner of the icon, which designates a shortcut.) Double-clicking this icon activates Paint.

Paint

Figure 9-1.
A shortcut to Paint.

A user can create a shortcut to an object by using the object's context menu or by using the File menu in Windows Explorer. You can also provide shortcuts programmatically, as part of your applications. You can set up shortcuts to many different kinds of objects, including files, folders, Control Panel, printers, and various applications.

Once a shortcut exists, the user no longer needs to know the object's name and location. Double-clicking the shortcut to a file, for instance, simply activates the file (the default action for that file). That is, if the user has a shortcut to a Microsoft Word document on the desktop, double-clicking the shortcut opens Word with the file specified as the current working document.

If you set up a shortcut to a printer and then change the printer's network location, the shortcut continues to work. End users will still be able to print to that printer using the shortcut and will never know that the server has changed, because the location is transparent to them.

Shortcuts are also useful in installation or setup programs. For example, the setup could place a shortcut to your release notes or to a README file on the desktop. This makes it easy for the user to browse through the information, and it's also more likely that the user will actually read the file instead of simply ignoring it. You could also provide a shortcut in a multiple document interface (MDI) application to help the user keep track of the last document opened. The user could subsequently click that shortcut at any time to run your application again in the context of that document.

Users can create shortcuts of their own and place them on the desktop. After finding the object that is the target of the shortcut, a user can set up a shortcut in any of these three ways:

- Use the right mouse button to drag the object to the desktop and drop it there. A context menu will pop up. Click Create Shortcut on the context menu, and the shortcut icon will appear on the desktop.

- Right-click the object to display the context menu (shown in Figure 9-2), and then click Create Shortcut. When the shortcut icon appears, drag it to the desktop and drop it there.

- Select the object, and then click Create Shortcut on the File menu in Windows Explorer (shown in Figure 9-3). When the shortcut icon appears, drag it to the desktop and drop it there.

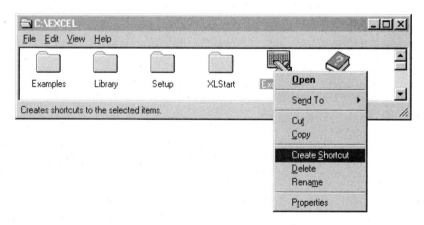

Figure 9-2.
The Create Shortcut item on a context menu.

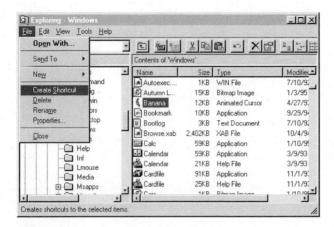

Figure 9-3.
The Create Shortcut item on the File menu.

> N O T E: If you create a shortcut to another shortcut, the system
> simply copies the shortcut—it does not create a new shortcut. Do
> not assume that shortcuts remain independent of one another.

How Shortcuts Are Implemented

Shortcuts are implemented through an OLE interface called IShellLink. If
you plan to create or manipulate shortcuts programmatically, it will be helpful to be familiar with some of the basic concepts of OLE, although you don't
need to be an OLE guru. To understand and use shortcuts, the most important topic to read up on is the Component Object Model. Reading the first
two chapters of *Inside OLE,* 2d edition, by Kraig Brockschmidt (Microsoft
Press, 1995), should give you sufficient background. For now, however, here
is a very brief overview of the Component Object Model.

The Component Object Model

The Component Object Model is a specification that describes the process
of communicating through interfaces, acquiring access to various interfaces
through the QueryInterface member function, determining pointer lifetime
through reference counting, and reusing objects by extending them. An object, in this context, is an item in the system that exposes interfaces (groups of
related functions) to manipulate the data or properties of the object. It is

created directly or indirectly by calling the CoCreateInstance function, which creates a new instance of the object and returns a pointer to an interface for the object.

When two objects within the system want to communicate with each other, one object calls member functions in the other object's interface by using a pointer to the interface. The call to CoCreateInstance returns this interface pointer. For instance, two objects might want to communicate with each other during a drag-and-drop operation. If one object is to be dropped on another object, the first one calls into the other's interface to request acceptance of the drop.

All interfaces used in the Component Object Model—including IShellLink, the one used to manipulate shortcuts—are derived from the base interface, IUnknown. All interfaces support three base member functions:

- QueryInterface, which determines whether a specific interface is supported for the object, increments the reference count, and returns a pointer to the interface.

- AddRef, which increments the reference count on an interface.

- Release, which decrements the reference count on an interface. Once an interface's reference count goes to 0, the object deletes itself, and the pointers to its interfaces are no longer valid. (If the reference count on all an object's interfaces is 0, the object can be freed because there are no longer any pointers to the object.)

An application that manipulates shortcuts must initialize the component object library with a call to CoInitialize or OleInitialize. When I created the SHORTCUT sample, I put this call in my InitInstance handler before calling any other functions. Each call to CoInitialize must be balanced with a call to CoUninitialize. CoUninitialize should be called when an application shuts down, because it ensures that the application won't quit until it has received all its pending messages. I normally put the call to CoUninitialize in the ExitInstance handler.

SHORTCUT: A Sample
That Manipulates Shortcuts

SHORTCUT is a simple MFC-based application in which the user can create a shortcut for a file selected from the current directory. When the user chooses the Create Shortcut menu item, the dialog box shown in Figure 9-4 displays a list of the files in the current directory. I filled the list box with file options by using a call to DlgDirList in my handler for the WM_INITDIALOG message, OnInitDialog. To create a shortcut to a text file named README, for example, the user would choose README.TXT from the list.

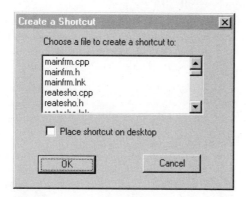

Figure 9-4.
The Create A Shortcut dialog box in the SHORTCUT sample.

The user indicates whether the shortcut should appear on the desktop by checking the Place Shortcut On Desktop option in the dialog box. After the user selects a file from the list and clicks the OK button, the application checks to determine whether the shortcut should be located on the desktop or in the current directory. If it should be placed on the desktop, the shortcut's default location is in a subdirectory (called DESKTOP) of the directory that contains Windows 95. For example, if your installation of Windows 95 is in the C:\WINDOWS directory, the shortcut file is placed in C:\WINDOWS\DESKTOP. This subdirectory is hidden; you can find it by opening an MS-DOS command prompt and typing *attrib desktop* or by going into your Windows installation directory and typing *dir desktop*.

If your system is configured to use a different profile per user, the location of the shortcut is different. You can set up a different profile per user by using the Passwords application in Control Panel. Open Passwords, click the User Profiles tab, and then check the Include Desktop Icons And Network Neighborhood Contents In User Settings option. This stores the desktop icons (and your desktop shortcut) in the Registry's Desktop subdirectory under HKEY_CURRENT_USER\Software\Microsoft\Windows\CurrentVersion\-Explorer\Shell Folders. The Desktop key will contain the fully qualified path to the icons. (Refer to Chapter 10 for a discussion of the Registry and its keys.) For example, if I set up my computer to support per-user profiles, the Desktop key will be located under C:\WINDOWS\PROFILES\NANCYCL\-DESKTOP. (The SHORTCUT sample does not support per-user profiles, so in this case all shortcuts targeted to the desktop are placed in the DESKTOP subfolder of the Windows 95 installation directory.)

The shortcut name is completed by retrieving the selected file through a call to DlgDirSelect, stripping off the filename extension, and replacing it with the LNK extension. All shortcuts have the LNK extension.

Then it's time to get down to the real work of creating the shortcut. The CreateShortCut::CreateIt function actually performs the task. It takes three parameters:

- *pszShortcutFile* is the file that the shortcut will point to.

- *pszLink* is the shortcut you are creating with a LNK extension.

- *pszDesc* is the description of the file. This is the string "Shortcut to *filename*", where *filename* is the name of the shortcut target.

Because this function makes a call to CoCreateInstance, it is assumed that CoInitialize has already been called. As you can see in the following code, this function uses both the IPersistFile interface, for actually saving the shortcut in the system, and the IShellLink interface, for storing the path and the description of the shortcut target:

```
HRESULT CreateShortCut::CreateIt (LPCSTR pszShortcutFile, LPSTR pszLink,
    LPSTR pszDesc)
{
HRESULT hres;
IShellLink *psl;

// Create an IShellLink object and get a pointer to the IShellLink
// interface (returned from CoCreateInstance).
hres = CoCreateInstance (CLSID_ShellLink, NULL, CLSCTX_INPROC_SERVER,
    IID_IShellLink, (void **)&psl);
if (SUCCEEDED (hres))
{
    IPersistFile *ppf;

    // Query IShellLink for the IPersistFile interface for
    // saving the shortcut in persistent storage.
    hres = psl->QueryInterface (IID_IPersistFile, (void **)&ppf);
    if (SUCCEEDED (hres))
    {
        WORD wsz [MAX_PATH];    // buffer for Unicode string
```

```
        // Set the path to the shortcut target.
        hres = psl->SetPath (pszShortcutFile);

        if (! SUCCEEDED (hres))
           AfxMessageBox ("SetPath failed!");

        // Set the description of the shortcut.
        hres = psl->SetDescription (pszDesc);

        if (! SUCCEEDED (hres))
           AfxMessageBox ("SetDescription failed!");

        // Ensure that the string consists of ANSI characters.
        MultiByteToWideChar (CP_ACP, 0, pszLink, -1, wsz, MAX_PATH);

        // Save the shortcut via the IPersistFile::Save member function.
        hres = ppf->Save (wsz, TRUE);

        if (! SUCCEEDED (hres))
           AfxMessageBox ("Save failed!");

        // Release the pointer to IPersistFile.
        ppf->Release ();
     }
     // Release the pointer to IShellLink.
     psl->Release ();
   }
   return hres;
}
```

Once you have created the shortcut, you might need to access and manipulate it programmatically. This is referred to as *resolving* the shortcut. I added a function to my sample that demonstrates how you can resolve a shortcut. I used the same type of dialog box that I used for creating the shortcut—and used almost exactly the same code to fill the dialog box with the names of the files in the current directory and prompt the user to choose a shortcut to resolve. The only difference was a simple check to ensure that the user actually picked a LNK file:

```
void ResolveShortCut::OnOK ()
{
char szFile [MAX_PATH];

// Get the selected item in the list box.
DlgDirSelect (szFile, IDC_LIST1);
```

(continued)

```
// Find out whether it is a LNK file.
if (strstr (szFile, ".lnk") != NULL)
    // Make the call to ResolveShortcut::ResolveIt here.
    ResolveIt (m_hWnd, szFile);

CDialog::OnOK ();
}
```

The ResolveShortCut::ResolveIt function resolves the shortcut. This function takes two parameters:

- *hwnd* is the handle to the window that currently has the focus. This is used in case the user must be prompted to take an action. For instance, a message box is displayed if the user needs to insert a floppy disk, if the shortcut is on unshared media, or if network problems arise during the resolution of the shortcut.

- *pszShortcutFile* is the fully qualified path to the shortcut.

Like the function that created the shortcut, this function calls CoCreate-Instance and assumes that CoInitialize has already been called. Notice that the following code needs to call into the IPersistFile interface. The IShellLink object implements this interface to store shortcut information. To get the path information requested later in the code, the shortcut information must be loaded first. Failing to load the shortcut information causes the calls to GetPath and GetDescription to fail.

```
HRESULT ResolveShortCut::ResolveIt (HWND hwnd, LPCSTR pszShortcutFile)
{
HRESULT hres;
IShellLink *psl;
char szGotPath [MAX_PATH];
char szDescription [MAX_PATH];
WIN32_FIND_DATA wfd;

// Get a pointer to the IShellLink interface.
hres = CoCreateInstance (CLSID_ShellLink, NULL, CLSCTX_INPROC_SERVER,
    IID_IShellLink, (void **)&psl);
if (SUCCEEDED (hres))
{
    IPersistFile *ppf;
```

```
// Get a pointer to the IPersistFile interface.
hres = psl->QueryInterface (IID_IPersistFile, (void **)&ppf);

if (SUCCEEDED (hres))
{
    WORD wsz [MAX_PATH];   // buffer for Unicode string

    // Ensure that the string consists of Unicode characters.
    MultiByteToWideChar (CP_ACP, 0, pszShortcutFile, -1, wsz,
        MAX_PATH);

    // Load the shortcut.
    hres = ppf->Load (wsz, STGM_READ);

    if (SUCCEEDED (hres))
    {
        // Resolve the shortcut.
        hres = psl->Resolve (hwnd, SLR_ANY_MATCH);
        if (SUCCEEDED (hres))
        {
            strcpy (szGotPath, pszShortcutFile);
            // Get the path to the shortcut target.
            hres = psl->GetPath (szGotPath, MAX_PATH,
                (WIN32_FIND_DATA *)&wfd, SLGP_SHORTPATH);
            if (! SUCCEEDED (hres))
                AfxMessageBox ("GetPath failed!");
            else
                AfxMessageBox (szGotPath);
            // Get the description of the target.
            hres = psl->GetDescription (szDescription, MAX_PATH);
            if (! SUCCEEDED (hres))
                AfxMessageBox ("GetDescription failed!");
            else
                AfxMessageBox (szDescription);
        }
    }
    // Release the pointer to IPersistFile.
    ppf->Release ();
}
// Release the pointer to IShellLink.
psl->Release ();
}
return hres;
}
```

Creating a Shortcut to an Object Other Than a File

The sample code demonstrates how to programmatically create a shortcut to a file, but it does not cover the steps you must take to create a shortcut to an object that does not have a filename, such as Control Panel or a printer. The major difference is that rather than setting the path to the shortcut, you will instead be setting the identification list (ID list) to the object. You do this by calling IShellLink::SetIDList and providing a pointer to an ID list.

You might well be thinking, "What the heck is an ID list?" Within the shell name space, each object that Windows Explorer can browse (such as files, folders, servers, and workgroups) has an identifier that is unique among the objects in its parent folder. These identifiers, referred to as *item IDs,* are stored as SHITEMID structures (defined in the SHLOBJ.H file). Each parent folder also has its own item ID. Therefore, any object can be uniquely identified by a list of item IDs, corresponding to the way a file can be uniquely identified by its path. Such a list of items, called an *ID list,* is defined as the ITEMIDLIST structure in SHLOBJ.H. It is important to remember that each item ID in an ID list is meaningful only in the context of the parent folder. (You'll find more information about ID lists in Chapter 14.)

> NOTE: If you plan to use the CreateIt function from the SHORT-CUT sample in your MFC-based application, you might run into problems with the conversion from multibyte to wide characters. If you do, take a look at "Technical Note 49: MFC/OLE MBCS to Unicode Translation Layer (MFCANS32)," available in the MSDN Development Library under Technical Articles, Visual C++ 2.0 (32-bit) Articles, MFC 3.1 Technical Notes. The MFCANS32 DLL provides ANSI interfaces to 32-bit OLE, which is primarily Unicode. This technical note will show you what you need to do if you experience this problem. You can also find helpful information on this topic in the Microsoft Visual C++ documentation.

IShellLink Details

The IShellLink interface provides a group of member functions that an application can access to provide shortcuts within the application. This section describes each function in detail, including syntax, parameters, and a description of the return value and any special uses for the function.

IShellLink::QueryInterface

Syntax:

QueryInterface (REFIID *riid*, LPVOID FAR **ppvObj*);

Parameters:

■ *riid* is the identifier of the interface requested. To access the IShellLink interface, this parameter should be *IID_IShellLink*.

■ *ppvObj* is the pointer to the variable that receives the interface. This parameter is filled in with a pointer to the IShellLink interface. The returned pointer can then be used to access the other member functions provided by IShellLink.

Description: Returns a pointer to the requested interface (IShellLink, in this case) if the interface is supported. Otherwise, it returns an error. Once this pointer is retrieved, the application can use it to gain access to the other member functions provided for the interface.

IShellLink::AddRef

Syntax:

ULONG AddRef (void);

Parameters: None.

Description: Increments a reference count for each new copy of an IShellLink interface pointer. The return value is the value of the reference count. Many applications use this value for testing or diagnostic purposes. The reference count is decremented when the Release member function is called.

IShellLink::Release

Syntax:

ULONG Release ();

Parameters: None.

Description: Decrements the reference count on the IShellLink interface. When the reference count reaches 0, the shortcut object is deleted and the pointer to the object becomes invalid. This member function returns the current reference count on the IShellLink object.

IShellLink::GetPath

Syntax:

GetPath (LPSTR *pszFile,* int *cchMaxPath,* WIN32_FIND_DATA **pfd,*
    DWORD *fFlags);*

Parameters:

- *pszFile* is a pointer to a text buffer that receives the path.

- *cchMaxPath* is the maximum number of characters for the path.

- *pfd* is a pointer to a structure containing information about the shortcut object.

- *fFlags* consists of the flags specifying the type of path information to retrieve.

Description: Gets the current fully qualified path for the shortcut object. The string containing the path is copied into the *pszFile* parameter. The *pfd* parameter is a pointer to a WIN32_FIND_DATA structure. This is the same information that is returned when making a call to FindFirstFile and FindNextFile, and it includes the file's attributes, creation time, and so on. The *fFlags* parameter can be set to SLGP_UNCPRIORITY to obtain the Universal Naming Convention (UNC) path to the file.

IShellLink::SetPath

Syntax:

SetPath (LPCSTR *pszFile);*

Parameter:

▪ *pszFile* is a pointer to a text buffer containing the new path for the shortcut object.

Description: Sets the current path of the shortcut object to the path specified by the *pszFile* parameter. For example, when an application creates a shortcut to a text file, STUFF.TXT, that resides in the C:\STUFF directory, the string passed to SetPath is *C:\STUFF\STUFF.TXT*.

IShellLink::GetIDList

Syntax:

GetIDList (LPCITEMIDLIST *ppidl*);

Parameter:

▪ *ppidl* is a pointer to an ID list.

Description: Gets the current ID list for the shortcut object.

IShellLink::SetIDList

Syntax:

SetIDList (LPCITEMIDLIST *pidl*);

Parameter:

▪ *pidl* is a pointer to an ID list.

Description: Sets the ID list for the shortcut object. This is useful when an application needs to set a shortcut to an object that isn't a file, such as Control Panel, another computer, or a printer.

IShellLink::GetDescription

Syntax:

GetDescription (LPSTR *pszName*, int *cchMaxName*);

Parameters:

▓ *pszName* is a pointer to a text buffer that receives the description.

▓ *cchMaxName* is the maximum number of characters that can be used in the description.

Description: Gets the description of the shortcut object. The description string is copied into the buffer to which the *pszName* parameter points.

IShellLink::SetDescription

Syntax:

SetDescription (LPCSTR *pszName*);

Parameter:

▓ *pszName* is a pointer to a text buffer containing the new description.

Description: Sets the description for the shortcut object to the text provided in the *pszName* parameter. The description can be anything the application chooses to provide. The description used by the SHORTCUT sample is simply "Shortcut to *filename*".

IShellLink::GetWorkingDirectory

Syntax:

GetWorkingDirectory (LPSTR *pszDir*, int *cchMaxPath*);

Parameters:

- *pszDir* is a text buffer that receives the working directory.

- *cchMaxPath* is the maximum number of characters for the working directory.

Description: Gets the current working directory for the shortcut object. The working directory is copied into the string to which the *pszDir* parameter points. If the working directory is larger than the buffer provided, the string is truncated.

IShellLink::SetWorkingDirectory

Syntax:

SetWorkingDirectory (LPCSTR *pszDir*);

Parameter:

- *pszDir* is a pointer to a text buffer that contains the new working directory.

Description: Sets the current working directory for the shortcut object to the path pointed to by the *pszDir* parameter. The working directory of the object needs to be set only if the shortcut object requires it. For example, if your application created a shortcut to a Microsoft Word document that used a template or another object that resided in a special directory, your application could use this member function to set the working directory.

IShellLink::GetArguments

Syntax:

GetArguments (LPSTR *pszArgs*, int *cchMaxPath*);

Parameters:

- ▨ *pszArgs* is a pointer to a text buffer that receives the arguments.

- ▨ *cchMaxPath* is the maximum number of characters that can be used for the arguments.

Description: Gets the current arguments that are associated with the short-cut object.

IShellLink::SetArguments

Syntax:

SetArguments (LPCSTR *pszArgs*);

Parameter:

- ▨ *pszArgs* is a pointer to a text buffer containing the new arguments.

Description: Sets the arguments for the shortcut object. This is useful when you need to create a shortcut to an application that takes special flags as arguments, such as a compiler.

IShellLink::GetHotkey

Syntax:

GetHotkey (WORD **pwHotkey*);

Parameter:

- ▨ *pwHotkey* is a pointer to a WORD to receive the hot key.

Description: Gets the hot key for the shortcut object.

IShellLink::SetHotkey

Syntax:

SetHotkey (WORD *wHotkey*);

Parameter:

■ *wHotkey* is a pointer to the hot key.

Description: Sets the hot key for the shortcut object. This allows you to specify that your shortcut is activated whenever the corresponding hot key is pressed. For example, you could set up a shortcut to a utility that backs up a specific directory when the user presses a key combination such as Alt-B.

IShellLink::GetShowCmd

Syntax:

GetShowCmd (int **piShowCmd*);

Parameter:

■ *piShowCmd* is a pointer to an integer to receive the Show command.

Description: Gets the Show command for the shortcut object.

IShellLink::SetShowCmd

Syntax:

SetShowCmd (int *iShowCmd*);

Parameter:

■ *iShowCmd* is the Show command to set.

Description: Sets the Show command for the shortcut object. The Show command is the show state of the window and can be one of the following:

SW_HIDE	Hides the window.
SW_MINIMIZE	Minimizes the window.
SW_RESTORE	Activates and displays the window, restoring it to its original size and position if it has been previously maximized or minimized.
SW_SHOW	Activates the window in its current size and position.
SW_SHOWMAXIMIZED	Activates and maximizes the window.
SW_SHOWMINIMIZED	Activates and minimizes the window.
SW_SHOWNA	Shows the window in its current state but does not activate it.
SW_SHOWNOACTIVE	Shows the window in its most recent size and position but does not activate it.
SW_SHOWNORMAL	Activates and displays the window. This style also includes the SW_RESTORE option and will restore the window to its original size and position.

IShellLink::GetIconLocation

Syntax:

GetIconLocation (LPSTR *pszIconPath*, int *cchIconPath*, int **piIcon*);

Parameters:

- *pszIconPath* is a pointer to a text buffer that receives the icon location.

- *cchIconPath* is the maximum number of characters in the icon location.

- *piIcon* is a pointer to the icon.

Description: Gets the icon location for the shortcut object.

IShellLink::SetIconLocation

Syntax:

SetIconLocation (LPCSTR *pszIconPath*, int *iIcon*);

Parameters:

▓ *pszIconPath* is a pointer to a text buffer containing the new icon location.

▓ *iIcon* is an index to the icon.

Description: Sets the location for the shortcut icon. Use this member function if you want to change the icon for the shortcut object.

IShellLink::Resolve

Syntax:

Resolve (HWND *hwnd*, UINT *fFlags*);

Parameters:

▓ *hwnd* is the handle to a window.

▓ *fFlags* consists of the flags that direct the system in resolving the shortcut.

Description: Resolves a shortcut. The system searches for the shortcut object and updates the shortcut path and its ID list, if necessary. If the system needs to display a dialog box asking the user for more information, it uses the handle to the window passed in the *hwnd* parameter as the parent window of the dialog box. The supported flags for this member function are listed on the following page.

SLR_NO_UI — Directs the system not to display a dialog box if it cannot resolve the shortcut.

SLR_UPDATE — When the Resolve member function is called, the system marks a shortcut as "dirty" if the object the shortcut points to has been changed (perhaps its location or size has changed, for instance). This flag directs the system to save the shortcut if the shortcut object has changed. The developer is thus saved the step of calling IPersistFile::Is-Dirty to determine whether the shortcut has changed.

Preserving Shortcuts

The Windows 95 user interface automatically attempts to resolve shortcuts whose targets have been renamed or moved. When you create a shortcut, the system saves information about the shortcut. Most of this information is the same as that found in the WIN32_FIND_DATA structure (file attributes, creation time, last access time, last write time, and file size). When the IShell-Link::Resolve member function is called, the system gets the path associated with the current shortcut by using a pointer to its ID list. The system then searches for the shortcut object in that path and resolves the shortcut if it finds the object.

If it does not find the shortcut object, the system then looks in the same directory for an object that has the same file creation time and file attributes but a different name. This will resolve a shortcut to an object that has been renamed.

If it still does not find the shortcut object, the system next searches the subdirectories of the current directory, recursively searching the directory tree for a match with either the filename or the creation time. If it does not find a match, it displays a dialog box that prompts the user for a location (a browse button). An application can suppress the dialog box by specifying the SLR_NO_UI flag when it calls the IShellLink::Resolve member function.

CHAPTER TEN

The Registry

Creating file viewers, using interface extensions, and working with the Microsoft Windows 95 user interface in other advanced ways all involve (at least to some degree) storing and accessing information in the centralized registration database called the Registry. Clearly, you as a developer will need to both use and understand the Registry. This chapter focuses on the Registry, with specific emphasis on how it applies to Windows 95 and how you can use it to integrate your applications with the new user interface.

What Is the Registry?

The Registry is a centralized, system-defined database in which applications and Windows system components store configuration data. In the past, applications based on Microsoft Windows 3.1 stored such information in the WIN.INI file or some other application-defined INI file, while the system stored its configuration data in SYSTEM.INI. Because this information was stored in ASCII files, a user could edit and view it in any simple text editor, such as Notepad. In the new Registry, the data is stored in binary files. Instead of using text editors to update the information contained in the Registry, applications can either use the Registry functions supplied by the system or create registration (REG) files that contain information to be stored in the Registry. These REG files are ASCII files that can be created with any text editor. The Registry Editor (REGEDIT) can read these files and store the information in the appropriate places in the Registry.

Why the change from easy-to-use ASCII files to more complex binary files? In the past, Windows-based applications used the GetProfileInt, GetProfileSection, GetProfileString, WriteProfileSection, and WriteProfileString functions to store information in the WIN.INI file. As more and more applications were written for Windows, however, problems with this method became apparent.

One big problem was the scope of the WIN.INI file. Each application was storing information in this file, and no rules governed what could be added or where it could be located. Data was placed in WIN.INI in no particular order. When the file was opened, it was hard to find or change an item. It was also difficult to determine exactly what needed to be changed and whether all the necessary changes had been made. In addition, INI files in Windows were limited in size to 64 KB, so if the file became too large, you were just out of luck.

One recommended solution was to have applications store their information in private INI files rather than in WIN.INI by using the GetPrivate-ProfileInt, GetPrivateProfileString, and WritePrivateProfileString functions. This got around the size issue and the potential confusion over which application uses what, but it didn't prove to be such a great plan. Because applications used different files, they were unable to share configuration information and other data easily. This caused problems for applications that were using dynamic data exchange (DDE) or OLE, because these applications need to share server names.

As a result, the registration database was created for version 3.1 of Windows. This database is the basis of the Registry now implemented in both Microsoft Windows NT and Windows 95.

The Structure of the Registry

The Registry stores data in a tree with a hierarchical structure. The tool that allows you to view, edit, and manage the Registry is called the Registry Editor, shown in Figure 10-1. The main screen of the Registry Editor displays the structured tree in—what else?—a tree view control. The data elements shown in Figure 10-1 are known as *keys* (HKEY_CLASSES_ROOT, HKEY_CURRENT-_USER, and so on). Each key can contain children, which are known as *subkeys*. (In Figure 10-1, Display is a subkey of HKEY_CURRENT_CONFIG, while Fonts and Settings are subkeys of the Display key.) Data entries are called *values* (BitsPerPixel, DPILogicalX, and so on). Each value consists of a value name and its associated data (if any).

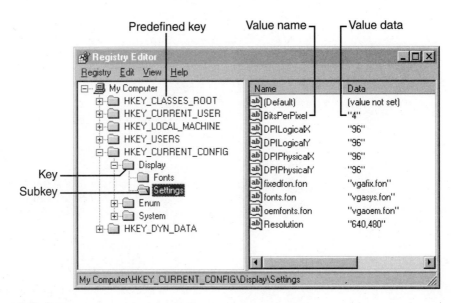

Figure 10-1.
The Registry Editor.

Keys don't necessarily have values associated with them. Sometimes, an application simply needs to know that a key exists; at other times, the application might need to associate many values with a specific key (as shown in Figure 10-1). A key can have any number of values associated with it, and the values can be in any form.

Just like dogs, keys have names. A key name consists of one or more printable ANSI characters (values in the range 32 through 127) and cannot include spaces, backslashes, or wildcard characters (* and ?). Key names beginning with a period (.) are reserved. This means that you can name both your dog and your key *Spot* if you so desire. These names are not localized into other languages, although values associated with the keys can be localized. Subkeys also have names. The name of a subkey must be unique with respect to the key immediately above it in the hierarchy.

The Registry supports several different data types for values, described in Table 10-1 on the following page. Your application can use any of these data types, depending on what you want to store.

Data Type	Description
REG_BINARY	Binary data in any form.
REG_DWORD	A 32-bit number.
REG_DWORD_BIG_ENDIAN	A 32-bit number in big-endian format (in which the most significant byte of a word is the low-order byte).
REG_DWORD_LITTLE_ENDIAN	A 32-bit number in little-endian format (same as REG_DWORD). Little-endian format (in which the most significant byte of a word is the high-order byte) is the most common format for computers running Windows NT.
REG_EXPAND_SZ	A null-terminated string containing unexpanded references to environment variables (for example, *%PATH%*). This value is a Unicode string or an ANSI string, depending on whether you use the Unicode functions or the ANSI functions. The Registry always stores strings internally as Unicode strings.
REG_LINK	A Unicode symbolic link.
REG_MULTI_SZ	An array of null-terminated strings, terminated by two null characters.
REG_NONE	No defined value type.
REG_RESOURCE_LIST	A device-driver resource list.
REG_SZ	A null-terminated string. This value is a Unicode string or an ANSI string, depending on whether you use the Unicode functions or the ANSI functions.

Table 10-1.
Data types for Registry values.

Predefined Keys

Predefined keys, which are defined by the system, help an application navigate in the Registry. You can also use them to develop tools that allow a system administrator to change whole categories of data. The following keys are defined at the root of the Registry:

- HKEY_CLASSES_ROOT

- HKEY_CURRENT_USER

- HKEY_LOCAL_MACHINE

- HKEY_USERS

- HKEY_CURRENT_CONFIG

- HKEY_DYN_DATA

These predefined keys are entry points to the Registry, and they are always open. This means that a developer does not have to call RegOpenKey first in order to work with the predefined keys. These keys are valid Registry handles for all Win32 implementations of the Registry, although use of the handles can vary from platform to platform.

HKEY_CLASSES_ROOT

In this key, the Registry entries define types (or classes) of documents and the properties associated with those types. Both conventional applications and OLE applications use data that is stored under this key. This key also provides backward compatibility with the Windows 3.1 registration database by storing information for DDE and OLE support. File viewers and user interface extensions store their OLE class identifiers in HKEY_CLASSES_ROOT, and in-process servers are registered in this key. (You'll find more information about in-process servers and how they work with file viewers and user interface extensions in Chapters 12 and 13.)

HKEY_CURRENT_USER

Current user preferences are stored in this key, including the settings of environment variables and data about program groups, colors, printers, network connections, and application preferences. This key makes it easier to establish the current user's settings; the key maps to the current user's branch in HKEY_USERS. In HKEY_CURRENT_USER, software vendors store the current user-specific preferences to be used within their applications. Microsoft, for example, creates the HKEY_CURRENT_USER\Software\Microsoft key for its applications to use, with each application creating its own subkey under the Microsoft key.

HKEY_LOCAL_MACHINE

Entries in this key describe the physical state of the computer, including data about the bus type, system memory, and installed hardware and software. HKEY_LOCAL_MACHINE contains subkeys that hold current configuration data, including Plug and Play information (the Enum branch, which includes a complete list of all hardware that has ever been on the system), network logon preferences, network security information, software-related information (such as server names and the location of the server), and other system information.

HKEY_USERS

This key stores information about the default user configuration and contains a branch for each user of the computer. The default configuration is supplied for new users on the local computer and for the default current user if the user hasn't changed preferences. Because Windows 95 also supports HKEY_CURRENT_USER, applications can access the user-specific information the same way they do under Windows NT. Each user's information is stored in a separate file, which can be stored locally or on a network server. Windows 95 can copy this file to the user's current system so that settings can move from one computer to another with the user.

HKEY_CURRENT_CONFIG

The HKEY_CURRENT_CONFIG key, which is mapped to a subkey within HKEY_LOCAL_MACHINE, stores non–user-specific configuration information that pertains to hardware. For example, an application can store a different server name for its data depending on whether the system is attached to a network.

HKEY_DYN_DATA

This key is used to store dynamic Registry data. The Windows 95 Registry supports both static data (which is stored on disk in the Registry) and dynamic data (which changes frequently, such as performance statistics). This dynamic data area is the mechanism that allows VxDs to provide real-time data to Win32 applications that can run remotely as well as locally. It also allows the system monitor to provide performance statistics on remote Windows 95 systems. VxDs are not limited to performance data. They can provide any data they want to pass from Ring 0 to Ring 3 efficiently without hogging the CPU. The Registry supports dynamic data by storing a pointer to a function that returns a value (or many values). When a Registry call queries values associated with a dynamic key, that function is called to return the desired value(s).

> **N O T E :** Dynamic keys have been introduced in Microsoft Windows 95 to handle dynamic Registry data. They are supported only in Windows 95.

Updating the Registry

It's not enough to know what is in the Registry; you'll also want to know how to store and retrieve information. You can access data in the Registry in any of these three ways:

- Use the built-in tools (the Registry Editor and Control Panel)
- Use the Win32 API
- Use registration files

Using Built-In Tools

The Registry Editor is a tool that lets you change settings in the Registry. If you are like me, you will like the Registry Editor so much that you will keep a shortcut to it on your desktop. (No, I'm not kidding.) If you are like other, not-so-masochistic people, you will take a look at it and shut it down fast.

In most cases, users can change system settings through Control Panel, without going into the Registry Editor. Actually, end users should never edit the Registry unless it is absolutely necessary. If you were to introduce an error into your Registry, the computer could become nonfunctional. It is true that the Registry can be restored, but let's face it—if you were to hose your whole system by playing with the Registry, would you want to go back in?

But if you are writing your own application and need to add settings to the Registry or make other Registry adjustments, Control Panel won't do the dirty work for you. Once you open the Registry Editor, you can use the menus to add keys and values. You can also import or export Registry data.

Using the Win32 API

The Win32 API provides a set of functions to access data stored in the Registry. Before it can add data to the Registry, an application must create or open a key. An application always refers to the key as a subkey of a currently open key, using the RegOpenKey or RegOpenKeyEx function to open a key and the RegCreateKey or RegCreateKeyEx function to create a key.

The RegCloseKey function closes a key and writes the data it contains into the Registry. The data cannot be written to the Registry before the function returns because it might take several seconds for the cache to be flushed to the hard disk. If the data must be written to the hard disk immediately, the application can use the RegFlushKey function. (Because this function uses many system resources, you should call it only when absolutely necessary.)

Using Registration Files

You can also use a registration file to import data into the system Registry. REG files are ASCII files that contain information about what values and keys should be added to the Registry and where to add the data. The following code shows the contents of a REG file that establishes the display settings shown in Figure 10-1 on page 257. I created this REG file by selecting the HKEY_CURRENT_CONFIG\Display\Settings key and choosing the Export Registry File item from the Registry menu:

```
REGEDIT4

[HKEY_CURRENT_CONFIG\Display\Settings]
"fonts.fon" = "vgasys.fon"
"fixedfon.fon" = "vgafix.fon"
"oemfonts.fon" = "vgaoem.fon"
"DPILogicalX" = "96"
"DPILogicalY" = "96"
"DPIPhysicalX" = "96"
"DPIPhysicalY" = "96"
"BitsPerPixel" = "4"
"Resolution" = "640,480"
```

If you have worked with REG files under Windows 3.1 or Windows NT, you will notice that the syntax here differs slightly. The first entry in the REG file is the word *REGEDIT4,* which specifies that the syntax of the file should follow the Windows 95 convention. This file will add the values specified (*fonts.fon, fixedfon.fon,* and so on) under the HKEY_CURRENT_CONFIG\-Display\Settings key. More details describing exactly how to create registration files can be found in the Win32 SDK documentation.

Differences Between the Windows 95 and Windows NT Registries

Because of certain system variances and differing design goals in Microsoft Windows 95 and Microsoft Windows NT, some features of the Windows NT Registry are not supported by Windows 95. The Windows 95 Registry is compatible with the Window NT Registry, but it has a completely different implementation.

The Windows 95 Registry differs from the Windows NT Registry in the following ways:

- The Windows 95 Registry has no security attributes and is therefore not secure.

- The Windows 95 Registry does not replace CONFIG.SYS, AUTO-EXEC.BAT, WIN.INI, or SYSTEM.INI files or Program Manager groups, although it does replace some information from these files through Plug and Play support. Older programs can still use the old-style configuration and initialization files.

- The Windows 95 Registry does not support the mapping of INI file functions (or the INI files themselves) into the Registry.

- The Windows 95 Registry layout is different from the Windows NT Registry layout.

Registry Functions in Windows 95

Windows 95 supports all the Win16 and Win32 Registry functions. Some Win32 functions return errors when called from Windows 95, however, just as some Win32 functions return errors when called from Win32s, as a result of system differences. Table 10-2 on the following page lists the Registry functions that Windows 95 supports, including numerous Win16 functions that are provided for compatibility with Windows 3.1.

Function	Description
RegCloseKey (Win16)	Closes the specified key.
RegCreateKey (Win16)	Creates the specified key. (Win32-based applications should use the RegCreateKeyEx function.)
RegDeleteKey (Win16)	Deletes the specified key.
RegEnumKey (Win16)	Enumerates the subkeys of the specified open key. (Win32-based applications should use the RegEnumKeyEx function.)
RegOpenKey (Win16)	Opens the specified key. (Win32-based applications should use the RegOpenKeyEx function.)
RegQueryValue (Win16)	Returns the value associated with the specified open key. (Win32-based applications should use the RegQueryValueEx function.)
RegSetValue (Win16)	Sets the value for the specified key. (Win32-based applications should use the RegSetValueEx function.)
RegCreateKeyEx (Win32)	Creates a key.
RegDeleteValue (Win32)	Deletes a value associated with the specified key.
RegEnumKeyEx (Win32)	Enumerates the subkeys of the specified open key.
RegEnumValue (Win32)	Enumerates the values of the specified open key.
RegFlushKey (Win32)	Writes all the attributes of the specified open key to the Registry.
RegOpenKeyEx (Win32)	Opens the specified key.
RegQueryInfoKey (Win32)	Returns information about the specified key.
RegQueryValueEx (Win32)	Returns the value associated with the specified open key.
RegSetValueEx (Win32)	Sets the value for the specified key.

Table 10-2.
Registry functions supported in Windows 95.

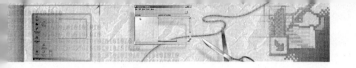

C H A P T E R   E L E V E N

The User Interface Library

Using the features of SHELL32.DLL, the user interface dynamic-link library, is an easy way to extend the functionality of the Microsoft Windows 95 user interface. SHELL32.DLL provides functions that allow your application to implement drag-and-drop operations, to gather information from the system about other applications and files, and to use some of the interface's special widgets such as taskbar notifications and access bars. (The user interface and its features are sometimes referred to collectively as the *shell*.)

This chapter discusses the programming techniques necessary to use the functions included in SHELL32.DLL. To illustrate some of what you can do with these functions, I created a small sample named SHELLFUN, which demonstrates the following functionality:

- Drag and drop
- The SHGetFileInfo function
- The ability to add, remove, and modify items in the taskbar notification area
- The ability to add, remove, and reposition an access bar

When you access SHELL32.DLL, you must use the SHELLAPI.H header file. You need to include this file at the beginning of your application in order to use this library's functions and messages.

Drag and Drop

The drag-and-drop functions in SHELL32.DLL allow an application to register itself with the system for drag-and-drop notifications, to query information about the file or files dropped, and to permit or prevent a drop. Before

265

an application can process a drop, it must register itself with the system by using the DragAcceptFiles function. In SHELLFUN, this happens in the processing of the WM_CREATE message for the main window:

```
case WM_CREATE:
    // Indicate that drag and drop is OK.
    DragAcceptFiles (hWnd, TRUE);
```

After making this call, the application receives notification of a drop in the form of the WM_DROPFILES message. In the *wParam* parameter of the message, the system packages a handle to a structure containing information about the drop object. Using this handle, the application can query information such as the number of files dropped, the filename(s), and the location of the drop. To query the number of files being dropped, you can pass a special value (−1) to the DragQueryFile function in the second parameter. The application can get the name of the file being dropped by subsequent calls to DragQueryFile, with the second parameter specifying the index to the file. The drop operation is completed with a call to DragFinish.

In the SHELLFUN sample, I allow only one file to be dropped at a time. The dropped file is opened and read into a data buffer, to be displayed in a multiline edit control.

```
case WM_DROPFILES:
{
    // A file is being dropped.
    int iFiles;
    char lpszFile [MAX_PATH];
    HDROP hDropInfo = (HANDLE)wParam;

    // Get the number of files.
    iFiles = DragQueryFile (hDropInfo, (DWORD)(-1), (LPSTR)NULL, 0);

    if (iFiles != 1)
        MessageBox (hWnd, "One file at a time, please.", NULL, MB_OK);

    else
    {
        HANDLE hFile;
        DWORD dwFileSize, dwBytesRead;
        char *lpBufPtr;

        DragQueryFile (hDropInfo, 0, lpszFile, sizeof (lpszFile));
        // Open the file.
        if ((hFile = CreateFile (lpszFile,
            GENERIC_READ,
            FILE_SHARE_READ,
            NULL,
```

```
            OPEN_EXISTING,
            FILE_ATTRIBUTE_NORMAL,
            (HANDLE)NULL)) == (HANDLE)(-1))
    {
        MessageBox (hWnd, "File open failed.", NULL, MB_OK);
        break;
    }

    // Get the size of the file.
    dwFileSize = GetFileSize (hFile, NULL);
    if (dwFileSize == 0xFFFFFFFF)
    {
        MessageBox (NULL, "GetFileSize failed!", NULL, MB_OK);
        break;
    }

    // Allocate a buffer to read the file into.
    lpBufPtr = (char *) malloc (dwFileSize);
    if (lpBufPtr == NULL)
    {
        MessageBox (NULL, "malloc failed!", NULL, MB_OK);
        CloseHandle (hFile);
        break;
    }

    // Read the file contents into the buffer.
    ReadFile (hFile, (LPVOID)lpBufPtr, dwFileSize, &dwBytesRead,
        NULL);

    if (dwBytesRead == 0)
    {
        MessageBox (hWnd, "Zero bytes read.", NULL, MB_OK);
        break;
    }

    // Update the multiline edit control with the file contents.
    SendMessage (hwndEdit, WM_SETTEXT, 0, (LPARAM)lpBufPtr);

    // Close the file.
    CloseHandle (hFile);

    free (lpBufPtr);
}

// Signal that the drag-and-drop operation is over.
DragFinish (hDropInfo);

break;
}
```

Figure 11-1 shows the result of dragging a file named *A Sample Text File* and dropping it in the SHELLFUN window. Because the SHELLFUN sample simply reads the file into a buffer and does no processing, it's easiest to do this with a text file. (You can drop a binary file, but it'll look funny.)

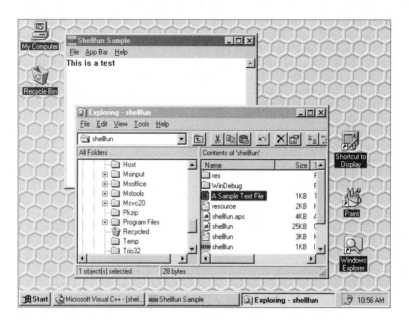

Figure 11-1.
The result of a drag-and-drop operation in the SHELLFUN sample.

When the application no longer needs to support drag and drop, it must unregister itself by using the DragAcceptFiles function as follows:

```
DragAcceptFiles (hWnd, FALSE);
```

To determine where a file is being dropped, the application can use another drag-and-drop function, DragQueryPoint. The DragQueryPoint function returns the drop point, and the application can then draw the item at that point, as you can see here:

```
// A file is being dropped.
POINT pt;
int idx;
char lpszFile [MAX_PATH];
HDC hDC;
```

```
// Find out where the drop is.
DragQueryPoint (hDropInfo, &pt);

// Get a DC.
hDC = GetDC (hWnd);

// For each file dropped, write its name out to the client.
for (idx = 0;
    DragQueryFile (hDropInfo, idx, lpszFile, sizeof (lpszFile));
    pt.y += 20, idx++)
    TextOut (hWnd, pt.x, pt.y, lpszFile, sizeof (lpszFile));

// Signal that the drag-and-drop operation is over.
DragFinish (hDropInfo);

// Release the DC.
ReleaseDC (hDC, hWnd);
```

> **NOTE:** What you've just seen is a message-based (Windows 3.1) method of using the drag-and-drop functions in the user interface library. A new, alternative method uses OLE to perform drag-and-drop operations. The message-based method is fine for simple drag-and-drop tasks, whereas the OLE method is far richer and allows more complex operations. This book does not cover the OLE-based method in detail, although Chapter 14 contains a sample that shows how to implement the IDropSource interface for drag and drop. (See "Supporting Drag and Drop," page 355.) For more information about drag and drop using OLE, you can refer to the Win32 SDK, the Microsoft Visual C++ 2 documentation, and *Inside OLE,* 2d edition, by Kraig Brockschmidt (Microsoft Press, 1995).

Retrieving File Information

Assuming that you want to learn a little bit about the files being dropped in your application, you'll appreciate the SHELL32.DLL functions that execute a file, get the name and the handle of an executable file, parse command-line arguments, extract icons, and get file information. Many of these functions existed in previous versions of Windows, but some are new.

The FindExecutable and ShellExecute functions, which are not new, take advantage of file associations to find and start applications or to open and print files. By specifying a filename, you can use FindExecutable to get the name and the handle of the executable file that is started when an open association is run. (This function is supported only for compatibility with previous versions of Windows; it is not recommended for Win32-based applications.) ShellExecute either opens or prints a specified file. Your application designates which operation is performed by specifying *open* or *print* in the *lpszOp* parameter of the function. Pretty simple.

To get the icon associated with an executable, you can use the Extract-Icon function. This function returns the handle of an icon from a file that you specify—an executable file, a dynamic-link library, or an icon file. Once you have this handle, you can use it to draw the icon.

Shh! Be Very, Very Quiet; We're Hunting New Functions

Windows 95 offers some new functions and structures that you can use to retrieve information about files. These functions all have an *SH* prefix, so, as Elmer Fudd would say, "Be vewy, vewy quiet...."

- The SHGetNameMappingCount function gets the number of file mappings for the specified file.

- The SHFreeNameMappings function frees the file mappings for the specified file.

- The SHFileOperation function allows the application to specify a file or printer operation (moving, copying, deleting, renaming, or changing a printer port) and how to perform the operation. The application can control operations such as allowing multiple destination files, specifying a silent operation (no papers flying between folders), or determining whether to complete the operation without user confirmation.

- The SHGetFileInfo function gets information about the specified file, including its display name, its icon, its type, its attributes, the icon location, and the large and small icons for the file.

In the SHELLFUN sample, the SHGetFileInfo function retrieves information about a file specified by the user. Not one to give advice that I don't take myself ("Don't do anything that the system will do for you"), I use the Open common dialog box to get the name of the file to query. When the user chooses the file, its display name and type name are displayed in the multiline edit control in SHELLFUN's main window:

```
void OnFileInfo (HWND hWnd, HWND hwndEdit)
{
OPENFILENAME OpenFileName;
char szDirName [MAX_PATH] = "";
char szFile [MAX_PATH] = "\0";
char szFileTitle [MAX_PATH] = "\0";

// The filter specification for the OPENFILENAME structure
char szFilter [] = {"All Files\0*.*\0"};

OpenFileName.lStructSize        = sizeof (OPENFILENAME);
OpenFileName.hwndOwner          = hWnd;
OpenFileName.hInstance          = (HANDLE)g_hInst;
OpenFileName.lpstrFilter        = szFilter;
OpenFileName.lpstrCustomFilter  = (LPTSTR)NULL;
OpenFileName.nMaxCustFilter     = 0L;
OpenFileName.nFilterIndex       = 1L;
OpenFileName.lpstrFile          = szFile;
OpenFileName.nMaxFile           = sizeof (szFile);
OpenFileName.lpstrFileTitle     = szFileTitle;
OpenFileName.nMaxFileTitle      = sizeof (szFileTitle);
OpenFileName.lpstrInitialDir    = NULL;
OpenFileName.lpstrTitle         = "Pick a file for information.";
OpenFileName.nFileOffset        = 0;
OpenFileName.nFileExtension     = 0;
OpenFileName.lpstrDefExt        = "*.*";
OpenFileName.lCustData          = 0;
OpenFileName.Flags              = OFN_PATHMUSTEXIST |
    OFN_FILEMUSTEXIST | OFN_HIDEREADONLY;

if (GetOpenFileName (&OpenFileName))
{
    SHFILEINFO sfi;
    char buff [2056];

    // The user chose to get the file information: display name,
    // type name, file attributes, icon location, and executable type.
    if (SHGetFileInfo (OpenFileName.lpstrFile, 0, &sfi,
        sizeof (SHFILEINFO), SHGFI_DISPLAYNAME | SHGFI_TYPENAME))
    {
        memset (buff, '\0', sizeof (buff));

        // Display the information.
        wsprintf (buff, "Display name: %s    Type Name: %s",
            sfi.szDisplayName, sfi.szTypeName);

        // Update the multiline edit control with the file description.
        SendMessage (hwndEdit, WM_SETTEXT, 0, (LPARAM)buff);
    }
}
}
```

The end result, shown in Figure 11-2, isn't the fanciest example of user interface design, but it does illustrate that the display name can be a long filename. The type name is the name registered for that type of file in the Registry.

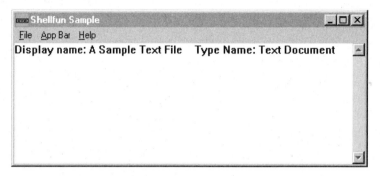

Figure 11-2.
Retrieving file information in SHELLFUN.

Taskbar Notifications

The Windows taskbar includes an area in which applications can display status information. In Figure 11-3, for instance, this *taskbar notification area* (sometimes called the *tray notification area*) includes an electrical plug icon to signal that my laptop is plugged in, another icon to indicate that my PCMCIA card is active, and a time display telling me that it's getting close to teatime.

Figure 11-3.
The taskbar notification area.

An icon in the taskbar notification area can have a ToolTip associated with it, which is helpful for displaying additional status information. For example, when my laptop is running off its battery, a battery icon replaces the electrical plug icon. If I allow my mouse to linger over the battery icon, a ToolTip pops up, indicating how much battery life is left. A printer icon and an associated ToolTip can also be useful. When you print a document, the printer icon appears in the notification area, and its ToolTip can tell you the status of the print job (whether it's spooling, printing, and so on).

In the SHELLFUN sample, the user can add an icon to the taskbar notification area. You need to provide an icon and, optionally, a ToolTip string. SHELLFUN uses the built-in Windows logo icon, IDI_WINLOGO. The user can add or remove the icon or modify its state in the taskbar notification area by choosing menu commands:

```
case IDM_ADDICON:
    TrayMessage (hWnd, NIM_ADD);
    break;

case IDM_STATECHANGE:
    TrayMessage (hWnd, NIM_MODIFY);
    break;

case IDM_REMOVEICON:
    TrayMessage (hWnd, NIM_DELETE);
    break;
```

TrayMessage is an application-defined function that fills out a NOTIFY-ICONDATA structure and sends the message passed in the second parameter through the Shell_NotifyIcon function. Notice that a member of the structure is filled in with flags. This member can be a combination of the following flags:

NIF_MESSAGE	Specifies that the *uCallbackMessage* member is valid
NIF_ICON	Specifies that the *hIcon* member is valid
NIF_TIP	Specifies that the *szTip* member is valid

The following code demonstrates how SHELLFUN fills out this structure and uses the Shell_NotifyIcon function:

```
void TrayMessage (HWND hWnd, UINT message)
{
NOTIFYICONDATA tnd;

// Change the state of the small icon in the taskbar.
if (g_State1)
{
    lstrcpyn (tnd.szTip, g_szState2, sizeof (tnd.szTip));
    g_State1 = FALSE;
}
else
{
    lstrcpyn (tnd.szTip, g_szState1, sizeof (tnd.szTip));
    g_State1 = TRUE;
}
```

(continued)

```
switch (message)
{
    case NIM_ADD:
        tnd.uFlags = NIF_MESSAGE | NIF_ICON | NIF_TIP;
        break;

    case NIM_MODIFY:
        tnd.uFlags = NIF_TIP;
        break;

    case NIM_DELETE:
        tnd.uFlags = 0;
        g_State1 = FALSE;
        break;
}

tnd.uID              = (UINT)IDI_WINLOGO;
tnd.cbSize           = sizeof (NOTIFYICONDATA);
tnd.hWnd             = hWnd;
tnd.uCallbackMessage = TRAY_CALLBACK;
tnd.hIcon            = g_hIconState;

Shell_NotifyIcon (message, &tnd);
}
```

Your application can send three messages using Shell_NotifyIcon:

NIM_ADD	Adds an icon to the taskbar notification area
NIM_MODIFY	Modifies an icon in the taskbar notification area
NIM_DELETE	Deletes an icon from the taskbar notification area

SHELLFUN permits the user to modify (change the state of) the icon in the taskbar notification area by choosing the Change State command on the AppBar menu. When the user does this, the ToolTip text changes from *State 1* to *State 2*, as illustrated in Figure 11-4.

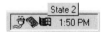

Figure 11-4.
Changing the state of an icon in the taskbar notification area.

The application can provide a special callback message that handles mouse messages intended for a taskbar icon. This is useful if you want a context menu to pop up when the user clicks the icon with the right mouse button.

The SHELLFUN sample displays a message box when the user clicks the icon with the left mouse button, as shown in Figure 11-5. Here is the callback function that SHELLFUN uses:

```
void TrayCallback (WPARAM wParam, LPARAM lParam)
{
UINT uID;
UINT uMouseMsg;

uID = (UINT)wParam;
uMouseMsg = (UINT)lParam;

if (uMouseMsg == WM_LBUTTONDOWN)
{
   if (uID == (UINT)IDI_WINLOGO)
      MessageBox (NULL, "Click!", "This sure is fun!", MB_OK);
}
}
```

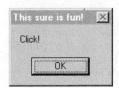

Figure 11-5.
SHELLFUN responds to the user clicking the taskbar icon.

> N O T E: A taskbar notification can be especially useful if you are writing an installer or a Control Panel application for a hardware item such as a sound card. It's nice to let users know when the hardware is up and running, allowing them to check status without having to open an application.

Access Bars

An *access bar* is a window that is much like the taskbar. Anchored to one edge of the screen, it usually contains buttons that give a user quick access to commands, applications, or windows. Although this might sound a lot like a toolbar, one key difference is that the system reserves the area occupied by an access bar (just as it does for the taskbar) and will prevent other applications from using that area. A user can have one or several access bars on the desktop at any time. Try to use access bars judiciously; it can get crowded.

The SHELLFUN sample allows the user to create or remove an access bar (also known as an AppBar) by choosing menu commands. SHELLFUN's AppBar menu is shown in Figure 11-6.

Figure 11-6.
SHELLFUN's AppBar menu.

Creating an Access Bar

You first need to decide what you want your access bar to do and what it should look like. I decided that mine should look a bit like the taskbar and that it should contain buttons that let the user change the bar's position (right, left, top, or bottom). To create the access bar itself, I used Create-WindowEx and the extended style WS_EX_TOOLWINDOW:

```
// Create the access bar.
g_hWndAppBar = CreateWindowEx (WS_EX_TOOLWINDOW,
   "AppBarClass", "AppBar",
   WS_POPUP | WS_THICKFRAME | WS_CLIPCHILDREN,
   0, 0, DEF_APPBAR_WIDTH, DEF_APPBAR_HEIGHT,
   NULL, NULL, hInstance, NULL);

// Now create the button children.
g_hwndBtn1 = CreateWindow (
   "BUTTON",            // create a button
   "&Right",            // window title
   BS_PUSHBUTTON | BS_CENTER | WS_VISIBLE | WS_CHILD,
   0, 0, 0, 0,
   g_hWndAppBar,        // parent window
   (HMENU)IDM_RIGHT,    // ID
   hInstance,           // instance
   NULL);
```

```
g_hwndBtn2 = CreateWindow (
    "BUTTON",               // create a button
    "&Left",                // window title
    BS_PUSHBUTTON | BS_CENTER | WS_VISIBLE | WS_CHILD,
    0, 0, 0, 0,
    g_hWndAppBar,           // parent window
    (HMENU)IDM_LEFT,        // ID
    hInstance,              // instance
    NULL);

g_hwndBtn3 = CreateWindow (
    "BUTTON",               // create a button
    "&Top",                 // window title
    BS_PUSHBUTTON | BS_CENTER | WS_VISIBLE | WS_CHILD,
    0, 0, 0, 0,
    g_hWndAppBar,           // parent window
    (HMENU)IDM_TOP,         // ID
    hInstance,              // instance
    NULL);

g_hwndBtn4 = CreateWindow (
    "BUTTON",               // create a button
    "&Bottom",              // window title
    BS_PUSHBUTTON | BS_CENTER | WS_VISIBLE | WS_CHILD,
    0, 0, 0, 0,
    g_hWndAppBar,           // parent window
    (HMENU)IDM_BOTTOM,      // ID
    hInstance,              // instance
    NULL);
```

Of course, it's not enough to just create the windows and wish upon a star for an access bar—you need to register it with the system. SHELLFUN does this when the user chooses to add the access bar. As I did for the taskbar notification, I filled out a structure, APPBARDATA, and used a special function, SHAppBarMessage, to register the access bar:

```
case IDM_ADD:
    if (! g_fRegistered)
    {
        // Fill out the structure needed to register the new access bar.
        g_appBar.hWnd = g_hWndAppBar;
        g_appBar.cbSize = sizeof (APPBARDATA);

        // Identifier for notifications
        g_appBar.uCallbackMessage = APPBAR_CALLBACK;
```

(continued)

```
    // Register the access bar.
    if (! SHAppBarMessage (ABM_NEW, &g_appBar))
        break;

    // Set the default size and position of the access bar.
    AppBarPosChanged (ABE_TOP, &g_appBar);

    ShowWindow (g_hWndAppBar, SW_SHOW);

    // Set the registered flag to TRUE.
    g_fRegistered = TRUE;
}
break;
```

The access bar initially appears anchored to the top of the desktop, as shown in Figure 11-7. Clicking one of the buttons on the bar will change its position.

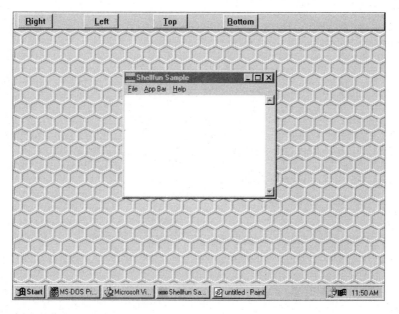

Figure 11-7.
The access bar in SHELLFUN.

To remove the access bar, you use the same SHAppBarMessage function, specifying the ABM_REMOVE message as the first parameter. In SHELL-

FUN, I don't actually destroy the window; I hide it in case the user chooses to add it again later. When the application closes, however, I do destroy the window in my cleanup code:

```
case IDM_REMOVE:
   if (g_fRegistered)
   {
      // Unregister the access bar.
      SHAppBarMessage (ABM_REMOVE, &g_appBar);
      ShowWindow (g_hWndAppBar, SW_HIDE);
      g_fRegistered = FALSE;
   }
   break;
```

Because an access bar is a window in its own right, it has its own window procedure, in which events such as activation, creation, and destruction (and lots of other words ending in *-tion*) happen. This is also where the callback message specified in the ABM_NEW message is sent. Here is the window procedure for SHELLFUN's access bar:

```
LRESULT CALLBACK AppBarWndProc (HWND hwnd, UINT msg, WPARAM wparam,
   LPARAM lparam)
{
static HWND hwndBtn1, hwndBtn2, hwndBtn3, hwndBtn4;

switch (msg)
{
   case WM_CREATE:
      g_fRegistered = FALSE;
      break;

   case WM_DESTROY:
      DestroyWindow (hwndBtn1);
      DestroyWindow (hwndBtn2);
      DestroyWindow (hwndBtn3);
      DestroyWindow (hwndBtn4);
      break;

   case WM_WINDOWPOSCHANGED:
   case WM_ACTIVATE:
   {
      APPBARDATA abd;
      abd.cbSize = sizeof (APPBARDATA);
```

(continued)

```
            abd.hWnd = hwnd;
            abd.lParam = (LONG)NULL;
            SHAppBarMessage (ABM_ACTIVATE, &abd);
            break;
        }

    case WM_COMMAND:
        if (HIWORD (wparam) == BN_CLICKED)
            AppBarClicked (LOWORD (wparam), (APPBARDATA *)&g_appBar);
        break;

    case APPBAR_CALLBACK:
        AppBarCallback (hwnd, msg, wparam, lparam);
        return 0;

    default:
        return DefWindowProc (hwnd, msg, wparam, lparam);
    }
}
```

Using the Access Bar Callback Message

As mentioned earlier, an application can specify that a callback message must be sent to it. SHELLFUN defines this message as APPBAR_CALLBACK (although an application can specify any message). This callback message is used for processing notifications that are sent to the access bar when the state of the bar changes (for example, from ABS_ALWAYSONTOP), when a full-screen application starts or closes, and when an event occurs that might affect the bar's size or position. SHELLFUN uses the following code to process the access bar's callback message. (It's very similar to code used as an example in the Win32 SDK.)

```
void AppBarCallback (HWND hWnd, UINT msg, WPARAM wParam, LPARAM lParam)
{
UINT uState;

switch (wParam)
{
    case ABN_STATECHANGE:
        // Check to see whether the access bar is still ABS_ALWAYSONTOP.
        uState = SHAppBarMessage (ABM_GETSTATE, &g_appBar);
```

```
SetWindowPos (hWnd,
    (ABS_ALWAYSONTOP & uState) ? HWND_TOPMOST : HWND_BOTTOM,
    0, 0, 0, 0, SWP_NOMOVE | SWP_NOSIZE | SWP_NOACTIVATE);
break;

case ABN_FULLSCREENAPP:
    // A full-screen application has started, or the last
    // full-screen application has closed. Reset the access bar's
    // z-order appropriately.
    uState = SHAppBarMessage (ABM_GETSTATE, &g_appBar);

    if (lParam)
    {
        SetWindowPos (hWnd,
            (ABS_ALWAYSONTOP & uState) ? HWND_TOPMOST : HWND_BOTTOM,
            0, 0, 0, 0, SWP_NOMOVE | SWP_NOSIZE | SWP_NOACTIVATE);
    }
    else
    {
        if (uState & ABS_ALWAYSONTOP)
            SetWindowPos (hWnd, HWND_TOPMOST, 0, 0, 0, 0,
                SWP_NOMOVE | SWP_NOSIZE | SWP_NOACTIVATE);
    }

case ABN_POSCHANGED:
    // The taskbar or another access bar
    // has changed its size or position.
    AppBarPosChanged (g_appBar.uEdge, &g_appBar);
    break;
}
}
```

Changing an Access Bar's Size or Position

The size or position of an access bar can change, usually as a result of the user resizing or moving it. In SHELLFUN, the user can change the position of the bar by clicking the Right, Left, Top, or Bottom button to align the access bar with the specified edge of the screen. The application must then determine whether that position is available. If another access bar is already anchored to the specified edge, you must recalculate the position of the new access bar so that it will appear next to the bar already occupying that edge.

In SHELLFUN, I had to consider the vertical or horizontal orientation of the access bar and then remember to reset the positions of the child buttons accordingly. (The buttons are placed crosswise on a horizontal bar, or up and down on a vertical bar.) When the user clicks a button on the SHELLFUN access bar, the message is sent to a function that filters out information about which button was clicked:

```
void AppBarClicked (UINT msg, APPBARDATA *pabd)
{
switch (msg)
{
   çase IDM_LEFT:
      AppBarPosChanged (ABE_LEFT, pabd);
      break;

   case IDM_RIGHT:
      AppBarPosChanged (ABE_RIGHT, pabd);
      break;

   case IDM_TOP:
      AppBarPosChanged (ABE_TOP, pabd);
      break;

   case IDM_BOTTOM:
      AppBarPosChanged (ABE_BOTTOM, pabd);
      break;
}
}
```

Once you have determined the new specified edge, you can do the real positioning:

```
void PASCAL AppBarPosChanged (UINT uEdge, APPBARDATA *abd)
{
RECT rcl;

// Get the screen coordinates.
rcl.left = rcl.top = 0;
rcl.right = GetSystemMetrics (SM_CXSCREEN);
rcl.bottom = GetSystemMetrics (SM_CYSCREEN);

switch (uEdge)
{
   case ABE_TOP:
      abd->rc.left = abd->rc.top = 0;
```

```
        abd->rc.right = rcl.right;
        abd->rc.bottom = DEF_APPBAR_HEIGHT;
        break;

    case ABE_BOTTOM:
        abd->rc.left = 0;
        abd->rc.top = rcl.bottom - DEF_APPBAR_HEIGHT;
        abd->rc.right = rcl.right;
        abd->rc.bottom = rcl.bottom;
        break;

    case ABE_LEFT:
        abd->rc.left = abd->rc.top = 0;
        abd->rc.right = DEF_APPBAR_WIDTH;
        abd->rc.bottom = rcl.bottom;
        break;

    case ABE_RIGHT:
        abd->rc.top = 0;
        abd->rc.left = rcl.right - DEF_APPBAR_WIDTH;
        abd->rc.right = rcl.right;
        abd->rc.bottom = rcl.bottom;
        break;
}

// Check to see whether this position is OK.
SHAppBarMessage (ABM_QUERYPOS, abd);

switch (uEdge)
{
    case ABE_LEFT:
        abd->rc.right = abd->rc.left + DEF_APPBAR_WIDTH;
        break;

    case ABE_RIGHT:
        abd->rc.left = abd->rc.right - DEF_APPBAR_WIDTH;
        break;

    case ABE_TOP:
        abd->rc.bottom = abd->rc.top + DEF_APPBAR_HEIGHT;
        break;

    case ABE_BOTTOM:
        abd->rc.top = abd->rc.bottom - DEF_APPBAR_HEIGHT;
        break;
}
```

(continued)

```
// Set the access bar position.
SHAppBarMessage (ABM_SETPOS, abd);

// Move and size the access bar so that it conforms to the
// bounding rectangle passed to the system.
MoveWindow (abd->hWnd, abd->rc.left, abd->rc.top,
   abd->rc.right, abd->rc.bottom, TRUE);

if ((uEdge == ABE_TOP) || (uEdge == ABE_BOTTOM))
{
   MoveWindow (g_hwndBtn1, 5, 0, BUTTON_WIDTH, BUTTON_HEIGHT, TRUE);
   MoveWindow (g_hwndBtn2, BUTTON_WIDTH * 2, 0, BUTTON_WIDTH,
      BUTTON_HEIGHT, TRUE);
   MoveWindow (g_hwndBtn3, BUTTON_WIDTH * 4, 0, BUTTON_WIDTH,
      BUTTON_HEIGHT, TRUE);
   MoveWindow (g_hwndBtn4, BUTTON_WIDTH * 6, 0, BUTTON_WIDTH,
      BUTTON_HEIGHT, TRUE);
}
else
{
   MoveWindow (g_hwndBtn1, 2, 5, BUTTON_WIDTH, BUTTON_HEIGHT, TRUE);
   MoveWindow (g_hwndBtn2, 2, BUTTON_HEIGHT * 2, BUTTON_WIDTH,
      BUTTON_HEIGHT, TRUE);
   MoveWindow (g_hwndBtn3, 2, BUTTON_HEIGHT * 4, BUTTON_WIDTH,
      BUTTON_HEIGHT, TRUE);
   MoveWindow (g_hwndBtn4, 2, BUTTON_HEIGHT * 6, BUTTON_WIDTH,
      BUTTON_HEIGHT, TRUE);
}
}
```

Getting Information About the Taskbar

You can also use SHAppBarMessage to get information about the system's taskbar—specifically, information about the taskbar's position. In SHELL-FUN, the user can do this by choosing a menu option.

```
case IDM_TASKBAR:
{
   APPBARDATA abd;
   char buff [MAX_PATH];

   memset (buff, '\0', sizeof (buff));
```

```
abd.cbSize = sizeof (APPBARDATA);
SHAppBarMessage (ABM_GETTASKBARPOS, &abd);

wsprintf (buff, "Left: %d, Right: %d, Top: %d, Bottom: %d",
    abd.rc.left, abd.rc.right, abd.rc.top, abd.rc.bottom);

// Update the multiline edit control.
SendMessage (hwndEdit, WM_SETTEXT, 0, (LPARAM)buff);
break;
}
```

The information returned from the call to SHAppBarMessage is displayed in the multiline edit control in the client area of the main SHELLFUN window, as shown in Figure 11-8.

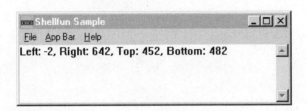

Figure 11-8.
Taskbar information retrieved by the SHELLFUN sample.

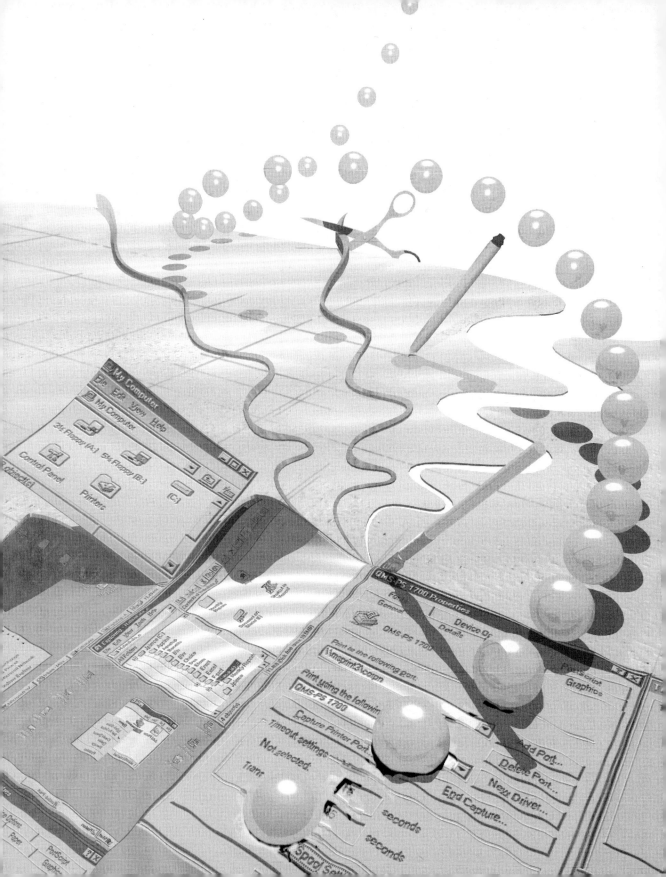

CHAPTER TWELVE

File Viewers

Let's say that you have created some Microsoft Word documents named STUFF1.DOC, STUFF2.DOC, and STUFF3.DOC. Now let's say that you want to give those files to a reviewer who doesn't use Word. (Heresy, I know, but there's always one in the crowd.) You can of course resave the documents as text files that can be read with any text editor. Or, if the reviewer happens to be running the Microsoft Windows 95 operating system, he or she can use a file viewer to check out the files.

A file viewer, one of the new features of Windows 95, allows a user to quickly see the contents of a file without having to run the full application that created the file—in fact, without even requiring the presence of that application. The file viewer not only displays a file's contents but also provides a user interface that can include items such as a menu, a toolbar, and a status bar.

To use a file viewer, you first right-click a file to display its context menu, which will look something like the menu shown in Figure 12-1 on the next page. Then simply choose the Quick View option from the context menu to display the file contents in a file viewer. (Alternatively, you can select the file and choose Quick View from the File menu in Windows Explorer.)

Before you go off and try this on your computer, however, be aware that the Quick View option will not appear on a file's context menu unless a file viewer is registered for that particular type of file (DOC, TXT, AVI, and so on). The option is displayed only if you have a file viewer installed and if that file viewer has registered itself properly in the Registry. When you right-click a file, the system checks the Registry to find a viewer for that file based on the file's extension and class. If no file viewer is registered for that file type, the Quick View option doesn't appear on the context menu.

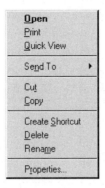

Figure 12-1.
A context menu containing the Quick View option.

If you install the sample I wrote for this chapter, MFCVIEW, you will have a rudimentary file viewer for text files, shown in Figure 12-2. You need to copy the dynamic-link library to your \WINDOWS\SYSTEM\VIEWERS folder and then run the MFCVIEW.REG file. The DLL is registered to reside in this path; if you want to place the DLL somewhere else, change the REG file to reflect the new location. (If you rebuild the project, the DLL file will automatically be placed in \WINDOWS\SYSTEM\VIEWERS. You can change this location by going to the Project menu, choosing Settings, clicking the Link tab, and changing the Output File Menu item. Then click the Debug tab and edit the Executable For Debug Session and the Working Directory items. You must alter these three items for both Win32 Debug and Win32 Release. Note that you must still change and run the REG file.)

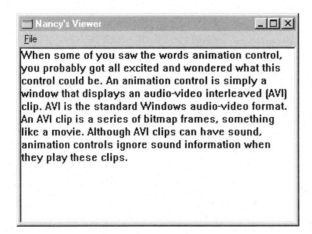

Figure 12-2.
Nancy's Viewer (a rudimentary file viewer).

How File Viewers Work

In the preceding explanation, I mentioned file classes. Technically speaking, file viewers are component objects implemented inside an in-process server DLL. In simpler, more human-understandable terms, file viewers live in a DLL that exports certain functions so that the system can make calls to the DLL to display file contents. The DLL is referred to as an *INPROC server,* which simply means that it runs only as an add-on to an existing application (in this case, as an add-on to the system-supplied application called QUIKVIEW), not as a stand-alone application.

When a user clicks the Quick View option for an OLE compound file, the system can use the file's class identifier (an OLE CLSID value) to figure out which viewer to use. If the file isn't a compound file, the system uses the file extension to determine which viewer to use.

Because a file viewer is a component object, you can add interfaces and augment functionality to support new features. For example, a file viewer can act as an OLE container application and can activate embedded objects in-place inside the file being viewed. Or you could beef up another file viewer to let the user make a selection in a document and copy the selection to the Clipboard or drag it to another location.

How File Viewers Are Instantiated

The system doesn't directly call a file viewer; instead, it starts an instance of QUIKVIEW.EXE for each file to be viewed. QUIKVIEW is a program that starts the file viewing process and creates a message queue for file viewers. The program then associates a path with a file viewer, instantiates the file viewer object, and tells the file viewer to load and display the file. At this point, QUIKVIEW turns over execution of the process it created to the file viewer until the file viewer shuts down. When determining which file viewer to instantiate, QUIK-VIEW uses one of these three methods:

- If the file is an OLE compound file, it contains a class identifier (CLSID) that identifies its type. QUIKVIEW uses this CLSID to determine the file type and which viewer to use.

- If the file is not an OLE compound file but begins with a consistent and unique byte pattern, the application that created it can register the byte pattern in the Registry and associate the pattern with a CLSID, which will determine the file type.

- If the file is not an OLE compound file (or if it is but lacks a CLSID), QUIKVIEW uses the filename extension to identify the file type.

If a file type is registered but the system can't find its file viewer, or if the Quick View operation fails, QUIKVIEW displays the message *There is no viewer capable of viewing* <type of file> *files.*

Registering File Viewers with the System

A file viewer can register itself for more than one file type if it can handle multiple file formats. But if a given file type has more than one registered file viewer, the system calls the file viewer that was registered most recently when the user chooses Quick View.

The Structure of Registry Entries

The following Registry structure is required if QUIKVIEW is to associate a file's class identifier or extension with the class identifier of a file viewer. If you deviate from this structure, QUIKVIEW won't find your file viewer, and you'll be one frustrated developer.

```
HKEY_CLASSES_ROOT
    \QuickView
        \<extension> = <human-readable document type>
            \{<CLSID>} = <human-readable viewer name>
            \{<CLSID>} = <human-readable viewer name>
            \{<CLSID>} = <human-readable viewer name>
            ⋮
        [More extension entries for additional file types]
        ⋮

    \CLSID
        \{<CLSID>} = <human-readable viewer name>
            \InprocServer32 = <full path to file viewer DLL>
            \ThreadingModel = <Model>
            ⋮
        [More class IDs for file viewers and other object servers]
        ⋮
```

How about some explanation?

▨ HKEY_CLASSES_ROOT is the root of the Registry.

▨ The QuickView key is the top-level key, where the file viewer associations are stored. It can have any number of extension subkeys (TXT, CPP, and so on), each representing a registered file type. Each extension subkey can have one or more class identifier subkeys, each representing a registered file viewer object. The most recently registered file viewer appears first in the list of class identifier subkeys, and it is the first one found when QUIKVIEW enumerates the registered file viewers.

■ The *<extension>* key is a three-character file extension preceded by a period (for example, *.WRI*).

■ The *<human-readable document type>* key is a string that can be displayed to the user, describing the file type associated with the class identifier or extension. A file viewer can change this string when it is installed so that the name always reflects the preferred viewer. For example, this string might be *Windows Write Document*.

■ The CLSID key is a 16-byte OLE class identifier spelled out in hexadecimal digits in the form 12345678-1234-1234-1234-1234567890AB, including hyphens. All class identifiers are surrounded by curly braces ({ }) when stored in the Registry. The file viewer class identifier should always differ from the file type class identifier because the application that created the file might already be using the file type class identifier to identify itself as a compound document server.

■ The *<human-readable viewer name>* key is a string that describes the vendor of the file viewer, as such a description might be displayed in an About box—*Company ABC Write Document Viewer*, for instance.

■ The *<Model>* subkey specifies the threading model as it relates to OLE objects. Under Windows 95, OLE is apartment-threaded. The term *apartment* describes a thread with a message queue that supports OLE/COM (Component Object Model) objects. Operations that yield to the message queue can cause further messages to be sent to any objects within the apartment. Apartment model threading simply allows multiple apartments where previously only one existed (the main application thread). By default, a single-threaded application consists of a single apartment (its single thread). When a process calls CoInitialize or OleInitialize from a thread, a new OLE apartment is created. Thereafter, each time CoInitialize or OleInitialize is called in a thread, a new OLE apartment is created. You can create in-process objects that are apartment-model-aware in any apartment. You mark the DLL as apartment-model-aware through the *ThreadingModel=Apartment* value of the InprocServer-32 key. In-process objects that are not apartment-model-aware are created in the main apartment of the application, the main apartment being the first thread that calls CoInitialize or OleInitialize.

Each CLSID stored under the file extension subkeys corresponds to an entry of that same CLSID stored under the top-level key, called (what else?) CLSID, the standard location for storing information about OLE objects. For file viewers, an InprocServer32 subkey is needed under the file viewer's class identifier key. The value of this subkey is the full path to the file viewer DLL. In my sample, the file viewer is stored in the \WINDOWS\SYSTEM\VIEWERS folder. InprocServer32 is a standard OLE subkey storing the path to an object. Using this subkey allows the QUIKVIEW program to use standard OLE APIs to access and create objects from file viewer servers.

An apartment-model-aware process must have thread-safe entry points because multiple apartments can call CoCreateInstance or CoGetClassObject simultaneously. In practice, this means that your application should do the following:

- DllGetClassObject must support supplying references to multiple class objects. If you implement your class objects dynamically, this shouldn't be an issue because any class object you supply will be called only from a single apartment. If you implement your class object as a static object, you must ensure that your AddRef and Release member functions use InterlockedIncrement and InterlockedDecrement rather than the $++/--$ operators.

- With both static and dynamic class objects, global lock-count, as implemented for IClassFactory::LockServer, must use InterlockedIncrement and InterlockedDecrement. If you're not using a global counter for this value now, you should start doing so.

- Carefully implement DllCanUnloadNow by using the global counter from InterlockedIncrement along with a global counter that keeps track of the total number of instances that have been created.

When you create a file viewer using MFC, you can let MFC initialize for you, as I did in the MFCVIEW sample.

An Example of Registering a File Viewer

Let's look at an example of registering a file viewer for text (TXT) files. The viewer is implemented in an in-process server DLL called MFCVIEW.DLL, whose class identifier is e83b63c0-6ff5-11ce-993c-00aa004adb6c. The actual Registry entries appear in the REG file shown here:

```
REGEDIT4

[HKEY_CLASSES_ROOT\CLSID\{e83b63c0-6ff5-11ce-993c-00aa004adb6c}]
@="Nancy's Viewer"
[HKEY_CLASSES_ROOT\CLSID\{e83b63c0-6ff5-11ce-993c-00aa004adb6c}
    \InprocServer32]
@="c:\\windows\\system\\viewers\\mfcview.dll"
"ThreadingModel"="Apartment"

[HKEY_CLASSES_ROOT\QuickView\.TXT]
@="txtfile"
[HKEY_CLASSES_ROOT\QuickView\.TXT\{e83b63c0-6ff5-11ce-993c-
    00aa004adb6c}]
@="Nancy's Viewer"

[HKEY_CLASSES_ROOT\txtfile\CLSID]
@="{e83b63c0-6ff5-11ce-993c-00aa004adb6c}"
```

The first line, *REGEDIT4*, specifies that the registration file follows a new (Windows 95) syntax. Notice the syntax of the entries, with square brackets ([ ]) surrounding each key and each value enclosed in quotation marks. This syntax allows you to specify the InprocServer32 and ThreadingModel subkeys. The threading model in this code is set to *Apartment*, which specifies that multiple threads in the executable can create OLE objects. (Although long lines in the REC file above are broken to fit on the printed page, you must enter each one as a single unbroken line. There is no continuation character.)

Basic Steps in Creating a File Viewer

You have two options when you decide to write your own file viewer: you can take the really hard way and use C, or you can use MFC version 3.1 or later and let MFC do a lot of the grunt work for you. Since one of the rules I live by is "Don't do anything that you can get someone else to do for you," I chose the MFC method. If you want to do all the work yourself, you aren't out of luck: the FILEVIEW sample in the Win32 SDK demonstrates exactly what you have to do to reinvent that wheel.

When I wrote the MFCVIEW sample, I followed the steps outlined in a technical article by Nigel Thompson, "MFC/COM Objects 1: Creating a Simple Object" (available on the Microsoft Developer Network Development Library CD), and the information in "Technical Note 38: MFC/OLE IUnknown Implementation" (one of the MFC technical notes found in the Visual C++ documentation). So if you think the steps look familiar and you've read Nigel's article recently, you'll know why.

Here is what I did to create Nancy's Viewer:

1. Create the project.

2. Generate GUIDs.

3. Create the object class.

4. Implement the basic object.

5. Implement the IUnknown interface.

6. Implement the IFileViewer interface.

7. Implement the IPersistFile interface.

8. Let MFC initialize the class factories for you.

9. Create the class to show the file contents.

10. Build, register, and run the file viewer.

Step One: Create the Project

I used Visual C++ version 2.1 (MFC 3.1) to create the project. In AppWizard, I selected *MFC AppWizard (dll)* as the type of project. I also selected the option called Use MFC In A Static Library, to specify how to link to the MFC library. With the default option (using MFC in a shared DLL), the MFC classes won't work correctly if your COM object is used by some non-MFC application. So you must use the static library instead.

I decided to include OLE Automation as an option in my sample file viewer. It's easier to add it when you create the project than to go back later and add it yourself.

At this point, I built the project to be sure that everything was OK.

Step Two: Generate GUIDs

There's no getting around it—to create a file viewer, you must create a globally unique identifier (GUID) for it. You can run UUIDGEN (from the Win32 SDK) to create a GUID, or you can let MFC do it for you and use a defined macro to get one each time you need one. Guess which option I chose?

I created both the GUIDS.CPP file, which includes the standard header files I needed, and the INITGUID.H file, an OLE header file which ensures that the GUIDs are unique and are built only once. Here is the entire source for the GUIDS.CPP file; the GUID for the object class is stored in the last file, VIEWERID.H.

```
#include "stdafx.h"
#include <initguid.h>

// Include the definition for the file viewer object.
#include "ViewerID.h"
```

Step Three: Create the Object Class

Next I created the object I needed, CFileView, by using ClassWizard. The CFileView object is derived from the CCmdTarget class. This class implements the IUnknown interface for you, which means one less thing to do. When I created the class, I selected the OLE Automation and OLE Createable check boxes and gave the class the external name Nancy's Viewer. ClassWizard created the FILEVIEW.CPP and FILEVIEW.H files.

ClassWizard puts a curious line in the CPP file:

```
IMPLEMENT_OLECREATE(CFileView, "NancyViewer", 0xe83b63c0, 0x6ff5,
    0x11ce, 0x99, 0x3c, 0x0, 0xaa, 0x0, 0x4a, 0xdb, 0x6c)
```

This is a macro that implements class factory support. The class factory allows other applications to create your objects. The numbers listed after the string *Nancy's Viewer* are combined to create a GUID for the class:

```
e83b63c0-6ff5-11ce-993c-00aa004adb6c
```

This line is also included in the VIEWERID.H file, albeit in a somewhat different form:

```
// ViewerID.H

#ifndef _CLSID_NancyViewer_
#define _CLSID_NancyViewer_

DEFINE_GUID (CLSID_NancyViewer, 0xe83b63c0, 0x6ff5, 0x11ce,
    0x99, 0x3c, 0x0, 0xaa, 0x0, 0x4a, 0xdb, 0x6c);

#endif  // _CLSID_NancyViewer_
```

Step Four: Implement the Basic Object

This is the big step. To implement the object, you must first add the interface definitions and member variables to the header file FILEVIEW.H. Another very helpful macro, DECLARE_INTERFACE_MAP, supplies the basic COM interface definition. Interface maps are similar to message maps. They provide the standard implementation of the IUnknown interface of the CCmdTarget class, maintaining a reference count and aggregation support.

After declaring the interface map, you need to define the interfaces your object will support—in this case, both IFileViewer and IPersistFile. The BEGIN_INTERFACE_PART macro marks the beginning of the definition, and the END_INTERFACE_PART macro marks the end:

```
class CFileView : public CCmdTarget
{
    ⋮
    // Declare the interface map for this object.
    DECLARE_INTERFACE_MAP ()

    // IFileViewer interface
    BEGIN_INTERFACE_PART (FileViewer, IFileViewer)
        // IFileViewer stuff
        STDMETHOD(ShowInitialize) (LPFILEVIEWERSITE lpfsi);
        STDMETHOD(Show) (LPFVSHOWINFO pvsi);
        STDMETHOD(PrintTo) (LPSTR pszDriver, BOOL fSuppressUI);
    END_INTERFACE_PART (FileViewer)

    BEGIN_INTERFACE_PART (PersistFile, IPersistFile)
        // IPersistFile
        STDMETHODIMP IsDirty ();
        STDMETHODIMP Load (LPCOLESTR pszFileName, DWORD dwMode);
        STDMETHODIMP Save (LPCOLESTR pszFileName, BOOL fRemember);
        STDMETHODIMP SaveCompleted (LPCOLESTR pszFileName);
        STDMETHODIMP GetCurFile (LPOLESTR __RPC_FAR *ppszFileName);
        STDMETHODIMP GetClassID (LPCLSID pClsID);
    END_INTERFACE_PART (PersistFile)

public:
    // Member variables
    LPFILEVIEWERSITE m_lpfsi;                    // file viewer site
    CLSID            m_clsID;                    // CLSID of this
                                                 // file viewer
    char             m_pszPath [MAX_PATH];       // path from
                                                 // IPersistFile::Load
    DWORD            m_grfMode;                  // open mode for file
    BOOL             m_fLoadCalled;              // Load already called?
    BOOL             m_fShowInit;                // ShowInitialize called?
    CMyFrame         *m_Wnd;                     // viewer frame window
    LPFVSHOWINFO     m_pvsi;
}
```

When creating your own file viewer, you need to be concerned about both the IPersistFile interface, which is used to get the path for the file, and the IFileViewer interface, which is notified when a file viewer should show or print a file. For your file viewer to work, it must implement functions for each interface. These interfaces also include the IUnknown member functions AddRef, Release, and QueryInterface.

N O T E : It is extremely important to specify the definitions of the interfaces exactly as they are defined in the header file (in this case, SHLOBJ.H). If you don't do this correctly, your object won't work.

In the FILEVIEW.CPP file, you must also use a few macros to implement a data table that CCmdTarget uses to implement IUnknown, including entries for both IFileViewer and IPersistFile. The first parameter is the name of the class containing the interface object; the second parameter is the IID that is mapped to the embedded class; and the third parameter is the name of the local class:

```
BEGIN_INTERFACE_MAP (CFileView, CCmdTarget)
    INTERFACE_PART (CFileView, IID_IFileViewer, FileViewer)
    INTERFACE_PART (CFileView, IID_IPersistFile, PersistFile)
END_INTERFACE_MAP ()
```

Step Five: Implement the IUnknown Interface

Both the IFileViewer and the IPersistFile interfaces implement the standard IUnknown interface. This is a snap once you know what to do. By using the macros in the preceding code, you create an embedded class through the local name (FileViewer and PersistFile), with an uppercase *X* prepended to the name (XFileViewer and XPersistFile). This means that the embedded class for FileViewer is XFileViewer.

Another macro that I use liberally is METHOD_PROLOGUE, which lets you access the parent—the CCmdTarget derived class, CFileViewer—through a special pointer, *pThis*. The AddRef, Release, and QueryInterface functions can delegate to the CCmdTarget implementation through a call to ExternalAddRef, ExternalRelease, and ExternalQueryInterface, respectively.

```
// IUnknown for IFileViewer
STDMETHODIMP CFileView::XFileViewer::QueryInterface (
    REFIID riid, void **ppv)
{
METHOD_PROLOGUE (CFileView, FileViewer);
TRACE ("CFileView::IFileViewer::QueryInterface\n");
return pThis->ExternalQueryInterface (&riid, ppv);
}
```

(continued)

```
STDMETHODIMP_(ULONG) CFileView::XFileViewer::AddRef (void)
{
METHOD_PROLOGUE (CFileView, FileViewer);
return pThis->ExternalAddRef ();
}

STDMETHODIMP_(ULONG) CFileView::XFileViewer::Release (void)
{
METHOD_PROLOGUE (CFileView, FileViewer);
return pThis->ExternalRelease ();
}
```

Step Six: Implement the IFileViewer Interface

To implement the IFileViewer interface, the file viewer must implement the three member functions FileShowInitialize, FileShow, and PrintTo.

FileShowInitialize   This is a pre-show function. It allows a file viewer to determine whether it can display a file and, if it can, to perform the necessary initialization operations. The system calls FileShowInitialize before calling IFileViewer::Show. FileShowInitialize must perform all operations that are prone to failure; if it succeeds, IFileViewer::Show will not fail. The system specifies the name of the file that will be displayed by calling the file viewer's IPersistFile::Load member function. This function returns NOERROR if it is successful; otherwise, it returns an OLE-defined error value. In my file viewer, this function calls AddRef, creates the windows it needs, loads the file, stores the filename, and returns the error status.

```
STDMETHODIMP CFileView::XFileViewer::ShowInitialize (
    LPFILEVIEWERSITE lpfsi)
{
METHOD_PROLOGUE (CFileView, FileViewer);
TRACE ("CFileView::XFileViewer::ShowInitialize\n");

HRESULT hr;

// Be sure that you have the file viewer.
if (pThis->m_lpfsi != lpfsi)
{
    pThis->m_lpfsi = lpfsi;
    pThis->m_lpfsi->AddRef ();
}

// Default error code
hr = E_OUTOFMEMORY;
```

```
// Create the windows.
pThis->m_Wnd = new CMyFrame;
pThis->m_Wnd->Create ();

// Load a file.
HGLOBAL hMem=NULL;
char szwFile [512];

if (pThis->m_pszPath == NULL)
   return E_UNEXPECTED;

// This file viewer is registered for a TXT extension that
// is either in a compound file (a single stream called "Text")
// or in a flat text file. This sample shows
// how to open and work with both types of files.

// Make a Unicode copy of the filename.
mbstowcs ((USHORT *)szwFile, pThis->m_pszPath, sizeof (szwFile));

// CAREFUL: StgIsStorageFile returns S_FALSE if the file doesn't
// contain an IStorage object. Don't use SUCCEEDED to test the
// return value!
if (StgIsStorageFile (szwFile) == NOERROR)
{
    LPSTORAGE pIStorage = NULL;
    LPSTREAM pIStream = NULL;
    STATSTG stat;

    // It is a compound file; open it and the text stream.
    hr = StgOpenStorage (szwFile, NULL, pThis->m_grfMode, NULL, 0,
        &pIStorage);

    if (FAILED (hr))
        return hr;

    mbstowcs ((USHORT *)szwFile, "Text", sizeof (szwFile));

    hr = pIStorage->OpenStream (szwFile, 0,
        STGM_DIRECT | STGM_READ | STGM_SHARE_EXCLUSIVE, 0, &pIStream);

    if (SUCCEEDED (hr))
    {
        // Determine the amount of text and allocate memory.
        hr = pIStream->Stat (&stat, STATFLAG_NONAME);
```

(continued)

```
      if (SUCCEEDED (hr))
      {
         hMem = (HGLOBAL) malloc (stat.cbSize.LowPart + 1);

         if (hMem != NULL)
            // Now load the text into the controls.
            hr = pIStream->Read ((LPVOID)hMem, stat.cbSize.LowPart,
               NULL);
          else
            hr = E_OUTOFMEMORY;
      }
      pIStream->Release ();
   }
   pIStorage->Release ();
}

else
{
   HANDLE hFile;
   DWORD dwFileSize, dwBytesRead;
   char *lpBufPtr;

   // Open the text file.
   if ((hFile = CreateFile (pThis->m_pszPath,
      GENERIC_READ,
      FILE_SHARE_READ,
      NULL,
      OPEN_EXISTING,
      FILE_ATTRIBUTE_NORMAL,
      (HANDLE)NULL)) == (HANDLE)(-1))
   {
      AfxMessageBox ("Failed to open file");
      return STG_E_FILENOTFOUND;
   }

   // Get the size of the file.
   dwFileSize = GetFileSize (hFile, NULL);
   if (dwFileSize == 0xFFFFFFFF)
      return STG_E_READFAULT;
```

```
   // Allocate a buffer into which the file will be read.
   lpBufPtr = (char *) malloc (dwFileSize);
   if (lpBufPtr == NULL)
   {
      CloseHandle (hFile);
      return STG_E_READFAULT;
   }

   // Read the file contents into a buffer.
   ReadFile (hFile, (LPVOID)lpBufPtr, dwFileSize, &dwBytesRead, NULL);

   // Update the multiline edit control with the file contents.
   pThis->m_Wnd->UpdateEdit (lpBufPtr);

   // Close the file.
   CloseHandle (hFile);
}

// Tell IFileViewer::Show it's OK to call it.
pThis->m_fShowInit = TRUE;


return NOERROR;
}
```

FileShow This function is used to display a file. The system specifies the name of the file to display by calling the file viewer's IPersistFile::Load member function. This function returns NOERROR if it is successful or E_UN-EXPECTED if IFileView::ShowInitialize wasn't called before IFileView::Show. This member function is similar to the Windows ShowWindow function in that it receives a Show command indicating how the file viewer should initially display its window.

```
STDMETHODIMP CFileView::XFileViewer::Show (LPFVSHOWINFO pvsi)
{
METHOD_PROLOGUE (CFileView, FileViewer);
TRACE ("CFileView::XFileViewer::Show\n");

if (! pThis->m_fShowInit)
   return E_UNEXPECTED;

pThis->m_pvsi = pvsi;

// If you could not view the file, go back to the message loop.
if ((pThis->m_pvsi->dwFlags & FVSIF_NEWFAILED) == 0)
```

(continued)

301

```
{
    if (pThis->m_pvsi->dwFlags & FVSIF_RECT)
        pThis->m_Wnd.MoveWindow (pThis->m_pvsi->rect.left,
            pThis->m_pvsi->rect.top, pThis->m_pvsi->rect.right,
            pThis->m_pvsi->rect.bottom);
    pThis->m_Wnd.ShowWindow (pThis->m_pvsi->iShow);

    if (pThis->m_pvsi->iShow != SW_HIDE)
    {
        pThis->m_Wnd.SetForegroundWindow ();
        pThis->m_Wnd.UpdateWindow ();
    }

    // If an old window exists, destroy it now.
    if (pThis->m_pvsi->dwFlags & FVSIF_PINNED)
    {
        pThis->m_lpfsi->SetPinnedWindow (NULL);
        pThis->m_lpfsi->SetPinnedWindow (pThis->m_Wnd.m_hWnd);
    }

    if (pThis->m_pvsi->punkRel != NULL)
    {
        pThis->m_pvsi->punkRel->Release ();
        pThis->m_pvsi->punkRel = NULL;
    }
}
return NOERROR;
}
```

PrintTo   This function prints a file. The system specifies the name of the file to print by calling the file viewer's IPersistFile::Load member function. This function returns NOERROR if it is successful; otherwise, it returns an OLE-defined error value. This member function resembles Show in that it does not return until it finishes printing or an error occurs. If a problem arises, the file viewer object is responsible for informing the user of the problem. This is not implemented in my file viewer—it's just a stub.

```
STDMETHODIMP CFileView::XFileViewer::PrintTo (
    LPSTR pszDriver, BOOL fSuppressUI)
{
// This is a stub. Printing isn't implemented.
TRACE ("CFileView::XFileViewer::PrintTo\n");

return E_NOTIMPL;
}
```

Step Seven: Implement the IPersistFile Interface

To implement the IPersistFile interface, the file viewer must implement the following member functions: GetClassID, Load, GetCurFile, IsDirty, Save, and SaveCompleted.

GetClassID   This function returns the document's CLSID.

```
STDMETHODIMP CFileView::XPersistFile::GetClassID (LPCLSID pClsID)
{
METHOD_PROLOGUE (CFileView, PersistFile);

*pClsID = pThis->m_clsID;
return NOERROR;
}
```

Load   This function loads the document contained in the given filename. Load only stores the filename; ShowInitialize actually opens the file.

```
STDMETHODIMP CFileView::XPersistFile::Load (
    LPCOLESTR pszFileName, DWORD dwMode)
{
METHOD_PROLOGUE (CFileView, PersistFile);

// No modifications are necessary to this code; it simply
// copies the parameters into the CFileView::m_pszPath and
// m_grfMode members for use in IFileViewer::ShowInitialize
// and IFileViewer::Show later on.

// You should never be called twice.
if (pThis->m_pszPath)
    pThis->m_fLoadCalled = FALSE;    // handle error case

if (pszFileName == NULL)
    return E_INVALIDARG;

// Copy the ANSI filename and the mode to use in opening it.
lstrcpy (pThis->m_pszPath, pszFileName);

// Remember that this function has been called.
pThis->m_fLoadCalled = TRUE;
return NOERROR;
}
```

GetCurFile This function returns either the absolute path of the document's currently associated file or the default filename prompt if there is no currently associated file. GetCurFile returns E_UNEXPECTED if the Load function has not yet been called; otherwise, it copies the path and returns NOERROR.

```
STDMETHODIMP CFileView::XPersistFile::GetCurFile (
    LPOLESTR __RPC_FAR *ppszFileName)
{
LPOLESTR psz;
ULONG cb;

METHOD_PROLOGUE (CFileView, PersistFile);

// No modifications are necessary to this code; it simply
// copies the CFileView::m_pszPath string into a piece
// of memory and stores the pointer at *ppszFile.

// Load must be called, of course.
if (pThis->m_fLoadCalled)
    return E_UNEXPECTED;

if (ppszFileName == NULL)
    return E_INVALIDARG;

cb = (lstrlen (pThis->m_pszPath) + 1) * sizeof (OLECHAR);
psz = (LPOLESTR) malloc (cb);

if (NULL == psz)
    return E_OUTOFMEMORY;

return NOERROR;
}
```

IsDirty This function checks a document object for changes that might have been made since the object was last saved. IsDirty can simply return S_FALSE because a file viewer does not modify the file.

```
STDMETHODIMP CFileView::XPersistFile::IsDirty (void)
{
return S_FALSE;
}
```

Save   The Save function saves a copy of the object to the specified filename. Both the Save and the SaveCompleted member functions should return E_NOTIMPL.

```
STDMETHODIMP CFileView::XPersistFile::Save (
    LPCOLESTR pszFileName, BOOL fRemember)
{
return E_NOTIMPL;
}
```

SaveCompleted   This function signals that the caller has saved the file with a call to IPersistFile::Save and has finished working with it.

```
STDMETHODIMP CFileView::XPersistFile::SaveCompleted (
    LPCOLESTR pszFileName)
{
return E_NOTIMPL;
}
```

Step Eight: Let MFC Initialize the Class Factories for You

In earlier days, the hapless developer was forced to register all class factories manually. Now this work is done for you when you create the project in App-Wizard in the InitInstance function.

```
BOOL CMfcviewApp::InitInstance ()
{
// Register all OLE servers (factories) as running. This enables the
// OLE libraries to create objects from other applications.
COleObjectFactory::RegisterAll ();

return TRUE;
}
```

Just to show you what you save, here is a peek at what the FILEVIEW sample must do in order to define the class factory object with the IClass-Factory interface and implement that interface completely to create a file viewer object:

```
STDMETHODIMP CFVClassFactory::CreateInstance (
    LPUNKNOWN pUnkOuter, REFIID riid, PPVOID ppvObj)
{
PCFileViewer pObj;
HRESULT hr;
```

(continued)

305

```
*ppvObj = NULL;
hr = E_OUTOFMEMORY;

// Verify that a controlling unknown asks for IUnknown.
if (NULL != pUnkOuter && ! IsEqualIID (riid, IID_IUnknown))
    return E_NOINTERFACE;

// MODIFY:  If you use an object other than CFileViewer,
// be sure to change the name and parameters here. I do
// recommend that you continue to follow this model, however,
// and just modify CFileViewer as necessary.
pObj = new CFileViewer (pUnkOuter, g_hInst, ObjectDestroyed);

if (NULL == pObj)
    return hr;

// MODIFY: Add other parameters to Init as necessary.
hr = pObj->Init ();

if (SUCCEEDED (hr))
{
    // Return the requested interface.
    hr = pObj->QueryInterface (riid, ppvObj);

    if (SUCCEEDED (hr))
    {
        // Everything worked; count the object.
        g_cObj++;
        return NOERROR;
    }
}

// Kill the object if anything failed after creation.
delete pObj;

return hr;
}
```

MFC 3.1 defines special entry points for in-process servers: DllGet-ClassObject and DllCanUnloadNow. AppWizard also provides them when you create your project.

```
STDAPI DllGetClassObject (REFCLSID rclsid, REFIID riid, LPVOID *ppv)
{
return AfxDllGetClassObject (rclsid, riid, ppv);
}

STDAPI DllCanUnloadNow (void)
{
return AfxDllCanUnloadNow ();
}
```

Step Nine: Create the Class to Show the File Contents

So far, you've seen the steps you need to implement to create a file viewer that is a COM object in an INPROC server. To actually show the contents of the file, however, you need to create some windows. In the MFCVIEW sample, I created a simple class named CMyFrame, derived from CFrameWnd. This class includes the frame window and a child multiline edit window:

```
class CMyFrame : public CFrameWnd
{
    DECLARE_DYNCREATE (CMyFrame)
    public:
        CMyFrame ();
        virtual ~CMyFrame ();
        void Create (void);
        void UpdateEdit (char *);

    // Attributes
    public:
        CEdit m_Edit;

    // Operations
    public:
        // Overrides
            // ClassWizard generated virtual function overrides.
            // {{AFX_VIRTUAL (CMyFrame)
            // }}AFX_VIRTUAL

        // Implementation
```

(continued)

```
protected:
    // Generated message map functions
    // {{AFX_MSG (CMyFrame)
    afx_msg void OnSize (UINT nType, int cx, int cy);
    afx_msg void OnFileExit ();
    // }}AFX_MSG
    DECLARE_MESSAGE_MAP ()
}
```

When the ShowInitialize member function is called, it makes a call to a function in the CMyFrame class in order to create the frame window and the multiline edit window:

```
void CMyFrame::Create (void)
{
// Create the frame window.
CFrameWnd::Create ("AfxFrameOrView", "Nancy's Viewer",
    WS_OVERLAPPEDWINDOW | WS_CLIPCHILDREN,
    CRect (CW_USEDEFAULT, CW_USEDEFAULT, 250, 250),
    NULL, MAKEINTRESOURCE (IDR_VIEWERMENU), WS_EX_TOPMOST);

// Create the edit window inside.
// Get the size of the parent window.
CRect wndRect;
GetClientRect (&wndRect);

// Create a child edit control to display the text.
m_Edit.Create (ES_MULTILINE | ES_AUTOVSCROLL | WS_CHILD |
    WS_VISIBLE | ES_AUTOVSCROLL, wndRect, this, ID_EDIT);
}
```

The multiline edit control is updated to reflect the contents of the current file through a call to a member function named UpdateEdit:

```
void CMyFrame::UpdateEdit (char *lpBufPtr)
{
::SendMessage (m_Edit.m_hWnd, WM_SETTEXT, 0, (LPARAM)lpBufPtr);
}
```

The sample file viewer I created simply displays the file contents and is resizable. In your own file viewer, you can add toolbars, status bars, font support, or anything else you like. You could use one of the new rich edit controls instead of a standard multiline edit control. The user interface is up to you.

Step Ten: Build, Register, and Run the File Viewer

You are now ready to compile (after fixing all those missing semicolons and misspelled names), link, register your file viewer, and try it out. If you have registered it correctly, your file viewer will pop up with the specified file loaded. If you need to do some debugging, you can change your project setting to specify QUIKVIEW.EXE as the executable and the directory where your file viewer resides as the working directory. Figure 12-3 shows how I set up my debugging sessions for the MFCVIEW sample.

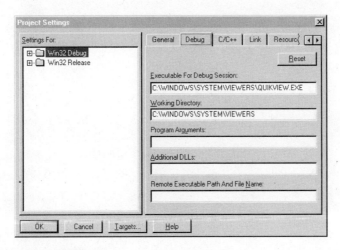

Figure 12-3.
Project settings for the MFCVIEW sample.

> NOTE: To remove the file viewer registered by the MFCVIEW sample in this chapter, please refer to the \README.TXT file on the companion disc.

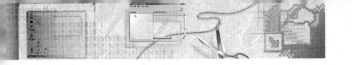

PART III

EXTENDING THE
USER INTERFACE

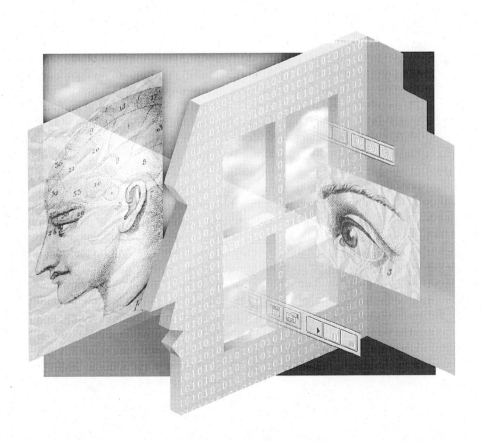

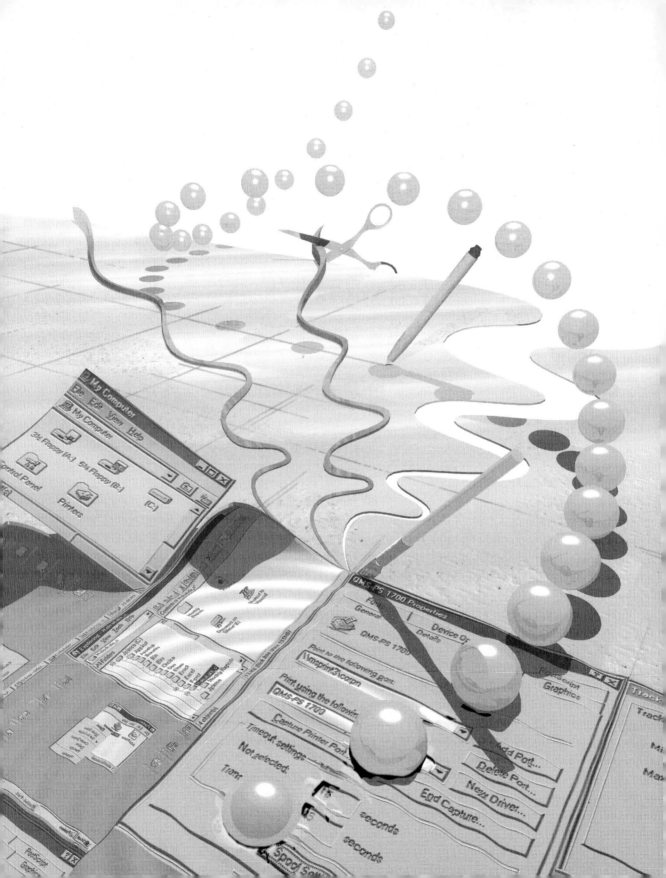

CHAPTER THIRTEEN

User Interface Extensions

The Microsoft Windows 95 user interface is extensible, giving you, as an application developer, access to tools that manipulate objects in the shell name space (which is discussed in detail in Chapter 14). You also have the ability to browse through the file system and networks. If you like, for example, you can create a user interface extension that adds items to the context menu of a specific file type or an extension that lets you assign an icon to a certain file type. This chapter explains the user interface extensions (often called *shell extensions*) and how to implement them. This discussion assumes that you have read Chapter 12, covering file viewers, and that you have at least a minimal understanding of the Component Object Model (COM).

The Windows 95 user interface supports seven types of user interface extensions (referred to as *handlers*):

- *Context menu handlers* add items to the context menu of a particular file object.

- *Drag-and-drop handlers* are context menu handlers that are accessed when a user drops a dragged object in a new location.

- *Icon handlers* add an instance-specific icon for a file object or an icon for a specific file class.

- *Property sheet handlers* add pages to the property sheet displayed for a file object.

- *Copy hook handlers* permit or prevent the copying, moving, deleting, or renaming of a folder or a printer object.

- *Drop target handlers* control the action that occurs when a dragged object is dropped on another object.

- *Data object handlers* supply the interface when files are being dragged and dropped or copied and pasted.

Like file viewers, all user interface extensions are implemented as COM objects. Once you understand the basics of how to implement COM objects, you'll need relatively little additional information to implement a user interface extension.

I wrote two user interface extension samples in MFC: PROPEXT (a property sheet handler) and CTXTMENU (a context menu handler). If you don't use MFC, you'll want to look at SHELLEXT (written by Greg Keyser), a sample from the Win32 SDK that demonstrates how to create various user interface extensions. (I included this sample on the companion disc.)

Registering User Interface Extensions

Like all COM objects, user interface extensions must be registered in the Registry, or they won't work. An extension must register its class ID (CLSID) under the Registry key HKEY_CLASSES_ROOT\CLSID. Within this key, the extension adds an InProcServer32 key that gives the location of the extension's DLL. The first statement in the following sample code registers the CLSID of my property sheet extension, NancyPropSheet. The second statement in the code specifies the location of the DLL containing the extension and the threading model:

```
[HKEY_CLASSES_ROOT\CLSID\{771a9da0-731a-11ce-993c-00aa004adb6c}]
   @="NancyPropSheet"
[HKEY_CLASSES_ROOT\CLSID\{771a9da0-731a-11ce-993c-00aa004adb6c}\
   InprocServer32]
   @="c:\\windows\\system\\propext.dll"
   "ThreadingModel"="Apartment"
```

The shellex key contains the information used to associate a user interface extension with a file type. You must also register your extension under this key. You can map the user interface extension to a particular class of file (based on the filename extension), or you can specify that it is valid for files of all types. To register the property sheet for files of a specific type—NWCFile, for example—specify the file type as shown here:

```
[HKEY_CLASSES_ROOT\.NWC]
   @="NWCFile"
[HKEY_CLASSES_ROOT\NWCFile]
   @="Shell Extension file"
[HKEY_CLASSES_ROOT\NWCFile\shellex\PropertySheetHandlers]
   @="NWCPage"
[HKEY_CLASSES_ROOT\NWCFile\shellex\PropertySheetHandlers\NWCPage]
   @="{771a9da0-731a-11ce-993c-00aa004adb6c}"
```

If you want all files to reap the benefits of your special property sheet page, specify an asterisk (*) after HKEY_CLASSES_ROOT, as I did in my property sheet handler, PROPEXT:

```
[HKEY_CLASSES_ROOT\*\shellex\PropertySheetHandlers]
    @="NWCPage"
[HKEY_CLASSES_ROOT\*\shellex\PropertySheetHandlers\NWCPage]
    @="{771a9da0-731a-11ce-993c-00aa004adb6c}"
```

> **NOTE:** To remove any of the user interface extensions that are registered by the samples discussed in this chapter, please refer to the \README.TXT file on the companion disc.

Implementing IShellExtInit

To initialize an instance of a user interface extension, the system uses one of two interfaces: IShellExtInit or IPersistFile. You must use the IShellExtInit interface to initialize context menu handlers, drag-and-drop handlers, and property sheet handlers.

Like all COM interfaces, IShellExtInit supports the three standard IUnknown member functions—QueryInterface, AddRef, and Release—as shown in the PROPEXT sample. (If the syntax looks a little odd, remember that this sample was written in MFC and uses the built-in macros that support COM objects and nested objects.)

```
// IUnknown for IShellExtInit
STDMETHODIMP CPropExt::XShellInit::QueryInterface (
    REFIID riid, void **ppv)
{
METHOD_PROLOGUE (CPropExt, ShellInit);
TRACE ("CPropExt::XShellInit::QueryInterface\n");
return pThis->ExternalQueryInterface (&riid, ppv);
}

STDMETHODIMP_(ULONG) CPropExt::XShellInit::AddRef (void)
{
METHOD_PROLOGUE (CPropExt, ShellInit);
return pThis->ExternalAddRef ();
}

STDMETHODIMP_(ULONG) CPropExt::XShellInit::Release (void)
{
METHOD_PROLOGUE (CPropExt, ShellInit);
return pThis->ExternalRelease ();
}
```

When you use the IShellExtInit interface, you must also implement the Initialize member function.

Initialize   This member function is passed a pointer to the IDataObject that represents the file object(s) being manipulated. My initialization code gets the name of the selected file. Because the system stores that filename in the same way that the filename is stored during a drag procedure, I can get the file by using the DragQueryFile function. The filename is saved in a member variable for the extension object.

```
STDMETHODIMP CPropExt::XShellInit::Initialize (
    LPCITEMIDLIST pidlFolder, IDataObject *pdobj, HKEY hkeyProgID)
{
METHOD_PROLOGUE (CPropExt, ShellInit);
TRACE ("CPropExt::XShellInit::Intialize\n");

HRESULT hres = E_FAIL;
FORMATETC fmte =
{
    CF_HDROP,              // use CF_HDROP format
    NULL,                  // no specific device required
    DVASPECT_CONTENT,      // embedded object
    -1,                    // must be -1 for DVASPECT_CONTENT
    TYMED_HGLOBAL          // how to transfer data
};
STGMEDIUM medium;

// No data object
if (pdobj == NULL)
{
    TRACE ("CPropExt::XShellInit::Initialize() no data object");
    return E_FAIL;
}

// Use the given IDataObject to get a list of filenames (CF_HDROP).
hres = pdobj->GetData (&fmte, &medium);

if (FAILED (hres))
{
    TRACE ("CPropExt::XShellInit::Initialize() can't get data");
    return E_FAIL;
}
```

```
// HDROP can contain more than one file. If the user selects
// multiple files and brings up a context menu, your handler
// will be called. Not all files will be your type! Only the
// first one will be that type.
if (DragQueryFile ((HDROP)medium.hGlobal, (UINT)(-1), NULL, 0) == 1)
{
    DragQueryFile ((HDROP)medium.hGlobal, 0, pThis->m_szFileName,
        sizeof (pThis->m_szFileName));
    hres = S_OK;
}
else
    hres = E_FAIL;

// Release the data.
ReleaseStgMedium (&medium);

return hres;
}
```

Initializing with IPersistFile

Icon handlers, drop target handlers, and data object handlers are initialized with the IPersistFile interface, which is used to load and save documents that are stored in disk files (as opposed to objects stored in IStorage instances). Once the document is loaded, the application opens it as needed. IPersistFile itself won't open the file for you; it has no way of knowing what type of data your file contains.

In addition to the standard IUnknown functions, the IPersistFile interface supports six other member functions. Five of these functions—IsDirty, Save, SaveCompleted, GetCurFile, and GetClassID—are part of the IPersist-File interface but are not required for user interface extensions. For each of these functions, you can simply return E_NOTIMPL. First, however, let's look at the Load member function, which does need to be implemented.

Load   This member function loads the document object that is specified in the *pszFileName* parameter. A user interface extension saves the filename for further processing. For example, an icon handler saves the filename to determine which type of icon to supply for the file.

Unlike the other functions listed here, the Load function is required for user interface extensions. The implementation, as you can see, is trivial:

```
STDMETHODIMP CIconExt::XPerFile::Load (LPCOLESTR pszFileName,
   DWORD dwMode)
{
METHOD_PROLOGUE (CIconExt, PerFile);

WideCharToMultiByte (
   CP_ACP,                        // codePage
   0,                             // dwFlags
   (LPCWSTR)pszFileName,          // lpWideCharStr
   -1,                            // cchWideChar
   pThis->m_szFile,               // lpMultiByteStr
   sizeof (pThis->m_szFile),      // cchMultiByte,
   NULL,                          // lpDefaultChar,
   NULL);                         // lpUsedDefaultChar

return NOERROR;
}
```

The following member functions, as mentioned earlier, are supported by IPersistFile but are not required by user interface extensions.

IsDirty   The IsDirty function checks a document object for any changes that might have been made since the document was loaded.

Save   This function saves a copy of the object to the given filename.

SaveCompleted   The SaveCompleted function simply signals that the object has been saved.

GetCurFile   This member function returns either the absolute path of the document's currently associated file or the default filename prompt (if no currently associated file exists).

GetClassID   The GetClassID function returns a document's class ID.

Context Menu Handlers

The first user interface extensions we'll look at are context menu handlers, which you can use to add items to a context menu. Figure 13-1 shows the result of installing the context menu handler in the CTXTMENU sample. I added the Test Context Menu item to the menu.

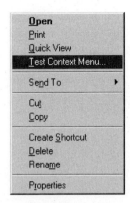

Figure 13-1.
The context menu after the CTXTMENU handler has been installed.

By adding items to an object's context menu, you are also adding verbs for that file type. *Verbs* are the set of operations supported by a particular object—open, save, or play, for instance. You can designate a menu item as either class-specific or instance-specific. Instance-specific context menus apply only to individual files. Generally, unless the menu items are dynamic (that is, they depend on the state of the object), it's much easier to simply add static verbs in the Registry than to add a context menu handler. The data exported from the Registry for the audio CD player on my system is shown here. The Play command is a static verb.

```
REGEDIT4

[HKEY_CLASSES_ROOT\AudioCD]
@="AudioCD"
"EditFlags"=hex:02,00,00,00

[HKEY_CLASSES_ROOT\AudioCD\DefaultIcon]
@="C:\\WINDOWS\\SYSTEM\\shell32.dll,40"

[HKEY_CLASSES_ROOT\AudioCD\shell]
@="play"

[HKEY_CLASSES_ROOT\AudioCD\shell\play]
@="&Play"

[HKEY_CLASSES_ROOT\AudioCD\shell\play\command]
@="C:\\WINDOWS\\cdplayer.exe /play %1"
```

Although you can use a context menu handler to alter items on a context menu or remove items from a context menu, it is not recommended. Think about it. Would you want other applications messing around with your menu items? Some context menu handlers might rely on others being added first, when in fact the last thing the system does is add an item to the context menu. As a result, a handler might be loaded, but the item might not appear on the context menu.

Registering Context Menu Handlers

Context menu handlers are registered with the system as described earlier ("Registering User Interface Extensions," page 314). You must use the ContextMenuHandlers key under shellex. The following code is from the REG file created for the CTXTMENU sample:

```
[HKEY_CLASSES_ROOT\*\shellex\ContextMenuHandlers]
    @="NWCMenu"
[HKEY_CLASSES_ROOT\*\shellex\ContextMenuHandlers\NWCMenu]
    @="{5fbcd2e0-73dd-11ce-993c-00aa004adb6c}"
```

Context Menu Handler Interfaces

To create a context menu handler, you must implement both the IShellExt-Init and the IContextMenu interfaces. In addition to the usual IUnknown functions, the context menu handler interface uses the QueryContextMenu, InvokeCommand, and GetCommandString member functions.

QueryContextMenu   The QueryContextMenu member function is called just before the system displays an object's context menu. A context menu handler inserts a menu item by position (MF_BYPOSITION) directly into the context menu by calling InsertMenu. In the call to InsertMenu, Query-ContextMenu passes the handle to the context menu in the *hMenu* parameter. The second parameter, *indexMenu*, specifies where to insert the menu item; and the third parameter, *idCmdFirst*, provides the first menu item identifier you should use for that context menu. Because menu items must be string items (MF_STRING), the *uFlags* parameter of InsertMenu must be *MF_BYPOSITION | MF_STRING* for each menu item the context menu handler inserts. The following example demonstrates how to add three new menu items (Sample Menu Item 1, Sample Menu Item 2, and Sample Menu Item 3) to a context menu:

```
STDMETHODIMP Sample::QueryContextMenu (HMENU hmenu,
    UINT indexMenu, UINT idCmdFirst, UINT idCmdLast, UINT uFlags)
{
int cVerbs = THREE_ITEMS;

for (int i = 0; i < cVerbs; i++)
{
    char szMenu [80];
    wsprintf (szMenu, "Sample Menu Item #%d", i + 1);
    InsertMenu (hmenu, indexMenu + i, MF_BYPOSITION | MF_STRING,
        idCmdFirst + i, szMenu);
}

return (HRESULT)cVerbs;
}
```

InvokeCommand   InvokeCommand is called when the user selects an item from the context menu for which you have registered a handler. This function is passed a pointer to the LPCMINVOKECOMMANDINFO structure, which contains information including the size of the structure (*cbSize*), the owner window for any message box or dialog box (*hwnd*), the validity of the *dwHotkey* and *hIcon* parameters (*fMask*), the command to be executed (*lpVerb*), the flag to be passed to ShowWindow (*nShow*), the hot key to be assigned to the application after it is opened (*dwHotkey*), and the handle to an icon (*hIcon*). Hot keys and icons are optional. The LOWORD of the *lpVerb* member contains the menu item identifier offset (the menu item ID minus *idCmd-First*), which is used to determine what command the user has chosen. In the following code from the CTXTMENU sample, this value is the new command, ID_NEWCMD, and a message box is displayed:

```
STDMETHODIMP CTxtMenu::XMenuExt::InvokeCommand (
    LPCMINVOKECOMMANDINFO lpici)
{
METHOD_PROLOGUE (CTxtMenu, MenuExt);
char szTest [MAX_PATH * 2];

if (HIWORD (lpici->lpVerb))
{
    AfxMessageBox ("E_FAIL");
    return E_FAIL;
}
```

(continued)

```
if (LOWORD (lpici->lpVerb) > ID_NEWCMD)
{
    AfxMessageBox ("Invalid Arg");
    return E_INVALIDARG;
}

if (LOWORD (lpici->lpVerb) == ID_NEWCMD)
{
    wsprintf (szTest, "Context menu for file: %s", pThis->m_szFileName);
    ::MessageBox (lpici->hwnd, szTest, "Context Menu Handler", MB_OK);
}
else
    ::MessageBox (lpici->hwnd, "ID != ID_NEWCMD", "Context Menu Handler",
        MB_OK);

return NOERROR;
}
```

After you install the context menu handler, click the item labeled Test Context Menu to see the dialog box shown in Figure 13-2.

Figure 13-2.
The Context Menu Handler dialog box.

GetCommandString A context menu handler must also implement Get-CommandString. This function is called to provide Help text for a context menu item. GetCommandString simply copies into the *pszName* string the text that will be displayed:

```
STDMETHODIMP CTxtMenu::XMenuExt::GetCommandString (
    UINT idCmd, UINT uType, UINT *pwReserved, LPSTR pszName, UINT cchMax)
{
if (idCmd > ID_NEWCMD)
    return ResultFromScode (E_INVALIDARG);

if (idCmd == ID_NEWCMD)
    lstrcpy (pszName, "Context Menu Test");

return NOERROR;
}
```

Drag-and-Drop Handlers

If you know how to implement a context menu handler, implementing a drag-and-drop handler is a piece of cake. Drag-and-drop handlers are context menu handlers that are accessed when a user drops an object after dragging it to a new location. The two kinds of handlers differ only in how you register them. You must use the DragDropHandlers key to register a drag-and-drop handler, as you can see in this sample REG file:

```
REGEDIT4

[HKEY_CLASSES_ROOT\CLSID\{<CLSID value>}]
    @="Sample Context Menu"
[HKEY_CLASSES_ROOT\CLSID\{<CLSID value>}\InprocServer32]
    @="c:\\windows\\system\\ctxtmenu.dll"
"ThreadingModel"="Apartment"

[HKEY_CLASSES_ROOT\.NWC]
    @="NWCFile"
[HKEY_CLASSES_ROOT\NWCFile]
    @="Shell Extension file"
[HKEY_CLASSES_ROOT\NWCFile\shellex\DragDropHandlers]
    @="NWCDD"
[HKEY_CLASSES_ROOT\NWCFile\shellex\DragDropHandlers\NWCDD]
    @="{<CLSID value>}"
```

Icon Handlers

An icon handler allows you to customize the icon that is displayed for a particular type of file. If you create a file whose extension is not registered for a specific icon, the standard Windows icon is associated with the file by default. Figure 13-3 on the next page shows three test files with the default icons.

To install the icon handler created by the SHELLEXT sample, copy SHELLEXT.DLL to the \WINDOWS\SYSTEM folder and run SHELLEXT.-REG. Then go to Windows Explorer, right-click one of the test files, choose Properties from the context menu, and select a GAK color. Finally, refresh Windows Explorer (by pressing the F5 key) to see the icons for the test files change to the ones that are specified in the handler, as shown in Figure 13-4 on the next page.

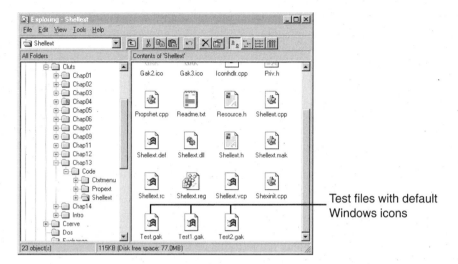

Figure 13-3.
Test files with default Windows icons.

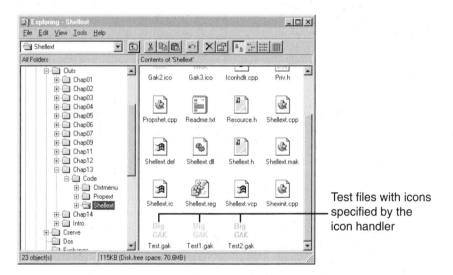

Figure 13-4.
New icons for the test files.

If you want to provide an icon for all files of a certain type, you don't need to write an icon handler. Instead, you can simply add the DefaultIcon key for your application to the Registry and set its value to the path of the executable or the DLL containing the icon and the index to the icon:

```
DefaultIcon = c:\Mydir\Myapp.exe,1
```

Under Windows 95, you can specify that each file instance of a certain type should have a different icon. To do this, specify %1 as the value for the DefaultIcon key, and then register the icon handler under the shellex\IconHandler key. An application can have only one IconHandler entry.

```
[HKEY_CLASSES_ROOT\NWCFile\shellex\IconHandler]
   @="{<CLSID value>}"
```

Icon Handler Interfaces

To create an icon handler, you must implement the IPersistFile interface (described earlier in this chapter) and the IExtractIcon interface. IExtractIcon supports the GetIconLocation and ExtractIcon member functions, in addition to the standard IUnknown functions.

GetIconLocation   This member function retrieves the location of the icon. Normally, this location is an executable or DLL filename, but it can be any file. The function fills in the *szIconFile* parameter with the fully qualified path of the file that contains the icon, the *piIndex* parameter with the index to the icon in the file, and the *pwFlags* parameter with the type of icon. In the following example, the flag is specified as GIL_PERINSTANCE, which means that different files of this type have different icons.

```
STDMETHODIMP CIconExt::XIconExt::GetIconLocation (UINT uFlags,
   LPSTR szIconFile, UINT cchMax, int *piIndex, UINT *pwFlags)
{
METHOD_PROLOGUE (CIconExt, IconExt);
::GetModuleFileName (AfxGetInstanceHandle (), szIconFile, cchMax);
*piIndex = 0;
*pwFlags |= GIL_PERINSTANCE;
return S_OK;
}
```

Other supported flags include GIL_SIMULATEDOC, which specifies that the icon is the one registered for this file type's document type; and GIL_PERCLASS, which stipulates that icons are the same for all files of this class. (As mentioned earlier, however, don't create an icon handler for all files of a certain class—just update the Registry entry instead.)

ExtractIcon   This member function is called when the interface needs to display an icon that does not reside in an executable or a DLL. When the icon for a file is in a separate ICO file (or any other type of file), the icon handler must extract the icon and return it. Since applications usually have file icons in executables or DLLs, icon handlers can simply implement ExtractIcon as a return-only function that returns S_FALSE:

```
STDMETHODIMP CIconExt::XIconExt::ExtractIcon (
    LPCSTR pszFile, UINT nIconIndex, HICON *phiconLarge,
    HICON *phiconSmall, UINT nIconSize)
{
return S_FALSE;
}
```

Property Sheet Handlers

When a user chooses Properties from the context menu of a file object, Windows 95 displays a property sheet for that file type. At a minimum, you'll see a General property sheet page with information about the file, including its type, location, size, and so on, as shown in Figure 13-5.

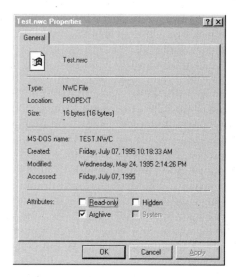

Figure 13-5.
The standard property sheet for a file object.

If you want to offer more information about files of a certain type (whether the file has been checked by an individual, for instance, or when the file was most recently backed up), you can customize the property sheet for that file type by implementing and registering a property sheet handler. I used a property sheet handler to add an extra page to the property sheet that is shown in Figure 13-6. This page simply serves to show that the property sheet extension has been installed and registered for NWC files.

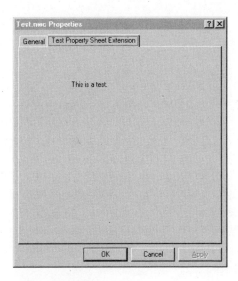

Figure 13-6.
A property sheet page added by a user interface extension.

Like the other user interface extensions you've seen, property sheet handlers must be registered in the Registry. These handlers use the Property-SheetHandlers key to store their CLSIDs. Here is the part of the REG file that registers the property sheet handler for NWCFile:

```
[HKEY_CLASSES_ROOT\NWCFile\shellex\PropertySheetHandlers]
   @="NWCPage"
[HKEY_CLASSES_ROOT\NWCFile\shellex\PropertySheetHandlers\NWCPage]
   @="{771a9da0-731a-11ce-993c-00aa004adb6c}"
```

To register the property sheet handler for all file types, as I did in the PROPEXT sample, substitute an asterisk (*) for the two instances of NWCFile in the preceding code.

You can also register multiple property sheet handlers for a file type. In this case, the order of the subkey names in the PropertySheetHandlers key determines the order of the additional property sheet pages. You can use a maximum of 24 (MAXPROPPAGES) property sheet pages.

Property Sheet Handler Interfaces

Property sheet handlers are initialized through the IShellExtInit interface and use the IShellPropSheetExt interface. In addition to the IUnknown functions, the IShellPropSheetExt interface includes the AddPages and Replace-Page member functions.

AddPages This member function adds pages to a property sheet. It is passed a pointer to a function that will add the property page and the *lParam* parameter that will be passed to the function. *lParam* is useful for passing application-specific data to the handler. The property sheet handler creates each added page by using the CreatePropSheetPage function and uses the handle that function returns in a call to lpfnAddPage. The following code adds a single property sheet page and provides a dialog procedure for the page:

```
STDMETHODIMP CPropExt::XPropExt::AddPages (
    LPFNADDPROPSHEETPAGE lpfnAddPage, LPARAM lParam)
{
METHOD_PROLOGUE (CPropExt, PropExt);
TRACE ("CPropExt::XPropExt::AddPages\n");

PROPSHEETPAGE psp;

psp.dwSize      = sizeof (psp);   // no extra data
psp.dwFlags     = PSP_USEREFPARENT;
psp.hInstance   = AfxGetResourceHandle ();
psp.pszTemplate = MAKEINTRESOURCE (IDD_TESTPAGE);
psp.pfnDlgProc  = (DLGPROC) pThis->PropExtDlgProc;
psp.pcRefParent = (UINT *)& (pThis->m_cRefThisDll);

pThis->m_hPage = ::CreatePropertySheetPage (&psp);
if (pThis->m_hPage)
{
    if (! lpfnAddPage (pThis->m_hPage, lParam))
        ::DestroyPropertySheetPage (pThis->m_hPage);
}
return NOERROR;
}

BOOL APIENTRY CPropExt::PropExtDlgProc (
    HWND hDlg, UINT message, UINT wParam, LONG lParam)
{

switch (message)
{
```

```
case WM_NOTIFY:
    switch (((NMHDR FAR *)lParam)->code)
    {
        case PSN_APPLY:
            SetWindowLong (hDlg, DWL_MSGRESULT, TRUE);
            break;

        case PSN_KILLACTIVE:
            SetWindowLong (hDlg, DWL_MSGRESULT, FALSE);
            return 1;
            break;

        case PSN_RESET:
            SetWindowLong (hDlg, DWL_MSGRESULT, FALSE);
            break;
    }
}
return FALSE;
}
```

ReplacePage   ReplacePage is called for Control Panel applications, allowing them to replace an existing property sheet page with their own page.
Standard property sheet extensions do not need to implement this function
and can simply return E_NOTIMPL.

Copy Hook Handlers

Windows 95 calls a copy hook handler before a folder object is moved, copied, deleted, or renamed. You can create a copy hook handler to provide approval or disapproval of a given action. The handler itself does not actually
perform the task; the system does that after it receives approval from the copy
hook handler. You cannot use a copy hook handler to monitor an action, such
as a copying operation, because the handler is not informed of the success or
failure of the action.

Like other user interface extensions, copy hook handlers are registered
in the Registry. A folder object can have multiple copy hook handlers. A copy
hook handler is registered under the directory\shellex\CopyHookHandlers
key. Here is a copy hook handler registered in the SHELLEXT sample:

```
[HKEY_CLASSES_ROOT\directory\shellex\CopyHookHandlers\GAKsCopyHook]
    @="{87b9bd00-c65c-11cd-a259-00dd010e8c28}"
[HKEY_CLASSES_ROOT\*\shellex\CopyHookHandlers\GAKsCopyHook]
    @="{87b9bd00-c65c-11cd-a259-00dd010e8c28}"
```

Copy hook handlers differ from other user interface extensions in that the copy hook handler interface is initialized directly—that is, without using an IShellExtInit or IPersistFile interface first. Because of this, you don't need to implement these interfaces. (Hooray! Less work!) You must, however, implement the ICopyHook interface. But this is easily done; you need to implement only the standard IUnknown member functions and ICopyHook's one function, CopyCallBack.

CopyCallBack   The system calls the CopyCallBack member function before it copies, moves, renames, or deletes a folder object. The operation is designated by the *wFunc* parameter as one of the following:

FO_COPY	Copies files in *pszSrcFile* to *pszDestFile*
FO_MOVE	Moves files in *pszSrcFile* to *pszDestFile*
FO_RENAME	Renames files in *pszSrcFile*
FO_DELETE	Deletes files in *pszSrcFile*

This function returns an integer value (IDYES or IDNO) that indicates whether the system should perform the operation. The system calls each copy hook handler registered for a folder object until all the handlers have been called or until a handler returns IDCANCEL.

Drop Target Handlers

A drop target handler controls the action that occurs when one object is dropped on another object. For example, if you drag a Microsoft Word document and drop it on the Word icon or on a shortcut to the Word icon, Word will start and open that document. A drop target handler makes this happen.

Unlike the other user interface extensions we have discussed so far, only one drop target handler at a time is supported. In those other cases, you could register many extensions. (Note that the Registry entries refer to them as, for example, PropertySheetHandlers.)

You register a drop target handler in the Registry under the Drop-Handler key, with the value being the CLSID of the drop target extension:

```
[HKEY_CLASSES_ROOT\SampleType\shellex\DropHandler]
    @="{<CLSID value>}"
```

A drop target handler is implemented through the IDropTarget interface and initialized with the IPersistFile interface. IDropTarget implements the DragEnter, DragOver, DragLeave, and Drop member functions as well as the standard IUnknown functions.

DragEnter   DragEnter signals the beginning of a drop. It determines both whether the target window can accept the dragged object and what effect the dragged object will have on the target window. The function is passed the state of the keyboard (whether one of the keyboard modifier keys is being pressed: MK_CONTROL, MK_SHIFT, MK_ALT, MK_LBUTTON, MK_M-BUTTON, or MK_RBUTTON), the cursor point, and a pointer to which drop effect should be used. The drop effect can be DROPEFFECT_NONE, DROP-EFFECT_COPY, DROPEFFECT_MOVE, DROPEFFECT_LINK, or DROP-EFFECT_SCROLL.

DragOver   This member function provides feedback to the user about the state of the drag operation within a drop target application.

DragLeave   DragLeave causes the drop target to remove its feedback if the mouse leaves the drop area or if the drop is canceled.

Drop   This member function, the most interesting of the four, is responsible for effecting the drop of the object onto the target. In the following code, the data for the object is retrieved, the name of the file being dropped is queried, and the function returns S_OK for success. If the data for the object cannot be retrieved, the function returns E_FAIL.

```
STDMETHODIMP SampleType::Drop (IDataObject *pDataObj,
    DWORD grfKeyState, POINTL pt, DWORD *pdwEffect)
{
HRESULT hres = E_FAIL;
FORMATETC fmte = {CF_HDROP, NULL, DVASPECT_CONTENT, -1, TYMED_HGLOBAL};
STGMEDIUM medium;

if (pDataObj && SUCCEEDED (pDataObj->GetData (&fmte, &medium)))
{
   char szFileDropped [MAX_PATH];

   DragQueryFile ((HDROP)medium.hGlobal, 0, szFileDropped,
      sizeof (szFileDropped));
   TRACE ("SampleType::Drop(%s,%s)", this->szFileName, szFileDropped);
   hres = S_OK;
```

(continued)

331

```
    if (medium.pUnkForRelease)
        medium.pUnkForRelease->Release ();
    else
        GlobalFree (medium.hGlobal);
}

return hres;
}
```

Data Object Handlers

A data object handler allows your application to supply the IDataObject interface for a file type when files are being dragged and dropped or copied and pasted. IDataObject is an important OLE interface that is responsible for transferring and caching data and presentations. IDataObject defines functions that retrieve, store, and enumerate data and that handle data-change notifications. A default IDataObject is available for all file types, so you don't have to implement this interface if you like the default implementation.

Like the drop target handler, only one data object handler is supported at a time. To register a data object handler, you use the DataHandler key in the Registry and give the CLSID value of your extension:

```
[HKEY_CLASSES_ROOT\SampleType\shellex\DataHandler]
    @="{<CLSID value>}"
```

A data object handler is initialized with the IPersistFile interface and implements the IDataObject interface. Aside from the standard IUnknown member functions, this handler must implement the following functions.

GetData   The GetData member function retrieves the data associated with the given object, in the format that is specified from a designated storage medium. Both the data format (FORMATETC) and the storage medium (STG-MEDIUM) are defined in detail in the OLE 2 Help documentation.

GetDataHere   This member function, like GetData, retrieves the data associated with the given object, in the format that is specified from a designated storage medium. In the GetData function, however, the callee provides the storage medium, whereas the caller supplies the storage medium in the GetData-Here function.

QueryGetData   QueryGetData looks at the format of the data and determines whether a call to GetData will succeed.

GetCanonicalFormatEtc   GetCanonicalFormatEtc retrieves a list of the formats supported for the object.

SetData   This member function sets the data in the specified format.

EnumFormatEtc   The EnumFormatEtc member function enumerates the formats that you can use to store data obtained by the GetData function or sent with the SetData function.

DAdvise   DAdvise creates a connection between the data transfer object and an advisory sink. The advisory sink is then informed when the object's data changes.

DUnadvise   The DUnadvise member function deletes the advisory sink connection that the DAdvise function establishes.

EnumDAdvise   The EnumDAdvise member function enumerates the advisory sink connections currently established for an object.

Like the IDropTarget interface, the IDataObject interface is fully explained and referenced in the OLE 2 documentation. If you aren't familiar with drop targets or data objects, however, it's probably not a good idea to think about creating an extension to implement these interfaces.

Debugging User Interface Extensions

Once you have written and registered your user interface extension, what do you do if it doesn't work? In most applications, you can simply run Microsoft Visual C++ in debug mode, set some breakpoints, and start debugging. But user interface extensions are loaded at startup for Windows Explorer, so you must find a way to start Windows Explorer without loading all its DLLs. Here's how:

1. Open your Project menu and choose the Settings item. Click the Debug tab, and type the path to EXPLORER.EXE in the Executable For Debug Session edit box.

2. Close all applications, and turn off your computer.

3. Restart Windows 95 and Visual C++, loading your user interface extension.

4. Click the Start button, and then choose Shutdown.

5. Hold down the Ctrl-Alt-Shift keys and simultaneously click No. (Sounds a bit like playing Twister, doesn't it?)

6. The desktop may go blank, and your heart may start palpitating, but don't worry. If you press Alt-Tab, you can get to your instance of Visual C++. At this point, you are ready to debug. Set your breakpoints and go.

If you don't want to exit Windows to debug your extension, you can force the system to unload DLLs very quickly by changing a setting in the Registry. Under HKEY_LOCAL_MACHINE\SOFTWARE\Microsoft\Windows\CurrentVersion\explorer, add the AlwaysUnloadDll key and set its value to 1. (I always set it to 1, but any value will do.) Adding this key sets the time-out value for DLLs to a very small value.

User Interface Extensions and Windows NT

You can use Windows 95 user interface extensions under Microsoft Windows NT version 3.51 running with its new shell. (The shell is still due to be released as of this writing.) You will, however, need to place the extension DLL in \WINDOWS\SYSTEM32 rather than in \WINDOWS\SYSTEM. You'll also need to add one step in your application's setup process and registration.

To have Windows NT recognize and run your user interface extension, the handler's CLSID must be listed under a new Registry key that contains a list of approved handlers. By default, only a person with administrator privileges is allowed to modify the list in this key. Here is the location where the CLSID must be registered in Windows NT:

```
HKEY_LOCAL_MACHINE\Software\Microsoft\Windows\CurrentVersion\
    Shell Extensions\Approved
```

To register the extension, you must add a named value to the Approved key. The name of the value must be the string form of the CLSID, which you can obtain by using the StringFromCLSID function.

If you haven't yet written applications for Windows NT, you might find it odd that your setup application would be unable to write to the Approved key. The ability to write to this key depends on the access privileges of the person installing the application. The setup application should attempt to open the key, requesting the KEY_SET_VALUE permission. If it succeeds, you can add the new CLSID to fully register the corresponding extension. If the request fails, with a security violation, the person installing the application does not have permission to register new extensions. In this case, the setup application might warn the user that some application features will not be available unless an administrator turns them on (by installing the application or by writing the Registry keys directly). Or, if the extension is crucial to the application's functioning, the setup application might cause the installation to fail completely, notifying the user that an administrator must install the program.

The following sample code demonstrates how an application can register its user interface extension under Windows NT:

```
// First, attempt to open
// the Registry key where
// approved extensions are listed.
long err;
HKEY hkApproved;

err = RegOpenKeyEx (
   HKEY_LOCAL_MACHINE,
   "Software\\Microsoft\\Windows\\CurrentVersion\\"
      "Shell Extensions\\Approved",
   0,
   KEY_SET_VALUE,
   &hkApproved);

if (err == ERROR_ACCESS_DENIED)
{
   // The user does not have permission to add a new value
   // to this key. In this case, you might warn the user that some
   // application features will not be available unless an administrator
   // installs the application. If the extension is central to the
   // application's functioning, tell the user that only an
   // administrator can perform the install, and stop the install.
   ⋮
}
```

(continued)

```
else if (err == ERROR_FILE_NOT_FOUND)
{
    // The key does not exist. This happens only if setup is running
    // on Windows 95 instead of Windows NT or if you are installing on an
    // older version of either operating system that lacks the Win95 UI.
    ⋮
}

else if (err != ERROR_SUCCESS)
{
    // Some other problem...
}

else
{
    // Assume that lpstrProgID contains your ProgID string.
    LPSTR lpstrProgID = "My Bogus Class";

    // Assume that clsidExtension contains the CLSID structure.
    // The following code creates a string from this CLSID.
    // If a string version of the CLSID is already handy,
    // skip this code.
    CLSID clsidExtension = {0x11111111, 0x1111, 0x1111,
        0x11, 0x11, 0x11, 0x11, 0x11, 0x11, 0x11, 0x11};
    HRESULT hr;
    LPOLESTR lpolestrCLSID;
    char rgchCLSID [40];

    CoInitialize (NULL);

    hr = StringFromCLSID (clsidExtension, &lpolestrCLSID);

    // StringFromCLSID returns a Unicode string, so convert to ANSI for
    // calling the Registry. Note that on Windows NT you can call the
    // Unicode version of the Registry API instead.
    WideCharToMultiByte (CP_ACP, 0, lpolestrCLSID, -1, rgchCLSID, 40,
        NULL, NULL);

    CoTaskMemFree (lpolestrCLSID);
    CoUninitialize ();
```

```
// Now add the new value to the Registry.
err = RegSetValueEx (
   hkApproved,
   rgchCLSID,
   0,
   REG_SZ,
   (const BYTE *)lpstrProgID,
   strlen (lpstrProgID));

// Finally, close the key.
err = RegCloseKey (hkApproved);
}
```

If you are registering your extension for Windows NT version 3.51 (with the new shell) by using a REG file, add the following line:

```
[HKEY_LOCAL_MACHINE\Software\Microsoft\Windows\CurrentVersion\
   Shell Extensions\Approved\{CLSID_VALUE}]
   @="My Shell Extension"
```

For *CLSID_VALUE,* insert the actual CLSID for your extension. For *My Shell Extension,* substitute the name of the exported user interface extension.

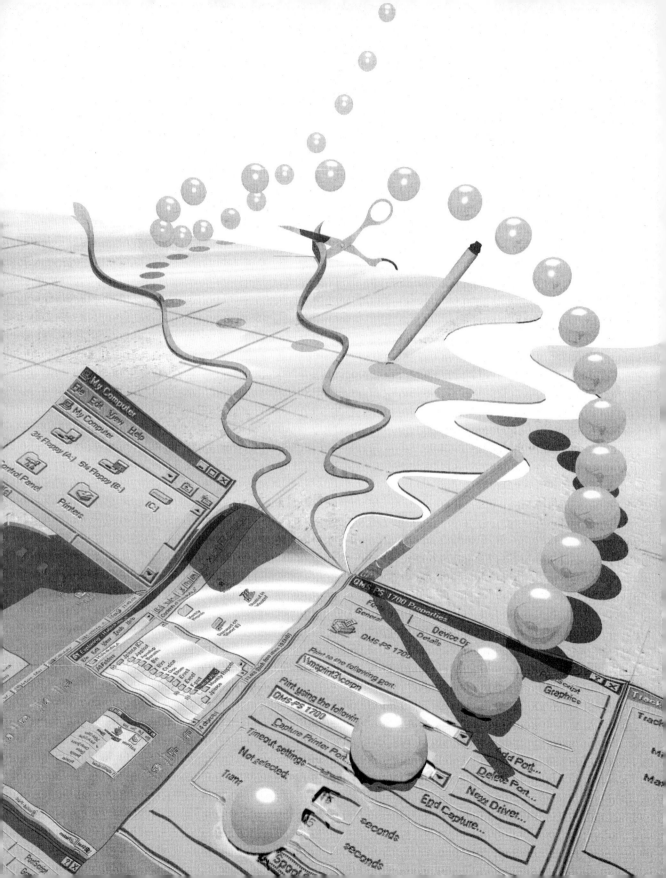

C H A P T E R   F O U R T E E N

The Shell Name Space

In this final chapter, we'll discuss the shell name space and how developers can take advantage of some of the built-in browsing functions in Microsoft Windows 95. The ability to browse the shell name space lets you scan, locate, or display information about the directory structure of the system or about particular folders.

The *shell name space* is a collection of symbols, such as filenames, directory (folder) names, or database keys. The system stores all these objects and others in a hierarchical structure and uses Windows Explorer to display the information. At the root of this structure is the desktop.

A developer not as savvy as you are might say, "So what? This is just a glorified directory structure." Bzzt! Thanks for playing. Next contestant, if you please.

The shell name space does include file system information, but it contains much more than files and folders. It also includes network resources, printers, Control Panel applications, the Recycle Bin, and so on. This arrangement makes it easy for the user to find an object without having to understand the underlying directory structure of the file system. Figure 14-1 on the next page, for instance, from the ENUMDESK sample (written by Greg Keyser), displays the contents of a Control Panel folder.

This chapter presents two samples that demonstrate how to use built-in functions to browse the shell name space. The first sample, Greg Keyser's ENUMDESK, is written in C using the Win32 API. The second sample is MFCENUM, the version I ported to MFC. In Figure 14-2, also on the next page, you can see the ENUMDESK main window. Looks like Windows Explorer, doesn't it?

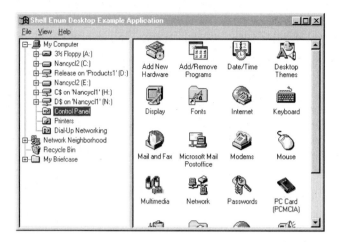

Figure 14-1.
The contents of a Control Panel folder.

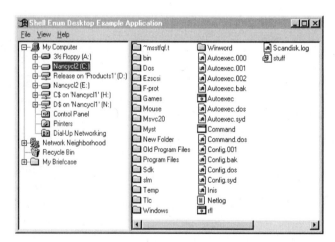

Figure 14-2.
The ENUMDESK main window.

Definitions

Before you begin looking at the samples, it will be useful to define some terms. You've seen many of the terms before, but these definitions emphasize how the terms are used in the context of this chapter.

Let's start with folders. A *folder* is simply a collection of objects in the shell name space. Although it is much like a file system directory, a folder can also be a container for remote computers, storage devices, the desktop, Control Panel, and so on. A folder can contain other folders as well as file objects, but each type of folder contains only certain types of file objects— for example, you cannot drag a Control Panel application into a file system directory folder. A *file object* is an object in a folder, such as an actual file, a printer, or some other type of object.

An *item identifier* (item ID) is a binary data structure that uniquely identifies an object in the object's parent folder. When you need to trace a path to an item from the desktop, you use an item ID list. The user never sees item IDs; display names are shown instead. A PIDL (pronounced "piddle"—stop giggling) is a pointer to an ID list, used with many of the functions that let you browse the shell name space.

Each folder is an OLE object that knows how to enumerate its contents and carry out other actions. To do this, folders implement the IShellFolder interface. When an application gets a pointer to the IShellFolder interface for a folder, this is referred to as *binding to the folder*. Your application can bind to the desktop folder by using the SHGetDesktopFolder function. Your application can also bind to a subfolder of any given folder by using the IShellFolder::BindToObject member function. With these two functions, an application can browse through the shell's entire name space, as you'll see later in the chapter.

Some folders are known as *virtual folders*. Virtual folders aren't actual file directories or storage devices. Rather, they are containers for a number of storage devices and network resources. Examples of virtual folders are the desktop folder, the My Computer folder, and the Network Neighborhood folder. Other virtual folders contain file objects, such as printers, that are not part of the file system.

File system directories also use some special folders. For example, the Programs folder contains the user's program groups, and the desktop directory physically stores files that have been copied to the desktop folder. You can find these special folders in the Registry under HKEY_CURRENT-_USER\Software\Microsoft\Windows\CurrentVersion\Explorer\Shell Folders.

An application uses the SHGetSpecialFolderLocation function to retrieve the location of a special folder, whether it is a virtual folder or part of the file system. The function returns a PIDL, which the application must eventually free by using the task allocator. If the folder is part of the file system, you can convert the PIDL to a file system path by using the SHGetPathFromIDList function.

Enumerating Items in the Shell

When an application has the IShellFolder interface for a folder, it can determine the folder's contents by using the EnumObjects member function. EnumObjects creates an *item enumeration object,* which is a set of item identifiers that can be retrieved by using the IEnumIDList interface.

After you get an item enumeration object, your application can retrieve all the item IDs one or more at a time from the enumeration object by repeatedly calling the IEnumIDList::Next member function. Using other member functions, you can skip items in the sequence, return to the beginning of the sequence, or "clone" the enumeration object to save its state. When your application has finished using the enumeration object, you must free the object by calling its Release member function.

The MFCENUM and ENUMDESK samples use a tree view control and a list view control to display items in the shell name space. These two controls are created when the application starts. The desktop folder is retrieved, and the tree view control is filled with the contents of the desktop.

```
void CMfcenumView::OnFill ()
{
LPSHELLFOLDER lpsf = NULL;
LPITEMIDLIST lpi = NULL;
HRESULT hr;
TV_SORTCB tvscb;

// Get a pointer to the desktop folder.
hr = SHGetDesktopFolder (&lpsf);

if (SUCCEEDED (hr))
{
   // Initialize the tree view control to be empty.
   m_TreeCtl.DeleteAllItems ();

   // Fill in the tree view control from the root.
   FillTreeView (lpsf, NULL, TVI_ROOT);

   // Release the folder pointer.
   lpsf->Release ();
}
```

```
tvscb.hParent = TVI_ROOT;
tvscb.lParam = 0;
tvscb.lpfnCompare = TreeViewCompareProc;

// Sort the items in the tree view control.
m_TreeCtl.SortChildrenCB (&tvscb, FALSE);
}
```

The application-defined FillTreeView function enumerates the items in the folder identified by the first parameter (a pointer to a shell folder). The second parameter is the fully qualified item ID list to the item (the PIDL of the item identified by the first parameter). The third parameter is the tree view parent item. This function will add only items that are folders or that have subfolders.

The FillTreeView function first calls SHGetMalloc. All user interface extensions must use the task allocator to allocate or free memory objects (such as item ID lists) returned across shell interfaces. SHGetMalloc does this.

```
void CMfcenumView::FillTreeView (
    LPSHELLFOLDER lpsf, LPITEMIDLIST lpifq, HTREEITEM hParent)
{
TV_ITEM          tvi;              // tree view item
TV_INSERTSTRUCT  tvins;            // tree view insert structure
HTREEITEM        hPrev = NULL;     // previous item added
LPSHELLFOLDER    lpsf2 = NULL;
LPENUMIDLIST     lpe = NULL;
LPITEMIDLIST     lpi = NULL, lpiTemp = NULL, lpifqThisItem;
LPTVITEMDATA     lptvid = NULL;
LPMALLOC         lpMalloc = NULL;
ULONG            ulFetched;
UINT             uCount = 0;
HRESULT          hr;
char             szBuff [256];
HWND             hwnd = ::GetParent (m_TreeCtl.m_hWnd);

// Allocate a shell memory object.
hr = ::SHGetMalloc (&lpMalloc);
if (FAILED (hr))
    return;

if (SUCCEEDED (hr))
{
    // Get the IEnumIDList object for the given folder.
    hr = lpsf->EnumObjects (hwnd, SHCONTF_FOLDERS | SHCONTF_NONFOLDERS,
        &lpe);
```

(continued)

343

```
if (SUCCEEDED (hr))
{
    // Enumerate through the list of folder and nonfolder objects.
    while (S_OK == lpe->Next (1, &lpi, &ulFetched))
    {
        // Create a fully qualified path to the current item.
        // The SH* functions take a fully qualified path PIDL,
        // while the interface member functions take a
        // relative path PIDL.
        ULONG ulAttrs = SFGAO_HASSUBFOLDER | SFGAO_FOLDER;

        // Determine what type of object you have.
        lpsf->GetAttributesOf (
            1, (const struct _ITEMIDLIST **)&lpi, &ulAttrs);

        if (ulAttrs & (SFGAO_HASSUBFOLDER | SFGAO_FOLDER))
        {
            // You need this next if statement to
            // avoid adding objects that are not real
            // folders to the tree. Some objects can
            // have subfolders but aren't real folders.
            if (ulAttrs & SFGAO_FOLDER)
            {
                tvi.mask = TVIF_TEXT | TVIF_IMAGE | TVIF_SELECTEDIMAGE |
                    TVIF_PARAM;

                if (ulAttrs & SFGAO_HASSUBFOLDER)
                {
                    // This item has subfolders, so put a plus sign in the
                    // tree view control. The first time the user clicks
                    // the item, you should populate the subfolders.
                    tvi.cChildren = 1;
                    tvi.mask |= TVIF_CHILDREN;
                }

                // Get some memory for the ITEMDATA structure.
                lptvid = (LPTVITEMDATA) lpMalloc->Alloc (
                    sizeof (TVITEMDATA));
                if (! lptvid)
                    goto Done;    // Error - could not allocate memory

                // Now get the friendly name to
                // put in the tree view control.
                if (! GetName (lpsf, lpi, SHGDN_NORMAL, szBuff))
                    goto Done;    // Error - could not get friendly name

                tvi.pszText = szBuff;
                tvi.cchTextMax = MAX_PATH;
```

```
            lpifqThisItem = ConcatPidls (lpifq, lpi);

            // Now make a copy of the ITEMIDLIST.
            lptvid->lpi = CopyITEMID (lpMalloc, lpi);

            GetNormalAndSelectedIcons (lpifqThisItem, &tvi);

            lptvid->lpsfParent = lpsf;    // pointer to parent folder
            lpsf->AddRef ();

            lptvid->lpifq = ConcatPidls (lpifq, lpi);
            tvi.lParam = (LPARAM)lptvid;

            // Populate the tree view insert structure.
            // The item is the one filled above.
            // Insert it after the last item inserted at this level,
            // and indicate that this is a root entry.
            tvins.item = tvi;
            tvins.hInsertAfter = hPrev;
            tvins.hParent = hParent;

            // Add the item to the tree.
            hPrev = m_TreeCtl.InsertItem (&tvins);
          }

          // Free the task allocator for this item.
          lpMalloc->Free (lpifqThisItem);
          lpifqThisItem = 0;
        }

        lpMalloc->Free (lpi);    // free the PIDL the shell gave you
        lpi = 0;
      }
    }
  }

else
    return;

Done:
    if (lpe)
        lpe->Release ();

    // The following two if statements will be TRUE only if you got here
    // on an error condition from the goto statement. Otherwise, free
    // this memory at the end of the while loop above.
```

(continued)

```
        if (lpi && lpMalloc)
            lpMalloc->Free (lpi);
        if (lpifqThisItem && lpMalloc)
            lpMalloc->Free (lpifqThisItem);

        if (lpMalloc)
            lpMalloc->Release ();
}
```

FillTreeView used the folder's IShellFolder interface to get the folder's contents and then used the IShellFolder::EnumObjects member function to create an item enumeration object. This function then called the IEnumID-List::Next member function to iterate through all the item IDs for all the folders in the name space.

Getting Friendly Names and Icons

As binary data structures, item IDs aren't much fun to look at or easy to remember. You need to get a friendlier name for an object when you display it to the user. Fortunately, each item in a folder has a display name and two icons associated with it. (One icon is displayed when the item is selected, and the other is displayed when the item is not selected.)

The code you just saw retrieved each item's display name and its icons by calling application-defined functions. The GetName function gets the object's friendly name by using the IShellFolder::GetDisplayNameOf member function. If necessary, GetName converts the display name to Unicode characters, filling a buffer that is either allocated by the task allocator or specified by the application. It then returns a pointer to this buffer. Otherwise, GetName simply returns the offset to the display name in the identifier.

```
BOOL CMfcenumView::GetName (LPSHELLFOLDER lpsf, LPITEMIDLIST lpi,
    DWORD dwFlags, LPSTR lpFriendlyName)
{
BOOL bSuccess = TRUE;
STRRET str;

if (NOERROR == lpsf->GetDisplayNameOf (lpi, dwFlags, &str))
{
    switch (str.uType)
    {
        case STRRET_WSTR:
            WideCharToMultiByte (CP_ACP,        // code page
                0,                              // dwFlags
                str.pOleStr,                    // lpWideCharStr
                -1,                             // cchWideChar
```

```
                lpFriendlyName,              // lpMultiByteStr
                sizeof (lpFriendlyName),     // cchMultiByte
                NULL,                        // lpDefaultChar
                NULL);                       // lpUsedDefaultChar
            break;

        case STRRET_OFFSET:
            lstrcpy (lpFriendlyName, (LPSTR)lpi + str.uOffset);
            break;

        case STRRET_CSTR:
            lstrcpy (lpFriendlyName, (LPSTR) str.cStr);
            break;

        default:
            bSuccess = FALSE;
            break;
        }
    }

else
    bSuccess = FALSE;

return bSuccess;
}
```

You can use the IShellFolder::SetNameOf member function to change the display name of a file object or folder. One side effect of changing the display name is that the item ID also changes.

Another application-defined function gets the selected and unselected icons for the item. You need these icons when adding the item to the tree view control so that the control can display the item's status correctly. This function fills in the *iImage* and *iSelectedImage* members of the tree view item passed in (in the second parameter) with the unselected icon image and the selected icon image, respectively. The GetIcon function, shown in this code, simply calls the SHGetFileInfo function to retrieve the correct icon:

```
void CMfcenumView::GetNormalAndSelectedIcons (
    LPITEMIDLIST lpifq, LPTV_ITEM lptvitem)
{
// Don't check the return value here.
// If GetIcon() fails, you're in big trouble.
lptvitem->iImage = GetIcon (lpifq,
    SHGFI_PIDL | SHGFI_SYSICONINDEX | SHGFI_SMALLICON);

lptvitem->iSelectedImage = GetIcon (lpifq,
    SHGFI_PIDL | SHGFI_SYSICONINDEX | SHGFI_SMALLICON | SHGFI_OPENICON);
```

(continued)

347

```
return;
}

int CMfcenumView::GetIcon (LPITEMIDLIST lpi, UINT uFlags)
{
SHFILEINFO sfi;

SHGetFileInfo ((LPCSTR)lpi, 0, &sfi, sizeof (SHFILEINFO), uFlags);

return sfi.iIcon;
}
```

Getting Object Attributes

The attributes of each file object and folder determine, among other things, what actions can be carried out on the item. For instance, in the code that filled the tree view control, you needed to get object attributes to determine whether the item had subfolders or was a folder itself. To determine the attributes of a file object or a folder, an application uses the IShellFolder-::GetAttributesOf member function. Table 14-1 lists some of the possible attributes of an object. (These attributes are defined in SHLOBJ.H.)

Attribute Flag	Description
SFGAO_CANCOPY	The object can be copied.
SFGAO_CANMOVE	The object can be moved.
SFGAO_CANLINK	The object can be linked.
SFGAO_CANRENAME	The object can be renamed.
SFGAO_CANDELETE	The object can be deleted.
SFGAO_HASPROPSHEET	The object has a property sheet.
SFGAO_DROPTARGET	The object is a drop target.
SFGAO_LINK	The object is a shortcut.
SFGAO_SHARE	The object is shared.
SFGAO_READONLY	The object is read-only.
SFGAO_GHOSTED	The object is displayed with a ghosted icon.
SFGAO_FILESYSANCESTOR	The object contains a file system folder.
SFGAO_FOLDER	The object is a folder.

Table 14-1.
Examples of object attributes.

(continued)

Table 14-1. *continued*

Attribute Flag	Description
SFGAO_FILESYSTEM	The object is a file system object (file/folder/root).
SFGAO_HASSUBFOLDER	The object has a subfolder.
SFGAO_REMOVABLE	Determines whether the object is removable media.

Filling the List View Control

Now let's look at how to fill the list view control in our samples with the contents of the folder selected in the tree view control. In Figure 14-3, the contents of my root C drive are displayed in a list view control in large icon view. (In Figure 14-2 on page 340, the same contents are displayed in list view.)

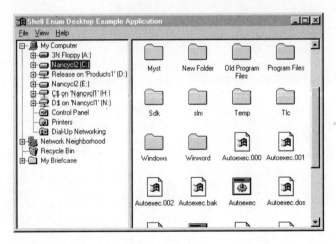

Figure 14-3.
The contents of the Nancycl2 [C:] folder in large icon view.

N O T E : You might have noticed that ENUMDESK, the C sample, contains a feature that is missing from the MFC version: a splitter bar. When I first ported the code to MFC, I ignored the splitter bar, thinking that I would add it later. But of course I ran out of time. So I leave the implementation of splitter bars in MFC to you, as an interesting exercise.

In the MFCENUM sample, I populate the list view control whenever a new folder is selected in the tree view control. The list view control first deletes all its current items. When the control is empty, the application uses the SHGetFileInfo function to retrieve the image lists (large and small) associated with the shell.

```
BOOL CMfcenumView::InitListViewImageLists ()
{
HIMAGELIST himlSmall;
HIMAGELIST himlLarge;
SHFILEINFO sfi;
BOOL bSuccess = TRUE;

himlSmall = (HIMAGELIST) SHGetFileInfo ((LPCSTR) "C:\\",
    0, &sfi, sizeof (SHFILEINFO), SHGFI_SYSICONINDEX | SHGFI_SMALLICON);

himlLarge = (HIMAGELIST) SHGetFileInfo ((LPCSTR) "C:\\",
    0, &sfi, sizeof (SHFILEINFO), SHGFI_SYSICONINDEX | SHGFI_LARGEICON);

if (himlSmall && himlLarge)
{
    ::SendMessage (m_ListCtl.m_hWnd, LVM_SETIMAGELIST,
        (WPARAM)LVSIL_SMALL, (LPARAM)himlSmall);
    ::SendMessage (m_ListCtl.m_hWnd, LVM_SETIMAGELIST,
        (WPARAM)LVSIL_NORMAL, (LPARAM)himlLarge);
}
else
    bSuccess = FALSE;

return bSuccess;
}
```

After you've associated the image lists, it is time to fill the list view control. This procedure is nearly identical to the procedure used to fill the tree view control: get a task allocator for the folder, enumerate the objects, and add those that can be displayed to the list view control.

```
BOOL CMfcenumView::InitListViewItems (
    LPTVITEMDATA lptvid, LPSHELLFOLDER lpsf)
{
LV_ITEM        lvi;
int            iCtr;
HRESULT        hr;
LPMALLOC       lpMalloc;
LPITEMIDLIST   lpifqThisItem;
LPITEMIDLIST   lpi = NULL;
LPENUMIDLIST   lpe = NULL;
```

```
LPLVITEMDATA lplvid;
ULONG        ulFetched, ulAttrs;
HWND         hwnd = ::GetParent (m_ListCtl.m_hWnd);
UINT         uFlags;

lvi.mask = LVIF_TEXT | LVIF_IMAGE | LVIF_PARAM;

hr = SHGetMalloc (&lpMalloc);
if (FAILED (hr))
   return FALSE;

if (SUCCEEDED (hr))
{
   hr = lpsf->EnumObjects (hwnd, SHCONTF_FOLDERS | SHCONTF_NONFOLDERS,
      &lpe);

   if (SUCCEEDED (hr))
   {
      iCtr = 0;

      while (S_OK == lpe->Next (1, &lpi, &ulFetched))
      {
         // Get some memory for the ITEMDATA structure.
         lplvid = (LPLVITEMDATA) lpMalloc->Alloc (sizeof (LVITEMDATA));
         if (! lplvid)
            goto Done;

         // Since you are interested in the display attributes
         // as well as other attributes, you need to set ulAttrs to
         // SFGAO_DISPLAYATTRMASK before calling GetAttributesOf().
         ulAttrs = SFGAO_DISPLAYATTRMASK;
         lpsf->GetAttributesOf (1, (const struct _ITEMIDLIST **)&lpi,
            &ulAttrs);
         lplvid->ulAttribs = ulAttrs;

         lpifqThisItem = ConcatPidls (lptvid->lpifq, lpi);

         lvi.iItem = iCtr++;
         lvi.iSubItem = 0;
         lvi.pszText = LPSTR_TEXTCALLBACK;
         lvi.cchTextMax = MAX_PATH;
         uFlags = SHGFI_PIDL | SHGFI_SYSICONINDEX | SHGFI_SMALLICON;
         lvi.iImage = I_IMAGECALLBACK;

         lplvid->lpsfParent = lpsf;
         lpsf->AddRef ();
```

(continued)

351

```
                // Now make a copy of the ITEMIDLIST.
                lplvid->lpi = CopyITEMID (lpMalloc, lpi);

                lvi.lParam = (LPARAM)lplvid;

                // Add the item to the list view control.
                if (m_ListCtl.InsertItem (&lvi) == -1)
                    return FALSE;

                lpMalloc->Free (lpifqThisItem);
                lpifqThisItem = 0;
                lpMalloc->Free (lpi);   // free the PIDL the shell gave you
                lpi = 0;
            }
        }
    }

Done:
    if (lpe)
        lpe->Release ();

    // The following two if statements will be TRUE only if you got here
    // on an error condition from the goto statement. Otherwise, free
    // this memory at the end of the while loop above.
    if (lpi && lpMalloc)
        lpMalloc->Free (lpi);
    if (lpifqThisItem && lpMalloc)
        lpMalloc->Free (lpifqThisItem);

    if (lpMalloc)
        lpMalloc->Release ();

    return TRUE;
}
```

The final step is to sort the list view control by using the LVM_SORT-ITEMS message or the CListCtrl::SortItems member function. Items can be sorted through a callback procedure that uses the IShellFolder::CompareIDs member function. This function compares two item ID lists and returns the result. Windows Explorer always passes 0 as the *lParam* parameter to indicate that the items should be sorted by name. The compare function returns 0 if the objects are the same, a negative value if *pidl1* should be placed before *pidl2*, and a positive value if *pidl2* should be placed before *pidl1*.

```
int CALLBACK CMfcenumView::ListViewCompareProc (
    LPARAM lparam1, LPARAM lparam2, LPARAM lparamSort)
{
LPLVITEMDATA lplvid1 = (LPLVITEMDATA)lparam1;
LPLVITEMDATA lplvid2 = (LPLVITEMDATA)lparam2;
HRESULT hr;

hr = lplvid1->lpsfParent->CompareIDs (0, lplvid1->lpi, lplvid2->lpi);

if (FAILED (hr))
    return 0;

return hr;
}
```

Displaying an Item's Context Menu

The ENUMDESK sample supports context menus for items in the tree view and list view controls. Figure 14-4 shows the context menu displayed when I right-click the Nancycl2 [C:] folder.

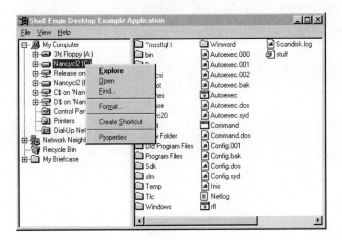

Figure 14-4.
The context menu for the Nancycl2 [C:] folder in the ENUMDESK sample.

When an application determines that the user has right-clicked a specific tree view or list view item, the application calls a helper function to display the item's context menu. The helper function is passed the handle to the parent window, a pointer to the folder, a pointer to the item ID list, and the location where the context menu should be displayed.

```
BOOL CMfcenumView::DoTheMenuThing (
    HWND hwnd, LPSHELLFOLDER lpsfParent, LPITEMIDLIST lpi, LPPOINT lppt)
{
LPCONTEXTMENU lpcm;
HRESULT hr;
char szTemp [64];
CMINVOKECOMMANDINFO cmi;
DWORD dwAttribs = 0;
int idCmd;
HMENU hMenu;
BOOL bSuccess = TRUE;

hr = lpsfParent->GetUIObjectOf (
    hwnd,
    1,   // get attributes for this many objects
    (const struct _ITEMIDLIST **)&lpi,
    IID_IContextMenu,
    0,
    (LPVOID *)&lpcm);

if (SUCCEEDED (hr))
{
    hMenu = CreatePopupMenu ();

    if (hMenu)
    {
        // Get the context menu for the item.
        hr = lpcm->QueryContextMenu (hMenu, 0, 1, 0x7fff, CMF_EXPLORE);
        if (SUCCEEDED (hr))
        {
            idCmd = TrackPopupMenu (
                hMenu, TPM_LEFTALIGN | TPM_RETURNCMD | TPM_RIGHTBUTTON,
                lppt->x, lppt->y, 0, hwnd, NULL);

            if (idCmd)
            {
                // Execute the command that was selected.
                cmi.cbSize       = sizeof (CMINVOKECOMMANDINFO);
                cmi.fMask        = 0;
                cmi.hwnd         = hwnd;
                cmi.lpVerb       = MAKEINTRESOURCE (idCmd - 1);
                cmi.lpParameters = NULL;
                cmi.lpDirectory  = NULL;
                cmi.nShow        = SW_SHOWNORMAL;
                cmi.dwHotKey     = 0;
                cmi.hIcon        = NULL;
```

```
        hr = lpcm->InvokeCommand (&cmi);
        if (! SUCCEEDED (hr))
        {
            wsprintf (szTemp, "InvokeCommand failed. hr = %lx", hr);
            AfxMessageBox (szTemp);
        }
    }
}

else
    bSuccess = FALSE;

DestroyMenu (hMenu);
}

else
    bSuccess = FALSE;

lpcm->Release ();
}

else
{
    wsprintf (szTemp, "GetUIObjectOf failed! hr = %lx", hr);
    AfxMessageBox (szTemp);
    bSuccess = FALSE;
}

return bSuccess;
}
```

With this code in place, the user can right-click an item, view the item's context menu, and choose a command from the context menu.

Supporting Drag and Drop

Although this book can't really cover OLE drag-and-drop operations in any detail, let's take a brief look at the basic steps used by ENUMDESK (and MFCENUM) to support the IDropSource interface. All applications containing data that can be dropped into another application must implement this interface. Our samples support IDropSource so that the user can pick up an object in a window and drop it on Windows Explorer or on the desktop.

In addition to the standard IUnknown OLE interface member functions, you must implement two IDropSource functions: QueryContinue-Drag, which determines whether a drag operation should continue; and GiveFeedback, which enables a source application to provide feedback during a drag-and-drop operation.

In ENUMDESK and MFCENUM, the QueryContinueDrag function determines whether the user has pressed the Esc key or released the mouse button (signaling a drop). If Esc has been pressed, the drop procedure is canceled; if the mouse button has been released, the drop is finished.

```
STDMETHODIMP CDropSource::QueryContinueDrag (
    BOOL fEscapePressed, DWORD grfKeyState)
{
if (fEscapePressed)
    return DRAGDROP_S_CANCEL;
else if (! (grfKeyState & MK_LBUTTON) && ! (grfKeyState & MK_RBUTTON))
    return DRAGDROP_S_DROP;
else
    return NOERROR;
}
```

The GiveFeedback implementation in the samples simply directs the system to use the default cursor for the drop operation:

```
STDMETHODIMP CDropSource::GiveFeedback (DWORD dwEffect)
{
return DRAGDROP_S_USEDEFAULTCURSORS;
}
```

INDEX

Italic page-number references indicate a figure or a table.

Special Characters

\ (backslash) in filenames, 222, 225, 228–29
: (colon) in filenames, 222, 225, 228
, (comma) in filenames, 224–25
= (equal sign) in filenames, 224–25
. (period) in filenames, 222–26, 228, 230–31
+ (plus sign) in filenames, 224, 231
; (semicolon) in filenames, 224–25
[] (square brackets) in filenames, 224–25
_ (underscore) in filenames, 222, 224

A

ABM_NEW message, 279
ABM_REMOVE message, 278–79
ABS_ALWAYSONTOP style, 280
access bars
    callback message for, 280–81
    creating, 276–80, *278*
    introduced, 275–76, *276*
    position of, 281–84
    size of, 281–84
ACS_AUTOPLAY style, 60
ACS_CENTER style, 60
ACS_TRANSPARENT style, 60
AddBitmap member function, 23, *31*
AddButtons member function, 23, *31*
adding items to tree view controls, 98–101
adding ToolTips to nonbutton controls, 27–29
Add member function, *72*
AddPages member function, 328–29
Add Printer wizard, 123, *124*
AddRef member function, 238, 297, 298, 315.
    See also IUnknown interface
AddString member function, *31*
AFXCMN.H header file, 5, 11, 40, 51, 61, 71,
    91, 105
alias, 8.3 (filename), 223–24
AlwaysUnloadDll key, 334
ANIMATE_CLASS, *5*, 60
Animate_Close macro, 66

Animate_Create macro, 60, *66*
Animate_Open macro, *66*
Animate_Play macro, *66*
Animate_Seek macro, *66*
Animate_Stop macro, *66*
animation controls
    creating, 60–65, *61, 63*
    introduced, xviii, *xix, 59,* 59–60
    macros and member functions, 65, *66*
ANIMAT sample, 61, *61,* 64–65. *See also*
        animation controls; MFCANIM sample
apartment threading in OLE, 291, 293
APPBAR_CALLBACK message, 280
APPBARDATA structure, 277
AppBars. *See* access bars
Approved key, 334–35
Arrange member function, *91*
ASSERT message, 15
Attach member function, *73*
audio-video interleaved (AVI) clips, 59–60.
        See also animation controls
AutoSize member function, 24, *31,* 204
AVI (audio-video interleaved) clips, 59–60.
        See also animation controls

B

backslash (\) in filenames, 222, 225, 228–29
BeginDrag member function, *72*
BEGIN_INTERFACE_PART macro, 296
binding to folder, 341. *See also* IShellFolder
        interface
BitBlt function, 15
bitmaps
    image lists and, 67–69, *68*
    toolbar, 24, *24–26, 26*
breaks, line, 148
breaks, word, 148
buddy controls, 53–55, *54*
ButtonCount member function, *31*

Nancy Winnick Cluts is the fourth of the seven children of Bronislaw and Anne Winnick, and the only one who really likes messing around with computers. She holds a degree in computer science from Indiana University.

After college, she was employed at Tandy Corporation, programming in 6809 assembler for the Color Computer on a software product called DeskMate, where she got her first taste of working all night to meet schedules and squeezing every last byte out of code to make it fit in a very tiny space.

Nancy joined Microsoft in 1990. When the opportunity arose to work with Microsoft Windows NT, she jumped at the chance to learn all she could about the new Win32 API and to help developers write applications using Win32. In 1993, she joined the Microsoft Developer Network, writing technical articles about programming for Microsoft's newest operating systems.

Nancy resides in Redmond, Washington, with her husband, Jonathan, and her son, Nicholas.

The manuscript for this book was prepared and submitted to Microsoft Press in electronic form. Text files were prepared using Microsoft Word 6.0 for Windows. Pages were composed by Microsoft Press using Aldus PageMaker 5.0 for Windows, with text in New Baskerville and display type in Helvetica Bold. Composed pages were delivered to the printer as electronic prepress files.

Cover Graphic Designer
Rebecca Geisler

Interior Graphic Designer
Kim Eggleston

Interior Graphic Artist
Michael Victor

Principal Compositor
Barb Runyan

Principal Proofreader/Copy Editor
Sally Anderson

Indexer
Foxon-Maddocks Associates

If you are developing or are considering developing applications for Microsoft® Windows,® this book is a key resource.

ISBN 1-55615-679-0
576 pages
$29.95 ($39.95 Canada)

THE WINDOWS® INTERFACE GUIDELINES FOR SOFTWARE DESIGN

Here are the Microsoft® guidelines for creating well-designed, visually and functionally consistent user interfaces for applications that run on the Microsoft Windows operating system. Completely rewritten for Windows 95 and Windows NT™, this new edition of THE WINDOWS INTERFACE GUIDELINES FOR SOFTWARE DESIGN is an essential handbook for all programmers and designers working in a Windows-based environment, regardless of experience level or development tools used.

Topics include:

- General input techniques—navigation, selection, viewing, editing, and creation, including both command and direct manipulation methods such as drag and drop.

- Windows—primary and secondary types and their components, including property sheets, dialog boxes, message boxes, palette windows, and pop-up windows.

- Menus, controls, and toolbars—types and their components and when to use them.

- Microsoft OLE—how to support design interfaces for OLE embedded and linked objects, visual editing, and other forms of activation.

- User assistance—how to use contextual forms of help, including tooltips and wizards.

- Integration with the system—designing your software so that its interface functions and operates consistently with Windows.

- Visual design—effective use of color, layout, fonts, and graphics.

Microsoft Press

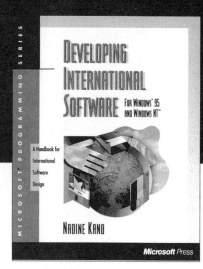

IF YOU'RE THINKING GLOBALLY, THIS IS AN ESSENTIAL REFERENCE. THIS BOOK PROVIDES INFORMATION NOT AVAILABLE ANYWHERE ELSE.

This comprehensive guide and reference will help you write global code and localize applications for Windows® 95 and Windows NT™ more easily, more quickly, and less expensively. You'll get important information about ways to save time and money in the translation process, the culture-specific issues you need to consider, international information pitfalls, and the way in which locale-specific laws may affect the feature set and product distribution.

DEVELOPING INTERNATIONAL SOFTWARE FOR WINDOWS 95 AND WINDOWS NT presents Microsoft's own guidelines for creating international software—guidelines that document years of collective international experience. Geared to programmers and interface designers who have some knowledge of Windows-based coding techniques and the C++ programming language, this book focuses on smart development strategies. Topics include:

- Designing a global program
- Working with character set encodings
- Localizing the user interface
- Supporting local cultural conventions
- Handling multilingual input/output
- Processing Far Eastern writing systems

More than half the book provides critical reference material on international standards and built-in Windows support for international applications. These include:

- Common Latin diacritics and ligatures
- Sort orders for selected languages
- Code-page support on Windows and locale-specific code-page information
- DBCS/Unicode™ mapping tables
- Code-page charts and tables
- Win32® country-specific and language-specific information
- Platform support for the Win32 NLSAPI
- Locale support on Windows
- Multilingual API functions and structures
- Font signature bit-field assignments
- Input Method Manager API functions, messages, and parameters
- Keyboard layouts
- International currency, date, time, and address formats
- Localized editions of Microsoft® Windows

ISBN 1-55615-840-8
768 pages
$35.00 ($46.95 Canada)

Microsoft Press

AND CONQUER.

The opportunities in programming for Windows® are booming. There are target platforms such as Windows 95, Windows NT™, Windows for Workgroups and Microsoft BackOffice— plus new tools and technologies.

With all that, you need a new way to stay informed, sharpen your skills, and get technical help — the Microsoft Developer Network (MSDN). An annual subscription program, MSDN is a quick, easy, and affordable way to access Microsoft development information and technology. And for learning and implementing Microsoft technologies, such as Win32®, OLE, MAPI, ODBC, and MFC, it's is absolutely essential.

Sign up for a **Level 1** MSDN subscription, and *every quarter* you'll get the Development Library — a CD packed with the most up-to-date development information for *all* Microsoft technologies and Windows platforms. Each new edition brings you *more than 150,000 pages* of technical articles,

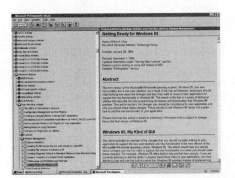

The Library is the quickest, easiest way to implement Microsoft technology.

white papers, product documentation, sample code, and more. *It's an incredible value.* And thanks to the Library's advanced, full-text search engine, you'll get the information you need fast! Additionally, every other month, you also receive the *Developer Network News*, with the latest on Microsoft's systems strategy and development products. All for just $195 a year — *less than the cost of a compiler.*

The Development Library is
"one of the 100 best CD-ROMs...a must have."
PC Magazine, 6/6/95

Sign up for **Level 2** MSDN subscription, and every quarter you get all the Level 1 benefits — *plus* the latest Microsoft SDKs and DDKs and the Windows and Windows NT Workstation operating systems. All for only $495 a year. And if you're developing client/server applications for Microsoft BackOffice, step up to a **Level 3** subscription for $1495 a year.

To sign up, call (800) 759-5474, 6:30 A.M. to 5:30 P.M. (Pacific time), Monday through Friday and ask for Offer # M5SB-MSP. With our money-back guarantee, you risk nothing.* (For more information, you can call, dial our fax-back service at (206) 635-2222 for Document 600, or e-mail us at msdn@microsoft.com.)

Try it and you'll agree. A Microsoft Developer Network subscription is the quickest, easiest and most economical way to conquer *any* Windows programming challenge.

END-USER LICENSE AGREEMENT FOR MICROSOFT SOFTWARE

IMPORTANT—READ CAREFULLY: This Microsoft End-User License Agreement ("EULA") is a legal agreement between you (either an individual or a single entity) and Microsoft Corporation for the Microsoft software product identified above, which includes computer software and associated media and printed materials, and may include "online" or electronic documentation ("SOFTWARE"). By installing, copying or otherwise using the SOFTWARE, you agree to be bound by the terms of this EULA. If you do not agree to the terms of this EULA, you are not authorized to use the SOFTWARE.

The SOFTWARE is protected by copyright laws and international copyright treaties, as well as other intellectual property laws and treaties. The SOFTWARE is licensed, not sold.

1. **GRANT OF LICENSE.** This EULA grants you the following limited, non-exclusive rights:

Use. Microsoft grants to you the right to make and use copies of the Microsoft software program included with this book (the "SOFTWARE") for your internal use solely to develop and test software products designed to operate with the Microsoft Windows operating system. The SOFTWARE is in "use" on a computer when it is loaded into temporary memory (i.e. RAM) or installed into permanent memory (e.g., hard disk, CD-ROM, or other storage device) of that computer.

Distribution. You have a royalty-free right to reproduce and distribute the Sample Images and Code (collectively "Sample Code") included with the SOFTWARE provided that you: (i) distribute the Sample Code only in conjunction with and as a part of your software product which is designed to operate with the Microsoft Windows operating system; (ii) do not use Microsoft's name, logos, or trademarks to market your software product; (iii) include a valid copyright notice for your software product; and (iv) agree to indemnify, hold harmless, and defend Microsoft and its authors from and against any claims or lawsuits, including attorneys' fees, that arise or result from the use or distribution of your software product.

Microsoft reserves all rights not expressly granted to you.

2. **COPYRIGHT.** All right, title and copyrights in and to the SOFTWARE (including but not limited to any images, photographs, animations, video, audio, music, text and "applets," incorporated into the SOFTWARE), and any copies of the SOFTWARE, are owned by Microsoft or its suppliers. The SOFTWARE is protected by copyright laws and international treaty provisions. Therefore, you must treat the SOFTWARE like any other copyrighted material except that you may either (a) make one copy of the SOFTWARE solely for backup or archival purposes, or (b) install the SOFTWARE on a single computer provided you keep the original solely for backup or archival purposes. You may not copy the printed materials accompanying the SOFTWARE.

3. **OTHER RESTRICTIONS.** You may not rent or lease the SOFTWARE, but you may transfer the SOFTWARE and accompanying written materials on a permanent basis provided you retain no copies and the recipient agrees to the terms of this EULA. You may not reverse engineer, decompile, or disassemble the SOFTWARE. If the SOFTWARE is an update or has been updated, any transfer must include the most recent update and all prior versions. Without prejudice to any other rights, Microsoft may terminate this EULA if you fail to comply with the terms and conditions of this EULA. In such event, you must destroy all copies of the SOFTWARE PRODUCT and all of its component parts.

4. **INTELLECTUAL PROPERTY RIGHTS.** Microsoft may have patents or pending patent applications, trademarks, copyrights, or other intellectual property rights covering subject matter in the SOFTWARE. You are not granted any license to these patents, trademarks, copyrights, or other intellectual property rights except as expressly provided in this EULA.

DISCLAIMER OF WARRANTY

The SOFTWARE (including instructions for its use) is provided "AS IS" WITHOUT WARRANTY OF ANY KIND. MICROSOFT FURTHER DISCLAIMS ALL IMPLIED WARRANTIES INCLUDING WITHOUT LIMITATION ANY IMPLIED WARRANTIES OF MERCHANTABILITY OR OF FITNESS FOR A PARTICULAR PURPOSE OR AGAINST INFRINGEMENT. THE ENTIRE RISK ARISING OUT OF THE USE OR PERFORMANCE OF THE SOFTWARE AND DOCUMENTATION REMAINS WITH YOU.

IN NO EVENT SHALL MICROSOFT, ITS AUTHORS, OR ANYONE ELSE INVOLVED IN THE CREATION, PRODUCTION, OR DELIVERY OF THE SOFTWARE BE LIABLE FOR ANY DAMAGES WHATSOEVER (INCLUDING, WITHOUT LIMITATION, DAMAGES FOR LOSS OF BUSINESS PROFITS, BUSINESS INTERRUPTION, LOSS OF BUSINESS INFORMATION, OR OTHER PECUNIARY LOSS) ARISING OUT OF THE USE OF OR INABILITY TO USE THE SOFTWARE OR DOCUMENTATION, EVEN IF MICROSOFT HAS BEEN ADVISED OF THE POSSIBILITY OF SUCH DAMAGES. BECAUSE SOME STATES/COUNTRIES DO NOT ALLOW THE EXCLUSION OR LIMITATION OF LIABILITY FOR CONSEQUENTIAL OR INCIDENTAL DAMAGES, THE ABOVE LIMITATION MAY NOT APPLY TO YOU.

U.S. GOVERNMENT RESTRICTED RIGHTS. The SOFTWARE and documentation are provided with RESTRICTED RIGHTS. Use, duplication, or disclosure by the Government is subject to restrictions as set forth in subparagraph (c)(1)(ii) of The Rights in Technical Data and Computer Software clause at DFARS 252.227-7013 or subparagraphs (c)(1) and (2) of the Commercial Computer Software—Restricted Rights 48 CFR 52.227-19, as applicable. Manufacturer is Microsoft Corporation/One Microsoft Way/Redmond, WA 98052-6399.

If you acquired this product in the United States, this EULA is governed by the laws of the State of Washington. Should you have any questions concerning this EULA, or if you desire to contact Microsoft Press for any reason, please write: Microsoft Press/One Microsoft Way/Redmond, WA 98052-6399.